Law's Stories

Law's Stories

Narrative and Rhetoric in the Law

Edited by Peter Brooks and Paul Gewirtz

Yale University Press/New Haven and London

Set in Times Roman type by The Composing Room of Michigan, Inc., Grand Rapids, Michigan. Printed in the United States of America by BookCrafters, Inc., Chelsea, Michigan.

Library of Congress Cataloging-in-Publication Data

Law's stories : narrative and rhetoric in the law / edited by Peter
  Brooks and Paul Gewirtz.
      p.   cm.
  Includes bibliographical references and index.
  ISBN 0-300-06675-9 (alk. paper)
  1. Law—Language. 2. Law—Methodology. 3. Forensic oratory.
4. Narration (Rhetoric). I. Brooks, Peter, 1938– .
K213.L398   1996
340′.1—dc20   95-26410
                       CIP

A catalogue record for this book is available from the British Library.

The paper in this book meets the guidelines for permanence and durability of the Committee on Production Guidelines for Book Longevity of the Council on Library Resources.

10 9 8 7 6 5 4 3 2 1

Contents

Acknowledgments, vii

INTRODUCTION

Paul Gewirtz Narrative and Rhetoric in the Law, 2

Peter Brooks The Law as Narrative and Rhetoric, 14

I STORYTELLING IN LEGAL DISCOURSE

Martha Minow Stories in Law, 24

Daniel A. Farber and Suzanna Sherry Legal Storytelling and Constitutional Law: The Medium and the Message, 37

COMMENTS

Anthony Kronman Leontius' Tale, 54

Harlon L. Dalton Storytelling on Its Own Terms, 57

II THE CONSTRUCTION OF CASES

Robert Weisberg Proclaiming Trials as Narratives: Premises and Pretenses, 61

Robert A. Ferguson Untold Stories in the Law, 84

Alan M. Dershowitz Life Is Not a Dramatic Narrative, 99

COMMENTS

Janet Malcolm The Side-Bar Conference, 106

David N. Rosen Rhetoric and Result in the Bobby Seale Trial, 110

III EXCLUDABLE STORIES

Peter Brooks Storytelling Without Fear? Confession in Law and Literature, 114

Paul Gewirtz Victims and Voyeurs: Two Narrative Problems at the Criminal Trial, 135

COMMENTS

Louis Michael Seidman Some Stories About Confessions and Confessions About Stories, 162

Elaine Scarry Speech Acts in Criminal Cases, 165

IV THE RHETORIC OF THE JUDICIAL OPINION

John Hollander Legal Rhetoric, 176

Sanford Levinson The Rhetoric of the Judicial Opinion, 187

COMMENTS

Pierre N. Leval Judicial Opinions as Literature, 206

J. M. Balkin A Night in the Topics: The Reason of Legal Rhetoric and the Rhetoric of Legal Reason, 211

Reva B. Siegel In the Eyes of the Law: Reflections on the Authority of Legal Discourse, 225

Catharine A. MacKinnon Law's Stories as Reality and Politics, 232

Notes, 239

Contributors, 279

Index, 281

Acknowledgments

The essays and comments in this volume were originally presented at a symposium entitled "Narrative and Rhetoric in the Law" held at the Yale Law School on February 10–11, 1995. The editors wish to thank the Law School and Dean Anthony Kronman for the generous support and advice given to the project, and the Whitney Humanities Center, cosponsor of the symposium, and its past and present directors, David Bromwich and David Marshall. The Secretary's Office of Yale University provided further needed support. We also thank Josephine Orio for her cheerful and efficient help with the logistics of this project and Mary Pasti for her admirable editorial assistance.

Most of the essays and comments have been much revised and expanded from their original oral form, and we thank all the contributors for their conscientious labors under a tight deadline.

Introduction

Paul Gewirtz

Narrative and Rhetoric
in the Law

Books about law typically treat it as a bundle of rules and social policies. This book
is different. It looks at law not as rules and policies but as stories, explanations,
performances, linguistic exchanges—as narratives and rhetoric. This approach
reflects a striking convergence of recent academic work about law and the general
public's enormous current interest in law. Both scholars and the public have increasingly been drawn to law as an arena where vivid human stories are played
out—where stories are told and heard in distinctive ways and with distinctive
stakes. There will always be great scholarly and public interest in law-as-rules-and-
policies, in law's vast array of general directives on economic welfare, security,
freedom, and justice. But there is virtually as much interest today in law's stories
and how those stories are told and interpreted by litigants, lawyers, courts, juries,
the media, the general public, and scholars themselves. Both the public and the
scholar have found absorbing the ways law brings together story, form, and power.

This is particularly true of criminal investigations and trials. The proliferating
portrayals of law in popular culture most commonly involve criminal cases—
whether in television programs such as *L.A. Law* and *NYPD Blue,* novels by John
Grisham and Scott Turow, movies ranging from *The Accused* to *The Verdict,* or the
news media's now-extensive coverage of law in real life. Similarly, it is no surprise
that so many of the essays in this volume concern criminal prosecutions. Of all of

law's narrative arenas, the criminal prosecution most fully engages the public's narrative desires and the scholar's narrative speculations. But as this volume illustrates, narrative and rhetoric pervade all of law and, in a sense, constitute law.

Examining law as narrative and rhetoric can mean many different things: examining the relation between stories and legal arguments and theories; analyzing the different ways that judges, lawyers, and litigants construct, shape, and use stories; evaluating why certain stories are problematic at trials; or analyzing the rhetoric of judicial opinions, to mention just a few particulars. But as a matter of general outlook, treating law as narrative and rhetoric means looking at facts more than rules, forms as much as substance, the language used as much as the idea expressed (indeed, the language used is seen as a large part of the idea expressed). It means examining not simply how law is found but how it is made, not simply what judges command but how the commands are constructed and framed. It understands legal decisionmaking as transactional—as not just a directive but an activity involving audiences as well as sovereign law givers; indeed, it emphasizes the ways legal processes involve speakers in exchange with audiences everywhere. It sees laws as artifacts that reveal a culture, not just policies that shape the culture. And because its focus is story as much as rule, it encourages awareness of the particular human lives that are the subjects or objects of the law, even when that particularity is subordinated to the generalizing impulses of legal regulation.

The new academic interest in narrative and rhetoric in law can be seen as part of a broader scholarly movement usually denominated "law and literature." As with so many young movements, political or scholarly, it remains an open question whether the participants in this one really have a common purpose. But for now, there is a group of scholars who at least do not disclaim the common label.

In a frequently used distinction, law and literature includes the study of both law *in* literature and law *as* literature. "Law in literature" usually refers to work that examines the representations of law and lawyers in fiction—for example, Melville's *Billy Budd,* Dickens's *Great Expectations* and *Bleak House,* Tolstoy's "Death of Ivan Ilych," Kafka's *Trial,* Aeschylus' *Oresteia.* In its least impressive forms, this sort of work can indulge in facile moralizing about law, using as a springboard a literary work whose focus on law is marginal and whose moral complexity is reduced to a simple humanistic message. But at its best, such work can help to illuminate the legal world in distinctive ways by attention to literature's narrative particularity, its focus on kinds of human understanding beyond reason alone, its capacity for provoking an empathetic understanding of others' inner life, its forms and its self-consciousness about language, and its critical perspective (or at least perspective of ambiguity) toward the phenomena it represents.[1]

If this book is seen as part of the law-and-literature movement, however, it falls into the second broad category, law *as* literature. Work in this category examines law and legal texts the way a literary text might be examined, sometimes with the help of tools provided by literary theory and literary criticism. Of course, there are fundamental differences between law and literature; most obviously, law coerces people. But both law and literature attempt to shape reality through language, use distinctive methods and forms to do so, and require interpretation—and therefore there may be things to learn from seeing how analogous problems are treated in the two disciplines. The most established writing in this category concerns the "interpretation" of legal texts, addressing such questions as how we should think about the "original intent" of the author, what the role of the reader is in creating the meaning of a legal text, and whether texts change meaning over time, how that occurs, and what that means (all of which have analogues in literary interpretation). But law can be treated "as literature" in a broader sense, by becoming more self-conscious about the form, structure, and rhetoric of legal texts, legal arguments, and other phenomena of the legal culture. That is what this book in large part tries to do in focusing on narrative and rhetoric in the law.

Nevertheless, the law-and-literature label may mislead as much as it helps in this context. Many of the contributors to this volume have no particular literary training or literary expertise and do not see themselves as using techniques of literary criticism in their examination of legal subjects. In writing about storytelling and rhetoric in law, they see themselves as addressing traditional and familiar parts of legal practice and study and believe that what is original in their work reflects a self-consciousness and reflectiveness that is not distinctively literary. That self-understanding, however, may itself confirm the considerable overlap of law and literature, for each area considers storytelling and rhetoric central parts of its practice and study—matters internal to its discipline, quite apart from interdisciplinary adventures.

Whether or not usefully characterized as part of the law-and-literature movement, this book reflects what might be called an interdisciplinary leap—an a priori commitment to the worth of engaging people from different disciplines to confront problems of common interest. Such a commitment needs only a relatively weak form of interdisciplinary faith: one may accept that such interdisciplinary confrontations are unlikely to achieve a grand new synthesis, and acknowledge that after such encounters the participants from the different disciplines return to their mostly separate intellectual projects. But something may still change because of an encounter. Even those who do not pursue interdisciplinary collaboration any further may return to their disciplinary solitude with some new tools and insights and analogies—devices to open up at least a few inches of fresh ground on their home turf.

There is also a cautionary dimension to the interdisciplinary commitment reflected here: the consideration of narrative in law must take explicit account of the distinctive context within which legal narratives occur. Storytelling in law is narrative within a culture of argument. Virtually everyone in the legal culture—whether a trial lawyer presenting her case to a court or jury, a judge announcing his findings about what happened in the case, even a law professor writing an article—is explicitly or implicitly making an argument and trying to persuade. Storytelling is, or is made to function as, argument.

In addition, the stakes of legal narrations are high, certainly in litigation. The goal of telling stories in law is not to entertain, or to terrify, or to illuminate life, as it usually is with storytelling outside the legal culture. The goal of storytelling in law is to persuade an official decisionmaker that one's story is true, to win the case, and thus to invoke the coercive force of the state on one's behalf. My late colleague Robert Cover probably overstated the point when he spoke of the "violence" of the words of a judicial decision; but he was right to underscore that the words of court decisions have a force that differentiates them from most other utterances. However provocative and generative it may be to treat law as literature, we must never forget that law is not literature.

The contributors to this volume include a broad range of legal scholars, many with extensive and ongoing involvements as practicing lawyers; several scholars of literature with substantial interests in law; and a judge, a full-time attorney, and an author-journalist who has written extensively about law. Not surprisingly, therefore, the essays in this collection show the diverse ways that narrative and rhetoric in the law may be studied and understood.

The first group of essays concerns, and is a contribution to, a growing body of legal scholarship that either itself consists of stories or defends storytelling by legal scholars as well as lawyers. These scholars typically claim that storytelling has a distinctive power for "oppositionists"[2] and other outsider groups, particularly racial and religious minorities and women. Telling stories (rather than simply making arguments), it is said, has a distinctive power to challenge and unsettle the legal status quo, because stories give uniquely vivid representation to particular voices, perspectives, and experiences of victimization traditionally left out of legal scholarship and ignored when shaping legal rules.

This storytelling movement raises many important challenges and questions, which are pursued in the essays by Martha Minow, Daniel Farber and Suzanna Sherry, Anthony Kronman, and Harlon Dalton. Do stories, compared to other kinds of discourse in law, have a distinctive power? Put another way, how are stories different from theories? Do stories have a distinctive power for outsider groups? If so, how does that power work and how do the stories gain their effect? How does this storytelling movement fit alongside other recent intellectual trends?

It seems clear that stories, and the empathy they often prompt, can increase the range of understandings among listeners. Moreover, when the listeners are judges or other decisionmakers who are from insider groups or have an insider's perspective, outsider stories can add fresh and valuable knowledge. But storytelling is an activity available to all individuals and groups, and in law a decisionmaker usually must choose among competing stories. How, then, is the choice to be made? Surely we cannot assume that just because a story is told by an outsider it is any more true or complete than a story told by an insider. If accounts conflict, how to decide among them?

Moreover, a sophisticated account of storytelling in law or legal scholarship must take account of the complex relationship between storyteller and listener. Storytelling, for example, can undoubtedly provoke new understandings and engagement from listeners. But storytelling (particularly storytelling self-styled as oppositional) can also divide teller from listener; drive the listener away in annoyance, fatigue, or disbelief; or leave the listener silent and unwilling to respond. How do stories gain their effect, or fail to do so? Specifically, are there attributes of the outsider stories championed by the legal storytellers that make them able to have an impact on listeners who, by hypothesis, are unreachable by traditional arguments?

The relation between stories and theories is also a complex one. Stories tend to be particularized, theories to be more general. The particularity of stories is often said to be the reason that they produce their distinctive effects (including the ways they give pleasure). Moreover, their particularity often consists of things left out of the simplifying character of general statements.[3] (These virtues of particularity should be familiar to lawyers, for the common-law method celebrates case-by-case and fact-dependent decisionmaking and reflects a certain distrust of the ability of general legal rules to regulate a complex and ever-changing reality.) But particularization has its own problems. Many stories make at least an implicit claim to be a typical or representative fact pattern, but they may not be. As we have learned from many public officials (Ronald Reagan is just one example), a story may be told with great effect as if it were a typical example, but it may distort the truth because in fact it is atypical. For every claim that the facts push legal decisionmakers to the right legal outcome (a claim by, say, Karl Llewellyn at his most German-romantic), one hears the counterclaim that facts are not values or that "hard cases make bad law." To move from story to action, we need theories too, theories that help us to assess the representativeness of a particular story, to choose among competing stories, to decide which facts are relevant. So, too, we need to appreciate the value of general rules as well as particular stories, for general rules, in spite of their imperfections, can protect against favoritism and unequal treatment.

Last, there are other questions of evaluation. By what criteria is it fair to judge a legal scholar's story? If aesthetic criteria are relevant, what are they? On matters of race, for example, does the legal scholar as storyteller have any comparative advantage over such storytellers as Ralph Ellison, James Baldwin, Toni Morrison, Richard Wright, and Walter Moseley?

The second and third groups of essays concern a quite different subject: trials and the narrative transactions at trials (for the most part, criminal trials). One group of essays considers the construction of cases—that is, how lawyers, witnesses, and judges put together and communicate stories at trial. The other group focuses on narratives that courts have considered problematic, so problematic that they have often been excluded from the trial setting—in particular, confessions and victim impact evidence. These are large and immensely rich subjects and, in some sense, familiar ones in the legal literature, where extensive consideration is given to trial procedures. But focusing on the trial process as a struggle over narratives can give even familiar trial phenomena a fresh look. Such analysis has yielded, and can continue to yield, insights that are descriptive, interpretive, instrumental, and normative.

As a descriptive matter, we all know that trials involve the telling of stories. But how, precisely, do the stories get told, and how are the forms of narrative at trial different from the forms of narrative in other contexts? Most obviously, narratives at trial are in competition. But one side does not tell its story, then the other side. Instead, the main part of each side's story must be presented through evidence, not by a single person in a continuous narrative. Each side has to present its story by calling witnesses to offer elements of the story piecemeal. These witnesses are sponsored storytellers, but their storytelling is framed by a ritual oath that the witness's whole obligation is to the truth, "nothing but the truth." For this and other reasons, these sponsored storytellers may wind up saying things quite damaging to the side that called them.

Witnesses, moreover, do not usually tell their stories as uninterrupted narratives. All stories must be elicited by a series of questions and answers, and the form of questioning and answering is governed by an elaborate system of rules. In addition, because a witness's knowledge of a case is usually selective, that person's story is rarely a narrative with beginning, middle, and end (rarely, at least, do its beginning, middle, and end correspond to those of the plaintiff's or defendant's narrative). Rather, a witness's story usually furnishes discrete pieces in a mosaic whose overall shape emerges only as the trial progresses. Neither side is allowed to keep its perspective uninterruptedly before the decisionmaker until its overall story can be fully presented. Instead, immediately after one side elicits a witness's story, the opposing side cross-examines, thereby introducing the opposing side's perspective even as the first side's story is unfolding.

In short, a trial consists of fragmented narratives and narrative multiplicity. To be sure, the skillful lawyer is always shaping the fragments and at least implicitly pointing to the whole. But often not until the very end of the trial, with the lawyers' summations, does either side have a chance to put the pieces together and to present a flowing, uninterrupted narrative to the decisionmaker. In addition, one side's narrative is constantly being met by the other side's counternarrative (or sidestepping narrative), so that "reality" is always disassembled into multiple, conflicting, and partly overlapping versions, each version presented as true, each fighting to be declared "what really happened"—with very high stakes riding on that ultimate declaration. It is the fragmentation and contending multiplicities of narrative, regulated by special rules of narrative form and shaping, that mark the central distinctiveness of narratives at trial—along with, obviously, the high stakes in how the narrative combat is resolved.

But even this rather complex account is only the beginning, even as a description. It leaves out, for example, the complex ways in which lawyers elicit and shape witnesses' stories, including a client's story.[4] It ignores other relational complexities of the lawyer's involvement with the production and presentation of the client's story—most interestingly, perhaps, the lawyer's simultaneous identification with and distancing from the client's story throughout the trial process.[5] It does not discriminate among the many audiences of the trial—jury, judge, potential clients, friends, television cameras, the general public—or analyze how audiences affect the presentation of the narrative, which is an aspect of Janet Malcolm's essay here. And it is simply the background for any consideration of the complex relation between the construction of courtroom narratives and the wider social narratives with which courtroom narratives intersect—a central aspect of the contributions of Robert Weisberg, Robert Ferguson, and David Rosen in this volume.

Beyond this sort of descriptive or interpretive analysis, studying trial narratives also opens up instrumental questions. What kinds of narratives and what ways of telling work for the various audiences at a trial—including what is usually the most important audience for the storytellers, the judge or jury who will decide the case? How do trial narratives gain their intended effects, or fail to?

In fact, we know little about how the stories at trial are received—in particular, how jurors decide what they believe to be the true story. There is some evidence that jurors tend to come to the trial with a set of stock stories in their minds and that they try to fit trial evidence into the shape of one of those stock stories. This suggests that lawyers will have an easier time persuading a jury that their side's story is true if they can shape it to fit some favorable stock story. Alan Dershowitz's essay in this collection, however, emphasizes how deceptive such stock stories can be—indeed, how misleading a juror's basic expectations about narratives can be—and for that reason he favors giving greater weight to statistical evidence.

The various narrative forms at the trial suggest other, perhaps more mundane, instrumental questions. How does the sequencing of certain kinds of evidence affect its reception—for example, the sequencing of favorable and unfavorable evidence or the sequencing of anecdotal and statistical evidence? How does the dialogic relationship between lawyer and witness affect the reception of the witness's evidence? Lawyer-witness rapport, for example, may produce a different effect from lawyer-witness confrontation, and different styles and contexts of confrontation may have different effects. What makes a story—or a storyteller—credible? For example, to what extent must stories display coherence and consistency to be believable? To what extent does emotion or imagery affect a judge or a jury? Analysis of trials as narrative transactions can make these instrumental issues—once touched upon in the lawyer's study of "rhetoric" and now mostly just part of experienced litigators' unspoken feel and craft—the renewed subject of reflective study.

Lastly, studying trials as narrative invites a variety of normative questions. Are the right people getting their stories told, to a sufficient degree and with adequate effectiveness? Do the multiplicities of narratives at trial (and on appeal) undercut the idea of objectivity or the idea that there is such a thing as the truth? Or does this narrative multiplicity suggest only that people are at times fallible or deceptive or at times so indifferent to truth that they may let people literally get away with murder? Should there be a lawyer's ethics of narrative, which forbids a lawyer from presenting a story he or she believes to be false?

This last question is just a piece of the much broader normative problem of limits on the kinds of stories that may be told at trial and on the ways stories can be told. Not every story may be presented in court. The entire law of evidence regulates whether and how stories may be told at trial, and can be seen as a law of narrative. This law of narrative also includes various constitutional principles that govern the admissibility of confessions, the right to remain silent, the fruits of police searches, the right to confront witnesses, and the appropriateness of victim impact statements at sentencing. Of unusual interest—and the focus of the third group of essays in this volume, by Peter Brooks, Paul Gewirtz, Elaine Scarry, and Louis Michael Seidman—are stories that are so problematic that they have often been flatly excluded at trial. Here, descriptive, interpretive, and normative analysis work together, because the normatively problematic character of these stories becomes clear only after one appreciates their place in narrative transactions, the ways these stories are produced or gain their effects.

The fourth and last section of this book is largely about the judicial opinion, especially the rhetoric of the judicial opinion. The contributors here are the law professors Sanford Levinson, Reva Siegel, and Jack Balkin, the poet-scholar John Hollander, and Judge Pierre Leval—with some concluding observations by Professor Catharine MacKinnon.

The judicial opinion is a central text in the American legal system. It not only states what a court believes to be the true facts of a case but also sets forth an explanation and justification for the legal conclusion reached. In stating the facts of a case, the judicial opinion inescapably shapes those facts to create an official account—definitive at least until an appellate court reshapes the facts once again. In interpreting the law, the judicial opinion becomes a part of the ongoing articulation of the meaning of the laws. It typically interprets other primary texts—a statute or a constitution—but over time the centrality of these other texts can become somewhat effaced by the authoritative texts of judicial opinions themselves. They have authority the way no literary critic's interpretation of a primary text can, even if that critic's interpretation becomes the dominant one: they become binding precedents with legal authority.

A judicial opinion serves three primary functions: first, to give guidance to other judges, lawyers, and the general public about what the law is; second, to discipline the judge's deliberative process with a public account of his or her decision, thus deterring error and corruption; and, third, to persuade the court's audiences that the court did the right thing. The opinion usually ends with the words "It is so ordered," emphasizing the coercive force that judges wield. But the written justification in the body of the judicial opinion is what gives the order its authority.

For all these reasons, judicial opinions are the legal texts most commonly studied in law schools today, and judicial opinions are what lawyers' arguments are mostly about. But this study and argument is mostly about the substance of what the court says, not how the court says it. Looking at the judicial opinion in a somewhat literary way brings into view the rhetoric and form of the opinion in ways traditional legal analysis has tended to ignore. The essays included here show the rich fruits of that sort of inquiry. As someone particularly interested in the problem of judicial authority, what stands out for me is that rhetorical analysis complicates and even destabilizes the authority that the court proclaims. This occurs in a variety of ways.

First, rhetorical ambivalence of a characteristic sort reveals the judges' anxiety about their authority. In their dominant rhetoric, judges typically try to root a new decision in some text that precedes the decision of the case at hand—the text of the Constitution or a statute or a prior judicial ruling. In this rhetorical mode, courts justify their actions as compelled by preexisting law, or at least closely continuous with it, even when a break is occurring. Compulsion and precedent—reasons of pedigree—give legitimacy and authority. On the other hand, as if such claims are insufficient to confer authority or are not altogether accurate, a court often goes beyond the rhetoric of compulsion and continuity and includes a much more comprehensive effort to persuade its audience that it is doing the right thing. This effort to be as broadly persuasive as possible means that the opinion usually includes not only reasons of pedigree but also reasons based on policy and social consequences, as well as attention to language and form. Attention to rhetoric in this latter sense may result in, for example, shaping facts so that the equities seem to favor the winning party; choosing a tone suited to specific persuasive purposes (such as Earl Warren's designedly plain, understated, and nonaccusatory tone to avoid inflaming the white South in *Brown v. Board of Education,* 347 U.S. 483 (1954), or, by contrast, the intensity and fine-tuned grandeur of Justice Souter's discussion of *stare decisis* in *Planned Parenthood v. Casey,* 505 U.S. 833 (1992); displaying a disarming candor to convince the audience of the judge's honesty and self-awareness; or using the sort of "literary" flourishes that disturb Judge Leval. Such comprehensive reasoning and rhetoric all reveal that the courts themselves are ambivalent about their authority: authority (as well as the ability to be effective) depends not only on a decision's pedigree but also on the courts' broader ability to generate prospective agreement that they are doing the right thing.

Second, the authority of the judicial opinion is complexified because today there are multiple opinions in many court cases. Individual judicial opinions are typically marked by a rhetoric of certainty and inevitability, a rhetoric that denies the complexity of the problem before the court and drives with a tone of self-assurance to its conclusion. Like the rhetoric of compulsion and pedigree, the rhetoric of certainty seems to result from the perceived need of judges to preserve the institutional authority of the court. Acknowledging complexity and ambivalence, on this account, threatens the legitimacy of a decision backed by state power.

But the opinion is not always successful in simplifying the complexities, for the contemporary form of judicial opinion writing tends to keep them visible. Nowadays the decision of a case by a multimember appellate court often brings not simply one opinion but multiple opinions, a series of concurrences and dissents by different judges. So the actual text of the case is typically multiple texts, multiple opinions, which simultaneously present multiple accounts of a single reality. The existence of multiple opinions defeats the ability of any single opinion to enshrine any particular version of reality as the undoubted truth. Multiple opinions containing different versions of the facts remind the reader that judicial opinions always create "the facts" in the sense that judges always select out from the profusion of details before them selected particulars that seem plausible and give an account coherence. Multiple opinions are also reminders that the sources of law at hand are far richer than any one account exhausts, that each account contains the shaping mind of its describer, and that judges come to different understandings about what the law means.

In short, in a case where there are multiple opinions, there is a debate occurring within the text itself. And there is often a debate within the text about its own meaning—what the case now being decided signifies for future cases, how it should be read as a precedent in the future. Here we see uncertainty even among those at the founding moment about what the founding means; a text announces the elements of its own indeterminacy. Not surprisingly, the fights over meaning continue after the opinions are announced. An opinion is typically offered as a fixed and stable object—its supposed stability as a precedent is another part of its authority—but in fact, an opinion is always being reinterpreted and reshaped in subsequent litigation. The activity of attempted appropriation and reshaping goes on indefinitely, for each new case becomes a generative precedent. This unrelenting struggle to reshape what opinions mean inescapably complicates their authority.

Lastly, the authority of the judicial opinion today is complicated by doubts about authorship. It is well known in the United States that judges nowadays frequently do not actually write the opinions that appear over their name; their law clerks do. As I mentioned earlier, a court's authority has partially rested on a requirement that the judge who decides a case must write an opinion justifying the decision, a requirement that the justifying role be fused with the decisionmaking role. That is one of the things that constrains and therefore legitimates judicial power. But if the justifying role is sharply separated from the decisionmaking role because law clerks write the opinions, then part of what has legitimated judicial power erodes.

Why, it might be asked, is there currently so much interest in narrative and rhetoric in law? The answer, I think, involves the convergence of a number of quite different forces and is quite revealing about some wider and not altogether consistent trends in both academic life and the broader culture.

For some people (I especially have in mind many of the "storytelling" legal scholars), the turn to narrative reflects a sense that traditional modes of legal analysis are linked in some way to preservation of the political status quo and are insufficiently responsive to the interests and concerns of certain social groups, particularly minorities and women. This turn to narrative is politically reformist.

But for others the interest in narrative may actually reflect a retreat from reformist ambitions in a conservative age—a turn to analyzing form and structure and rhetoric that arises from a frustration with the capacity of substantive legal argument to change the real world of law as one would like, or perhaps even a loss of faith in substantive reform itself.

To some extent, I also think the turn to narrative among legal academics, like their interest in law and literature generally, is a reaction against the two most important contemporary movements in legal scholarship: law and economics, with its reinvigorated scientistic approach to law, and critical legal studies, with its own form of abstraction. Those who are drawn to the subject of narrative and rhetoric in law frequently see themselves as resisting the scientism and abstraction of these other legal movements.[6]

But because interest in narrative has grown in virtually all intellectual disciplines, part of the explanation must also be nonspecific to law. Here, I think, the turn to narrative is a clear offshoot of the further loss of faith in the idea of objective truth and the widespread embrace of ideas about the social construction of reality. Narrative, in other words, is seen *as* the social construction of reality.

I also suspect that the interest in narrative in so many academic disciplines may reflect the recent high prestige and influence of literary theory, a field in which important intellectual insights of general usefulness have been made. Certainly this helps to explain the openly interdisciplinary explorations of literary theory by those in other fields. It may also help to explain the interest in narrative by some scholars who do not self-consciously borrow from literary theory. Most of us, after all, use and profit from ideas, concepts, and vocabularies that are in the air, particularly if they have been validated as useful and important within the academic world generally.

Lastly, I think the academic lawyer's interest in narrative is fueled by the noticeably broader cultural interest in law itself. This broader cultural interest in law—which rests in significant part on the compelling stories that law tells—understandably pushes both legal academics and practicing lawyers to attempt a more self-conscious examination of how law's stories work. Virtually all of the essays in this volume are touched by and react to this broader public engagement with law. Perhaps these essays will speak to some of the broader public, not simply as an imagined audience but as an actual one.

Peter Brooks

The Law as Narrative
and Rhetoric

"Narrative and Rhetoric in the Law": it has become evident that topics traditionally studied by literary scholars and critics have taken a place in legal studies. Rhetoric, the art of persuasion and, by extension, the organization of discourse, is a property of all statements. Narrative appears to be one of our large, all-pervasive ways of organizing and speaking the world—the way we make sense of meanings that unfold in and through time. The law, focused on putting facts in the world into coherent form and presenting them persuasively—to make a "case"—must always be intimately intertwined with rhetoric and narrative. Yet only recently have the implications of law's dependence on narrative and rhetoric become an object of intense investigation and interrogation. Many lawyers, judges, and legal scholars would no doubt acknowledge the presence of rhetoric and narrative in their disciplines but then ask, So what? What follows? Does it follow that legal studies should let themselves be invaded by the concerns of literary criticism? And if so, how?

It is no secret that "law and literature" has become something of a movement, a subject addressed in scholarly journals and even an occasional law school course. But the rubric covers different uses of that "and." For some, and perhaps most obviously, the "and" means law *in* literature: study of representations of the law in literature, law as a recurrent and important literary theme. This is not a negligible topic, since literature, from Aeschylus to Kafka, keeps encountering the law as that which speaks most profoundly of its own nature as a reflection on the human condition. Tragedy is always the story of the discovery of the law—perhaps the Law—and in this manner it makes clear, maybe more than any other genre, that literature's exploration of the individual's destiny always encounters those systems of constraint, those basic interdictions, that both frustrate individual endeavors and constitute irrefutable elements of the definition of the human condition.

The "and" has also meant literature *in* the law: a use of literary representations of persons struggling with the law in order to make the legal profession more acutely aware of the effects of its actions on human actors. When judges, for instance, gather in seminars to discuss literary texts—as they now sometimes do—the intent is to make them respond with a fuller imaginative range to the predicaments and entanglements of human actors before the law. In this understanding, law and literature is much like the movement for medicine and literature: a use of literature as a humanizing device.

But the most powerful claim for an "and" linking law and literature is different. It has been a claim that interpretive methods developed in literary study can, and should, be imported into the study of the law. Maybe because literary theory gained a certain prestige, or notoriety, in recent decades from its flamboyant and well-publicized debates about interpretation, legal scholars have turned, with enthusiasm or bemusement, to issues raised by hermeneutics and various forms of poststructuralism, including deconstruction, asking, for instance, whether the grounds of legal interpretation are as stable as they traditionally are claimed to be. Are there any grounds of interpretation that do not themselves derive from the practice of interpretation? Lawyers and judges tend to assume that, as professionals, they work in reference to an objective standard or original intention that stands outside the rhetorical system. But one may ask whether there is any outside of rhetoric—meaning the norms, the *topoi,* the commonplaces that govern legal thinking as a professional discourse.

On the other hand, literary critics—who often harbor a bad conscience about their profession—have displayed a desire to break out of the realm of fictions, to engage large cultural issues: to make their interpretive techniques work on something closer to "reality." And law, in contemporary American culture, offers an exceptional intersection of textuality and social power. If literary analysis can offer insights into the law, it might prove anthropologically useful.

Issues of interpretation, intentionalism, rhetoric, and objectivity have been explored from various perspectives by such scholars as Richard Posner, Stanley Fish, Ronald Dworkin, and Owen Fiss; and a number of students in both law and literature are pursuing work that crosses the borders between the two fields. More recently, another kind of intersection of law and literature has gained attention: the claim that narrative—storytelling—is a central component of legal practice and thinking. Here, it seems, there has been less sustained critical attention paid to a concept and an issue in which law and literature could find crucial common ground.

The concept of narrative has entered legal studies largely with an emphasis on its use as a vehicle of dissent from traditional forms of legal reasoning and argumentation. In this view, storytelling serves to convey meanings excluded or marginalized by mainstream legal thinking and rhetoric. Narrative has a unique ability to embody the concrete experience of individuals and communities, to make other voices heard, to contest the very assumptions of legal judgment. Narrative is thus a form of countermajoritarian argument, a genre for oppositionists intent on showing up the exclusions that occur in legal business-as-usual—a way of saying, you cannot understand until you have listened to our story. This currently popular use of narrative in legal discourse bears analysis for both its revisionary force and its limitations.

The place of the concept of storytelling in legal talk was thus the starting point for the symposium that resulted in this volume, and the subject of its first session, where presentations by Daniel Farber and Suzanna Sherry and Martha Minow consider the claims urged for storytelling and the impact of these claims, with comments offered by Harlon Dalton and Anthony Kronman. The legal storytelling movement has tended to valorize narrative as more authentic, concrete, and embodied than traditional legal syllogism. But as many of the contributors here point out, storytelling is a moral chameleon, capable of promoting the worse as well as the better cause every bit as much as legal sophistry. It can make no superior ethical claim. It is not, to be sure, morally neutral, for it always seeks to induce a point of view. Storytelling, one can conclude, is never innocent. If you listen with attention to a story well told, you are implicated by and in it.

Attention to the place of narrative in legal thinking is only a starting point. When one reflects on the role of storytelling at the law in general, the topic proliferates, showing its pertinence on every head. It need not take an O. J. Simpson trial to remind us that the law is in a very important sense all about competing stories, from those presented at the trial court—elicited from witnesses, rewoven into different plausibilities by prosecution and defense, submitted to the critical judgment of the jury—to those retold at the appellate court, which must pay particular attention to the rules of storytelling and the conformity of narratives to norms of telling and listening, on up to the Supreme Court, which must tress together the story of the case at hand and the history of constitutional interpretation, according to the conventions of *stare decisis* and the rules of precedent, though often, because dissents are allowed, presenting two different tellings of the story, with different outcomes.

Narrative is indeed omnipresent in the law, something that has no doubt always been recognized but has rarely been attended to in an analytic manner. The more's the pity, for the analysis of narrative is one area in which literary study has produced a body of work that has a certain coherence and force. What came during the 1970s to be known as narratology—the analytic study of the phenomenon of narrativity and its various discursive manifestations—has developed some hypotheses, distinctions, and analytic methods that could be useful to legal scholars, if they were to pay attention. Early in the history of literary theory, Aristotle told us the obvious but important fact that stories must have beginnings, middles, and ends and to be so constructed that the mind of the listener, viewer, or reader could take in the relation of beginning, middle, and end. Aristotle implies that we need to see the end as entailed by a process and to view it as casting retrospective illumination on the process of the middle and, indeed, defining the beginning as that which eventually leads to the end.

In our own century, starting from the Russian Formalists' distinction between *fabula* (the order of events as they took place in the world referred to by the narrative discourse) and *sjužet* (the order and the manner in which events are presented in the narrative discourse), literary analysts have reflected on the ways in which discourse reorganizes stories to give them a certain inflection and intention, a point, perhaps even an effect on their hearers. The fabula-sjužet distinction leads to a further reflection: that all we, as readers or listeners, have to work with is the presentation of events in the vehicle of narrative discourse, that our understanding of events as they happened out there, in the world, is an inference we make, a normalized chronology and causality we intuit from what the narrative tells us—a process that, in the case of a Conrad or a Faulkner, for instance, can be inhabited by doubt. The study of the modalities of narrative presentation—use of points of view, verb tenses, flashbacks, and the like—induces a sense of the uneasy relations of telling and told, an awareness of how narrative discourse is never innocent, but always presentational, a way of working on story events that is also a way of working on the listener or reader.

No doubt any courtroom advocate knows the importance of narrative presentation instinctively. The courtroom lawyer's task would seem to be to take an often fragmentary and confusing fabula and turn it into a seamless, convincing sjužet. But this is not a simple process of addition, stringing the beads of events into a necklace of narrative. There are contradictions and incoherencies to be dealt with, alibis and excuses to be found, gaps to be filled. Hypothetical narratives are formed to cover and explain events; they are narratives that themselves modify events, change their status, produce other events to fill the gaps, lend intention to action. The lawyer with her or his client must at once elicit and construct a story, and the distinction between the elicited and the constructed is by no means clear. How could it be, in an adversarial system that expects prosecution and defense to tell different stories, and leaves it to listeners—the jury, however instructed by the judge—to judge the plausibility of the results?

Part II of this volume addresses the narrative construction of cases in the law, with presentations by Robert Weisberg, Robert Ferguson, and Alan Dershowitz and comments by Janet Malcolm and David Rosen. Their extraordinarily rich and varied explorations of this issue—ranging from Henrico County, Virginia, in 1800 to *The Thin Blue Line,* from Bobby Seale to the judicial side-bar conference—give a sense of the prodigious variety of narrative artifacts and genres confronted and created by the operations of the law. When one probes the storytelling elements of legal business-as-usual, the narratives proliferate vertiginously. There is matter for a whole volume, so many questions does the probing raise.

How is it, for instance, that a case decided by a jury "beyond a reasonable doubt" can then go on to appeal, and have the narrative that won out in the courtroom reversed? Appeals court judges are not supposed to second-guess the triers of fact. They look for judicial error, or story events overlooked or excluded from the jury's attention, or, on the contrary, events illegitimately brought to its attention or items wrongly given the status of events. So it is that one sees appellate courts retelling the story with a different outcome, using a different narrative glue to bind events together. And when the majority opinion is countered by dissent, two retellings are in competition, the one uneasily, though conclusively, victorious because it convinces at least one more of these professional listeners than did the other. The law fascinates the literary critic in part because people go to jail, even to execution, because of the well-formedness and force of the winning story. Conviction in the legal sense results from the conviction created in those who judge the story. Because some narratologists have meditated on the issue of how stories create conviction, one can argue that here the work of literary critics could usefully be read within the legal community.

The plea for attention to narrative—the formal, analytic sort of attention brought by the literary critic—may take on particular cogency when we confront the radical question of the pertinence of the very notion of narrative to the law. Alan Dershowitz raises this radical question in his contention that the whole notion of a well-formed narrative—as exemplified in Chekhov's rule that a gun introduced in act I must by act III be used to shoot someone—is misleading in the court of law, for it leads jurors to believe that real-life stories must obey the same rules of coherence. If we allow into evidence the narrative of spousal abuse, then the eventual murder of former wife by former husband becomes a logical narrative conclusion to the story. But Dershowitz wants to argue, Who is to say that life provides such narrative logic? Dershowitz offers here his version of a theory of narrative advanced by Jean-

Paul Sartre (among others), in his contention that narrative, as opposed to living, really starts at the end of the story, which is there from the beginning, transforming events into indicia of their finality, their making sense in terms of their outcome. For the critic and theorist Roland Barthes, narrative is a kind of sentence writ large, which reaches its conclusion with a full predication of the initial subject. Or, as Barthes also puts it, narrative is a large-scale demonstration of the logical error of the *post hoc ergo propter hoc:* that because something follows something else, it is caused by it, follows from it.

It is indeed in the logic of narrative, as one of our large ways of speaking the world, to explain by way of etiology, to show by way of the enchainment of events how we got to where we are. Dershowitz may be right to protest that life is blinder and more formless than that. Yet his protest may be in vain. For our literary sense of how stories go together—of their beginnings, middles, and ends—may govern life as well as literature more than he is willing to allow. Our very definition as human beings is very much bound up with the stories we tell about our own lives and the world in which we live. We cannot, in our dreams, our daydreams, our ambitious fantasies, avoid the imaginative imposition of form on life. Life is in many respects narrativized in series and bunches of intersecting stories—never complete until our death, of course, but nonetheless oriented toward the significant chapterization of our existence. Life in this manner is made to imitate art. It would be an important, though no doubt impossible, task to address the legitimacy of our sense of story, and our need for narrative plots, at the law. If Dershowitz utters a significant caveat about putting too much trust in our sense of how stories turn out, it is not clear that we could even put together a story, or construe a story as meaningful, without this competence—acquired very early in life—in narrative construction. If narrative form were to be entirely banished from the jury's consideration, there could be no more verdicts.

Since the law at least implicitly recognizes the power of storytelling, it has been intent, over the centuries, to formalize the conditions of telling—to assure that narratives reach those charged with judging them in certain rule-governed forms. Against what may often appear as the fragmented, contradictious, murky unfolding of narrative in the trial courtroom stand formulas by which the law attempts to impose form and rule on stories. The judge must know and enforce these rules. And when stories are culled from the trial record and retold at the appellate level, it is to evaluate their conformity to the rules. At this level, all narratives become exemplary: they illustrate a point of law, a crucial issue in justice, a symbolic moment in the relations of individual and state. So it is that the law has found certain kinds of narrative problematic and has worried about whether they should have been allowed a place at trial or what place they should have been allowed. All the rules of evidence, including the much-debated exclusionary rule, touch on the issue of rule-governed storytelling.

Two striking instances of narratives that have caused the law intense uncertainty and anxiety are the age-old problem of confession and the more recent question of victim impact statements. When and how can a confession be certified as voluntary, both uncoerced and—therefore?—true to the facts? Can the law create contextual rules that will assure that these most intimate and damaging of personal stories be correctly told and listened to? Where victim impact narratives are concerned, how does one balance the need to include the story of harms done with the need to do evenhanded, dispassionate justice? And if one is to allow the victim's narrative of harm, what is its place at trial? The issues here turn on calculations of the effect of stories told on their listeners—first and last, the jurors, the listeners who matter. Hence these issues point us toward other, related ones, for instance, how judges may instruct juries to listen to stories. These are some of the questions taken up in the presentations by Peter Brooks and Paul Gewirtz and commented on by Louis Michael Seidman and Elaine Scarry.

In U.S. law, all the issues—including those that concern the telling of and the listening to stories—find their ultimate commentary in the judicial opinion, especially the Supreme Court opinion. And so it is with discussion of the judicial opinion, with presentations by John Hollander and Sanford Levinson, comments by J. M. Balkin, Pierre Leval, and Reva Siegel, and concluding remarks by Catharine MacKinnon, that we end. By focusing on the rhetoric of the judicial opinion, we intend no trivial or pejorative sense of rhetoric. Rather, we would call attention to the fact that the judicial opinion, like other forms of legal discourse, belongs to rhetoric and uses certain rhetorical forms—indeed, as some of the contributors here point out, rhetoric was originally conceived as the art of argument in law courts. When one uses language, there is no escape from rhetoric. The point is to know where one is in it, what topoi one is using, and what their effect may be.

"It is so ordered," the opinion of the court typically concludes. This rhetorical topos inevitably fascinates the literary analyst, who normally deals with texts that cannot call on such authority. Much literature, one suspects, would like to be able to conclude with such a line—to order an attention to its message, to institute a new order or a new point of view on the basis of the imaginative vision that it has elaborated. It is powerless to do so, except insofar as it has been rhetorically persuasive. Literary narratives, especially those that stage the reactions of listeners to a story told, sometimes contain marks of their intended effect, of the change in the lives of their readers they would hope to bring about. The judicial opinion appears to start from the other end, to announce an effect that has the force of law and then find the rhetoric that will persuade its audience that this effect has behind it an inexorable logic leading to an inevitable result.

But the authority of the court opinion is not a given—it must be earned; and the audiences from which assent must be won are often multiple. In many a Supreme Court opinion—*Miranda v. Arizona* is a good example—one can detect the Court's attempts to address different listeners: dissenting Brethren first of all, then lower court judges, then state legislatures and the police forces of the nation, then the public at large. The rhetoric of persuasion has several prongs in such an opinion. And there are moments when the Court's authority to order appears so threatened by the noncompliance of its audiences that the rhetoric of persuasion is tensed in defense of the very notion of the Court's legitimacy, as, notably, in *Cooper v. Aaron*, where the Court faced the open defiance of the state of Arkansas to its school desegregation decisions. In such cases, the story of rule and precedent told by the Court must be so overwhelmingly persuasive (and in all the important desegregation cases of the 1950s and 1960s, backed by a unanimous Court) that resistance is made to appear aberrant.

Even in less dramatic cases, courts must attempt to present their opinions as seamless webs of argument and narrative. The story of the case at hand must be interwoven with the story of precedent and rule, reaching back to the constitutional origin, so that the desired result is made to seem an inevitable entailment. If narrative may be said to start at the end—in that we know an end is coming and that beginning and middle will retrospectively make sense in its terms and seem an enchainment of cause and effect—constitutional adjudication claims to start from the beginning, in first principles laid down in the Constitution itself. Constitutional adjudication is always in some measure a story of origins, reaching back to our founding text and ur-myth. Yet as with so many stories of origin, this may be something of a trompe l'oeil. What the Court must do is rule on a present matter in a plausible and persuasive way, according to established principle, then find the connecting thread of narrative to take it back to origins. As in Sartre's description of narrative, the story really proceeds in the reverse: its apparent chronology, from beginning to end, may cover up its composition, from end to beginning.

In *Planned Parenthood v. Casey,* Justice Souter, writing for the plurality, eloquently states: "Our Constitution is a covenant running from the first generation of Americans to us and then to future generations. It is a coherent succession" (505 U.S. 833, at 2837). The covenant is a master narrative, into which each new narrative episode must be fitted. How does this work? In Justice Souter's words again, "[T]he Court's legitimacy depends on making legally principled decisions under circumstances in which their principled character is sufficiently plausible to be accepted by the Nation" (at 2814). The narrative of the covenant relies on precedent and stare decisis in order that change or innovation appear to be principled, so that sequence appears not random but consecutive. The most apt words in Souter's sentence may be "sufficiently plausible." What does suffice here? Only that which is rhetorically effective, that which persuades, that which assures conviction. "Sufficiently plausible" invites assent, but also a degree of awareness of how one is being worked on by rhetoric. "Sufficiently plausible" offers a pretty good definition of what we, as listeners, demand of any narrative proposed to our attention.

At the end of the symposium, I felt that we were ready to begin. By this I mean that in the manner of successful conferences—and this one was marked by an exceptionally high level of thinking, storytelling, and rhetoric—"Narrative and Rhetoric in the Law" had begun to clear the terrain, define the issues, provide the terms for a more sustained consideration of the questions raised. One would have liked to be able to shut all the participants in a room and make them work through to further definition and clarification. Still, what had emerged clearly enough by the end of the sessions was not only that the law is consubstantial with narrative far more than is usually acknowledged but that the law turns on what we might call narrative in situation: stories in their dynamic transaction between tellers and listeners. How stories are told, listened to, received, interpreted—how they are made operative, enacted—these are issues by no means marginal to the law nor exclusive to theory; rather, they are part of law's daily living reality. If the essays and comments in this book succeed in making this point—as I believe they do— they open the way to continuing research that would make imperative the closer cooperation of legal and literary analysts. Here, I think, we find a shock of recognition as two disciplines with disparate aims discover that they have important matter of common concern and that transgressing the boundaries that separate them has a real logic, indeed a certain necessity.

Part I

Storytelling in Legal Discourse

Martha Minow

Stories in Law

One of my favorite stories is an old one about the walled city of Verona. Over time, the population inside the wall grew and the city became overcrowded. The problems from this circumstance mounted, until one day the Bishop decided something had to be done, and called a meeting with the Chief Rabbi.

The Bishop said, "The overcrowding in Verona has become unbearable. The Jews must leave."

The Chief Rabbi said, "Leave? But we have lived here for generations! Surely we should talk about so drastic a measure."

The Bishop replied, "But who should talk? We could have a debate. But everyone in town cares about the subject."

The Rabbi proposed, "We could hold it in the amphitheater; there is room for everyone."

But the Bishop said, "No one could hear us there. It will have to be a silent debate."

They agreed, and the big day arrived. Everyone turned out and watched expectantly as the Bishop began.

He raised his right hand up to the sky.

The Rabbi brought his right hand down and pointed to his left palm.

The Bishop held up three fingers.

The Rabbi held up one.

The Bishop reached under his chair and brought out a wafer and ate it, and a glass of wine and sipped it.

The Rabbi pulled out an apple and took a bite.

At that moment, the Bishop leapt up and said, "You are right, the Jews can stay. We in Verona will have to find another way to solve our problem."

A crowd gathered around the Bishop, excited and perplexed. "We followed the debate very closely," one person said, "but what exactly was said?"

"Ah, the man was brilliant," said the Bishop. "I said, 'The Lord of All commands that the Jews leave Verona today.' He replied, 'But the Lord is here in Verona with the Jews, too.' I answered, 'The three aspects of the Trinity—the Father, Son, and Holy Ghost—guide us on this matter.' And he answered, 'But there is just one Almighty, one King of the Universe.' I responded with the wafer and the wine to say, 'Jesus died for our sins so the Christians could be saved.' But he responded with the apple, noting 'We are all children of Adam and Eve.' And indeed we are; we are in this together; we will work it out together."

Meanwhile, another crowd surrounded the Rabbi. "Rabbi, Rabbi, Rabbi, what happened? " they cried. "I have no idea," said the Rabbi. "The Bishop said, 'The Jews of Verona must leave here today.' I answered, 'We are staying right here.' He returned, 'I will give you three days to pack.' I offered, 'We'll take a week,' and then he ate his lunch and I ate mine."

This story has endured for some time; and I confess, I never tire of it. I have used it in talking about problems in the adversary system, the difficulties of bilingual education, and the elements of luck in persuasion. Like a rich common-law decision, the story has multiple features that can be highlighted, depending on the context in which it is invoked.

At the most basic level, then, I suggest that storytelling offers real continuities with common-law reasoning; it dwells on particulars while eliciting a point that itself may be molded or recast in light of the story's particulars reviewed in a different time.

The story of Verona has something particular to say in this moment, in this discussion of narrative and law. It is a story about reaching agreement without full understanding; it is a story about the importance of perspective to human capacities to understand and to communicate; it is a story about the influence of experience and situation on perception, and the making of meaning out of human actions.

Each of these themes appears in contemporary debates about the place of stories in legal scholarship.[1] Some writers advocate the use of stories to promote practical problem-solving; some admire and some criticize the power of stories in conveying particular points of view or perspectives; some celebrate and others worry about the disproportionate use of storytelling genres by women of various races and men of color in legal writing. Rather than review those debates, I mean here to comment on them in three ways: First, I will review a recent effort of my own to approach a legal controversy by telling some stories about it; I will ask what works and what does not work in this effort. Second, I will consider how Hannah Arendt's defense of the political theorist as storyteller illuminates the motives and methods of story-telling in and around law. Finally, I will consider the promise and limits of story-telling as an approach to a legal problem in light of Hannah Arendt's conception of political theory as storytelling.

But before I do this, let me offer some opening observations. Stories seem to work, when they do, on many levels; they can produce an experience, an insight, and one or more emotional responses. With any given story, some people get it and some people do not. Some of those who get it do not like the experience and are troubled by it. Perhaps the story prompts a response that feels inconsistent with other strongly held views or intuitions. Perhaps the experience of a response to the story is itself troubling because it occurs on levels not easily summarized by principles, logical analysis, or other specific modes of reasoning that seem more generally accessible or rationally defensible. But the walled-city-of-Verona story raises questions about the accessibility of a given form of rational argument in a world of human and group differences. I will return to these observations when I conclude.

THE STORY OF KIRYAS JOEL

THREE STORIES

I recently wrote a paper telling three stories about the Supreme Court's 1994 decision in the case of *Board of Education of Kiryas Joel Village School District v. Louis Grumet*.[2] You may know it as the Hasidic school case. The Supreme Court struck down a state statute creating a special school district for the disabled children of an ultraorthodox Jewish community in upstate New York. Construed as a viola-tion of the establishment clause, the statute triggered five opinions in the Court and revealed the recurring disagreements about how to formulate legal doctrine in this area.

In conversations about the case, I was most struck by how many people thought the case was an easy one—and nearly all agreed with the Supreme Court's conclu-sion. Although unsure of my conclusion, I felt that the case was a hard one. I set out in my essay to communicate why and found myself telling stories. The first story is a short version of the history of the Jewish Diaspora—the dispersion of Jews from Palestine after the destruction of the Second Temple in A.D. 70. As a people without a nation, the Jews—and the governing authorities—devised ways to live apart that sometimes led to a certain amount of autonomy and self-governance and sometimes led to distrust, regulation, violence, and expulsion. Thus, the Jewish communities of Babylonia and medieval Europe retained control over domestic legal affairs, such as religion, education, family law, and civil litigation.[3] The tradition-bound segregated Jewish communities provided some psychological sustenance and preserved collective Jewish identity in societies that largely despised Jews, excluded them from the economic and social worlds opened to others, and threatened them with physical violence.

The story I then told focused on the perhaps ironic turn of events presented by the Enlightenment and the ultimate emergence of constitutional democracies in Europe: in several countries Jews encountered opportunities to join the larger societies, but only if they surrendered their religious traditions. As a story within a story, I told of Moses Mendelssohn, who argued that Jews could "adopt the mores and constitutions of the country in which you find yourself, but be steadfast in upholding the religion of your fathers, too." And it was the conventionally Jewish-looking Moses Mendelssohn who was walking down a busy street in Berlin in the 1790s when he accidentally bumped into a large Prussian officer. The officer yelled, "Swine!" Mendelssohn returned with a courtly bow, replying, "Mendelssohn." It is a bittersweet commentary, perhaps, on what happens when members of a despised group claim equality while retaining their group membership. I explored similar tensions posed for Jews by the French Revolution and Napoleon's code; Jews repeatedly faced the invitation to citizenship if they would reconcile their religious beliefs and practices with the duties and conduct of the French people.[4] The destruction of the Jews during World War II, for many Jews, demonstrated the impossibility of this invitation.

I told this first story to frame the second story—the story of the village of Kiryas Joel in New York that led to the Supreme Court controversy. The first story gives a context to the effort by a group of Hasidic Jews to live in an enclave by themselves, to speak Yiddish, to dress in clothes more typical of medieval communities than late twentieth-century America, and to educate their children in private, single-sex religious schools. Called the Satmar, these people obtained incorporation of their residential area near the Catskill Mountains as a separate local government under New York law. Named for their founder, the village of Kiryas Joel, like similar communities of Satmar Hasidim, is viewed by its inhabitants as a form of homage to those who died in the Holocaust and as a living testament to the vitality of the way of life the Nazis tried to eradicate.[5] They also sought publicly funded educational and related services for their children with disabilities, as authorized by federal and state law. During the mid-1980s the state provided such services in the religious schools run by the Satmar, but Supreme Court decisions then forbade the provision of such public services in religious schools on the grounds that this could advance sectarian ends or entangle the government in religious activities.[6]

Some of the parents of disabled Hasidic children sent their children to the public school in the next town but found this an unacceptable option because of the "panic, fear, and trauma" experienced by children sent away to school with people who viewed them as very different from themselves.[7] So at the request of residents of Kiryas Joel, the New York legislature authorized the village to set up its own public schools. The village exercised this authority to set up a school solely for students with disabilities, because the residents had no interest in having any other public schools. Citizen taxpayers and the New York School Board Association challenged the statute in court and claimed that this special school district violated the requirement to separate church and state.

The school itself is administered by people from outside the community, with entirely secular instruction under the direction of a non-Hasidic superintendent with twenty years' experience in bilingual and bicultural education in the New York City public schools.[8] Nonetheless, the entire student enrollment in the school comprises Hasidic Jews, some from within Kiryas Joel and some from neighboring communities. There is some evidence, though not in the record of the case, that whatever franchise is enjoyed by the villagers is effectively controlled by the rebbe through the auspices of his son, the rov.[9] The son announced his slate of candidates for school board and instructed all eligible voters to vote for them.[10] Dissent within the community exists, but it also tends to be followed by expulsion from the communal institutions.[11] Such facts were not in the record, because the challengers objected to the sheer creation of the special school district as an impermissible union of church and state.

The New York trial court, appellate court, and Court of Appeals all found the statute a violation of the establishment clause by using various versions of the Supreme Court's precedents in the area. Four members of the Supreme Court treated the statute as an impermissible "fusion" of governmental and religious functions;[12] the legislature, in this view, improperly delegated civic authority on the basis of religious group membership rather than general and neutral principles. One member sought to reestablish the precedent of *Lemon v. Kurtzman*,[13] which once guided establishment clause decisions, but received no attention by a majority of the Court across the several opinions. Justice Stevens found several specific factual points justified finding this an instance of establishment rather than accommodation of religion; Justice O'Connor agreed, but in her own opinion recommended revisiting the decisions made in the 1980s that prevented the provision of public services on the site of parochial schools. Justice Kennedy wrote separately, with the view that accommodation of the Satmar is a permissible goal, but the legislature impermissibly configured a school district along religious lines.

The dissenting Justices Scalia, Rehnquist, and Thomas reasoned that the school itself posed no problems for the establishment clause, that the civil authority over the schools was explicitly distinct from religious authority, and that the motivation for the legislation was either secular or else a permissible accommodation of religion. Rather than pursue these or other doctrinal lines of argument, my story proceeded to consider why all organized Jewish groups, except the Orthodox, joined in opposing the school district in Kiryas Joel. I speculated that this lineup echoed the dilemma of assimilation created by the Enlightenment for Jews and other subcommunities.

Finally, my third story told the contrasting tale of the struggle for desegregation of schooling and other institutions in this country. Social movements, using lawyers, have struggled for both racial equality and inclusion of people with disabilities during the twentieth century. With this story as a larger context, the village of Kiryas Joel could be faulted both for secluding all of its students from integration with other kinds of children and for isolating its children with disabilities from education with its nondisabled children in the religious schools.

I myself struggle for a conclusion in the paper. I argue, perhaps weakly, that however much we may criticize the Satmar for failing to shoulder the financial costs of fully educating their children with disabilities in the religious schools (with no public aid), this is surely a decision the Constitution entitles them to make. Just as parents may choose private religious schools for some of their children, they may choose public schools for others. I also suggest that as desirable as desegregation may be as a public policy, the courts have curbed it at the limits of city boundaries, and it would be both curious and unfair to make an exception to this rule where disabled Hasidic children are involved. It is their education and their interests that must be considered. Thus, if the Satmar parents are viewed as making a good-faith request for secular public education within a secular town recognized by the state, their children are entitled to it. I tweak the Satmar by suggesting that their bilingual programs for Yiddish-speaking disabled children should be opened to their archenemies, the Lubavitch Hasids, but mainly I ask questions about how subgroups can both respect and resist the state in a liberal society committed to both inclusion and religious liberty. More generally, I propose evaluating similar proposals for special public schools for African-American males only, for military academies for boys only, and for math classes for girls only at least in part by reference to competing narratives of particularity and narratives of inclusion.

WHAT WORKS AND WHAT DOES NOT WORK

What works about the stories I tell about Kiryas Joel? I think that they can shake up some assumptions. The case looks harder with than without the narrative of the Diaspora. Indeed, the case looks harder because of the emphasis on the details of the school for disabled Hasidic children: many people who read about the case did not realize that the school was for children with disabilities; others did not realize that the entire instruction in the school is secular and under the control of secular authorities. Some people tell me I have convinced them that the Court's decision was wrong.

Such comments make me nervous, because I am not sure I have convinced myself. Not that it matters much in terms of Kiryas Joel itself: within a month of the Supreme Court's decision, the New York legislature adopted a new law, written to permit any municipality to apply for a special school district, and granted approval under this statute to Kiryas Joel. The new statute is under challenge and will raise questions of motive and effect, but it is a new framework for the debate. But when we turn to other claims by groups to have accommodations in public schools that produce segregation, what terms of evaluation should prevail? I imply in my essay that the juxtaposition of the story of the particular group with the story of social movements for inclusion can prompt wise judgments. Can good judgments indeed emerge simply with the collision of stories and narratives of the societal struggles for desegregation and integration? Must good judgments follow from such collisions, or might poor conclusions also be reached? How is this process of decision through contrasting stories better and worse than application of one set of norms, and how are stories better and worse in gathering together potentially conflicting norms?

On reflection, I think that good judgments *could* emerge when people turn over in their minds competing narratives about both a particular claimant and a larger social struggle, but there is no guarantee. Being able to appeal to some overarching principles and even some mid-level concepts lends at least the sense of some consistency in judgments across contexts and over time, which matters to the rule of law.[14] These kinds of consistency seem especially important where relations between the state and subgroups are involved; otherwise favoritism, unfair discrimination, and unreasoned whimsy seem only too likely. Yet stories implicitly identify some principles that can be universalized in the sense that any group meeting the terms of those principles should be treated the same way. Two such principles direct observers of the case of the school district of Kiryas Joel to consider and to treat as weighty (1) the needs and interests of children, especially those with disabilities, and (2) the meaning of the proposed action in the lives of the subgroup and in the lives of others in the society. Whose meanings should receive state endorsement or state rejection?[15]

Perhaps my turn to storytelling stems from my own understanding that neither of these principles currently receives acknowledgment, much less a place of priority in prevailing legal analysis. I and others could and in fact do work directly on the project of advocating these principles,[16] but in that long period called the meantime, shifting from the fight over principles to the insights of stories offers another technique for persuasion. So the incompleteness of storytelling as a mode for decisionmaking may be both a defect and a virtue, a defect if one seeks articulated norms to guide future decisionmakers, but a virtue if one knows that prevailing articulated norms are not the right ones.

There is for me a more troubling shortcoming of the storytelling mode. By itself, it gives no guidance or suggestion about which stories to tell. Here are small examples. In my published account of the Satmar Hasidim, I detailed divisions within the community and negative views held by others about it.[17] I also reported on earlier litigation by the Satmar objecting that the neighboring public school system failed to fully accommodate local Yiddish-speaking disabled children. I did not, however, report on an earlier suit brought by the Satmar in Kiryas Joel challenging the use of female bus drivers when male students were transported to the neighboring public school,[18] nor of their failed effort to assure that Satmar girls would be taught in the public school only by female public-school teachers who spoke Yiddish.[19] Why not? I viewed them as irrelevant given that the public school set up in Kiryas Joel is itself coed with both male and female teachers, in sharp contrast to the sex segregation usually demanded by the Satmar.[20] But there is also no question but that these additional stories convey unattractive features of the community that I was trying to paint in a sympathetic light. Storytellers (and advocates) may do this, and there is no rule or guiding principle of selection for storytelling. To be sure, there are problems of selectivity in any human endeavor, including efforts at systemic theory building, because the limits of time, space, and attention invariably force authors to select which features, objectives, examples, and objections to discuss explicitly and which ones not to. In the very moment of treating one or another starting point as plausible, an author has selected, knowingly or unknowingly, from a range of possibilities.

The biggest check on selectivity problems in storytelling lies in the availability of another story, perhaps told by someone else. Indeed, as anyone who has told a story to a child—or been a child—may recall, the likely response to one story is the call to tell another. I tried to check the partiality of the stories of the Diaspora and Kiryas Joel with a counterstory about the social movements for school desegregation and integration in the United States. But the availability of counterstories does not indicate which counterstories should be elicited, obtained, or heeded.[21] If the counter or alternative stories are simply those told in response to an initial story, we face the specter of warring stories with no methods for testing them or for resolving disputes that they reflect.

In another context, I have worried about this problem, given the contemporary prevalence in legal and political arenas of victim stories.[22] One who claims to be a victim invites, besides sympathy, two other responses: "I didn't do it," and "I am a victim, too." No wonder some describe contemporary political debates as exhibitions of "one-downmanship" or as the "oppression Olympics." Victim stories risk trivializing pain and obscuring the metric or vantage point for evaluating competing stories of pain. Victim stories also often adhere to an unspoken norm that prefers narratives of helplessness to stories of responsibility, and tales of victimization to narratives of human agency and capacity.

Intriguingly, Seyla Benhabib argues that Hannah Arendt's commitment to an existential sense of human choice helps to explain her own defense of storytelling,[23] and it is to Hannah Arendt's views that I now turn.

HANNAH ARENDT ON THE STORYTELLER AS POLITICAL THEORIST

A quirky, original thinker, Hannah Arendt is perhaps best known for her studies of totalitarianism in general and of Nazism in particular.[24] Recently, several scholars have explored how what may seem quirky or undisciplined in her work actually manifests a methodological commitment that Arendt made to narrative, in contrast to the prevailing methods of social science.[25] Thus, for example, she interwove narratives about individuals and discussions of works of literature in *The Origins of Totalitarianism* not as faulty pursuits of the empirical method but instead as commitments to narrative as the mode for lending meaning and understanding to human action.[26] Arendt distinguished action, which is creative and free of causal necessity, from behavior, through which individuals become predictable creatures of the mass;[27] she further identified social science as well suited to describing behavior, but narrative as crucial to capturing the meaning of human actions and conveying the availability of choices to each individual.[28]

Seyla Benhabib traces Arendt's commitment to narrative to her effort to connect her commitments as an existentialist with her identification as a German-Jewish intellectual living through the twentieth century.[29] From these vantage points, Arendt struggled specifically with the very problem I recounted in the story of the Diaspora. States so often accord rights to members of their own nation but not to members of other nations, like Jews, who reside within their boundaries. Drawing on the legacies of modernism and antimodernism, and the traditions both German and Jewish, Arendt experienced a great tension between universalism and particularism.[30] This tension is manifest in the contrast between Arendt as the modernist and Arendt as the storyteller of revolutions and witness to totalitarianism.[31]

More basically, Benhabib and others suggest that Arendt defended storytelling as the proper mode for political theory after totalitarianism, compared with rationalist social science techniques that look for laws of human behavior. Those techniques risk dulling the mind of observers against what is new and unprecedented.

Social science rationality could treat horrors such as the concentration camps as capable of being explained and accepted by reference to prior events, rather than as radical departures that require a sense of rupture.[32]

Not only would such an explanation be wrong in Arendt's view, but it would also yield the worst moral response—passivity and acceptance rather than resistance and outrage.[33] Hence, in her explorations of the "banality of evil," the ordinariness of life within bureaucratic regimes, she adopted, perhaps paradoxically, the surprising view that horror can take the form of bureaucratic rule, with no one feeling accountable, as a way to shake up listeners so they would be on guard against future horrors. She struggled for modes of explanation that would demonstrate how every person can and must participate in the task of politics against the backdrop of totalitarian and mass societies that impair the capacity of people to act together as citizens.[34]

The task of the political theorist, as pursued by Arendt, is to confront the community with the challenge to think freshly in the face of the unprecedented and to reorient people to permit them to build a new future.[35] The method to be used must resist the tendency to present history as inevitable and analogous to the past or as the unfolding of historical necessity. Human beings are too unpredictable for these images to be correct, and, in any case, such images have poor moral implications, yielding compliance and predictable behavior rather than unpredictable and courageous human actions.

Storytelling can disrupt the illusion that social sciences create in the service of rational administration, the illusion that the world is a smoothly managed household.[36] Storytelling invites both teller and listener to confront messy and complex realities—and to do so in a way that promotes communication and thinking about how to connect the past and the future by thinking about what to do.[37] Rather than taking the view that only experts understand and act in the political world the political theorist who tells stories thinks about politics in a way that remains faithful to the capacity of citizens to act together.[38]

Arendt further suggested the moral resonance of the narrative form itself. This view seems to be echoed in works by James Boyd White and Martha Nussbaum, who emphasize the ethical relationship between author and reader, which is modeled especially in fictive narratives.[39] For Arendt, narratives are crucial in constructing a sense of the self in the face of traditions that have crumbled and human hopes that risk being forgotten.[40] The problem of selection does not trouble Arendt; she acknowledges that the storyteller selects and necessarily judges while excavating the past, just as a deep-sea diver finds pearls.[41] The storyteller uses bits of the past to unsettle the present and deprive it of peace of mind.[42] The story form is itself well suited to portraying the plurality of human viewpoints on any given event.

Arendt argued that the narrator should never pretend to reproduce the standpoint of past actors, because that would disguise the standpoint of the author.[43] She also maintained that only through the variety of relationships constructed by many people seeing from different perspectives can truth be known and community be created.[44] Attentiveness to the partiality of any story, then, as well as to the perspectival nature of a shared social world, follow from the commitment to narrative.

As may be obvious, these interpretations of Hannah Arendt's work bolster my own struggles with the case of *Board of Education of Kiryas Joel* (not to mention the walled city of Verona). Like Arendt, I notice and value the capacities of storytelling to draw attention and disrupt the tendency to assimilate a new problem to the past and submerge it under general schemes.[45] Like Arendt, I see in the mode of storytelling the possibility of enacting and expressing insights about the partiality of any individual's viewpoint, as well as the hope that we can come to imagine the viewpoint and experiences of others. Like Arendt, I look to storytelling to arrest the ready reaction, to reorient people's minds to confront the future, rather than to accept the past. Like Arendt, I look to stories, which I acknowledge that I select, as a way to create a heuristic for making meaning of the past and pointing toward ways to act in the future.

Like Arendt, I find myself struggling with the limits of Enlightenment universalism, or what some call political liberalism, given the historical events of the twentieth century. In the name of universalism, particular groups have been oppressed; in the name of Enlightenment rationality, particular groups have been exterminated. At the same time, as more recent history suggests, the war of all against all is a likely result of a revival of particularisms.

Indeed, there seem to be a series of nested dilemmas or multiple versions of the same dilemma. There is the "Jewish question": How much of their own identity must Jews (or any other subgroup) give up in order to enjoy the benefits of citizenship in a liberal state? The promise of inclusion in the world of rights-bearing individuals offers freedom from group-based oppression, but if the price is assimilation, it is too high. That price also gives a dark hint that inclusion, equality, and dignity are not truly in the offing.[46]

Similarly, there is the issue of modernity, which seems to invite the fluid movement of persons, capital, and ideas under the rubrics of political, economic, and intellectual freedom. Yet this same modernity seldom discloses the corrosive effects of mobility of people, investments, and ideas.[47] The mobilities that seem rational and compelling—and seem to fulfill contemporary political and economic theories—may neglect the places of meaning, coherence, stability, and commitment in people's lives.

There is, in addition, a parallel contest between intellectual methods, such as those of social science and some forms of philosophy, that seek the general and the universal but risk suppressing differences and disagreements. In contrast, commitments to narrative revel in particularity, difference, and resistance to generalization.

Finally, there is the tension between the general and the particular as goals for both intellectual focus and legal regulation. Should we desire explanations that are bigger than each particular, and laws that run across a vast range of particulars in search of predictability, power, coherence, and control, or do any general forms simply install one particular over others, suppressing by subsuming, neglecting by abstracting?

Hannah Arendt's work suggests that at stake in these dilemmas are both the meaning we choose to make of the twentieth century and the actions we hope to enable in the future. I do not want to sound grandiose but I do think that something like this is at stake in the contemporary debates over storytelling in legal scholarship. Storytelling similarly has resurged in other fields, such as medicine, history, religion, and political theory, biography and autobiography, fiction, and entertainment. If Arendt is right, these are causes for celebration.

Still, let me repeat the concerns already raised: Stories alone do not articulate principles likely to provide consistency in generalizations to guide future action; stories do not generate guides for what to heed or what additional stories to elicit. Stories on their own offer little guidance for evaluating competing stories. I might as well state explicitly another favorite story, and old one.

The Rabbi hears in his study a dispute between two congregants. He listens to the first person carefully and comments, "You're right." Then he listens to the second person and concludes, "You're right." The Rabbi's wife, overhearing it all from the kitchen, calls out, "They can't both be right." "You're right also," says the Rabbi.

Offered as an illustration of the limitation of stories themselves to guide the evaluation of stories, this story also suggests a guide to the entire set of dilemmas that I have described. The guide is a posture of humility and acknowledgment of the partiality of truths. To generalize far beyond the context of that story, let me suggest the following: Modes of analysis and argument that maintain their exclusive hold on the truth are suspect. By casting doubt on alternative modes, they shield themselves from challenge and suppress alternative ways of understanding. They also render ordinary and explicable all they encounter: "To a hammer, everything looks like a nail." But some things are extraordinary and call for extraordinary responses. Methods of analysis that smooth out the bumps and subsume all under generalizations risk not only making this mistake but hiding it from view.

Some forms of social-science reasoning—for example, the form of microeconomics recast as law and economics—run this danger. So do some forms of philosophic argument that convert all problems into terms amenable to a preexisting framework, whether it be one inspired by John Rawls or one developed by Jeremy Bentham. So do some forms of legal doctrinal analysis that crank a fact pattern through the judicially crafted test.

Storytelling offers a worthy challenge to these modes. Stories disrupt these rationalizing, generalizing modes of analysis with a reminder of human beings and their feelings, quirky developments, and textured vitality. Stories are weak against the imperializing modes of analysis that seek general and universal applications, but their very weakness is a virtue to be emulated.[48] A story also invites more stories, stories that challenge the first one, or embellish it, or recast it. This, too, is a virtue to be copied. And stories at the moment seem better able to evoke realms of meaning, remembrance, commitment, and human agency than some other methods of human explanation. All this might change if theorizing picks up some of the themes of stories, but, then again, it might not.[49]

I suggest, in conclusion, that the revival of stories in law is welcome, not as a replacement of legal doctrine, economic analysis, or philosophic theory but as a healthy disruption and challenge to them. This is not about which must leave, stories or law, stories or social science, stories or philosophy, but about how they can live together, in and outside the walled city of Verona.

Daniel A. Farber and Suzanna Sherry

Legal Storytelling and Constitutional Law: The Medium and the Message

Traditional legal scholarship was primarily doctrinal. It essentially attempted to synthesize confusing or complex areas of law, offering harmonizing principles or clarifying distinctions. In the past two decades, this form of scholarship has increasingly been supplemented by interdisciplinary work, often arguing for significant legal reforms. This interdisciplinary work retained the conventional forms of scholarship, familiar to professors of law, history, and economics alike. Most recently, however, a new form of legal scholarship has arisen. Rather than relying solely on legal or interdisciplinary authorities, empirical data, or rigorous analysis, legal scholars have begun to offer stories, often about their own real or imagined experiences. Thus, today, one might open a leading law review and find a dialogue between the author and an imaginary radical friend or a recollection of some incident in the author's past. Often the story recounts how the author was mistreated because of race, gender, or sexual orientation.

Although no one contests that these stories are more readable than typical law-review fare, the consensus about their value stops there. Advocates of storytelling believe that stories can play a fundamental role in advancing social reform. Only through stories, they contend, can the fundamental racist, sexist, and homophobic structures of our society be confronted and changed. Critics, including ourselves, have raised concerns about the storytelling movement. In particular, critics have been concerned about the risk that stories can distort legal debate, particularly if those stories are atypical, inaccurate, or incomplete. The critics have called for greater care and rigor in the use of narratives within the framework of scholarly analysis. In turn, storytelling advocates have argued that these criticisms implicitly posit the very intellectual framework that stories are designed to challenge.[1]

Our purpose on this occasion is not to continue our debate with the storytellers about the merits of narrative but rather to situate that debate within a much broader dispute. In particular, we would like to show that more is at stake than merely a squabble about a new scholarly methodology. This methodological dispute is intimately related to the confrontation between aspects of critical theory and the Enlightenment tradition.[2]

Substantively, storytelling is closely tied to calls by radical feminists and critical race theorists for regulation of some forms of speech and for changes in discrimination law. On a more philosophical level, the storytelling movement is a natural outgrowth of the attack on legal reasoning conducted by critical legal scholars. The conventional view is that legal arguments persuade their audience through the force of logic.[3] If legal argument is logically vacuous, as the indeterminacy thesis suggests, we need some other explanation of how people become persuaded to adopt or change their beliefs about constitutional issues. Storytelling provides an answer to this dilemma by positing another, nonargumentative method of persuasion. In short, we will try to show how storytelling resolves a conundrum posed by the interminacy thesis and how that answer in turn has implications for the law governing hate speech and pornography.

We leave to another day the task of evaluating critical theory. Our purpose is not to critique critical theory but simply to shed light on its structure. We believe that the storytelling movement draws on a coherent perspective of the relation between language and law, which pulls what might seem disparate strands of critical theory together. At least for those who place value on intellectual coherence, this account may serve to strengthen the appeal of critical theory.[4] Be that as it may, we hope at least to show how the dispute between the storytellers and critics such as ourselves relates to a broader range of issues.

We begin by sketching the indeterminacy thesis and explaining how it makes persuasion problematic. We then show how advocates of storytelling have explained the role of stories in forming and changing beliefs. Because the particular forms of the indeterminacy thesis endorsed by the critical legal studies (CLS) movement are specific to arguments as opposed to other forms of expression, narratives are seen as having the power to change beliefs, for good or evil, in a way that argument cannot.[5] Thus, stories provide the Archimedean lever with which to move the world.

We then turn to the relation between this view of the workings of language and various disputes about legal doctrines. Just as "stories from the bottom" have the power to shift belief in progressive directions, stories from the top—pornography, hate speech, and symbolic government actions—can entrench racism, sexism, and other evils. Indeed, these "stories" from the top can be said not only to transmit but actually to constitute these evils. Not surprisingly, critical theorists advocate strong legal restrictions on these activities as a key to social change. Without such restrictions, they question whether fundamental social change is possible.

Finally, we sketch for purposes of contrast how the Enlightenment tradition addresses these issues. We do not, however, attempt to resolve the dispute between the Enlightenment tradition and critical theory. Our purpose is only to set the two approaches side by side in order to highlight the distinctive approach taken by critical theory. The chapter closes with a few thoughts about how to begin a fruitful dialogue between these two approaches.

INDETERMINACY, PERSUASION, AND STORIES

THE INDETERMINACY THESIS

Of all the aspects of critical legal studies, perhaps none gave rise to as much dispute as the indeterminacy thesis. In simple terms, the indeterminacy thesis holds: "The starting point of critical theory is that legal reasoning does not provide concrete, real answers to particular legal or social problems. . . . The ultimate basis for a decision is a social and political judgment incorporating a variety of factors. . . . The decision is not based on, or determined by, legal reasoning."[6]

There is a large jurisprudential literature on this thesis. That literature focuses on the relation between the indeterminacy thesis and liberal political theory—in a nutshell, on whether CLS has disproved the possibility of the rule of law.[7] Our focus, however, is quite different. Our subject is not political theory. It is not directly relevant for our purposes whether legal rules or judicial decisions are determinate in a way needed to maintain a liberal legal order. Instead, we are concerned with the process of persuasion—how it is that judges or ordinary citizens become convinced of a legal proposition, such as that pornography is (or is not) constitutionally protected. Thus, we focus on the indeterminacy thesis as it bears on arguments rather than on outcomes.

For similar reasons, we need not be troubled with the much-mooted question about the existence of "easy" cases in which legal reasoning produces clearly determinate results, and whether their existence would disprove the indeterminacy thesis. Our concern is with how individuals form or change their beliefs about legal issues. Whether a particular part of this process (legal reasoning) singles out a logically correct answer in some cases is only indirectly relevant. In other words, we are not particularly concerned with the question of what emerges from the legal system or with whether those outcomes satisfy the demands of liberal political theory. Instead, our concern is with how a lawyer can use words to influence a judge's view or, more generally, with how anyone can persuade someone else about the best answer to a legal question.

The conventional view is that the lawyer can persuade the judge through the use of valid legal arguments drawing upon such authoritative legal texts as precedents and statutes. It is this picture of persuasion that the indeterminacy thesis challenges. Obviously, lawyers do use legal arguments, but the indeterminacy thesis holds that these arguments lack the power to compel the audience to a particular conclusion.

It would be a massive task to sort through the various versions of the indeterminacy thesis and the supporting arguments offered in its behalf. Rather than undertake that task here, we refer the reader to the useful synthesis presented by Larry Solum in an article several years ago.[8] He catalogues the following reasons why legal reasoning might be indeterminate: First, individual rules of law themselves may be ambiguous or indeterminate, thereby providing no foothold for argument. Second, legal rules taken as a group may be circular or contradictory, or they may embody contradictory policies. Third, using legal rules may require reference to meta-rules, which suffer from the same flaws and provide the continual option of overriding existing legal rules.[9] The indeterminacy thesis holds that these factors combine to deprive legal reasoning of its power to constrain outcomes in significant cases.

INDETERMINACY AND THE PROBLEM OF PERSUASION

If these flaws in legal reasoning are ubiquitous, legal reasoning lacks logical force. In the jurisprudential equivalent of Newton's law of motion, every legal argument is matched by a logically equal and opposite legal argument. The opposing arguments thus cancel out logically.[10] Thus, if the indeterminacy thesis is correct, it is unclear how legal arguments have persuasive effect.

The strongest version of the indeterminacy thesis would be that the opposing arguments are not only equally valid logically but also equally effective rhetorically. This position seems problematic. It seems to fly in the face of the reality that arguments by lawyers do affect outcomes, which is why lawyers are sometimes paid large amounts of money to make those arguments. Also, some cases at least seem easy, whether or not this appearance is correct. Not surprisingly, critical scholars do not actually endorse this form of the indeterminacy thesis. Although the indeterminacy thesis holds that there are always (in the appropriate range of cases) opposing and equally valid arguments available, critical scholars do not believe that these opposing arguments are in practice equally effective.[11] It seems to be universally conceded that in fact judges will not find all arguments equally plausible and that sometimes a case seems easy because opposing arguments, though logically valid, are uniformly unacceptable to real-life judges.[12]

Thus, there is a certain degree of determinacy in the operation of the legal system, but it does not derive from the content of legal rules or arguments. What, then, is the external source that supplies the legal system with predictability?

One possibility is that the missing determinacy is supplied by a political or moral theory, so that legal rules are manipulated consciously or unconsciously to produce socially desirable results. Possible candidates might include Richard Posner's economic theories or the political theories of Robert Nozick or John Rawls. Critical legal scholars generally have been skeptical of this possibility, because they view such theories as suffering from much the same indeterminacy as the legal system.[13] More recently, Richard Delgado and Pierre Schlag have claimed that all normative argument suffers from inherent flaws like those that earlier critical scholars attributed to the legal system.[14] In their view, arguments based on moral claims simply lead nowhere, with or without an articulated theory. If morality, too, is indeterminate, it cannot supply determinacy to the legal system.

What, then, does account for the apparent determinacy of the legal system in operation? Critical scholars have found it difficult to articulate an answer. Joseph Singer points to the context of the judicial decision, which includes "the institutional setting (for example, court or legislature), the customs of the community (such as the standard business practices), the role of the decisionmaker (judge, legislator, bureaucrat, professor), and the ideology of the decisionmaker." Robert Gordon speaks of "stabilizing conventions," and Clare Dalton refers to "cultural values and understandings" as they impinge on and are created by our decisionmakers. Similarly, Mark Tushnet speaks of the image of the judicial role as the deciding factor, while Steven Winter refers to gestalts.[15]

These varying formulations suggest an account of how language does its most important work. On the surface, people make assertions and offer arguments, which they then assess in some purportedly rational way. But at a more fundamental level, language bypasses this process of rational consideration; it instead creates the structure or mindset in which what society calls rationality takes place. In some sense, when language is doing its most crucial work, it proceeds outside what we consider rational thought. We will refer to this as the mindset theory.

The mindset theory is inherently difficult to articulate because it is an attempt to describe how it is we "go on," as Wittgenstein put it, when rules run out.[16] Whatever enables us to proceed, often quite confidently, in this situation, cannot itself be reducible to rules, for then it would be equally indeterminate. For the same reason, it cannot be learned by mastering a collection of rules or by making logical inferences from those rules. In short, whatever kind of knowledge is involved here cannot be propositional—it cannot rely on assertions about the truth or falsity of statements about the world (including statements about rules of law). It is, however, apparently communicated in some way, in some nonpropositional form.[17]

On this view, one cannot be persuaded to change one's view on basic matters through argument, because what needs to be changed is the mindset controlling which arguments are received as persuasive and which are rejected. As Singer points out, this critical thesis makes the enterprise of persuasion problematic. Singer suggests that stories sometimes provide a method of persuasion that avoids this dilemma.[18] Although Singer discusses the use of stories only in one narrow situation, his comments have considerably broader implications. They suggest that the tacit understandings that determine mindsets may be transmitted through stories. Admittedly, there are other possibilities, but the suggestion is not an implausible one, particularly if the term "stories" is considered to include narratives, images, and similar types of communication.[19] From the mindset theory of law, it is only a small step to the view that mindsets are created by and changed through stories.

As we will see, the legal storytelling movement reflects a view of language quite compatible with the views of the indeterminacy theorists. We are in no position to know whether, as a matter of historical fact, the attention of critical theorists turned to storytelling because of the implications of the indeterminacy thesis. By and large, the leaders of the legal storytelling movement have been feminists or critical race theorists rather than members of critical legal studies. On the other hand, the indeterminacy thesis clearly reflected a corrosive skepticism about the conventional views of reasoning and argument, and this skepticism created a space in which storytelling and other forms of expression could take root. If the indeterminacy thesis is false, legal reasoning can claim some integrity as a form of thought. Storytelling could then either accept a role subordinate to legal reasoning or face the task of contesting a powerful and autonomous method of thought. But if the indeterminacy thesis is correct, then legal reasoning is a paper tiger, ready for replacement with more "progressive" methods of persuasion.

LEGAL STORYTELLING

The new storytellers believe that stories have a persuasive power that transcends rational argument. Indeed, one of the standard claims about stories is that "there are some things that just cannot be said by using the legal voice." The metaphors used to describe the effect of stories reflect this nonrational aspect of storytelling. Stories "explode" "stock stories" or "received knowledge," "disrupt" the established order, "shatter complacency," and "seduce the reader." They provide a "flash of recognition" and "resonate" with the reader's experience. Outsiders' stories recount the experiences of those who have "seen and felt the falsity of the liberal promise." Storytelling is also described as psychic "therapy."[20] All of these evocative metaphors refer to sensory experiences or physical effects, confirming that storytelling exerts its effects outside the level of logic.

Many advocates of storytelling explicitly contrast rational argument and the more directly emotive power of stories. As Gerald Lopez tells us, "Stories and storytelling de-emphasize the logical and resurrect the emotive and intuitive." The "epistemological claim" of feminist narratives, according to Kathryn Abrams, is that there are ways of knowing other than "scientific rationality." Radical feminist scholars—especially those using narrative as a methodology—thus reject the linearity, abstraction, and scientific objectivity of rational argument. Mari Matsuda similarly recommends noncognitive ways to know the good. Robin West questions whether purportedly rational theories are not instead rooted in emotion. She writes that "images, sometimes articulate, sometimes not, of what it means to be a human being . . . become the starting point of legal theory" and that those images derive from such noncognitive experiences as "school yard fights, armed combat, sports, games," and "the male child's memory of his mother."[21]

Others question the very distinction between reason and emotion. Mirroring the critical view of how judges really decide cases, Steven Winter suggests that the "cognitive process" proceeds by imposing narratives on experience, rather than through top-down reasoning.[22] If so, then traditional legal scholarship, with its linear, rational arguments, fundamentally fails to capture the essence of human reasoning. The cure, of course, is storytelling: according to Jane Baron, storytelling is designed to question the received definitions of such things as "reason" and "analysis," and to deny the distinction between "reason and analysis" and "emotive appeal."[23]

Whether the epistemological basis for storytelling is that it supplies a supplementary form of knowing missing from traditional scholarship or, more radically, that it better reflects our primary way of knowing, it clearly resonates with the critical view of persuasion. Both critical legal scholars and storytellers find the emotive or nonrational aspects of language much more persuasive than rational argument. And these nonrational aspects depend on context—the mindset of the speaker and the listener. Here again the storytellers' descriptions of their project mirror critical theory. They suggest that stories, unlike rational arguments, have the potential to change the mindset underlying legal rules. Richard Delgado says that "[s]tories, parables, chronicles, and narratives are powerful means for destroying mindset—the bundle of presuppositions, received wisdoms, and shared understandings against a background of which legal and political discourse takes place."[24]

Thomas Ross similarly notes that narrative is useful in the struggle to change assumptions and ideas, which are inevitably intertwined with rhetoric and language.[25] The storytelling literature is rife with claims of transformation and construction;[26] both terms are well suited to a methodology that operates at the level of mindsets rather than rational rules.

Storytellers thus present a coherent view of language as operating primarily in nonrational ways. This view of language, which underlies the use of storytelling as a methodology, is very much the heir of earlier critical theory. It elaborates on earlier views about how language works, and offers an escape from the paradox of indeterminacy created by the earlier theory. As the next section will show, a similar view of language underlies many of the substantive proposals of the new storytellers and other critical theorists.

CONSTITUTIONAL LAW, SOCIETAL STORIES, AND CRITICAL THEORY

The debate about storytelling has focused on methodology—what techniques may be legitimately used in legal scholarship, for what purposes, and how these techniques may be evaluated. Similarly, the indeterminacy debate focused on issues of legal methodology. Other bodies of scholarship address substantive issues raised by some of the same writers, particularly their vehement demands for the suppression of hate speech and pornography. So far, the methodological and substantive literatures have remained quite distinct. The argument for storytelling, however, has a deep connection with the arguments on these substantive legal issues. Both are founded on what we have called the mindset theory.

As we have seen, critical theorists have argued that stories can change the mindsets that underlie current social institutions. But not all stories are necessarily benign. Critical theorists have also asserted that existing mindsets like racism and sexism have been created by stories told by dominant groups; these assertions in turn serve as a basis for demanding government intervention to eliminate these malignant stories. We will consider three areas of law in which this demand has been made: pornography, hate speech, and equal protection doctrine.

MACKINNON'S VIEW OF PORNOGRAPHY

We begin with pornography. Since the early 1980s, a debate has raged between radical feminists and civil libertarians about the regulation of pornography, with other writers taking sides or adopting intermediate positions.[27] This debate has centered on proposed legislation designed by Catharine MacKinnon and Andrea Dworkin to regulate pornography as a civil rights violation.[28] Our present concern is less with the merits of this debate than with how proponents of the ordinance view the operation of pornography. We will focus on Catharine MacKinnon, who is unquestionably the leading academic advocate of this viewpoint.[29]

In MacKinnon's view, pornography plays a central role in the construction of gender inequality. Her view is based on a more general perspective on language that she shares with the legal storytellers. Society, she says, is "made of language,"[30] and language provides the foundation for oppression.

> Social inequality is substantially created and enforced—that is, *done*—through words and images. Social hierarchy cannot and does not exist without being embodied in meanings and expressed in communications. . . . Elevation and denigration are all accomplished through meaningful symbols and communicative acts in which saying it is doing it.[31]

Or, putting it another way:

> In the context of social inequality, so-called speech can be an exercise of power which constructs the social reality in which people live, from objectification to genocide. The words and images are either direct incidents of such acts . . . or are connected to them, whether immediately, linearly, and directly, or in more complicated and extended ways.
>
> Together with all its material supports, authoritatively *saying* someone is inferior is largely how structures of status and differential treatment are demarcated and actualized. Words and images are how people are placed in hierarchies, how social stratification is made to seem inevitable and right, how feelings of inferiority and superiority are engendered, and how indifference to violence against those on the bottom is rationalized and normalized. Social supremacy is made, inside and between people, through making meanings. To unmake it, these meanings and their technologies have to be unmade.[32]

In short, oppression is ultimately constructed through language.

Of the oppressive forms of language, the most effective is pornography. Pornography communicates the inferiority and subordination of women.[33] It plays an especially potent role in creating misogyny because of its connection with sex, which allows it to circumvent the conscious mind and exercise its effects without any awareness of the ideas it is transmitting. It is naive, MacKinnon says, to think that "anything other words can do is as powerful as what pornography itself does." Pornography changes people rather than persuading them. It bypasses the brain for the penis, for "an erection is neither a thought nor a feeling but a behavior." Pornography makes rational discussion of gender impossible: "Try arguing with an orgasm sometime." Because of pornography, "consumers see women as less than human, and even rape them, without being aware that an 'idea' promoting that content, far less a political position in favor of the sexualized inequality of the sexes, is being advanced."[34] To put it another way, pornography is the ultimate exercise in noncognitive storytelling.

Thus, MacKinnon views sexism as a mindset that is inculcated through stories that bypass conscious thought. Like the legal storytellers, she views the creation of societal mindsets as fundamental to social structure, although her focus is on evil rather than benign stories. Because pornography does not operate at the level of reason but at this deeper and more powerful level, she views it as a "speech act" in need of government regulation. Ultimately, for MacKinnon, sex inequality is not merely caused by pornography; it *is* pornography.

Although MacKinnon views pornography as uniquely powerful, she also believes that other forms of inequality are based on societal mindsets created by speech acts. Describing a brief she co-authored in a Canadian hate speech case, she says: "We argued that group libel, most of it concededly expression, promotes the disadvantage of unequal groups; that group-based enmity, ill will, intolerance, and prejudice are the attitudinal engines of the exclusion, denigration, and subordination that make up and propel social inequality; . . . that stereotyping and stigmatization of historically disadvantaged groups through group hate propaganda shape their social image and reputation, which controls their access to opportunities more powerfully than their individual abilities ever do."[35] In short, "[h]ate speech and pornography do the same thing: enact the abuse."[36] Both kinds of "stories" create subordination, although MacKinnon thinks that pornography is more powerful because of its connection with sexual arousal.

CRITICAL RACE THEORY ON HATE SPEECH AND EQUAL PROTECTION

Other critical theorists have focused their attention on racist speech rather than pornography. One of the most distinctive tenets of critical race theory has been its advocacy of the suppression of hate speech.[37] These writers contend that systems of oppression are inseparable from these verbal acts: "As critical race theorists, we do not separate cross burning from police brutality nor epithets from infant mortality rates. We believe there are systems of culture, of privilege, and of power that intertwine in complex ways to tell a sad and continuing story of inside/outsider." This argument, like MacKinnon's, views hate speech as fundamental to creating subordination. Or, to put it another way, "[R]acist speech constructs the social reality that constrains the liberty of nonwhites because of their race." By providing unconscious cues, hate speech subtly distorts thinking and behavior.[38]

The evil effects of hate speech on its victims or its audience do not occur because of its persuasive effects on the conscious mind. The direct impact on its victims has nothing to do with rational persuasion. Rather, it produces physiological shock reactions in its victims, subtly distorting their view of their world and themselves and even twisting their childrearing practices.[39] Nor can its malignant effects on the thinking of the white majority be countered through the marketplace of ideas, for (like pornography) it does not operate at the level of conscious reason. Instead, like a computer virus, it alters our programming without our knowledge: "[I]t is not just the prevalence and strength of the idea of racism that make the unregulated marketplace of ideas an untenable paradigm for those individuals who seek full and equal personhood for all. The real problem is that the idea of the racial inferiority of nonwhites infects, skews, and disables the operation of a market (like a computer virus, sick cattle, or diseased wheat). It trumps good ideas that contend with it in the market. It is an epidemic that distorts the marketplace of ideas and renders it dysfunctional."[40]

Among the invidious effects of hate speech is that it shapes the results of legal reasoning. Law formation is largely controlled by values,[41] and those values are shaped by racist speech. For instance, the "all deliberate speed" mandate for desegregation may "have relied on some assumptions that were significant in the dominant racist ideology" as reasons for avoiding immediate integration.[42] Again, as with the indeterminacy theorists, the focus is on the role of mindsets rather than logic in shaping judicial decisions.

The arguments for controlling pornography and hate speech parallel the claims made for the curative powers of storytelling.[43] What pornography and hate speech do, legal storytelling seeks to undo. Thus, within the storytelling literature itself, there are references to counterstories designed to combat the dominant stories.[44] Not surprisingly, the theories of language employed to support both the substantive and the methodological positions are the same.

The most sustained effort to work out the implications of mindset theory is found in a major article by Charles Lawrence.[45] He begins with a fuller exploration of the formation of mindsets, drawing on Freudian and cognitive schools of psychology to explain how hate speech shapes mindsets. He views racism as primarily an unconscious phenomenon. The extent of its irrationality is shown by the willingness of racists and anti-Semites to give hostile responses even when asked about entirely fictitious groups. Freudian mechanisms such as repression, denial, projection, reaction formation, and reversal are involved in racism.[46] Lawrence also makes use of cognitive psychology:

The content of the social categories to which people are assigned is generated over a long period of time within a culture and transmitted to individual members of society by a process cognitivists call "assimilation." Assimilation entails learning and internalizing preferences and evaluations. Individuals learn cultural attitudes and beliefs about race very early in life. . . .

Furthermore, because children learn lessons about race at this early stage, most of the lessons are tacit rather than explicit. Children learn not so much through an intellectual understanding of what their parents tell them about race as through an emotional identification with who their parents are and what they see and feel their parents do. . . . If we do learn lessons about race in this way, we are not likely to be aware that the lessons have even taken place.[47]

These mechanisms occur outside consciousness and are mutually reinforcing.[48] Note the recurrence of two key themes: beliefs take the form of tacit understandings or mindsets rather than propositions about the world, and they operate at a level deeper than that of conscious reason.

Not surprisingly, Lawrence finds in mindset theory a strong basis for banning hate speech.[49] He has also made creative use of the theory in rethinking equal protection doctrine. He begins with an innovative reading of *Brown v. Board of Education*.[50] Observing that the *Brown* opinion stressed the stigmatizing effect of segregation, Lawrence contends that precisely this stigmatizing effect constitutes the direct harm of hate speech on its victims. In essence, *Brown* was a hate speech case, in which the Court not only allowed but mandated the suppression of a racist message of inferiority.[51] The real question in the segregation cases was not racial separation as such but rather the messages of inequality communicated by particular forms of separation in a specific historical context.

Lawrence also uses mindset theory to revise the role of intent in discrimination law. Under the governing precedent, unless a statute refers to race on its face, it is unconstitutional only if enacted with discriminatory intent.[52] This rule has been sharply criticized by a number of commentators.[53] Lawrence shares these criticisms but offers his own alternative to the intent test. In his view, the real question is not the intent of the legislature but the message carried by a statute—its "cultural meaning." If a statute is understood by the public to invoke notions of racial inequality, then the court should presume racist intent.[54] Such a statute not only has a dubious provenance but functions much like hate speech: "[A]ctions that have racial meaning within the culture are also those actions that carry a stigma for which we should have special concern. . . . The association of a symbol with race is a residuum of overtly racist practices in the past. . . . And stigma that has racial meaning burdens all blacks and adds to the pervasive, cumulative, and mutually reinforcing system of racial discrimination."[55]

Lawrence's work is noteworthy in its creative application of the arguments in the hate speech debate beyond the area of First Amendment doctrine. In doing so, he has shown how mindset theory can be used to justify a broad agenda for legal change.

TOWARD A UNIFIED CRITICAL THEORY

As we have seen, Lawrence has integrated hate speech (and, by extension, pornography) with issues of equal protection law. By weaving together the views of Lawrence and other writers on these substantive issues with the indeterminacy thesis and the storytelling movement, we can begin to articulate a unified critical viewpoint on the legal system. It is not clear whether any single scholar accepts all of this viewpoint. Nor do we claim that someone who endorses some single aspect of this view is logically committed to endorsing the whole. But the theoretical pieces do fit together in an interestingly coherent way.

Beginning with the indeterminacy thesis, we see that the conscious process of legal reasoning is not really what accounts for the results in cases, nor is it truly capable of changing the beliefs and values of legal actors. Rather, beliefs are formed at a deeper level involving unarticulated social values and mindsets—values and mindsets that are inarticulate not only in the sense of being not yet stated but also in the stronger sense of being irreducible to any finite set of propositions or rules. The literature on substantive legal issues that we have just reviewed suggests that these tacit understandings are communicated through images, stories, and other symbols (sometimes including government actions, like segregation, which can function as hate speech). This transmission takes place at an unconscious level and is distinct from the conscious process of reasoning.

Any effort to persuade people to change their views must take place at a similarly deep level and clearly cannot put its main reliance on the indeterminate process of legal reasoning. Hence, as the storytelling literature teaches, the way to proceed is not through traditional forms of rational argument. Instead, persuasion must take place through the use of stories, which can operate at a deep level of mindset construction, just like the societal racist and sexist stories they seek to combat. At the level of methodology, this means legal storytelling. At the level of substantive law, it means that the government must suppress messages of bias and instead express affirmative support for oppressed groups.

A full-scale critique of this unified theory would obviously be a large task. The task would be complicated by the necessity of making the theory itself far more precise; this in turn would require making careful distinctions between the more radical versions of critical theory and more mainstream views shared in part by pragmatists and others. We will not undertake that task here. On the other hand, we think the stakes in this debate can be illuminated by contrasting this view with an alternative vision of law. We turn to this alternative vision in the next section and show how it offers another perspective on a broad range of problems ranging from the workings of legal reasoning, to the uses of stories, to the regulation of speech.

THE ENLIGHTENMENT ALTERNATIVE

Storytelling has encountered significant resistance in the legal academy.[56] Our purpose here is not to review or evaluate those responses but merely to note that they are based on a view of language that differs substantially from the view espoused by the storytellers. Whereas storytellers view language as operating most powerfully beyond the realm of reason, many of those who oppose either the methodology or the substance of the storytellers' proposals celebrate the use of language as a tool of rational argument.

Indeed, it should not be surprising that storytelling has been the object of resistance in the legal academy. Both law and the academic world have long been viewed as bastions of reasoned argument within a broader world that relies less on reason and more on power or rhetoric. Universities increasingly came to be treasured as enclaves of reason in an unreasoning world, as they grew from institutions designed to train young men for "the clergy and other gentlemanly professions" to scholarly communities dedicated to the proposition that "reason could grasp the essentials of human activity."[57] Felix Frankfurter praised Harvard—then, as now, the mythologized epitome of academic life—as a place where reason and intellectual merit reigned supreme. Many today still see the university as "an island of intellectual inquiry and robust discourse." Robert Post, for example, has noted the "fidelity to reason" that underlies the university's long-standing commitment to the pursuit of truth. Edward Rubin characterizes scholarship as unique because of its dependence on the "cognitive faculty that we identify as reason." The conventional view is thus that within the university, persuasion must be "on the basis of reason and evidence," not "social standing, physical strength, or the raw vehemence of argument."[58]

Law, too, has often been seen as the province—whether in reality or only in aspiration—of reason rather than emotion. Before the advent of critical theory, there was the paradigm of law as the domain of principle, not power.[59] The image of even the least powerful among us using the reason of law to force capitulation by such Goliaths as government and industry is captured in cases from *Brown v. Board of Education* and *Gideon v. Wainwright* to *INS v. Chadha* and *TVA v. Hill*.[60] Like the university, law has traditionally been viewed as preserving the power of rational argument in the face of nonrational forces.

This belief in the primacy of reason rather than rhetoric underlies much of the resistance to both the message and the medium of storytelling. The few direct critiques of storytelling that have been published so far have argued for the primacy of reasoned argument in scholarship.[61] Larry Alexander, while not addressing storytelling specifically, condemns much recent feminist and critical race theory scholarship as "fail[ing] the test for rational discourse." Henry Louis Gates, Jr., makes an analogous point when he accuses critical race theorists of replacing "the citizen at the center of the political theory of the Enlightenment . . . [with] the infant at the center of modern depth psychology and its popular therapeutic variants."[62]

Similarly, many of the most eloquent opponents of hate speech regulations clearly view reasoned deliberation as more significant or more legitimate than the use of language for emotional effect.[63] Robert Post, for example, grounds his regretful but firm rejection of most university hate speech regulations on a view of democracy that begins with the concept of "public reason." Carlin Meyer's impassioned denunciation of the feminist antipornography movement ends with a call to "analyze and reform" sexist ideology rather than to ban sexist images. Burt Neuborne opposes attempts to ban campus speech that causes "bruised emotions, even rage or anguish" unless the speech also causes "a demonstrable, tangible adverse effect on academic performance."[64] All these scholars endorse a view of language and thought that privileges the rational aspects of language over the emotive.

Put in a broader context, the debates over the regulation of hate speech or pornography are in part conflicts over the legitimacy of the "marketplace of ideas" as a justification for the First Amendment. The doctrines and positions that have grown out of Holmes's famous metaphor necessarily take as their starting point that in the long run the persuasive power of language lies primarily in its potential for rational argument. The economic metaphor indeed reflects the deep synchronicity between the view of humans as rational actors and the view of language as their uniquely rational tool.[65] The leading proponents of hate speech regulations, in contrast, reject the idea that speech persuades by rational argument and thus have no faith in the marketplace of ideas.[66] The domain of public speech is not a free market but rather an oligopoly: whoever has control of the most insidious and emotionally manipulative language will prevail, regardless of the "truth" of the ideas.

We have, then, two contrasting views of how humans react to language. These opposing views, in turn, spawn two different views of both law and scholarship. Under the critical paradigm, language is used most powerfully for subconscious or rhetorical effect; scholars in their writing and government in its legislation should recognize and respond to this primarily noncognitive aspect of language. For proponents of the traditional Enlightenment paradigm, on the other hand, language is (or should be) primarily a tool for rational argument. For that reason, scholars who seek to persuade others should rely on rational argument, and the government— which draws its legitimacy from the consent of the governed—should not limit the very tool that allows the populace to reach considered judgments.

Given the vast epistemological gap between these two worldviews, it is unsurprising that storytellers and Enlightenment traditionalists have been unable to resolve their differences. Indeed, the rancor with which the debate has occasionally been conducted[67] is understandable in such a context, where each side disputes not only the claims of the other but even whether the very form of those claims is legitimate.

CONCLUSION

We have attempted to show how various strands of critical theory can be woven together into a coherent whole. Each strand, in its own way, challenges the Enlightenment view of reason and its role in human institutions. The indeterminacy thesis holds that legal rules can provide no footing for logical argument. Hence, the legal system cannot be guided by rational thought; instead, its predictability derives from the unconscious mindsets of lawyers and judges. Legal storytelling seeks to break the hold of these mindsets, not through rational argument but through narrative power. In the realm of constitutional doctrine, this view about mindsets and how they are formed leads to demands for the suppression of malignant "stories," such as hate speech and pornography.

In contrast, the Enlightenment view is that the legal system can and should rely on the use of reason to resolve disputes, that viewpoints are best changed through reason rather than rhetoric, and that all forms of communication are presumptively immune from government regulation. This Enlightenment faith in "reason" (a term that we have no intention of trying to define here)[68] is sharply challenged by critical theorists, who find it a weak reed on which to rely in law, scholarship, and political discourse.

All this is, of course, an oversimplification of complicated intellectual terrain. To speak of the Enlightenment tradition is to invoke dozens of major thinkers whose mutual quarrels may nearly equal their agreements. And critical theory also contains a diversity of viewpoints, many of them individually complex. Our discussion consciously ignores these nuances in the interest of providing a useable roadmap to contemporary legal scholarship. We mean our description to be taken as a rough overview of two idealized modes of thought, not as full-blown intellectual history. Still, we believe that this overview provides insight into the intellectual issues at stake in the ongoing debate between critical and mainstream legal scholars.

If we are right, disputes about such constitutional issues as hate speech or such methodological issues as storytelling may reflect global disagreements about the operation of language and thought. Consequently, attempts at dialogue may often misfire because the disputants share less common ground than they may believe. It is not easy to know how to continue a productive dialogue under these circumstances. Each side, operating in the safety of its own intellectual framework, can trash the other. We believe, however, that the community of scholars should not readily abandon the idea of productive dialogue between opposing viewpoints.

How, then, might one proceed in the face of such a deep intellectual divide? We see three potentially constructive possibilities, which we might summarize as translation, synthesis, and comparison shopping.

The first possibility is for each side to attempt to speak the other's language. Mainstream scholars would attempt to persuade critical theorists through the use of stories; critical scholars would deploy conventional scholarly methods against mainstream views. This approach has some promise but also some problems, for it requires each side to operate on the territory claimed by the other, a territory that is in some sense foreign . Nevertheless, this approach does offer some possibility for fruitful interchange.[69]

A second possibility is to try to enunciate an alternative approach in which both reason and mindset play a role—or rather, in which the two are not seen as dichotomous. Some forms of pragmatist and feminist thought seem to be attempting to create such an alternative, but the conceptual problems are substantial, and it remains to be seen whether the attempt can succeed.[70]

A final possibility is simply to clarify the exact nature of the dispute. Perhaps, if the contesting positions are stated clearly enough, many people may find one rather than the other compelling. This kind of clarification might at least reduce hostilities by increasing each side's understanding of the other side's views. Ideally, clarification might also lay the groundwork for synthesis. Such a clarification, in any event, is the goal of this chapter.

Perhaps when disagreements become as fundamental as this one, there is nothing useful for the contestants to say to one another. As both lawyers and academics, however, we are temperamentally incapable of following Wittgenstein's famous injunction: "That of which one cannot speak, thereof one must remain silent."[71]

Anthony Kronman

Leontius' Tale

Stories often have a potent emotional effect. They please us, disturb us, make us cry and laugh, strengthen our attachments or dissolve them. Martha Minow and Daniel Farber recognize the emotional power that stories possess, but they also remind us of something else—the moral indeterminacy of storytelling. Some stories have good effects and others bad ones. Some stories strengthen good practices and good institutions, and others do the opposite. Moreover, stories do not contain within themselves the criteria for distinguishing the good ones from the bad. It seems, in fact, that the criteria for assessing the goodness and badness of stories must come from outside the realm of storytelling. What could their source be? Because any such criterion needs to be broad enough to encompass the whole field of storytelling, it must possess the same abstractness that principles and theories do. Hence it is plausible to think that the criteria required for the moral evaluation of stories must come from the realm of theory. That is a claim that many advocates of narrative resist.

Let me amplify the claim by retelling a story from Plato's *Republic*. You will recall that in the early books of the *Republic* Socrates and his interlocutors are busy constructing an imaginary city in speech, the perfectly just city, and that their arguments lead eventually to a city with three hierarchically ordered classes. Having concluded this part of their inquiry, the participants in the *Republic* return to the topic with which they began, the nature of the human soul. How is the human soul composed? What does it look like? Does it, in particular, have a structure similar to that of the imaginary city that Socrates and his friends have constructed?

For most of book 4 and a good part of book 5, this is what Glaucon and Adeimantus and Socrates discuss. They begin by quickly identifying two different parts of the human soul. On the one hand, there is the theoretical part, the part that is engaged in the business of reasoning and calculation. On the other hand, and at the opposite extreme, there is the appetitive part of the soul, which is filled with longings and desires of a literally thoughtless kind.

Having reached this point in the discussion, Socrates asks his companions if these two parts are all the soul contains. Adeimantus replies that he doesn't know, and Socrates himself admits he is not so sure. But then he says he has heard a story that suggests there is more to the soul than this, and proceeds to tell it.

Once upon a time, Socrates says, a man named Leontius was coming back to Athens from a trip abroad and happened to notice, outside the walls of the city, an enormous mound of corpses that had been left behind after a series of public executions earlier in the day. Leontius, who told the tale that Socrates repeats and that I am retelling now, reported to his friends that he wanted desperately to go and look at the bodies piled by the wall. There was something about this awful spectacle that drew his eye, but at the same time Leontius felt ashamed to look. At first he covered his eyes and started to walk away, but at last he could not resist. He was drawn back to the sight. So he went and looked, but then immediately struck himself on the chest and exclaimed, "Shameful eyes, fill yourselves, if that's what you desire."

What does Socrates infer from Leontius' story? That there must be a range of feelings in the human soul different from the brutish desires that are pulling Leontius to look at the corpses by the wall. There must be such feelings, Socrates says, because Leontius' feeling of shame is in conflict with his desire to look. Socrates concludes that there has to be a third part of the soul, in between the reasoning and appetitive parts, which is reducible to neither. Today we would call this intermediate part of the soul the realm of the emotions.

Emotions are complex things. They certainly have an affective component— they are feelings, not theories or arguments. But they also possess an intellectual or ideational dimension that brute desires lack. Anger, for example, is different from thirst, because it contains an idea as one of its constituent elements (the idea of improper treatment, which itself depends on further ideas of courtesy, justice, and so on). Emotions are a mixture of thought and feeling, and so Socrates properly puts them in a middle part of the soul, in between the brutish, unthinking, appetitive part, on the one hand, and the purely theoretical part, on the other.

It is to this intermediate domain of the soul that storytelling appeals, and the fact that Socrates identifies its existence through a story is itself significant in this regard. Why do stories characteristically direct themselves to this part of the soul? Because—like the emotions themselves and unlike both theories and appetites—stories combine thought and feeling and cannot make do with either alone.

What follows from this? Something important, I think, which I can bring out by adding a coda to my Socratic tale. Having retold the story of Leontius and used it to identify the previously unnoticed middle part of the soul, Socrates makes the following observation. The appetitive and theoretical parts of the soul are constantly at war, he says. The appetites pull us down, into a bestial existence, and thought draws us up toward something sublime. The emotional part of the soul, in between these other two, serves as an ally sometimes of one and sometimes the other. Sometimes the emotions link arms with the brutish feelings and seduce the thinking part of the soul into relinquishing command. But sometimes the emotions serve as an ally and helpmate to thought, checking the appetites and allowing reason to achieve the dominion that, on Socrates' view, it ought always to enjoy.

The emotional part of the soul, to which storytelling appeals, is therefore morally ambivalent. Sometimes it is the companion of the thinking part of the soul, sometimes of the appetitive part, and it makes all the difference, Socrates says, which side the emotions take in the endless battle between theory and desire.

From this I draw two conclusions. First, the faculty of reason, which provides the criteria we need to distinguish good stories from bad ones, is unable by itself to move us to action. It lacks the power to compel us to embrace and follow its own prescriptive norms. Reason is needed to guide us, but is incapable of inducing us to follow. It depends on the emotions, and hence on stories, to help carry us along, to provide the force that moves us to do as reason commands.

But second, stories and storytellers are always in a position of moral dependency, and what they do has value only when it follows the dictates of a part of the soul that transcends narrative and storytelling and the emotions that stories arouse. Reason is in command; stories contribute no independent moral insight of their own, and the most that they can do—an essential but limited function—is to energize the convictions of right reason, which come from outside their domain.

Is this Platonic view sound? I am unsure. But I do believe that no account of narrative can improve on Plato's view without first establishing where and why it is wrong.

Harlon L. Dalton

Storytelling on Its Own Terms

"One of my favorite stories is an old one." Thus begins the chapter by Martha Minow. At the symposium she related the tale based on the threatened expulsion of Jews from the ancient walled city of Verona. As I listened to her oral rendition, I was immediately drawn in, even though I had heard the story before. Truth to tell, I had even heard Minow tell it before. Nevertheless, it all seemed fresh and new, in part because Minow is such a terrific yarn spinner and in part because the neurons that I had pressed into service on the prior occasion had apparently been rewired in the interim, or perhaps fried.

Notwithstanding my enchantment, midway through the presentation a vagrant notion stole into my consciousness. "Hey," I thought, "this isn't a story. It's a joke." Instantly, I turned vigilant. I stared at Minow with newfound suspicion. Why? you might well wonder. Because if I had known that Minow's story was really a joke, I would have had my analytic tools at the ready. From the very start I would have been trying to figure out the punch line. If I had failed to anticipate it, I would have given Minow credit for telling a good joke. And if I had succeeded in completing the joke before she did, I would have patted myself on the back for being so brilliant.

My interaction with stories is wholly different. When a story is well told, I park my analytic faculties at the door. I suspend judgment rather than employing it to best the speaker. At the end of a good story, I want to ponder it and not just figure out who won the implicit battle of wits. By this measure, Minow's opening tale turns out, upon reflection, to have been a story after all (as well as a good joke), for in addition to being wonderfully evocative it shifted the analytic framework in useful ways.

What interests me most is the relation between storytelling and reasoning from principles. Although the latter is popularly thought to be the legal profession's bread and butter, both are, to my mind, critically important ways of knowing. Because they involve radically different modes of meaning generation, they are often thought of as at odds with one another. But it is their very difference that makes for the possibility of healthy symbiosis.

When we engage in traditional legal reasoning, we operate from within existing categories, both with respect to the rules laid down and in terms of our mental preset, or "mindset," to use the term favored by Farber and Sherry in their chapter. We take doctrinal and procedural building blocks as more or less given (even if our goal is to manipulate them, stand them on their heads, or cause them to disappear); we operate from within a particular point of view that we take to be general; and we scarcely notice the ways our thinking is structured and cabined. In contrast, when we listen to stories well told, we step outside the existing categories and the prevailing mindset. We go with the flow. We know that once the story is over, there will be time enough to sort out the meaning of it all.

As a consequence, stories (as Martha Minow informs us) cause people "to think freshly." They "draw [our] attention" and cause us "to arrest the ready reaction." They can "shake up some assumptions" and "deprive [the present] of peace of mind." Given this disturbing quality, storytelling has much to offer those who are committed to reasoning from principles. Far from being a substitute for it, storytelling provides a means of interrogating the reasoning process. Moreover, it provides an occasion for considering which principles should guide us and a way of discovering how the prevailing principles came to be.

To the contribution of Daniel Farber and Suzanna Sherry I react in the same three ways I always respond to their work on legal storytelling. As someone who cares about, believes in, and utilizes the genre, I am genuinely flattered by their attention. They take the work of storytellers seriously, read widely in the field, and offer a critique that is friendly rather than hostile. At the same time, I find myself mystified and frustrated by their deep and continuing misapprehension of the storytelling enterprise. Although my natural inclination is to lay the blame for this disconnect at their feet (an impulse I will indulge in just a moment), their work also causes me to wonder whether, just maybe, the legal storytelling corpus is not as developed, persuasive, or perhaps even as worthy as it ought to be.

Whatever the weaknesses of the genre and its current manifestations, it cannot be fairly faulted for failing to accomplish that which it does not set out to do. Yet Farber and Sherry continue to criticize storytelling, and in this essay the entire critical theory enterprise, for not satisfying the tests laid down for traditional scholarship and for failing to engage it on its own terms. That is a little like asking Miles Davis to play the notes as written.

Similarly, Farber and Sherry make the mistake of searching for a unified critical theory. With no sense of irony, they boldly proclaim their intention. "By weaving together the views of [Charles] Lawrence and other writers on these substantive issues with the indeterminacy thesis and storytelling movement, we can begin to articulate a unified critical viewpoint on the legal system. It is not clear whether any single scholar accepts all of this viewpoint. Nor do we claim that someone who endorses some single aspect of this view is logically committed to endorsing the whole. But the theoretical pieces do fit together in an interestingly coherent way." Wow! No self-respecting "crit" would ever attempt such a thing. How thoroughly un-postmodern!

To seek intellectual coherence across such a wide band of views, approaches, and projects is to indulge in intellectual play. That is fine, so long as no one mistakes it for meaningful critique. Although Farber and Sherry disclaim any interest in presenting a "full-blown intellectual history" of those they lump together, they surely must have noticed what a motley crew they have assembled. Moreover, they ignore the difficulties posed for their "unified critical viewpoint on the legal system" by the actual views of the scholars on whom they rely. For example, they quite properly acknowledge Mark Tushnet's leading role in the development of the indeterminacy thesis and recognize that he is one of the more visceral critics of legal storytelling. Yet they insist that indeterminacy and storytelling are of a piece.

In sum, Farber and Sherry are so possessed of the systematizing impulse and so hungry for "intellectual coherence" that they round off many of the most interesting corners in the legal academy. What binds together crits of every stripe is not their slavish adherence to any line but rather their penchant for improvisation and their resistance to categorical imperatives. To observe those qualities in action one need look no further than the outpouring of Richard Delgado, one of the godfathers of critical race theory. Richard has many fine qualities as a person and as a scholar, but coherence is not necessarily one of them. His work over time shows an extraordinarily creative mind branching out in many different directions. To cram Richard into a single pigeonhole would be to do his work a great disservice. All the more so the entire critical oeuvre.

Part II

The Construction of Cases

Robert Weisberg

Proclaiming Trials as Narratives:
Premises and Pretenses

In what sense is law narrative? First, there is a mundane question of taxonomy: What does the topic "legal narrative" include? There is the judicial opinion or trial presentation as a narrative of the facts about the parties; there is legal scholarship reviewing the history or background of judicial decisions by treating that history as narrative; there is, with increasing frequency these days, the legal scholar rendering insights in the form of narrative rather than conventional analysis and abstraction; there is the subtler issue of discovering hidden narratives underlying legal pronouncements that purport to have no history, or a different history.

At the level of legal doctrine, to tell a story about law, or to suggest that legal texts have underlying narratives, is to engage in a species of historical criticism of law. As Robert Gordon has shown, mainstream legal scholars believe that legal rules and principles are capable of intellectual coherence and practical utility at some general level independent of historical circumstances, yet scholars perennially confront the contingency of these rules and principles on specific human events at specific times.[1] Gordon then shows how rationalizers or apologists of law adopt a variety of strategies for finessing the tension between abstract authority and historical circumstance.

These strategies include (1) "denial" of the apparent historical contingency of law, relying on either sophisticated methods of induction from apparently changing legal practices that reveal subtler but still-universal legal principles, or a rigid constitutional originalism which argues that legal changes from foundational rules are simply illegitimate; (2) "Cartesianism," which treats law as a universal set of policy algorithms for addressing apparently different but essentially generic and recurring patterns of social needs; (3) "adaptationism," which finds the timeless component of law in a method for identifying, enhancing, and helping to implement the rationality inherent in the structure of any particular society or culture; (4) or "resignation," an ironic acceptance of law in a desperate existential effort to sustain some notion of meaningful order in the face of a social reality that challenges that notion at all turns.[2]

At another level, where legal scholars set out less committed to universal or timeless principles of law and more committed to observing how positive law emerges and operates, we can tell narratives of law to show that there exists outside the mundane or abstracted world of law a deeper story that truly "reveals" the norms of the culture. This is usually a story of struggle, oppression, redemption, or heroism about the establishment of a society's legal rules and may entail continual updating as morally or politically charged events in that society reenact those stories and myths.[3]

Thus, as Robin West has observed, even if we are speaking of legal doctrine itself, as opposed to "statements of facts" guided by doctrine, law assumes mythical commanders, mythical communities, and nightmares and fantasies about the powers of reason and authority.[4] Commercial law doctrine entails narratives or myths of the progress of commercial instrumentalism; criminal law may entail stock horror stories of civil unrest; any vaguely originalist theory of constitutional law carries a narrative of the solemn coming together of the framers. As the Christian reads in the Old Testament summaries of legal doctrines the traces of an unfolding story of a coming salvation, those who affirm a nation's secular laws may read in its texts the revelational traces of heroic actions that created the laws or a continuing plot of progress to perfect them.

Conversely, telling a legal narrative may be antirevelational, serving to demystify law, to demonstrate its contingency, its made-up quality, yet also to motivate us to be the artificers of our own law. Such a project may purport to be merely explanatory, as when Charles Beard explains the actions of the constitutional framers as strategies to protect their economic interests.[5] It can be both explanatory and brutally polemic, as when Douglas Hay explains the apparently merciful discrepancy between rule and enforcement of eighteenth-century English criminal law by telling a cynical story of the Crown's viciously brilliant plan to legitimate its terrifying power.[6]

This antirevelational notion of telling legal stories is, in a particular context, the flip side of the first notion. An apologist for legal formalism may narrate a story of the development of nineteenth-century commercial law as an evolving act of consensus of lawmakers and merchants to construct and refine efficient, public-interested rules for preserving property and enhancing socially useful transactions; a Morton Horwitz may then retell that story as a hypocritical effort to justify regressive capitalist exploitation of workers, artisans, and small merchants in the name of economic and social progress.[7]

These narrative projects to enhance or subvert legal authority may appear to be matters of historical analysis with no aesthetic implications. But modern theorists of narrative often argue that every historical rendering of events is an aesthetic project, as well as an empirical one, and that every aesthetic strategy has ethical premises and effects.[8] That is, certain ethical, political, and legal values manifest themselves or operate only in the medium of narratives by which a culture or nation defines itself. In this essay I consider what is at stake in narrative criticism from one perspective: contemporary views of the criminal trial. With the trial as the main focus, I argue that the prolific commentary on narrative is engaged more in ethical or political self-congratulation than in teaching us new truths about law and for that reason overlooks some dangerously unexamined ethical and political consequences of "narrative affirmance." I end with an example of the greater potential of narrative-in-law scholarship when it honestly confronts issues of the relation between legal forms, and nationalism and cultural identity.

PROFESSING LEGAL NARRATIVE

In one sense, to say that law is narrative is to share in the more general kind of plea that law ought to find some association with literature: the plea is really an expression of hope for spiritual redemption. To utter a popular trope like "law is essentially narrative" is simply to plead that law be treated as having a spiritual or emotional quality that might redeem the life of lawyers. As Richard Sherwin suggests, lawyers frustrated by the constraints of rationalism "crave enchantment," because they find it a likelier source of belief and meaning than rationalism, even though they recognize the concomitant risk of deception.[9] Thus, when lawyers and legal scholars utter one of the common tropes about law and narrative, they are offering what a linguist might call a performative rather than a "constative" remark;[10] they are not so much describing or explaining law or rendering a normative view of it as they are dramatically presenting themselves as having a particular moral or political or spiritual character with respect to law.

The law-is-narrative trope seems to be an especially useful performative speech act when uttered by trial lawyers or by legal scholars about trials, conveying more information about the feelings or fears or aspirations or delusions of the speaker than about trial lawyering. What the performative performs depends on who is saying it. When uttered by the trial lawyer, it tends to be a profession of worldly sophistication, of a desire to somewhat condescendingly correct whatever the average person's view of trial lawyering supposedly is. And sometimes it is a profession of the lawyer's purportedly deeper understanding of human character and psychology. Thus, the lawyer who lectures the layperson on the narrative nature of trial law may be thereby claiming either a greater cynicism or a greater wisdom or compassion.

When uttered by the scholar about trials or about law more generally, the statement may perform or express something else—something to do with the wider phenomenon of legal scholars professing the connection between law and literature. It is often a way to affirm a posture of humane passion or compassion as against a hard, cold world of legal abstraction, or to express the writer's sensitivity to the contingent or creative aspects of law. To some extent, the scholar is merely repeating or confirming what the trial lawyer has said, though perhaps with a bit more intellectual detachment. For others, it is an intellectual claim that we will understand the law in action far better if we study trials as anthropological phenomena rather than as adversarial procedures following legal rules.

Sometimes the trope's intended implication is simply wrong. Many observers of criminal trials who are sophisticated enough to understand the theory that a trial is essentially an aesthetic contest will say that the claim is wildly exaggerated. In this view, juries decide most cases on the basis of commonsense inferences from facts exactly the way the system is supposed to operate, and despite chic claims that "common sense is itself a social construction," there is a verifiable thing called common sense. This is especially true in run-of-the-mill cases—and implicitly so in those that are so one-sided for the state that they end up as guilty pleas.[11] Sometimes the trope is true but trivial. It would hardly shock lawyers who lived before the era of high critical theory in American academia to discover that the winner in some trials is the more sophisticated or compelling storyteller. In some uses, the trope is particularly obvious once we correct a definitional problem: Rhetoric is associated with and sometimes uses narrative; but lawyers have always used rhetorical tropes and formulas in their arguments. Indeed, that is what legal training once stressed, and narrative is different from rhetoric. But it may simply be that lawyers have implicitly learned the art of storytelling the way they once learned the rhetorical tropes. Either way this is still conventional lawyering.

Sometimes the law-is-narrative trope is meant to suggest something profound or iconoclastic about the law or about our species, but we so often see the statement made with a sense of its self-proving significance that we may fail to notice that no great significance has been established. Does it show that humans tend to think more narratively than conceptually and deductively? Doubtless true. Does it mean that progressive legal reform or a moral enlightenment or political revolution will occur when we stress and celebrate the narrative part of law and condemn as reactionary or irrelevant the supposedly old world of cold abstraction? This seems highly questionable, yet it is exactly what many scholars posit as the logical—and correct—consequence of enhancing the link between law and literature.

The past decade of law reviews has produced tens of articles that constitute what we might call a genre of narrative affirmance.[12] Typically an article begins by denigrating the supposedly traditional and rarely questioned view that law's authority is objective, deductive, linear, abstract, and acontextual. Next we get an allusion to developments in the social and even natural sciences, where traditional modes of analysis are now understood as forms of discourse, as being "situated" or "produced," as being constructed as rhetoric or literature. Almost always we see the ritual citation to Thomas Kuhn for the principle—which Kuhn has never actually espoused—that even physics is essentially a form of fiction.[13] Somewhat more plausibly, the writer alludes to John Dewey or Richard Rorty for the notion that narrative is an element of the pragmatic approach to truth that animates much American legal thinking. Often the article then proceeds to a *Rashomon*-like story: A legal event—most often a crime—is replayed from several perspectives. We are asked to admit a sense of disturbance and even revelational enlightenment that this can be true, however obvious it should be that this has always been the nature of trials.

Several conclusions frequently follow. First, and this is especially ironic, the writer adheres to the very traditional compulsion of legal scholars to draw practical conclusions from their hypotheses. In this case, the very scholar who has professed a theoretical or aesthetic view of matters once thought to be mundanely instrumental then reassures the audience that mundane conclusions can be drawn, as, for example, advice to the practitioner to make sure that a client's story is well formed and draws sufficiently on emotion, imagery, and theme. Second, a political lesson or moral lesson is drawn—often that the more morally deserving and usually politically or economically subordinated antagonist in the proceeding has been heard, or could only conceivably be heard (if she is allowed to speak, or if she is sensitively heard), in the language of narrative or some other literary form.

Third, larger cultural themes may be intimated. The scholar is likely to express concern that he has essentially refuted the possibility of objective, testable value in law and so has invited nihilism. Next, as a saving effort, the scholar finds a middle ground of sensible constructivism: he argues that for us to draw on traditional literary formulas or conceive new stories to achieve some instrumental legal goal does not entail descent into moral chaos and cynicism. "Constructed" principles and values are still values. Finally and more mundanely, the scholar may make the perfectly sensible point that the wise lawyer—or perhaps any lawyer automatically—will participate in the culture while also serving personal instrumental goals by drawing on established cultural sources of mental and aesthetic framing.

NARRATIVE, LAW, AND MORAL CRAFT

Narrative is a form of legal practice; legal practice and judging are partly ethical tasks, hence much of the recent scholarship about legal narrative is focused on what might be called the moral artistry of the judge or lawyer. Some scholars have focused on the appellate opinion to show the superior "moral craft" of these judges who can discover the "true" narrative underlying legal abstraction or the artificial narrative of official sources. Yet this sort of moral-legal artistry, as the very notion of a pragmatic craft might suggest, is as much a form of making as a form of discovering. It is a skill in devising rhetoric to capture appropriate moral outcomes or to craft fair legal results. It differs from the mythic notion of narrative in that the moral discoveries have less to do with discovering the immanence of the primal or sacred in the mundane than with observing or crafting narrative patterns as a matter of situation-sense in conventional social settings where conventional moral issues may appear.

In this vein, the most conventional focus of the trope that law is narrative is the appellate case that brings law to bear on facts, and the rendering of the facts in the appellate case is usually narrative in the weak, sequential sense. Law is narrative in the sense that cases, at least, have factual bases in human events that can be rendered in conventional narrative form. This, of course, comes dangerously close to the banality that cases all have explicit or implicit statements of facts. Numerous scholars have of late uttered the performative affirmation of law as narrative with little more in mind than noting that the statement of facts in an appellate case is a contestable and selective rendition of supposedly raw data. It is a staple of legal practice that where facts are disputed, lawyers narrate a version most conducive to their legal arguments without violating credibility or ignoring or negating those facts that are unequivocally established. To say that lawyers construct their stories is not very subversive. The truly subversive power of legal narrative does more than undermine a supposedly widespread belief that lawyers tell the objective truth. It has more to do with taking a society's narratives so seriously as to carry their immanent possibilities of meaning beyond the limits that lawmakers who use narratives impose.

Some scholars in this narrative-pragmatic vein have classified cases according to standard narratives. A good example is the bankruptcy discharge—the master narrative of consumer bankruptcy. David Ray Papke refers to Justice Sutherland as the Conan Doyle of this genre. For example, Papke describes the 1934 case of *Local Loan Co. v. Hunt* as a ritualized Dickensian story of freeing a family from living hell. In this stereotypical narrative, the bankrupt may be temporarily wayward, but he is fundamentally honest, industrious, and repentant.[14] Another example is Isabel Marcus's history of New York divorce law, which relies on stock narratives about the women figures in these one-sided disputes. She organizes both judicial and legislative action around narratives of women, ranging from legal nonentities under their husband's control, to adulterous whores whose immorality sufficiently threatens images of marital harmony to warrant fault-based divorce, to passive unloved martyrs who must yield to their adulterous husbands' need for legal and sexual freedom.[15] These legal stories tend to be deadeningly generic, for they exhibit no discrepancy between standard plot and particular story; moreover, they suggest the presence of the judge as a paternalistic, omniscient narrator, reassuring a happy ending in the mode of a romantic comedy under Northrop Frye's anatomy of genres.[16]

Some scholars have gone a step further in using this "discovery" about narrative as an evaluative device. They assume that there is good narrative and bad. Good narrative is concrete; it identifies the social and political facts that belie traditional legal categories. Bad narrative deceives with the illusion of concreteness, selecting and deleting facts and naming people and things to distort them to fit a conventionally acceptable legal conclusion. The more concrete and sensitive narratives have more than ornamental literary significance in the appellate decision: they directly affect the moral, intellectual, or legal quality of the decision. Whether as cause or effect, good narrative is associated with good decisions. In this sense, to say that law is narrative is to say either that underneath legal doctrine is a true story suppressed by the official narrative assumptions of the doctrine or that there is a contestable set of stories suppressed by the doctrine's claim of timeless Cartesian truth. Either way, the good narrative-pragmatic lawyer makes better legal arguments by uncovering what the doctrine may suppress.

The best argument for narrative is thus also the least original, and the turn to narrative apprehension of law has nothing very aesthetic about it but is simply a species of practical reasoning, an application of simple pragmatism or cognitive structuralist psychology.[17] Cognitive psychology, like legal doctrine, suggests that expertise requires not just knowledge but also skill at picking relevancies—a skill learned largely through experience—and that it includes nonintuitive articulation of interpretations. To some extent, if we add a moral component to this sense of relevance, narrative is a form of situation ethics, though, again, this simple Aristotelianism is not ambiguous or subtle enough to constitute anything literary. A simple statement of this notion comes, appropriately, from William James, writing on pragmatism:

> The individual has a stock of old opinions already, but he meets a new experience that puts them to a strain. Somebody contradicts them; or in a reflective moment he discovers that they contradict each other; or he hears facts with which they are incompatible; or desires arise in him which they cease to satisfy. The result is an inward trouble to which his mind till then had been a stranger, and from which he seeks to escape by modifying his previous mass of opinions. He saves as much of it as he can, for in this matter of belief we are all extreme conservatives. So he tries to change first this opinion, and then that (for they resist change very variously), until at last some new idea comes up which he can graft upon the ancient stock with a minimum of disturbance of the latter, some idea that mediates between the stock and the new experience and runs them into one another most felicitously and expediently.
>
> This new idea is then adopted as the true one. It preserves the older stock of truths with a minimum of modification stretching them just enough to make them admit the novelty, but conceiving that in ways as familiar as the case leaves possible.[18]

Perhaps the gist of the matter is that the scholars promoting the link between narrative and pragmatism vaguely assert that the choice of aesthetic form has ethical implications, but they tend to stop at the point of suggesting that lawyers with better narrating skills have better chances of winning reasonable but otherwise unconvincing legal arguments.

The implicit premise—or promise—of this scholarship has been captured best by the literary scholar Wayne Booth.[19] As Booth has argued, every choice of a story is ethical. Narrative is metaphoric and critical of other narratives. Each has a whole web of interpretations that compete with others. As Booth notes, every hour you spend with a narrative is a criticism of the life unlived during that time. Life is whatever the narrative narrates rather than whatever else you thought it was, and if the narrative is sufficiently picaresque, the world you return to, the world that the narrative implicitly criticizes, will disappoint you. Narratives are, in a sense, all stories of genesis; to tell them is to offer a standard for judging other metaphoric views of life.

As I noted, the commonest venue for the law-and-literature movement's narrative pragmatism is the commonest and easiest venue for all treatment of law—the appellate opinion. Thus, we see Kim Scheppele commenting that the key to understanding the evolving law of rape is to examine the conflicting narratives, the editing of facts, and the manipulation of time frames in conflicting appellate opinions treating matters of consent.[20] Truth, she argues, is not the property of an event; rather, it is a property of an account of an event. Women's stories continue to be disbelieved in court, but whereas law used to be sexist in its abstract doctrine, now it is sexist in its particular facts. That is, before the recent reform of rape laws women had to prove that the man used aggressive force or that the man knew they had not consented, whereas now they have trouble convincing courts that they in fact did not consent. As Mark Kelman has shown in his exposition on critical legal studies, these cases turn on the particular time-framing assumptions of the courts.[21] Almost any outcome of a factual dispute in a rape case can be reversed by expanding or contracting the time frame in which we view the action.

Scheppele argues that the subtle premise of the misogynist legal narrative is that truth is singular, immediately apparent, and permanent. In fact, she argues, apprehension of factual truth is often precarious and fragile and subject to distortion and decay over time—as in the now-conventional criticism of eyewitness identification testimony. She argues that a more accurate epistemology of sexual assault cases reveals that although there is at the core an objective set of facts, those facts appear through a complex sequence of silences, revisions, and counterstories. When women are attacked, among many harms they suffer is the loss of their grasp of the conventional coherence of an event, because the attack disrupts their normal expectations of reality. Their stories therefore do not comfortably jibe with the culturally available narratives of provocation, passion, or insanity under the premise of normal rationality. Before a new story becomes acceptable to courts and juries, we must see larger numbers of tellers and corroboration and even expert testimony that the story makes sense. Thus, Scheppele believes that legal narratives are based on epistemological premises and that the choice of narrative form often determines control over legal outcome.[22]

This argument is carried a step further by Alan Dershowitz, who offers the refreshingly anomalous argument (anomalous for a defense lawyer) that the very premise that facts take narrative form is unjust.[23] Countering the common talk of competing narratives in criminal cases, Dershowitz argues that the role of the defense lawyer—at least in a case where the defendant had obvious motive and opportunity for the crime but claims a total alibi—is to refute any claim of narrative form in the case, because he sees narrative form as an uninformed fantasy of the jury wholly exploitable by the prosecution. In his view, a jury will only convict if the prosecution case exhibits some Aristotelian coherence, and, rather than offer a counternarrative, the defense lawyer must convince the jury that the crime may be the result of random or inexplicable action or circumstance—that the true facts are either confusing or aesthetically disappointing.

Thus, if the jury hears that O. J. Simpson once assaulted Nicole Brown Simpson, and if it sees physical evidence at least consistent with Simpson's guilt, the prosecution urges it to use this information to form a well-wrought story with a resolute climax. But, Dershowitz argues, the overwhelming majority of men who assault their wives do not kill them, and if we start an imaginary videotape at the moment, say, that a jealous ex-husband encounters his ex-wife under circumstances where he might feel jealous, in "real life" (as opposed to prosecution narrative art), the encounter will usually end in boring anticlimax: they will talk and he will leave.[24]

Dershowitz faces a counterargument: Although it is true that most wife abusers do not kill, and it is therefore irrelevant that most wife killers have been abusers, it is also true that few abused wives are killed by anyone. Thus, once we know both that a woman has been abused by her husband and that she has been brutally murdered, it is no longer implausible or statistically unfair to look to the ex-husband as the major suspect. At this point, Dershowitz would argue that the constitutional presumption of innocence requires us to resist a narrative temptation we might otherwise think is reasonable. Dershowitz continues to insist that the apparently neutral and natural human penchant for narrative order serves as a prosecution device for unjust legal order.

It is obviously desirable that law should be informed by the voice of the concrete, the particular, the empathetic, the passionate. But to make this point about legal discourse should hardly require recurrence to the great works of the humanities. In effect, this part of law-in-literature scholarship constitutes a kind of remedial reading. Lawyers or law students are or should be perfectly aware even from conventional case analysis that human pain underlies doctrinal abstraction, that the general rules of common-law doctrine live in tension with and are often undone by the particular stories of the parties to the case.

A good example is the well-known case of *State v. Williams,* in which an American Indian couple was charged with involuntary manslaughter for keeping their child from life-saving medical care.[25] Many commentators on this case have argued that the "reasonable person" standard applicable in criminal negligence doctrine should be "particularized" down to the matters of the specific, socially ingrained reactions of Indian parents to government doctors. This point has often been treated as if it offered a striking insight into the role of narrative or voice in legal opinions: The court's view of the negligence standard, it is said, is based on a bourgeois-Anglo perspective about attitudes toward government and medical care. It thereby suppresses the voice or narrative of the parents, who would, if fully permitted, tell a story about their experiences with the federal government, their reasons to distrust Anglo doctors, and their culturally based justifications for withholding the child from the authorities who might take him away.[26]

This is a vital point in understanding the case, but it is a point readily revealed by conventional doctrinal analysis. Indeed, it is perhaps the only important issue to discuss about the case in a basic criminal law course. To say that we need to read works of imaginative literature to see this point is odd. It should be unnecessary, because normal human minds and sensibilities should realize the point even by reading the bare facts of the case—so long as the bare facts are made available—and in any event, as I have said, relatively conventional rules-standards analysis would make the point anyway.

EXAMPLE OF THE POVERTY LAW NARRATIVE

One distinct body of writing—one might now treat it almost as a formulaic genre—concerns the voice of the subordinated person facing the harsh power of the state bureaucracy and the struggle of the lawyer to recognize and give power to that voice.[27] Because poverty law is such a tense and volatile venue for the application of law to earthy human need and because it presents an apparently wide discrepancy in power and sophistication among the actors (client, lawyer, and state official), it has been the subject of much of the writing about "narrative competition" in law. This genre has often been promoted as a form of critical storytelling that generates theory out of practice.

In one review of this genre, Christopher Gilkerson classifies the types of legal narratives according to the various pairings of legal actors: clients and lawyers, lawyers and judges, lawyers and legislators, and so on. He recognizes that certain narratives are "universalized"—sometimes in the form of doctrines, sometimes in the form of social stereotypes, and, significantly, sometimes the two at once. An overly general narrative, by this measure, it likely to celebrate abstract rules of law.[28] Gilkerson deems law a "social institution through which people tell stories about their relationships with others and with the state and an authoritative language, or discourse, with the power to suppress stories not articulated in accepted forms." He adds that "the storytelling dilemma in law arises when authoritative discourse and knowledge impede the transfer of the storyteller's meaning and images." But the key feature of legal narratives is a carefully staged contest between the authentic and the inauthentic narrative voices.

Gilkerson then offers a brief taxonomy of poverty law narratives: stories told by clients to lawyers, stories told by lawyers to judges, universalized narratives, and stories told by judges to justify their decisions. His goal is both descriptive and normative—to determine whose stories should be told in advocacy and why. Gilkerson assumes that the client always speaks to the lawyer in narratives; he thus risks either the condescension that the client is a "natural" who cannot think in legal categories or, rather, if we assume that narratives uttered in courts are often the best strategies, that the client is a slicker or more effective lawyer than the lawyer. Obviously, Gilkerson prefers the former, because he suggests that the interwoven stories and identities that we see in legal narratives constitute the "subjective essence" of the human reality underlying legal issues.[29]

Anthony Alfieri also explains the gist of this genre.[30] The client tells the lawyer her welfare story. Ultimately, the story is reconstructed and cleaned up from the hearing transcripts. The lawyer suspects that he has falsified the client's story, so he seeks to retrieve it through literary techniques that he calls suspicion, metaphor, collaboration, and redescription. Suspicion is the practice of investigating the poverty lawyer's interpretation and its premise of client dependency, which are contradicted by the client's public and private assertions of power. The lawyer can transcend this falsification through suspicion and thereby come to share interpretive power with his client. By "metaphor" he means deciphering the doubleness of events—in this case, the narrative of family struggle immanent in the otherwise dry facts of the case. Collaboration is the sharing of storytelling. Redescription is the reconstruction of the client's image to discredit the traditional images of dependency. Encased by a traditional norm of detachment, poverty lawyers do not see the relevance of an individual client's struggle and do not encourage its production and reenactment, nor do they search for the conditions that brought it about. They, in fact, presuppose that narratives of client struggle are unusable in advocacy. A better lawyer, enlightened by sensitivity to the critical narrative of the client, can seize for the client a limited autonomy from the violence of the law's interpretive practices.[31]

In Lucie White's essay on the hearing of Mrs. G., we get critical storytelling in the form of antischolarship, or a narrative of law designed as antiprofessionalism.[32] Superficially, this piece seems more sophisticated than the simple sentimental genre in which law is seen as inherently procrustean and the human reality in which it purports to do justice as inherently resistant to procrustean legal categories. Although White speaks unpromisingly of the "humanist" view of law as opposed to the "instrumental" view of law, she argues that the former sees legal procedure not as a device to achieve legitimate outcomes but rather as a "normative horizon" that beckons us to create stronger and more valuable opportunities for participation than the bureaucratic state normally allows.

To demonstrate, she tells the story of Mrs. G. Summarized, it goes like this. Mrs. G., a single mother of four children who lives on AFDC (Aid to Families with Dependent Children) money received a six-hundred-dollar insurance settlement for an auto accident. She told her caseworker (another black woman) about it, and the caseworker wrongly reassured Mrs. G. that this settlement did not have to be set off against her monthly welfare payments. Later, the supervisor discovered the error and ordered Mrs. G. to pay back the six hundred dollars, which she had already spent on personal articles and shoes for her children.[33]

White, then a legal aid lawyer, represented Mrs. G. in the hearing at which she was to contest the reimbursement order. White rehearsed Mrs. G. to tell two stories to support her legal claim. First was the "estoppel" story, in which the caseworker clearly told Mrs. G. that no setoff was necessary; second was a "necessities" story, in which the payment was used to buy, for example, new shoes, the children's older shoes being beyond repair. To White's shock, at the hearing Mrs. G. chose not to follow the script. She refused to blame the caseworker for estoppel, now saying that she was unsure whether she ever even told the caseworker of the payment. As for necessities, Mrs. G. now said that the children's older shoes were adequate but that she had wanted the children to have finer ones for church.

White views Mrs. G.'s improvisation as an act of heroic self-assertion. On the estoppel story, White surmises that Mrs. G. refused to grovel or perhaps was protecting a black sister. As for the shoes, Mrs. G. did not want to equate material objects with life's true necessities. Rather, she wanted to affirm the necessity of religion as central to the spirit of Southern Black life.[34]

Surprisingly, Mrs. G. won her appeal. What does this signify about law and the norms of narrative? White cannot conclude that Mrs. G.'s was a successful legal strategy in some generalizable sense. She admits that she has no idea why the welfare department ruled in Mrs. G.'s favor. Did Mrs. G.'s paradoxical strategy morally disarm the examiner? Did Mrs. G. induce fear or respect? Did the examiner condescend to her? White concedes that Mrs. G.'s performance did nothing much to change her life or the local political landscape. What, then, are we to learn from this brilliant story-reversing maneuver by Mrs. G.?

The most obvious problem in answering this question is that we do not know which story was true after all. Had Mrs. G. dissembled to her lawyer because she thought her lawyer needed to hear the more conventional story and then, out of spontaneous and heroic honesty, blurted the truth to the hearing examiner? White could have gone back to ask the examiner, but maybe that would have disrupted the desired ambiguity. Or, on the contrary, was the original story true? If so, Mrs. G. may have proved herself both a better storyteller and better lawyer than White, but the value of the second narrative would be of a different sort: it would be a heuristic of aesthetic imagination—and rhetorical savvy—to win over the examiner. But was it done with the goal of morally educating the examiner to appreciate the multiplicity of motives and complexity of interests that welfare clients can have, or was it to snooker him with a story that would work? White does not address the more vexing "literary" problems in the case. Would enabling Mrs. G. to participate in the hearing with more authentic informality have deluded her into thinking that the state was a benevolent partner in her self-assessment? Would Mrs. G. have been acting more authentically after all, or must we recognize that Mrs. G., for perfectly good reasons, wanted to act out her own carefully scripted story as well?

The only lesson that White is willing to draw is admittedly negative: Mrs. G.'s victory was more attributable to the mysteries of human character than to the rule of law.[35] But at the end, White suggests that the due process doctrine of *Goldberg v. Kelly* should be extended to tailoring the procedures of a welfare hearing to take into account the insecurity of the claimant.[36] She even suggests "accent" or "discourse" due process. This might require coaching judges to restate powerless speakers' words into dominant discourse style, interpreters or expert witnesses to educate jurors, or even affirmative action representation on juries. This lame set of conclusions ends up detracting from what should be the main interest of the story: its cultural specificity.

White concedes that these measures might be impractical and might even widen cultural divisions. Thus, more subtly, she suggests expanding the "logic of proof" so that "conversational and narrative styles of subordinated groups are no longer deemed 'irrelevant' to the decision process."[37] Uncertain or "other-oriented" speech might be revalued in legal rituals that seek to build community rather than punish the transgression of legal rules. But White acknowledges that this approach, too, would not address the underlying economic and political facts. Thus, she suggests that perhaps the answer lies in some version of hate speech laws which directly attack the cultural imagery that subordinates Mrs. G. Finally, to the extent that the problem is bureaucracy itself, we must turn our energies to imagining a postbureaucratic world where formal procedures will be replaced by face-to-face deliberations among free but interdependent individuals.

White inadvertently tells us a great deal about law-and-narrative scholarship. In its embrace of concrete human facts over the distortions of abstract legal categories, it reveals great ambivalence about the welfare-bureaucratic state. Is the state the enemy of the individual? The savior? The unquestioned authority that must be made to receive the narrative message? Is it the individual at all we speak of, or a deeper sense of the person in social context? That is, did the state err at first by stereotyping Mrs. G. as a welfare chiseler, failing to recognize her individual humanity, or by treating her as an autonomous individual in a free market for goods, failing to recognize her as a member of a religious community? And what is the role of the lawyer in a world of legal narrative? White is implicitly ambivalent about whether lawyers can learn anything from narrative, because it is the very narrative authenticity of the story—even though the story is possibly a lie—that makes Mrs. G. so powerful, and any effort to do the translation for her would have to be inauthentic. Thus, after dallying with some bizarrely formalistic procedural remedies for the ills that Mrs. G.'s story uncovers, White has to make a leap to imagine the interdependent world where Mrs. G. would not suffer abstract constraints on her legal claims—but presumably would not need a lawyer either.

In that regard, White invites the implicit criticism offered of these poverty law narratives by William Simon.[38] Simon takes their premise to be that only respect for narrative difference and only the effort to establish the authentic client story enables the lawyer to respect the client's sense of autonomy. But, argues Simon, the perfectly rational purpose for having a lawyer for many people is to delegate their autonomy to the lawyer. The poverty-narrative genre turns the lawyer's role into story reader or archaeologist of authentic narrative and value, so that if she digs deep enough she renders her own role invisible; she carries out the client's wishes after witnessing the client's drama of self-presentation. The problem is that many clients deeply want to exercise their free choice to rely on someone else's judgment even though, or precisely because, that lawyerly judgment does not represent any well-worked-out choice by the client.[39] In clinical narratives like White's, the lawyer typically thinks she understands the contradiction between the life-destroying abstraction of the state and the natural humanity of the client. Thus, the lawyer's job is to efface herself as an image of the state and thereby help integrate the client safely into the legal regime. But does the lawyer understand her relation to the state any better than the client does?

THE NARRATIVE TRIAL AND NATIONAL HISTORY

I have offered several examples of commentary discovering narrative in legal practice and professing the ethical and political significance of that discovery. I have suggested that often in this work the commentator is overly engaged in the rhetoric of ethical or political self-congratulation, often lapsing into banality or sentimentality, and fails to appreciate the more discomfiting truths that narrative reveals about law. I will end by placing legal narrative in the broader context of recent debates about the role of narrative in historical scholarship. The key themes of this historiographic debate have been the relation between supposedly objective historical narration and frankly fictional literary narrative, and the role of narrative in describing and promoting cultural identity. These debates illuminate the complicated and ethically and politically volatile relationship between history, literature, and culture, and thereby point us toward deeper aspects of narrative in law.

Certainly, much of the recent law-as-narrative scholarship has viewed narrative as a means of enhancing a sense of cultural, racial, or ethnic identity.[40] In particular, the critical race theory school of legal scholarship suggests that writing narratives about law or discovering narratives in law shows that political struggles between dominant and subordinated groups often manifest themselves in competitions between dominant and suppressed cultural narratives.[41] Although the critical race scholars thereby argue that narrative is a contested area of law and not a transparent medium for uncontroversial legal values, the implication of much of their work is that there exist outside law wholly authentic criteria of cultural experience and identity that are then competitively represented in the legal arena; or, put differently, although marginal groups must often use indirection and suffer suppression in their efforts to give voice to their legal values, those values enjoy an authentic integrity and coherence outside the legal arena in which they compete. But law-as-narrative scholarship would do well to recognize that the relations among legal authority, narrative form, and cultural identity are far more complicated.

In a critical study of narrative and historiography, Lawrence Stone has suggested that confidence in narrative as the appropriate mode of historical writing waned early in this century and has now returned, and the reasons for this revival may prove fruitful for our examination of legal narrative.[42] Why did narrative disappear at all? Stone suggests that early modern scientific history derided narrative as unscientific when modern science became the most prestigious model of all scholarship. Supposedly, narrative told us the what and how but not the why.[43] Narrative history was superseded by the advent of Marxism, social science, French demographics and structuralism, Parsonian functionalism, Malinowskian anthropology, and economically-based cliometrics.[44] So why do we now have narrative again?

The revival of narrative, says Stone, suggests a loss of faith in those scientific projects, widespread disillusionment with any economic determinist model, and frustration over the split between social and intellectual history. Further, says Stone, we see the general decline of ideological commitments, especially the old Marxist debates about slavery, industrialization, and the rise of the working class and the gentry.[45] The advent of mixed economies throughout Europe and North America has weakened debates over Marxism, and if brute military power now seems to explain events, contemporary historians view that power as an example of individual or group "agency" that invites a return to older narratable history. Power, for the modern narrative historian, is really exercised by wills and can be exercised or thwarted by personal and political decisions. Relying on anthropology as the newly dominant social science, the new historian studies the nature of power, charisma, and authority in concrete, narrated situations. Indeed, Stone wonders whether future history students will have to be trained in rhetoric, in textual criticism, or in symbolic anthropology.[46]

Stone also hints, however, at what is the most salient aspect of the new narrative history: its use of narrative to illuminate the provenance of national or ethnic identity as the sustaining force in modern political conflict. Narrative has found energy in the combination of exacerbated self-consciousness about narrative method in the social sciences and the utility of narrative in promoting symbolic national or group identity over abstract ideological or governmental structure. And therein, I believe, lie the most promising, if the most abusable, opportunities of narrative legal scholarship.

The most aggressively post-modernist view of narrative comes from Hayden White.[47] As White notes, philosophers have sought to justify narrative as a mode of explanation different from the scientific; theologians and moralists have recognized the relation between a specifically narrativistic view of reality and the social vitality of any ethical system; anthropologists have reexamined the role of narrative in their work; and cultural critics, both Marxist and Fanonist, have announced the death of master narratives. Yet even though the traditional distinction between history and fiction—whereby historians only invent rhetorical flourishes and do not report facts—has been dissolved by recent theories that deny any ontological difference, even postmodernism is ironically committed to the return of narrative as an "enabling proposition" for a culture.[48]

Historians themselves, White argues, traditionally did not have to worry about the problem of narrative, because traditional history would presume no speaker but would rather engage the pretense that events are supposed to tell themselves. More precisely, White describes the three very old forms of history—the annals, the chronicle, and the history. The annals are just a chronological list, while the chronicle appears to tell a story but achieves no closure. Hence we move from the nonstory to the unfinished story to the story—or the modern history. But the key link in this chain of narrative development is, appropriately enough, law, or, more precisely, the rise of formal nation-states that must narratively control their histories in order to impose legal order on their peoples. For this view of the history of narrative history, White points us toward Hegel.[49]

In his *Lectures on the Philosophy of History,* Hegel directly links historical narrative with law, noting that prehistorical societies had no law governing transactions.[50] For Hegel, there is no possibility of objective history without law, because there is no impulse to record for posterity outside a law-bound society, for only in law-bound societies do definable and hence recordable social transactions take place. In that sense, the proper, if implicit, subject of all history is the legal nation itself and the endless conflict between law (or authority) and desire. Only where there is law can there be a subject or kind of event that lends itself to narrative, or a legal subject to serve as the agent, agency, and subject of historical narrative. The urge to tell stories derives either from a desire for national law and order or a desire to challenge that law and order.

Narrativity, for Hegel, presupposes a legal system against which or on behalf of which the typical agents of a narrative account militate. Hence, narrative deals with law, legality, legitimacy, or, more generally *authority*. The desire to narrate is the desire to represent authority, whose legitimacy depends on establishing certain grounding facts.[51] For Hegel, what history tells us is not the real story of what happened but rather the relation the legal state has established between a public present and a past that a state endowed with a constitution made possible. In traditional societies, narrative per se did not distinguish historiography from other kinds of discourses, nor did the reality of events recounted distinguish historical from other kinds of narrative. It was the interest of a specifically political mode of human community that made a specifically historical mode of inquiry possible, and the political nature of this mode of community required narrative for its representation. Thus, the proper subject of history was the collision between established duties, laws, and rights and the human contingencies that challenge them, and its aim was to depict those kinds of conflicts in prose narrative.

But the literary critic Homi Bhaba has offered a concept of nationhood that joins Hegel's with a more cynical contemporary view of history. Says Bhaba, "Nations, like narratives, lose their origins in the myths of time and only fully realize their horizons in the mind's eye."[52] We suffer ambivalence about the idea of the nation—an awareness that despite the certainty with which historians speak of the origins of the nation as a sign of modernity in society, the cultural temporality of the nation suggests a much more transitional social reality. As a matter of political history, the nation may come into being as a distinct legal personality, subject to customary law, but legal history must equally take account of the nation as an unstable system of social life, not a polity. Therefore, narrators and historians must finesse their way through conflicts over inclusion and exclusion, customs of taste, and rules of justice in trying to comprehend the nation and offer a coherent history as well. Traditional histories do not take the nation at its own word, but, for the most part, they do assume that the problem lies with the interpretation of "events" that have a certain transparency or privileged visibility. And in Bhaba's literary version of history, a nation emerges into political rationality through narrative—with its textual strategies and "metaphoric displacements."[53]

For Bhaba, "strategies of discourse" that function in the name of the people render narrative temporal rather than historical, to "resist the transparent linear equivalence of event and idea that historicism proposes."[54] National myths and stories slip and slide between categories like the "people," a specific ethnic group, or the collective of individuals. Nations are metaphors for imagined communities, and the historical necessity of the idea of the nation conflicts with the contingent and arbitrary signs and symbols that signify the affective life of a national culture. For Bhaba, the "people" are not simply historical events or parts of a patriotic body politic. They are imaginative conceptions and self-conceptions.[55]

The "people," argues Bhaba, live in double time: at one level they are essentially what they are, by virtue of some cloudy history, but they are also constantly rewriting themselves. They are "historical objects of national pedagogy" but also subjects erasing their history to show how national life can enjoy continual redemption. The scraps and patches of daily life must be repeatedly turned into the signs of a national culture. People follow the lesson of their received historical narrative, yet they also continually perform new narrative acts of self-definition. And the social authority of the nation then become the basis of law, but it also acts through the devices of lawmaking to do so. The people are an amorphous collection of actors and artists who continually address the conflict between the abstract powers of law and government and the competing and unequal interests and identities within the population.

The promise of legal scholarship about narrative or using narrative may lie in its power to describe law and statehood in this unstable condition. I close then, with a promising example drawn from American history.

In *Story and Transcription in the Trial of John Brown,* Robert Ferguson demonstrates how the legendary and infamous abolitionist hero Brown exploited the eclectic narrative and dramatic materials of the American criminal trial, while also drawing on the conventions of the literary romance, to embed himself forever in historical memory as a sacrificial hero.[56] Brown was, in Ferguson's view, enacting a myth of sacred inevitability, making it up as he went along; he was exploiting the artistic resources of the criminal law to establish a set of legal and moral principles that would haunt and constrain Americans thereafter. As Ferguson says: "[T]he underlying homologies between courtroom performance and the genre of the American Romance helped to turn Brown into Emerson's "hero of romance." The result was a story of mythopoeic proportions. . . . On trial for his life, John Brown achieved a special imaginative power by mixing legal artifice with religious understanding."[57]

As Ferguson shows, Brown was perhaps the first celebrity in American history in that he was the first to control the public perception of a major event through self-dramatizing manipulation of the press. He transformed himself from a man of questionable character, a feckless loser in both business and the military, into a mythic hero by artfully blending legal rhetoric, courtroom dramaturgics, and shards of junk culture from popular American romances.

Ferguson's key point is that narrative is multiple and polymorphous, not so much involving competing political narratives (the usual view of the new storyteller-scholars) as eclectically simultaneous narratives. Brown apotheosized himself by mixing legal artifice with religious understanding, with the special license of narrative romance as a frame of reference. Though incompetent as a revolutionary,

Brown roused visions of both cultural fulfillment and purification, mixed with images of armed invasion. His trial performance blended political, religious, legal, and racial stories in a grand strategy of exaggeration. Drawing largely on Hawthorne's store of romantic tropes, a bungling bankrupt transformed himself into a cultural icon.[58]

What deeper nation-story was Brown reenacting? In *The Slave Power Conspiracy and the Paranoid Style,* David Brion Davis examines the structure of the paranoid style in U.S. politics, a peculiarly (though not uniquely) American form in which ideas are believed and advocated.[59] The persistence of the paranoid style derives from a deep cultural belief that the United States should be morally pure. Indeed, the fundamental source of the American Revolution, by this measure, was not so much practical concern about control and taxes as an almost primal sense that the British represented a corruptly European defilement of colonial values.

The Civil War manifests two opposed yet closely related forms of the paranoid style. To the abolitionists, slave power was a dangerous atavism of European corruption. To the South, abolitionism threatened the defilement of civilized American society by encouraging slave rebellion. Each side accused the other not just of malevolent intentions but also, as is true of most alleged conspiracies, of subtle deceptions that made the malevolence even more insidious. To the abolitionists, the evil of slave power was obscured by a thin veneer of Southern etiquette and civility. To the Southerners, the evil subversive force of the abolitionists was obscured by their pretense to zealous humanitarianism.

Only in the 1850s, in response to the Missouri Compromise of 1850 and the Kansas-Nebraska Bill, was the defensive rhetoric transmuted into hardened conviction, which required a reassessment of American history and a mobilization of sectional power. The Fugitive Slave Law, the repeal of the Missouri Compromise, and the *Dred Scott* decision suggested a degree of Southern unity, premeditation, and control that would have been incredible years earlier. At the same time, the emergence of black Republicans and the appearance in Kansas of emigrant aid societies confirmed Southern fears that abolitionist conspirators had nearly gained control of the North.[60]

A cultural anthropologist (at least one with a functionalist bent) would say of this paranoid style that it helped stabilize the world of shifting social roles in a period of unprecedented fluidity and growth.[61] Garrisonian crusades struck at the heart of the morally expedient accommodations of a nation that had long defined slavery as a necessary evil, so proslavery forces had to portray abolitionists as fanatics, not humanitarians. The notion of a slave power conspiracy thereby solved a cultural problem for Northerners, who were now able to accept the appearance of Southern gentility and civility but to pierce through to the evil underneath. On the other hand,

Brown's conduct revived the Southerners' belief in a demonic plot by abolitionists, and Northern resistance to the Fugitive Slave Law aroused in the South nightmare images of vast organizations of slave stealers who would drain the South of all wealth. By the 1840s, American slaveholders had become increasingly aware of their own appearance-reality problems, so they turned the deception argument against the abolitionists. They could thereby shore up their communal values, and sharpen their regional and perhaps national self-definition.[62]

Thus, in a nation lacking transcendent national forces to check the conditioning influences of local environments and regional interests, the paranoid style enabled each side to perform an ideological finesse. The national fixation on extremes of aggression and guilt ironically tied in with the notion that a rational, purposive plan could be imposed on American life and with the Protestant messianic notion that the American mission was to save the world. Hence, the institution of slavery conformed to the story of the anti-Christ, with millenarian fantasies of persecution and suffering, of absolute power and absolute emancipation from violence. The abolitionist jeremiad became the key instrument for castigating the existing political and economic structure for its expediency and self-interest.[63]

As Ferguson describes the events leading to Brown's end, the great event was not the raid itself. Not only was that a failure, but it was a lucky failure. Had Brown died in the raid, he would have missed the chance for iconography; had it succeeded at all, Brown would have aroused too much wrath and fear, even in the North. Instead, he lived just long enough to make his death the most ritually important nonpresidential death of the century, and he caused a sea change in the national debate over slavery. After Brown's death the anomaly of slavery in a republic ceased to be a matter of negotiation. Once he raised the issue in the fiercely adversarial context of a criminal trial, slavery debates became, in Ferguson's view, truly adversarial.[64]

Brown exploited all the narrative resources (and apparent constraints) of the formalities of the trial. The rules of evidentiary relevancy enabled him to erase his unsavory past, and series of procedural concessions from the judge and prosecutor—designed to calm him down and lend an image of generous legitimacy to the trial—enabled him to embellish his life with heroic speeches and fabrications. His insensitivity became a quality of fierce principle, and his financial failure became a matter of transcendence over the material life. (Oddly, his sordid experience with the bankruptcy courts is what gave him experience in the courtroom.) A past full of grimy compromise was transformed into a life of rigid moralism in the trial question of innocence versus guilt, good versus evil.

Ferguson compares Brown's trial performance with his brief epistolary autobiography, which was itself a shameless act of romance fabrication, where, Gatsby-like, Brown made himself into a rising young businessman, a swashbuckling western adventurer, a descendant of revolutionary warriors, a Quaker pacifist, a humble shepherd, a great leader, and a martyr.[65] The remarkable thing is not the originality or sophistication but the shameless conventionality of Brown's writing—and later his trial performance. All his passionate expressions of idealism and belief were tropes out of popular romance literature, full of stereotypical excessive passion and self-righteousness. It was only a few years later, says Ferguson, that Brown's trite expressions were transformed into the moral and scriptural discourse of Lincoln.

As Ferguson shows, a trial by or in a community is also a trial *of* that community. Virginia authorities felt that an image of rigorous legal decorum would quell any fear of abolitionist violence. Thus, in a ritual battle over forms and tropes, Brown decried the denial of his various trial rights, and the court in turn made remarkable legal concessions to him, which he then used as further opportunities to denounce the trial as a mockery. In this regard, the state appears partly as the magnanimous, self-legitimating hander-down of favors and partly as a narrator itself, telling a story about the proper constraints on emotion in the courtroom. ("One more outburst, and I'll . . .") Decorum was not really the absence of emotion so much as a particular structure of boundaries of emotion designed to vindicate the communal majesty of the law. When Brown threatened distortion, he won more concessions, and soon he became an independent agent, free to engage in colloquies with witnesses and prosecutors.[66]

Brown crossed all the boundaries of legal formality and thus became the legal version of the frontier romance hero. He rhetorically declaimed the lack of fairness in the trial and accepted it rhetorically, even as he was granted concessions. He challenged the trial as mere form and yet it was the form of the trial that he so brilliantly exploited. In an absurd non sequitur, he proclaimed the selflessness of his actions, and after an exasperated prosecutor permitted him these hysterical irrelevancies, Brown fended off later attacks on relevancy grounds by resort to a sort of estoppel or waiver. One great irony is that his lawyers were constantly dismissed and rehired and dismissed on various grounds of conflict, so that Brown could lament that he was denied counsel, all the while preferring no counsel because he wanted to be able to speak his own voice in the trial. He exploited his wounded condition so that although he was able to stand, he managed to appear lying on a hospital cot.

Ralph Waldo Emerson himself recognized that Brown's ideal character, formed in the trial, could then be re-formed forever in the American imagination. A final, wonderful irony is that the famous song "John Brown's Body" was originally written about another John Brown—a feckless Confederate soldier who drowned unheroically—and that the song then got adapted to the heroic Brown.[67]

Hence, for Ferguson, a double act of interpretation inheres in law-and-literature scholarship: both of legal and historical events and of narrative. Ferguson pregnantly quotes Roland Barthes for the view that narrative is really a "prodigious variety of genres."[68] The trial transcript is raw data, to be read into a variety of narratives according to the stories people know how to tell. The relation between cultural and legal understanding is haphazard as well as political. Ferguson's brilliant essay can thus be read as a corrective to the sentimental invocations of legal narrative as identifying the simply authentic story or truth or the dialectic between two competing narratives. In fact, legal narrative is more artificial and polymorphous than any of these. Legal storytellers, including self-styled legal heroes like John Brown, must beg, borrow, and steal available materials, but if they are cleverly artistic with the forms of law and lucky enough to work at crucial moments in political history, they may become what Shelley called poets: the "unacknowledged legislators" of a nation.

Robert A. Ferguson

Untold Stories in the Law

A continuum of publication marks a courtroom trial—from indictment, to transcript, to judicial decision and on from there to newspaper report, journal article, historical account, and fictional projection—and this continuum supplies the major source of explanation in understanding the role of trial events in a republic of laws. The standard extrapolations from this continuum—accusation, verdict, opinion, and holding—control official perception, but these professional rubrics, all from the first part of the continuum, tell us little about the transmission of a trial into the realms of communal recognition and understanding. Very few citizens ever so much as glance at an indictment, a transcript, or a judicial opinion. Popular perception, at least until the advent of Court TV, has come through external reportage and commentary. The cultural work of interpretation in courtroom analysis lies, therefore, in the relation *between* legal and nonlegal narratives, where better critical tools are needed for revealing the hidden and neglected connections of the one with the other. This essay seeks to theorize one aspect of the relation between legal and nonlegal narratives at trial and to provide a practical demonstration of a methodology in courtroom analysis—what "reading a trial" can accomplish.

We can begin by combining a recent theoretical insight with an ancient maxim of legal study. The insight, while simple enough, has far-reaching implications: trials always function through a framework of storytelling.[1] Critics suggest that we are driven to tell and listen to stories through a "narrative desire," or passion for meaning.[2] By extension, trials depend on the familiar form of story—beginning, middle, and end—in their own quests for meaning. To the extent that they try to reveal and define questioned behavior, they must tell a credible story of what happened in the events held in dispute. So, too, the procedural forms of the trial find parallels in the craft of storytelling. In both settings, the incoherence of mere occurrence requires a superimposed and value-laden narrative before meaning can be achieved.[3] Likewise, the stories told in a courtroom are deliberately placed in direct competition with each other. Prosecution and defense necessarily offer contrasting accounts of the same event in the advocacy system, and one side or the other will eventually lose its audience under the assumption that procedural integrity rewards the account closest to the truth. Judges and juries must choose between accounts in reaching a decision. The bifurcation of guilt or innocence does not allow them to mediate or split the difference between tellings.

The substitution of "story" for "account" in these generalizations is useful because it underlines the ramifications of setting, form, presentation, and reception. The legal priorities placed on truthtelling not withstanding, a story succeeds only when it is well told. Lawyers in conflict look for a story that jurors will believe, and they understand that the most believable story will already appear familiar to their listeners. By the same token, the competition in storytelling caters to the lowest common denominator with competing stereotypes about crime as the gauge for choices to be made.[4] Thinking about trials in this manner raises painful but important questions. What are the appropriate standards in an artful presentation? Where does the legal requirement of the "whole truth" meet the dictates of a believable story? Is the best story necessarily the truthful one? What sacrifices in detail can be made in a truthful story to make it more generically appealing? How do we evaluate the presumed integrity of the storyteller when we must acknowledge that crafting a story involves certain made-up components? And what of the many audiences that listen to a trial? What choices can and should be made between them by the storyteller who would be heard?

Appropriate answers to these questions depend in part on the aforementioned legal maxim. Law students imbibe one of their first lessons through an anecdote of Chief Justice Theophilus Parsons, early constitutionalist and first "giant of the law in Massachusetts." Quoth Parsons: "A plaintiff brings an action against a neighbor for borrowing and breaking the iron pot in which he cooked his dinner. The defendant says he never borrowed any pot; and that he used it carefully; also, that the pot was broken and useless when he borrowed it; also, that he borrowed the pot of somebody not the plaintiff; also, that the pot in question was the defendant's own pot; also that the plaintiff never owned any pot, iron or other; also that the defendant never had any pot whatever."[5] Taken as prima facie evidence of pettifoggery by outsiders, this anecdote never fails to rouse a certain cynical pride when quoted within the profession, and it is important to grasp the dynamic behind such internal regard.

Certainly, the dynamic itself continues to thrive. If Parsons's anecdote came to life in a contemporary American courtroom, the lawyer for the defendant could claim that the plaintiff should have warned the defendant that the iron pot might explode in a microwave oven and that the plaintiff should sue the manufacturer rather than the defendant because no warning label had been affixed; *also,* that the defendant suffers from an obsessive-compulsive syndrome brought on by the "cultural psychosis" of fast food ingestion and that any taking of plaintiff's pot should be viewed as a therapeutic gesture in need of adjustment; *also,* that punishment would plunge the defendant more deeply into the very handicap that had caused social dysfunction in the first place; *also,* that the plaintiff, in openly ridiculing the defendant, tore up the moral contract that bound the two parties together as eating companions, forcing the defendant to act beyond the reassuring safety zone of an egalitarian ethos. In short, the lawyer of today might argue that the defendant represents the real victim in this sad case and that the plaintiff should be expected to bear the brunt of a mutual loss.[6]

What have we learned from this demonstration? First, advocacy leads to a natural proliferation of stories at trial. Lawyers like to put every conceivable account on the table. An indictment is the first story, and through it, the plaintiff or prosecution must raise every available permutation of relevant offense to guard against a non-suit; the defendant can escape simply by showing the inapplicability of the specific counts named therein. From the other side of the case, the defendant faces a different presumption, but one that encourages a comparable propagation of story. In one of the many imbalances in a balanced process, the defendant need not confirm *any* account in challenging the initial burden of proof placed on the plaintiff. It suffices to cast doubt on the accusation, and one means of doing so runs to other explanations of the plaintiff's case. If any combination of stories shakes the preponderance of evidence required of a plaintiff in a civil case or raises a reasonable doubt in a criminal case, the defendant will be found not guilty. The prospect makes counternarratives standard fare in a courtroom.

Second, and just as important, the competition between stories gives high priority to timeliness in courtroom storytelling. The most believable story, by definition, will tally with what competing lawyers are always searching for: a contemporary understanding. Not one of our embellishments on Parsons's time-honored, common-law action in trover would have been an effective story before 1950, but all are commonplace in a postmodern "ethos of victimization." Product liability cases, personality disorder defenses, environmental and genetic justifications for personal behavior, and arguments from social justice flourish in today's courtroom.[7]

The priority placed on timeliness in storytelling contains two subpremises. On the one hand, the struggle of attorneys to find the best accounts for their clients turns courtroom transcripts into excellent barometers of what is said and thought in a culture at any given moment of time. Anyone who has read such a transcript observes the maturation of a story line as counsel winnow through alternative accounts looking for the story that will win. Because courtroom stories exist only within the stark nominations of guilty or innocent, lawyers are cast entirely within a win-lose situation, and like anyone else in that context, they emphasize what seems to be working and quickly discard an ineffective narrative for a better or more timely one. On the other hand, advocates also know that jurors must first recognize the developing contours of a story to accept it, and the perception makes them practical students of preexisting narrative forms. The genre of a story, its familiar form in the telling, is a crucial factor and often the hidden ingredient in courtroom belief.[8] Notably, lawyers have masked the real importance of generic considerations through their appeals to the common sense of a situation. But common sense, as anthropologists have begun to show, is basically a culturally constructed use of experience to claim self-evidence; it is neither more nor less than "an authoritative story" made out of the familiar.[9]

To summarize, the dogged thoroughness of courtroom storytelling, its competitive format, its pragmatic attention to specific audiences, and its firm commitment to generic recognitions are controlling characteristics that we can identify and use to help read courtrooms trials. Identification also brings us to our present inquiry, "untold stories in the law." For if these same characteristics are intrinsic to the advocacy system, we should be surprised when one of them does *not* appear at trial. More specifically, in the proliferation and refinement of courtroom stories, what does it mean when an available and viable account is *not* raised in courtroom debate? What, in effect, happens when a relevant story is actively repressed in a republic of laws?

The act of repression to be examined here involves an untold story of a trial following a slave insurrection in Virginia in 1800, an event sometimes called Gabriel's rebellion. I choose this example because it remained submerged within the national consciousness until the twentieth century and because the long hiatus between event and recognition illustrates both the power and the inevitable costs of repression in a consensual culture dedicated to freedom of speech. The story itself, imputed to a slave who is simultaneously on trial for his life and under scrutiny as a defective piece of property, is set in the special slave court of oyer and terminer of Henrico County, Virginia, and it is just three sentences long:

> I have nothing more to offer than what General Washington would have had to offer, had he been taken by the British and put to trial by them. I have adventured my life in endeavouring to obtain the liberty of my countrymen, and am a willing sacrifice to their cause: and I beg, as a favour, that I may be immediately led to execution. I know that you have pre-determined to shed my blood, why then all this mockery of a trial?[10]

But before analyzing the story itself, we must first determine what repression can mean as a concept applied to the notion of courtroom story.

The historical fact of repression in 1800 and after is clear on a variety of levels. A figure like James Monroe, governor of Virginia at the time and later fifth president of the United States, would subsequently refuse to discuss the slave rebellion trials with anyone. Pressed toward the end of his life, he would admit only that "several of the conspirators were hanged," a figure well short of the twenty-six official executions bearing his signature in 1800. Nor do Monroe's words correspond with earlier ones. Chilling private letters between Monroe as governor and Thomas Jefferson as presidential nominee in 1800 exhibit the founding fathers of one revolution squelching another and discussing "whether mercy or severity is the better policy in this case." Their main calculation consists of a telling question: "when to arrest the hand of the Executioner."[11] On a more general social scale, repression can be found in the mobs and roving bands of white vigilantes that terrorize blacks in the aftermath of the rebellion.

Politically and legally, repression takes a variety of forms: the scourging of slaves who refuse to confess or bear false witness in the trials of Gabriel and his fellow conspirators, the creation of a police force, increased restrictions on the movements of blacks, new limits on their vocational opportunities, more pointed laws against the literacy of slaves, added stipulations against the rights of free blacks, and the vigorous enforcement of existing statutes against assembly and miscegenation.[12] After repression comes intellectual resistance: as late as 1975, Gabriel's rebellion is a relatively ignored event in American history. Daniel Sisson's monumental study, *The American Revolution of 1800,* fails to mention the insurrection, even though the unrest between Federalists and Republicans in that election year contributes to both the climate and the fact of rebellion.[13]

The points to remember, for present purposes, are that repression outlives its original context and that it returns to haunt the consciousness that created it. Admittedly, the implied connection between social repression and a psychological dynamic of explanation is a problematic one, but carefully used, it provides useful tools in a methodology of courtroom analysis—particularly when applied to the resolutely ratiocinative priorities in legal discourse. The surface narrative of a courtroom transcript is not unlike the consciousness of an individual; both offer the official record of what passes for explanation, and both know themselves to be under distinct pressure from other levels of explanation that need to be contained.

The classic theoretical parallel between the psychological development of the individual and civilization appears in *Civilization and Its Discontents,* where it receives a decidedly legal formulation. Sigmund Freud uses the parallel to carry social development from its inception in "justice" as "the decisive step" and "first requisite of civilization" to its logical conclusion, or "final outcome," in "a rule of law." In this process, civilization is both the ultimate source of salvation and the fountain of all individual frustration, and, as such, it creates a veritable force field of repression, "an irremediable antagonism between the demands of instinct and the restrictions of civilization." In another analogy, this one between the "Eternal City" of Rome and the human mind, Freud provides the key to recovering these patterns of repression by maintaining that nothing perishes in mental life: "[E]verything is somehow preserved and . . . in suitable circumstances . . . it can once more be brought to light."[14] Elsewhere, this return of the repressed takes the form of the uncanny, something secretly familiar that has undergone repression and then returned to consciousness all of a sudden in sometimes frightening and recurring patterns.[15]

Alternatively, the repressed can be thought of in sociological and anthropological terms. Mary Douglas writes convincingly about how "institutions create shadowed places in which nothing can be seen and no questions asked." The result is a kind of "structural amnesia." The social scientist unravels these structures by learning "the processes of the public memory," by examining "the storage system for the social order," by asking "what are the impossible thoughts?" and by discovering the principles of institutional "coherence" that allow some repressed thoughts to escape oblivion.[16] Just as repression is a multi-faceted phenomenon, so a variety of disciplines are relevant in the explanation of it.

The actual pattern of repression in the untold story under investigation can be seen in the nature of its transmission. The primary utterance of the speaking slave in Henrico County is at least thrice removed. The unnamed defendant may have used the exact words ascribed to him in court, but they do not appear in any of the relevant trial transcripts of 1800. We know, however, that these words could have been uttered there. The typical slave trial of the period relied on a turncoat who, in seeking a pardon, informed on fellow conspirators, and the trials in Henrico County were no exception. The convicting testimonies of the two main informers, themselves conspirators, indicate that the several hundred slaves actively involved in the conspiracy were led by literate artisans versed in the revolutionary rhetoric of their time. Gabriel, a black blacksmith who could read and write, planned to march on Richmond under the banner "death or liberty," a conscious inversion of Patrick Henry's famous rallying call. Furthermore, he was fighting "for his Country" as well as black freedom when he divided his followers into military units.[17]

Even so, the printed words that survive are not the slave defendant's but those of an English Quaker traveling in America in 1804, and they could have been written in their present form as late as 1811. Robert Sutcliff, a commercial traveler on business near Richmond, records his own conversation with an unnamed Virginia lawyer who, in turn, claims to have heard the words spoken at the trial "by one of them being asked, what he had to say to the court in his defence."[18] The actual words of our untold story depend, then, on a double transmission, and they belong for a period of time to an oral tradition of the Virginia aristocracy that suppressed the rebellion—an oral tradition that only a sympathetic foreigner dared to record and publish. And yet the effect of transmission in a dynamic of repression has made the slave who spoke at trial as eloquent as possible; his words are the *only* words that twentieth-century culture retains or repeats in summaries of the event.

The nature of that eloquence deserves careful attention. Unmistakably, one of the hidden virtues of the statement resides in its concision. Brevity in a recorded statement is suitable to the memory of an oral tradition and to the needs of a casual journalist in transcription, but the higher value of concision also flows from the honed or refined language of repetition. How many times did the unnamed member of the Virginia gentry hear and repeat the story among his peers in the four years before he encountered Robert Sutcliff? No one can say, but if there were originally excess words, they have been removed, and we are left with the most concise statement against slavery in the America of its time. Every word taken from this doomed slave's mouth counts.

True, the best of the Virginia planter class understood its own dilemma over slavery and could express it with power and conviction. As early as 1767, Arthur Lee warned Virginia that it lived on "the very brink of ruin" from slave rebellion. "On us, or on our posterity," he wrote in the *Virginia Gazette,* "the inevitable blow, must, one day, fall." In Lee's view, the "Bondage of the Africans" superseded every relative moral consideration. "There cannot be in nature, there is not in all history, an instance in which every right of men is more flagrantly violated."[19] Thomas Jefferson's more famous cry of despair over the possibility of a slave rebellion came in 1787, in *Notes on the State of Virginia:* "I tremble for my country when I reflect that God is just: that his justice cannot sleep for ever. . . . The Almighty has no attribute which can take sides with us in such a contest." Later, in 1797 and with feelings of "terror," he would write, "[W]e have the wolf by the ears, and we can neither hold him, nor safely let him go."[20] But while these statements are trenchant and informed by a rhetoric of revolution, they are shaped by a fear of its implications rather than the "spirit of '76" that early republicans liked to claim for themselves.

The words of the slave defendant survive because they coincide exactly in 1800 with, in Mary Douglas's terms, an institutional "principle of coherence."[21] Early republican culture insists on the right to rebel against tyranny in the name of freedom. In the one moment of required speech at trial, the moment when a defendant must respond to formal accusation, the Gabriel conspirator uses that principle to give the best conceivable answer available to him from the field of ideological concerns established twenty-five years before in the Revolution. "I have adventured my life in endeavouring to obtain the liberty of my countrymen," he tells the court. Having failed to achieve liberty, he is prepared, as Patrick Henry claimed to be, for death: "I beg, as a favour, that I may be immediately led to execution." This request, part of the personal right of revolution, is strongly fortified by the formal circumstance in which it is uttered. The legal platform of the trial and the slave defendant's response in procedural context magnify his words and turn them into a colossal statement within and about the republic of laws.

The five judges in the Henrico County courtroom have no choice but to agree with the defendant before them on the level of ideology. His rhetoric is theirs with a life of its own in the body politic. Indeed, for their own inconsistency, they would have needed only to glance at the state seal that they used regularly to ratify their judgments. The Virginians of 1776 devised that seal to depict "VIRTUS, the genius of the commonwealth . . . treading on TYRANNY, represented by a man prostrate, a crown fallen from his head, a broken chain in his left hand, and a scourge in his right." Affixed to it was the state motto: "*SIC SEMPER TYRANNIS*," or "thus always to tyrants."[22] Stripped of all place in the Revolution, American slaves supplied a negative example in the imagery and language of colonial rebellion. They appeared as the disembodied presence in their masters' litanies against the dangers of enslavement—literal reminders of the prospect of liberty in chains. Slaves were the nightmare presence behind a white quest for independence, and the speaker in the Henrico County courtroom of 1800 is the repressed reality in that nightmare come to life. Figuratively, the chains on his body are *meant* to be broken.

These judges would also have understood that the deepest underpinnings of their own discipline, natural law, sided with the defendant and against them. When they ask him what "he had to say to the court in his defence," his words echo the reigning theorist of Anglo-American culture, John Locke. In *An Essay Concerning the True Original, Extent, and End of Civil Government*, the condition of slavery is "nothing else but the *State of War continued*," and a slave retains the right to resist "whenever he finds the hardship of his Slavery outweigh the value of his life." That is exactly the claim of the defendant in this case. He would rather die than remain a slave, and he accepts the price of fighting for his freedom. "I know that you have pre-determined to shed my blood," he tells them. Power and not law holds him in place, "Absolute, Arbitrary Power" constituting the greatest evil in the social contract.[23]

Nonetheless, the same five judges condemn the defendant and twenty-five others like him to death, and they do it easily and quickly. They convict and sentence, reaching the required unanimous decision in a slave court for capital punishment in under an hour for most of the cases brought before them on charges of conspiracy and insurrection. In what connotation, then, are the answering words of the doomed slave peculiarly troubling—so troubling as to be carefully retained within "the processes of the public memory"? Why, in fact, *are* the slave defendant's words retained in the manner that they are? One answer lies in the return of the repressed in an official court of law. The defendant's voiced analogy to a black George Washington fulfills rather precisely one definition of the uncanny. Here, if anywhere, is the sudden appearance of something familiar but not known and, therefore, terrifying—something repressed that comes to the light in a recognizable but threatening, because alienated, form.[24]

How the uncanny manifests itself depends on what has been repressed, and the Southern jeremiads on slavery already noted help to provide that insight. As leaders of the Virginia slavocracy, Arthur Lee and Thomas Jefferson agree that "freedom is unquestionably the birth-right of all mankind," and they acknowledge that the dissemination of knowledge through the Enlightenment means that their slaves will evince an ever-growing capacity to seize that right. Both writers recognize the fact and implications of injustice, morally and practically, so what can possibly prevent their logical acceptance of emancipation? They respond with racist constructs against what Lee calls "those unfortunate and detestable people." To the extent that American slaves are "unfortunate" or, in Jefferson's understanding, "inferior," they may be seen to lack the capacity to act for their own freedom, and if they are also "detestable," then their moral right to freedom is also qualified or at least less disturbing emotionally.[25] Timing is everything in an Enlightenment understanding of the spread of knowledge, and repression in the mind of the slavocracy takes the form of "not yet." Accordingly, when a black person actually appears to demand equality, that person can be seen only in twisted or unnatural form.[26]

The black George Washington in the Henrico County courthouse stands against these evasions and for the proposition that already in that moment, in 1800, he is the equal, morally and physically, of the best of his masters. He is at once an ideological claimant as speaker and a twisted representation in the sight of his horrified listeners—a representation that they cannot forget. When the slave defendant announces that he has "nothing more to offer than what General Washington would have had to offer, had he been taken by the British and put to trial by them," he is also a Virginian speaking to Virginians about another Virginian at a moment when Washington, who died at Mount Vernon less than a year before the trial, has entered a complex process of transfiguration. Moreover, this slave defendant's claim is so forthright as to be virtually unique for its time. Nineteenth-century variations on the theme of a minority founding father tend to be uneasy ones that mediate the notion of violence through virtue and social success.[27] In this court case, however, the hope for a black Washington and its corollary, the fear of a black Washington, meet unavoidably in the logic of rebellion, and the politics of both emotions reside in the story before us.

Any deconstruction of the iconography around the figure of Washington must recall that the untold story in question is a multilayered text. The uncanny resides in the interstices of a narrative that contains, at once, the repressed voice of a speaking slave, the reiterated oral tale of an apprehensive Virginia lawyer, the receptive recapitulation of a Quaker Englishman, our own reactions, and the critic's realization of all four. There are, as well, three facets of the Washington figure embedded in this tale: martial glory, service to country, and the Virginia planter as slaveowner.

The speaking slave reminds us first that military power defines Washington's personal success. We would think less of the revolutionary soldier if he had been beaten and captured in the 1770s and then hanged as one of many disappointed rebels in a still-thriving British Empire. The conditional perfect verb form—"what General Washington *would have had* to offer"—catches this implication nicely. Meanwhile, the reference to rank—"General" rather than "George" Washington— emphasizes the rebellious activist over subsequent and more benign images of the later national leader as constitutional framer and first president. Significantly, the aspect of the slave rebellion that bothers the judges most in Henrico County comes in testimony that the leading conspirators have formed a military organization and assigned to themselves official military rank. Gabriel is elected general and his direct subordinates are colonels and captains in a revolutionary army that would have taken Richmond except for a violent rainstorm that delayed their plans just long enough for their plot to be exposed.[28] Asked what he has to say, the speaking slave does not hesitate. He deliberately draws attention to these parallels.

George Washington's military career figures in one other fashion. The leader of the American revolutionary army was a stern disciplinarian who flogged his soldiers much in the way that he scourged slaves at Mount Vernon. He once wrote that neither bravery nor hope of reward but "fear of punishment" distinguished the real soldier from others, and in 1776 he quickly demonstrated that he would "punish every kind of neglect, or mis-behavior," whether in officers or men. Big and physically very powerful, he brought a forceful presence to the position of commander in chief, and his rare bursts of anger intimidated those closest to him, filling them with dread and alarm.[29] Even in casual social interaction with his peers, Washington aroused feelings of awe akin to fear. Thomas Jefferson once observed that Washington possessed a temper "naturally high-toned" and that when "it broke its bounds, he was most tremendous in his wrath."[30] The Virginia elite in the Henrico County slave court would have known this side of Washington firsthand. For them, a black Washington carried connotations of a personal ascendancy lost to a modern appreciation.

The second and more familiar facet of Washington's import for early republicans, that of the selfless father of his country, also receives a twist in the defendant's response at trial. When the speaker, oral transmitter, and journal keeper of this story reveal that the defendant has "adventured . . . to obtain the liberty of my countrymen," the possessive attached to the word "countrymen" anticipates a separate nation. The defendant at trial is the father of *another* country, one that implicitly raises a new but still-familiar dimension. A "willing sacrifice to their [his countrymen's] cause," the defendant is no outlaw after vengeance. He is, rather, a visionary seeker after justice with all of the social ramifications that a fresh founding of black freedom would entail. Disinterested service, the eighteenth-century ideal of public virtue that defines Washington's reputation, remains intact in the slave about to be executed.

The remaining facet of Washington's public persona is even more illuminating when caught in the prism of the trial process. If there is one area where Washington appeared to fall squarely on the side of the judges in Henrico County, it would surely be in the daily life of the Virginia planter as slaveowner, but that presumption had already crumbled on December 14, 1799, the date of Washington's death. For while the rest of the country mourned the man "first in the hearts of his countrymen," his neighbors would have been reeling with the news that he had emancipated his slave force in his last will and testament. In the end, Washington deserted the slavocracy of Virginia in order to vindicate his revolutionary reputation, writing in his own hand: "Upon the decease [of] my wife, it is my Will and desire th[at] all the Slaves which I hold in [*my*] *own right,* shall receive their free[dom]."[31] Given one chance to speak in the Henrico County courthouse nine months later, a rebelling slave could well have realized that what General Washington finally "had to offer" was nothing less than the liberty of his countrymen.

There was a last reason for suppressing this story in 1800. The confidence with which the unknown speaker wields his arguments is a matter of record. Although the Virginia lawyer gives no description in transmitting the speech, he was impressed by the "manly tone of voice" of the responding defendant.[32] This degree of confidence follows naturally from the strength of the speaker's arguments, but it also leads that speaker to another level of rhetorical performance in the courtroom. Knowing what he knows, the defendant can reject altogether the authority of a court that holds his body but not his mind. Asked a question, he asks one of his own in return: "[W]hy then all this mockery of a trial?" We can close the analysis of this passage by answering that question for him.

Courts, even very oppressive or totalitarian courts, feel compelled to leave an orderly record of their proceedings. They need to believe in that order, and they count on the responsiveness of all concerned to accomplish these ends for them. Trials, in this sense, are both contests and rituals with the important technical distinction that these terms invoke. In Claude Lévi-Strauss's formulation, contests or games have "a *disjunctive* effect; they end in the establishment of a difference between individual players or teams." The reference of difference is to winners against losers, an inescapable by-product in courtroom decisions. "Ritual, on the other hand, is the exact inverse; it *conjoins,* for it brings about a union (one might even say communion in this context) or in any case an organic relation between two initially separated groups."[33] The contest in a trial decides winners and losers, and it extracts punishment and sometimes revenge. Ritual, by way of contrast, bespeaks a more strategic, if vaguer, notion of participation, one in which notions of resolution, closure, publication, the status quo ante, and recognition play themselves out in the consensual forms that define a republic of laws.

The judges in Henrico County needed the minimal cooperation of question and answer from the defendants before them, but they did not get it in this case, and the alternative response given—"why then all this mockery"—is intolerable to their ears. Without primal concurrence, they cannot assure themselves that they *do* govern by law; nor can they convince the governed that they are fairly governed. Procedurally, these judges are left with naked power in the place of consensual, validating process. In the words of Mary Douglas: "[I]nstitutions survive by harnessing all information processes to the task of establishing themselves. The instituted community blocks personal curiosity, organizes public memory, and heroically imposes certainty on uncertainty. In marking its own boundaries it affects all lower-level thinking, so that persons realize their own identities and classify each other through community affiliation."[34] Courtrooms as institutions are vulnerable to mockery when they face the task of establishing themselves. The elaborate give-and-take of legal procedures leaves numerous opportunities for breakdown, and the antagonistic participant, one who also has courage, can achieve a profound level of disruption by violating the fragile decorum and sense of ritual in the sequence of question and answer.

The defendant in the Henrico County courthouse has the fortitude to resist the information, the certainties, and, most of all, the frame of thought that existing structure would impose on him as his ticket for admission to the ritual of trial performance. His voice mocks that ritual, destroying its delicately complicit rhythms and leaving mutually recognized ideological contradictions in a judge and a defendant who are also master and slave. The speaker is soon silenced, but the implied thoroughness of courtroom narrative signifies that his voice will be heard again when the contradictions involved become culturally intolerable.

All of these observations lead back to the original question of this inquiry: What, in effect, happens when a relevant story is actively repressed in a republic of laws? The simple answer would seem to be that it always returns, but on what terms? Whose terms? In the rugged exchanges of courtroom advocacy, a relevant story that is effectively told belongs to the republic of laws for ready use and further manipulation. Ideologically, it remains available to everyone. But when such a story is actively repressed in a forum that prides itself on its thoroughness and fairness, it belongs to the agent of the repressed.

The notion of owning a story in these propositions should sound disturbing. To be sure, casual references using this kind of expression abound. Phrases taking the possessive form—"it is your story to tell" or "your story deserves to be heard"—appear in daily conversation, and storytellers copyright their work all of the time. But it is a different matter to claim that certain stories—particularly stories of discrimination—carry implicit prerogatives and burdens and that they do so because the law has repressed them in the past. In failing to tell these stories, the law has lost control of them on its own terms.[35] Perhaps, in consequence, a growing number of black legal scholars now believe that it is both a prerogative and a burden to speak about the failures of the law in a personal or confessional mode. Writing the story of discrimination is simultaneously therapy and hard duty, part of "recovering from the degradation of being divided against [oneself]" and part of the pressure of a world "full of black women who have never really been heard from."[36]

The price of repression in a republic of laws can be very high. Urged to speak when captured as the leader of the rebellion of 1800, Gabriel apparently refused to do so. In the words of Governor James Monroe: "It appeared he [Gabriel] had promised a full confession, but on his arrival here he declined making it. From what he said to me, he seemed to have made up his mind to die, and to have resolved to say but little on the subject of the conspiracy."[37] We can admit the factual accuracy of Monroe's account without, however, accepting its implications. What, after all, could "a full confession" have meant for a charismatic leader whose followers, the rank and file of a new revolutionary army, had voted "to give him the voice for General?"[38] Gabriel obviously had much to say to those compatriots who wanted to receive his message. Who, then, speaks for the eighteenth-century Gabriel today? This last question has been a subject of implicit debate in the literary criticism of modern times. In the continuum of publication around a trial, imaginative literature provides the zone where the repressed can lurk. To use Freud's own words, the uncanny in literature "is a much more fertile province than the uncanny in real life."[39]

It should surprise no one that the greatest national story of a slave insurrection skirts the issue of speech altogether. Writing in 1855, Herman Melville sets *Benito Cereno* in 1799, the time period of the Gabriel rebellion, but his story never enters the mind of the arch conspirator Babo, who, like Gabriel, refuses to speak when captured. Instead, Melville provides an endless series of external misreadings of the rebel leader alongside a deliberately defective official transcript of his later trial. Readers know that Babo is the "plotter from first to last" and the "helm and keel of the revolt," but they ponder these matters only through the executed slave's severed head, "that hive of subtlety," and through the traumatized Benito Cereno's continuing dread of "The negro."[40]

The difference in the most visible twentieth-century novelization of a slave rebellion is striking. William Styron's *The Confessions of Nat Turner* from 1966 has been controversial precisely because the author presumes to enter and understand the mind of Nat Turner, the leader of a slave rebellion in Southampton, Virginia, in 1831.[41] Many critics have deplored this perceived impertinence, claiming that "Nat Turner still awaits a literary interpreter worthy of his sacrifice," and the ensuing search for the real Nat Turner has become something of an academic cottage industry.[42] Clearly, there is no easy return of the repressed. But if the uncanny comes to light through anger and anxiety, nevertheless it comes. "Time is not a river. Time is a pendulum," Arna Bontemps asserts in his own novel based on the Southampton rebellion, *Black Thunder*.[43] Or, translating into the terms of this inquiry, a story wrongly refused by the law will return in a republic of laws as cultural narrative and, often enough, as renewed legal event. The law does not get beyond what it has not worked through. The pendulum swings back because the culture has made an ideological commitment to social justice and because the expectation of justice causes injustice to loom large.[44]

Who ultimately can speak for Gabriel? When all is said and done, Gabriel speaks for himself, but through two conflicting levels of understanding. First, the obscure eighteenth-century blacksmith who fought and died for his freedom remains a prototype and example of revolutionary aspiration. Somewhere at this very moment, another rebel, perhaps the leader of a street gang from the ignored underclass of any one of a number of urban ghettoes, is preparing to seek justice, and Gabriel will be an inspiration.[45] Second, Gabriel continues to speak through the dominant culture's own realization of racial unrest. Glimpses of injustice, past and present, have forced Americans to contemplate the still-present danger of racial cataclysm. Typifying this state of mind in a description of the actual uprising of blacks against whites in *Benito Cereno,* Melville writes that "past, present, and future seemed one."[46] Here, fears tied to a repressed past, but then realized in the present, have brought an utter collapse in time categories. Put another way, injustice in a republic of laws always finds the present tense.

Paying closer attention to the full continuum of publication around the trials of Gabriel and his fellow conspirators offers the opportunity to bring these conflicting understandings of hero versus nemesis into a socially productive tension with each other. Rereading the all-too-brief trial records of these slave defendants represents an act of partial recovery in American legal history. Methodologically, it divulges an untold story and brings that story to bear upon a larger understanding of an important event. Philosophically, it yields new insight into the ideology of race and revolution in early America and into the high level of slave engagement in those issues.

A final psychological dimension applies more directly to the republic of laws. Fresh understandings of these trials may help the country to face its repressed fears without panic—without the collapse of the future into a bitter past. Gabriel himself seems to have had some hope for that better future. In the conflicting testimony against the doomed but silent leader at trial, one slave witness offers a startling prospect. Gabriel meant to take Richmond by force, but what then? Even the refracting testimony of an informer cannot hide the optimism that follows—an optimism that in 1800 looks back to successful revolutions in Haiti and France as well as America. "If the white people agreed to their freedom," the rebel leader tells his slave recruits, "they would then hoist a white flag, and he would dine and drink with the merchants of the city on the day when it should be agreed to." There is a tangible poignancy in this appeal. When he asks others "to join him in fighting for his country," Gabriel may have had all Americans in mind.[47]

Alan M. Dershowitz

Life Is Not a Dramatic Narrative

The case involved a businessman named Hamilton who had taken out a life insurance policy on his partner ten days before the partner was gunned down by a professional hit man. The DA was finding it easy to persuade the jury that the timing could not possibly be coincidental, and Abe had been racking his mind for an answer. Emma [Abe's seventeen-year-old daughter], finding that she simply couldn't get his attention, had decided to try to help him figure out a common-sense rebuttal to the DA's circumstantial case.

And she had.

"Daddy," she said, popping into his home office late one night, "the answer is Chekhov."

"Why Chekhov?" Abe asked, his head still buried in the books.

"Because Chekhov once told an aspiring dramatist that if you hang a gun on the wall in the first act, you had better use it by the third act. We read it in lit class."

"So what does that have to do with the Hamilton case . . . ?"

"Your jurors see Chekhov's theory on TV and in the movies every day. Don't you get it, Daddy? On TV, when they show a businessman or a wife buying life insurance on someone, every viewer knows there's going to be a murder, and they know who the murderer will be. It's a setup."

"You've got a point. Sure, on TV, when a character coughs or has a chest pain, you know he's dying. There's no such thing as a cold or indigestion. Everything has to be relevant to the drama."

"But in real life, Daddy, the world is full of irrelevant actions and coincidences. People take out insurance policies all the time, and then the person lives till Willard Scott can put him on the *Today* show."

"You've really got something there, Emma. I think I may use it."

And Abe had used it. He'd convinced the jury not to look at the Hamilton case as if it were a made-for-TV movie, but rather as a slice of real life, full of irrelevant actions and coincidences. He'd asked the jurors how many of them had taken out life insurance on a loved one and what their neighbors would have thought if that loved one had died shortly thereafter.

After he'd won, several jurors had told him that his TV argument had turned them around.[1]

What Anton Chekhov actually told the writer S. S. Schovkin was, "If in the first chapter you say that a gun hung on the wall, in the second or third chapter it must without fail be discharged."[2] It should not be surprising that this canon of classic drama traces its origin back to biblical and other religious narratives. If we are part of a purposive universe—governed by God's law or by the Cosmos—then the stories within that universe must have meaning.[3]

Many literary, biblical, and even constitutional scholars live by a rule of teleology that has little resonance in real life—namely, that every event, character, and word has a purpose. "To everything there is season, and a time to every purpose under heaven," says Ecclesiastes (3:1). God does not engage in redundancy, say the Talmudists.[4] Freud, whose forebears came from that tradition, similarly believed that all words, even those dreamed or spoken in error, have meaning.[5] Some lawyers who view our Constitution in near biblical terms—and who seek to discern the true meaning of those near deities who wrote it—fall into the same teleo-theological trap: every word of that secularly sacred text must have a purpose, a meaning, and if we only had the wisdom of the framers, we could discern it.[6]

But life does not imitate art. Life is not a purposive narrative that follows Chekhov's canon. Events are often simply meaningless, irrelevant to what comes next; events can be out of sequence, random, purely accidental, without purpose. If our universe and its inhabitants are governed by rules of chaos, randomness, and purposelessness, then many of the stories—if they can even be called stories—will often lack meaning. Human beings always try to impose order and meaning on random chaos, both to understand and to control the forces that determine their destiny. This desperate attempt to derive purpose from purposelessness will often distort reality, as, indeed, Chekhov's canon does.

In Chekhovian drama, chest pains are followed by heart attacks, coughs by consumption, life insurance policies by murders, telephone rings by dramatic messages. In real life, most chest pains are indigestion, coughs are colds, insurance policies are followed by years of premium payments, and telephone calls are from marketing services.

My colleague Stephen Jay Gould, in his magnificent narrative of the earth aptly entitled *Wonderful Life,* teaches us that much of life, both on the micro and macro levels, is so random and without purpose that if we were to rewind the tape of life and replay it, it would come out differently every time.[7] *Homo sapiens* is not the preordained, logical, purposeful end of evolution. It is the accidental, random result of a series of historical contingencies that would never be replicated even if we could return to the time of the Burgess Shale and, like Michael Finnegan, begin again. Most of what happens—from the dinosaur extinction to the Holocaust, to the AIDS epidemic, to random killings, to brain tumors, to the lottery—are not part of any plan. To believe otherwise is to accept a particularly nasty variant of the "naturalistic fallacy."[8]

To be sure, after the fact, we may be able to offer a plausible retrospective account, a story or a narrative of what happened. As Sartre put it: "When you tell about life . . . you seem to start at the beginning. . . . But in reality you have started at the end."[9] Narrative often starts at the end. But rarely can we employ such retrospective accounts to predict their reoccurrence. Nor is this lack of prophetic ability merely a function of our relative ignorance. Often it is simply in the nature of things.[10] Quantum physics corroborates on the micro level what paleontology teaches on the macro level. The most important rule in the game of life is that generally there are no knowable rules. Perhaps it is the often-unspoken recognition of this nihilistic reality that drives us so powerfully toward prescriptive human laws by which we can exercise some control over our mostly random destiny and toward purposive narratives by which we seek to impose an order on the largely disordered events of life.

This critical dichotomy between teleological rules of drama and interpretation, on the one hand, and the mostly random rules of real life, on the other, has profoundly important implications for our legal system. When we import the narrative form of storytelling into our legal system, we confuse fiction with fact and endanger the truth-finding function of the adjudicative process. Fact finders are familiar with the dramatic form—not only from Chekhov but also from pulp novels, mysteries, movies, and television shows.[11] They expect a beginning, a middle, and an end to each story. Life, in drama, unfolds in acts or chapters or between commercials. There is an internal logic to the structure. Every narrative, like Churchill's pudding, must have a theme. Even surprise endings must be foreshadowed, at least in retrospect.[12] False clues, deliberately planted by the author to throw the reader off, are frowned upon by critics. Even the deus ex machina of Greek literature has a purpose, though we may not be blessed with the insight to comprehend it fully.[13]

Among the most pervasive narratives in the human experience have been the stories of justice. In these stories virtue is rewarded, vice punished, and justice achieved. The Psalmist reports, "I was a child and then grew old, but I never saw a righteous person abandoned or his children begging bread." This is a narrative of justice. But it is a perversely false narrative. It is false because the history of humankind is replete with the abandonment of the righteous and their children. It is perverse because it implies that those who are abandoned must necessarily have been unrighteous.

As a matter of historical reality, there has been precious little justice in the history of the world. Most Nazis, even hands-on perpetrators of genocide, lived good lives after the war; many Holocaust survivors did not.[14] There is absolutely no empirical correlation between righteousness and reward or unrighteousness and punishment. Indeed, it is precisely because of that lack of correlation—the factual untruth of the narrative of justice—that human beings have been driven to create another narrative, one that cannot be proved or disproved. That is, of course, the narrative of Heaven and Hell, of punishment and reward in the world to come. By creating this narrative of faith, we can insist that virtue is rewarded and vice punished, if not here on earth, then somewhere else, where we can never apply the tests of empirical truth or falsity. Because the narrative of justice cannot be observed here on earth, we create an unobservable world where we can simply declare that the narrative of justice will come true.

The biblical story of Job is a wonderful example of the power of the justice narrative. God tests Job by killing his children (and taking his wealth) despite his—and their—righteousness. Job passes the test of faith, and he is given new children (and wealth). Only in such a primitive narrative of justice would replacement children make up for the death of other children, but even this primitive ending was apparently not in the original narrative. It was added later on to satisfy the demands of the justice narrative.[15]

The concept of natural law, and its many variations, presupposes a narrative of justice and a teleological approach to drawing normative conclusions from natural phenomena. If there is a God whose laws ought to govern behavior, then the job of the natural lawyer is merely to discern these laws in divinely inspired texts, accounts, or the "nature" of human beings or God. Once these natural laws are discerned, the purposive narrative of justice may be implemented. But if there is no God, if there is no purpose to "nature," if there are only "laws" of science—such as the laws of energy and gravity—then human beings must invent, not discover, laws of morality and governance to regulate human conduct so that a narrative of justice can be enforced.[16]

All too often fact finders employ the canons of literature and interpretation in the search for truth, generally without any conscious awareness that they are doing so.[17]

A contemporaneous misuse of narrative, at least to this advocate, may have been at work in the O. J. Simpson case. The prosecution sought to persuade the jury that the canons of drama required it to conclude that O. J. Simpson's alleged history of spousal abuse inevitably led him to murder his wife. Why, after all, would the editor of the narrative—who is called a judge in our legal system—allow the jury to hear evidence of alleged abuse in the first chapter unless it resulted in murder by the third chapter? Surely these past incidents must be highly relevant to the question before the jurors: Did O. J. Simpson kill his wife? The prosecutor tried to strengthen this connection by working backward from the murder—employing Sartre's rule of narrative or the legal equivalent of the dramatic flashback—and arguing that in a large proportion of cases in which a man kills his present or former spouse, the killing is preceded by a narrative of abuse and control. The defense tried to get the jurors to work forward from the alleged abuse by explaining that fewer than one-tenth of 1 percent of spousal abusers escalate to homicide and that no one can accurately predict which ones will actually commit murder, even by using such criteria as a pattern of controlling behavior.

In the words of our previous discussion, the prosecutor tried to show that there is an internal logic, a sequential progression, to its narrative of abuse, control, and murder. The defense tried to show that in real life, as contrasted with fictional drama, the isolated acts of abuse only appear to be relevant because we now know that Nicole Brown Simpson was, in fact, murdered. But because we do not know by whom she was murdered and because this is real life filled with coincidences, randomness, and illogic, we cannot comfortably conclude that *this* alleged abuser became the one of more than one thousand whose acts culminated in murder.

Put another way, if we had a case—as we often do—where a defendant admitted that he killed his spouse, it might be logical to conclude that he probably abused her first, for a large proportion of the fifteen hundred or so annual spousal murderers were abusers first. But in a case where the question is, Did *this* alleged spousal abuser (one of several million each year) become one of those very rare spousal murderers? the logic of the narrative is not particularly compelling.[18] Again, the analogy to the dramatic narrative, with its literary license, is heuristically useful. In drama, if a character is shown having several scotches in the first act, you can safely assume that she will become an alcoholic by the third. And it is true that all alcoholics begin with several drinks. But only a small percentage of those who have two drinks become alcoholics. In fictional narrative, however, there would be no dramatic reason for showing the two drinks unless they were a prelude to a dramatic denouement. The same can be said of spousal abuse. If several instances of abuse are shown in the first act of a play, you could reliably predict that either the abuser will kill the abusee or vice versa by the third act. But in real life, such a lethal result is so rare as to be empirically insignificant (though morally significant, of course). That is why "bad man" evidence—a history of prior criminality—is always relevant in literature and rarely in criminal trials. And it is precisely because of its prevalence in literature that it is so prejudicial in court.

A related example of confusing narrative with real life in the Simpson case was the judge's ruling that the jurors should hear about the defendant allegedly dreaming that he would kill Nicole. In literature, dreams come true. Indeed, in support of the argument, the prosecutor Marcia Clark cited a song entitled "A Dream Is a Wish Your Heart Makes," from the Walt Disney cartoon movie *Sleeping Beauty*. In real life, however, dreams do not come true. They are not even wishes. They are "primary-process" primitive images, which are ambiguous. As one court put it, this ambiguity "leaves the meaning of the dream in the realm of mere conjecture, surmise, and speculation, and one surmise may be as good as another. Nobody knows."[19] Yet despite the lack of any empirical relation between dreaming about killing and actual killing, there was the danger that some jurors might have applied Chekhov's canon—or Walt Disney's fantasy—and assumed that unless the dream was relevant, it would not have been presented. This would be especially dangerous in a case where the facts follow the narrative form: in the first act the defendant dreams about killing his wife; in the second act, she is killed; and in the third act the defendant is placed on trial for the killing. Regardless of the empirical reality that only an infinitesimal percentage of people who dream about killing do kill, some jurors might have ended the drama by convicting the dreamer of being a killer.[20]

Jurors, like most people, are not good at thinking statistically or probabilistically.[21] They are much more comfortable thinking literarily, teleologically, religiously, narratively. But such thinking is often misleading and inapt, at least when it comes to answering empirical questions in a world governed more by randomness than by canons of narrative drama.

An example of an area where the law has tried to remedy possible confusion between fantasy and reality relates to the rape shield law. In the literature, when a young woman is shown in act I living a life of "promiscuity" (to use an anachronistic word from the world of literature), that life will become important to the plot: either she will continue her downward spiral toward a dissolute end, or she will be "saved." In act II if she has sex with an acquaintance which she claims was coerced and which he claims was consensual, surely the reader will regard the history of promiscuity as relevant on the issue of consent. Why else would it have been presented in act I? But our legal editors have correctly concluded that, unless special circumstances are present, the prejudicial impact of this history outweighs its probative value. For this (and other) reasons, the jury is not presented with this history. In life, unlike in art, a promiscuous woman does not always consent to sex.

To paraphrase Holmes, the life of the law should not be teleo-logic or theo-logic (neither of which is *logic* at all); it should be human experience. And human experience cannot be cabined into the structure of narrative. Let literature continue to borrow from law and life (though it would borrow more accurately if it looked less to Chekhov for its canons of structure and more to Proust and Mamet).[22] But let law develop its own rules of structure and editing—of evidence, relevance, and prejudice—by looking to the vagaries of real human experience. And let fact finders, especially jurors, be warned that life is not a Chekhovian narrative.

Janet Malcolm

The Side-Bar Conference

The side-bar conference is the sotto voce discussion between the trial judge and the competing trial lawyers in which the conflicting claims of narrative and legal procedure—of stories crying out to be told and the law's constraints on their telling—are argued and adjudicated. Because neither the jury nor the spectators can hear what is said, and because the press cannot report on what is said, these discussions are largely absent from the public consciousness of what happens in a trial. But as the lawyers and judges know, what is said and decided in these conferences can be crucial to a trial's outcome.

I remember my own rather startled first glimpse into the world of the side-bar conference. It occurred during my reading of the transcript of the Jeffrey R. Mac-Donald versus Joe McGinniss trial of 1987, in preparation for the writing of my book *The Journalist and the Murderer* (1990). *MacDonald v. McGinniss* was the strange case of a physician who had been convicted of murdering his pregnant wife and two small children and who, while serving three consecutive life sentences, sued the author of a best-selling "true crime" novel called *Fatal Vision*. Before the murder trial that ended in his conviction, MacDonald had struck a deal with McGinniss: he would give him full and exclusive access to his story and to his defense strategy—in fact, McGinniss became a member of the defense team—and in return, MacDonald would share in the proceeds of the book that McGinniss would write after the trial. Naturally, MacDonald hoped that he would be acquitted, but when he wasn't, he went to prison in the serene knowledge that McGinniss would write a book declaring his innocence and protesting the injustice of his conviction—a book that would pave the way for (as well as help pay for) the overturning of the verdict. During the four years it took McGinniss to write the book, he allowed—indeed encouraged—MacDonald to believe that he was writing the book MacDonald would have written himself had he been a writer. In fact, McGinniss was writing a book that depicted MacDonald as a psychopathic killer. During the murder trial, in Raleigh, North Carolina, McGinniss had become convinced of MacDonald's guilt. Like the jury, he had bought the prosecution's narrative, had accepted its reconstruction of what had happened on the night of the crime, and had rejected the defense's narrative. MacDonald's story was that four drugged-out hippies had committed the crimes after wounding him and knocking him out. The prosecution said there had been no hippies, that MacDonald's wounds were self-inflicted, and that circumstantial evidence (bloody footprints, holes in a pajama top, and so forth) proved MacDonald's guilt. But McGinniss never told MacDonald of his change of heart. He strung him along for four years, and only when the book was in print and about to be shipped to bookstores did MacDonald learn of McGinniss's perfidy.

MacDonald did not sue McGinniss for libel. He couldn't. He had signed a release that protected McGinniss from libel action. Instead, he sued McGinniss for fraud and breach of contract. His case rested on a sheaf of letters encouraging him in his delusion—letters that McGinniss had written to him in prison over the years, letters of such flagrant deceitfulness that they make anyone who reads them cringe, and persuaded five of the six jurors in the civil trial that MacDonald deserved some reparation. The sixth member of the jury, after declaring her sympathy for McGinniss, refused to deliberate with the rest and caused a mistrial; the case was then settled for $325,000.

The trial lasted six weeks. The plaintiff's lawyer was Gary Bostwick, and this was his first trial; he had been an engineer and then a Peace Corps volunteer before becoming a lawyer. The defense lawyer was Daniel Kornstein, a graduate of the Yale Law School, a *Yale Law Journal* editor, and an experienced trial lawyer. The judge was William J. Rae, who had become a federal judge three years earlier, had been a state judge previously, and had been a professional baseball player in his youth. Each lawyer took high moral ground in his opening statement and remained on it throughout the trial. "This is a case about a false friend," Bostwick said. "What you are going to see is evidence of a person who betrayed a friend, evidence of a person who brought himself into the situation of Dr. MacDonald and promised to do certain things and then for four years told Dr. MacDonald certain things which were not true." "This lawsuit is the spiteful product of a vengeful murderer," Kornstein said. "In the end this is really a case about barbarism and civilization, about death and life."

During the trial, with relentless artfulness, Bostwick developed his narrative of false friendship and drew his devastating portrait of McGinniss. Kornstein, with equal art and ardor, developed his narrative of a murderer's chutzpah in suing a good man who had only done what was necessary to protect his book. (So he lied.) In *The Journalist and the Murderer,* in a scene in which Bostwick talks to me about the lawsuit, I pause to comment on the bitterness of the struggle between him and his adversary: "I was interested to see that, even though the lawsuit was settled, Bostwick was still in the grip of the dislike and contempt for the defendant which had informed his work in the courtroom. Evidently, to be a good trial lawyer you have to be a good hater. A lawsuit is to ordinary life what war is to peacetime. In a lawsuit, everybody on the other side is bad. A trial transcript is a discourse in malevolence."

Now let me return to the side-bar conference and to what it was that startled me when I read a record of the side-bar conferences (the court reporter had transcribed most of them) in the transcript of the MacDonald versus McGinniss trial. What surprised me was the way everyone's mask suddenly dropped. Out of the hearing of the jury, the lawyers were free to change from dire antagonists to men calmly discussing business. They were free to talk about their competing narratives rather than to enact them. They were like actors sitting around the dressing room putting cold cream on their faces and arguing points of craft and turning to the director to decide who was right. I had been reading the transcript as if I were a juror listening to testimony, carried along by its rhetorical urgencies, swayed this way and that, feeling sympathy first for one side and then for the other. The side-bar conferences were rather shocking reminders that what was going on here—what goes on in all trials—is something like what goes on in wrestling matches on television. The wrestlers act as if they hate each other and want to hurt each other, but in fact they are colleagues, they belong to the same profession, and they are simply doing what they are paid to do, which is to fake violence. The feeling of esprit de corps that emanates from the side-bar conference is its most conspicuous feature. And the feeling of betrayal that I felt—the sense that these men were being themselves when talking among themselves and dissembling when speaking publicly—only, in fact, confirms the wisdom of the person or persons who invented the side-bar conference, who provided the shelter in which lawyers' (and judges') masks may be dropped but safeguarded the jury's suspension of disbelief by making the shelter soundproof. The juror, no less than the reader of a novel, needs to be protected from disbelief. The law protects plaintiff and defendant alike from narratives that tell their opponent's story too persuasively; each side's story is always being a little spoiled by the law. But in relegating to a private place the trial antagonists' negotiations over the limits of storytelling—over the containment of hating and blaming within crisp rules of procedure (the rules of fair play)—the law restores something of what it has taken. By so clearly denoting what is backstage and what is onstage, by keeping the illusion-destroying activities of backstage firmly hidden, the law, with a kind of moving clumsiness, signals its acknowledgment of a possibly higher power than its own: the power of the imagination.

David N. Rosen

Rhetoric and Result in the Bobby Seale Trial

Much of the power of narrative of the defendant in the Gabriel rebellion case comes from his refusal to participate in the trial. His rhetorical stance—denouncing the whole sham proceeding—is enormously powerful, but as a lawyer, I think immediately of the obvious fact that he did not win his case. Not that he was trying to. That is the point: he was not trying to. His was the freedom of having nothing left to lose, and he made the most of it. But what if the defendant is trying to win? What happens to the narrative then? What happens is an often-unheroic, sometimes-painful compromise or mutation, a repression, of the defendant's voice.

Let me illustrate my point with a case that the case of the Gabriel defendant brings to mind. In New Haven in 1970 the chairman of the Black Panther Party, Bobby Seale, was tried for murder. The Black Panthers were direct descendants of the Gabriel rebels. They, too, adopted a military structure, with official titles like Field Marshall and Minister of Defense. They sought to organize the black under-class, the "brothers off the block." And they directly adopted the rhetoric of that other Virginia farmer Thomas Jefferson, including much of the text of the Declaration of Independence in their ten-point platform.

Seale had come to New Haven to give a speech at Yale. While he was in New Haven, members of the Black Panther Party were holding captive and torturing a suspected police informant named Alex Rackley, whom they shot after Seale returned to California. Seale was charged with ordering the killing. As in the Gabriel rebellion, the critical evidence was offered by a turncoat party member. The trial attracted massive national and international attention and transfixed New Haven. The May Day demonstration in support of the defendants was preceded by rumors and threats of massive violence, and the National Guard was called up and assembled behind the Yale Co-Op.

Seale was brought for trial from Chicago, where he had been on trial with the Chicago Eight defendants, led by Abbie Hoffman, who were charged with disrupting the Democratic National Convention of 1968. For Seale, the Chicago trial had been a rhetorical triumph. He had insisted on his right to represent himself, and when the trial judge denied that right, Seale refused to stop speaking for himself, denouncing the tribunal and causing the judge to have him bound and gagged in the courtroom, shackled like a slave. Seale became an emblem of the black radical protest against American racism, and, to boot, the U.S. court of appeals ultimately reversed his contempt-of-court conviction.

New Haven was a different story, one in which I participated. At the time of the trial, I had been a graduate of the Yale Law School for several months and had started my first job, as a legal-aid lawyer. These credentials somehow qualified me to be one of the three lawyers at trial for Bobby Seale and his codefendant, a young woman named Ericka Huggins. We won our case, and instead of facing the death penalty, our clients returned to their families. But I felt acutely then and am reminded again by the story of the Gabriel rebellion that the needs of the trial left the defendant victorious but inevitably diminished by the tension between a trial as a place for telling important stories and the trial as the mechanism for springing our client.

In contrast to the defendant's regal resistance at the Gabriel rebellion trial and the enthusiastic, determined subversion in Chicago, at the Black Panther trial there was an extended negotiation with the court. When Seale arrived in New Haven, the trial judge allowed his lawyer, Charles Garry from San Francisco, to represent him *pro hac vice,* a nearly unprecedented ruling for Connecticut state courts at that time, and both Seale and Garry pledged that there would be no disruption. Nor was there: the lawyer was in charge; the lawyer wanted to be in charge; and whereas in Chicago disruption was an effective act of political theater, in New Haven the strategy was to forgo disruption in order to focus on winning the case through lawyering, as well as in exchange for various kinds of latitude from the judge. In fact, Seale did not testify; he did not open his mouth during the whole trial. He left it to his white lawyers to do his talking for him.

Even outside the courtroom, good strategy was the question. The May Day rally was a kind of bargaining chip. The rally was not violent because it was very much in the interest of the defense that it not be violent—both to show the Black Panthers as peaceable to prospective jurors and, again, to gain more leeway from the court. This was a point that the lawyers emphasized insistently to our clients, who in turn passed it on to their supporters. The Panthers organized to Free Bobby, but their menacing slogan, By Any Means Necessary, was given an ironic twist when the best available means turned out to be not revolutionary violence but standard lawyering to expose the weaknesses of a very thin prosecution case.

To be sure, the defense enunciated important themes that the defendants themselves felt passionately, most notably the obsessive desire of the state and federal governments to crush the Black Panthers. But however central such themes were, the point is that they were invoked only to the extent that they were useful within the structure of the trial. The drama of the Black Panthers as militant, even military, warriors against that governmental oppression, so central in Chicago, was jettisoned. In its place were themes that, while not false, could not have felt to the defendants like their most authentic stories. For example, Seale was depicted as that now well-known figure, the benign, somewhat distant and forgetful chairman of the board. And certainly it was not the defendants who were the storytellers.

As decisions were made about what stories would be told at the trial, the defendants sometimes looked even to my inexperienced self for guidance. That is because I was their lawyer. My job was, and is, to help clients formulate the most persuasive story from the evidentiary materials available. That is what lawyers do for a living. It requires careful listening to the client's own story to see if it matches a tried-and-true legal claim or trial story or, on the other hand, suggests a way a legal theory ought to be expanded or a new one developed. It also involves offering the client the stories that work in court to see which of them may match up with a part of the client's experience that may not have seemed worth mentioning, or emphasizing—and even arguing with the client about the extent to which conventional legal claims do in fact have resonance in her or his own experience. There is a wonderful resonance—a feeling of rightness—when a good legal narrative seems to coincide with what the client feels and wants most deeply to express. We search for the one true narrative that will capture the client's deepest truth and dazzle the jury. But the reality is that there is no such thing. There is only a compromise, a best-available fit between narratives, between the stories that our clients have to tell and what it is in their interest for a jury to hear.

Part III

Excludable Stories

Peter Brooks

Storytelling Without Fear?
Confession in Law and Literature

Mea culpa belongs to a man and his God. It is a plea that cannot be exacted from free men by human authority.
—Abe Fortas

I have only one thing to fear in this enterprise; that isn't to say too much or to say untruths; it's rather not to say everything, and to silence truths.
—Jean-Jacques Rousseau

A certain kind of narrative has long held a particularly problematic status in the law. As a kind of prologue to my remarks, let me mention the record of a criminal case that I stumbled on in the Yale Law Library, a case from 1819 in Manchester, Vermont, where the disappearance of the cantankerous Russell Colvin led to an accusation that his feuding neighbors, Stephen and Jesse Boorn, had murdered him—to which, after their conviction, they eventually confessed, only to have it discovered that Colvin was not dead, but had gone to live in Schenectady, New York. The subtitle of a narrative of the events gives the essential information: "A Full and Veracious Account of the Amazing Events in Vermont: How Stephen and Jesse Boorn, two Brothers, were Accused, Arrested, Indicted, Tried, Convicted and Sentenced to Die by Hanging for the Wilful Murder of Russell Colvin of Manchester, Having confessed the Crime; how, while the Condemned Men Languished in Prison, it was Proved that Colvin had not been Murdered, but was Alive and in

Good Health and how He Returned to Manchester and Saved the Unfortunate Doomed Men from a Terrible Fate."[1] The confession narrative is a dramatic instance of a story that needs to be told, but needs to be told right, voluntarily, in the correct context, according to the rules. I want to ask why it is that confession—specifically, the context in which confession is acceptable, certifiably voluntary, and thus admissible in evidence—has been such a problem to the law, and see whether the long tradition of literary confession may offer any illumination.

In *Miranda v. Arizona* (1966), the Supreme Court, in a 5–4 decision, issued its most far-reaching and controversial ruling on the place and use of confessions in the criminal law. It established rules for determining what might be considered a "true confession"—rules that immediately entered the popular consciousness as the "Miranda warnings," familiar from arrests in almost any television cop show: You have the right to remain silent; any statement you do make may be used as evidence against you; you have the right to the presence of an attorney; if you cannot pay for an attorney, one will be appointed to represent you. In establishing these "prophylactic standards" (as it later termed them) for confession, the Court was attempting to create, for itself and for the police stations of the nation, a set of guidelines that would permit a judgment of whether a confession had been given "voluntarily" or, on the contrary, had been "compelled" or "coerced."[2]

Voluntary versus compelled had long been the Court's major test of the admissibility of a confession at trial. But the due-process voluntariness test had proved very problematic in practice—in *Culombe v. Connecticut* (1961), Justice Frankfurter produced a sixty-seven-page "treatise" on the subject without reaching a resolution—and the Court found itself presented with more and more petitions for review of individual cases.[3] With *Massiah v. United States* (1964) and *Escobedo v. Illinois* (1964), the Court moved toward more specific rules—primarily the right to counsel in pretrial questioning—to govern the situation in which confessions could be said to be voluntary rather than coerced. *Miranda* takes a leap forward, specifying those conditions without which no confession will be admitted as voluntary. A cynical interpretation of the Court's decision in *Miranda* would say that the Court cut the Gordian knot of the problem of voluntariness by saying to the police: If you follow these forms, we will allow that the confession you obtained was voluntary. And there is considerable post-*Miranda* evidence indicating that the police quickly learned to play by the new rules and that they produced as many confessions as before. A more generous interpretation would see the Court's decision as a well-intentioned, if not entirely adequate, attempt to deal with a problem as old as the history of criminal prosecution. What are the criteria that allow us to know that a confession has been voluntarily made—and therefore that it may be accepted on its face as reliable, as a confession of the truth? Behind this question may lie another one, implicit rather than explicit in the Court's statements on confession: What is it about confession that makes it such a difficult and slippery notion to deal with? Why do we worry about confessions and their truth value, not only in the law but in literature and in daily life?[4]

Chief Justice Warren, writing for the majority, claims that the rules and warnings established by *Miranda* "enable the defendant under otherwise compelling circumstances to tell his story without fear" (384 U.S. 436, at 466). To this ideal of storytelling without fear—an unconstrained context for confession—stands opposed Justice White's comment, in his dissenting opinion, that "it is by no means certain that the process of confessing is injurious to the accused. To the contrary it may provide psychological relief and enhance the prospects for rehabilitation" (538). I detect here two fundamentally opposed views of how confession works and how it is to be valued—as well, no doubt, as two incompatible views of human nature and volition. White exaggerates only slightly when he argues, "The obvious underpinning of the Court's decision is a deep-seated distrust of all confessions" (537), which he finds in excess of the Fifth Amendment injunction against compelling someone to bear witness against himself. The issue joined here turns on the question of whether storytelling—in the confessional mode—should and even can take place without fear.

Justice Harlan, in his dissenting opinion, allows that the context of custodial questioning never can be wholly without fear. "The atmosphere and questioning techniques, open and fair though they be, can in themselves exert a tug on the suspect to confess, and in this light"—here he quotes Justice Jackson, dissenting in *Ashcraft v. Tennessee* (1944)—" '[t]o speak of any confessions of crime made after arrest as being "voluntary" or "uncoerced" is somewhat inaccurate, although traditional.' . . . Until today, the role of the Constitution has been only to sift out *undue* pressure, not to assure spontaneous confessions" (515). Justice Jackson's view of the "inaccurate but traditional" view of confession as voluntary or uncoerced will need further meditation. To stay with Harlan's opinion, the tug on the suspect to confess needs juxtaposition to one of the most effective moments of Warren's opinion: the moment when he invents what one might call the story of the closed room.

Warren founds this story on its inherent resistance to telling. It is essential, he says, to understand what has gone on when the defendant was questioned by police officers, detectives, or prosecuting attorney "in a room in which he was cut off from the outside world" (445). But: "The difficulty in depicting what transpires at such interrogations stems from the fact that in this country they have largely taken place incommunicado." After reviewing earlier examples of police use of "third degree" tactics—including beating, hanging, whipping, and prolonged incommunicado interrogation—to extort confessions, Warren allows that in modern interrogation physical brutality has largely given place to psychological coercion, then cites *Blackburn v. Alabama* (1960) to the effect that "the blood of the accused is not the only hallmark of an unconstitutional inquisition" (448). He continues: "Interrogation still takes place in privacy. Privacy results in secrecy and this in turn results in a gap in our knowledge as to what in fact goes on in the interrogation rooms." Privacy produces secrecy, which produces a gap in our knowledge. As literary scholars know, especially from the work of Wolfgang Iser, a "gap" (*Leerstelle*) demands to be filled; it activates the interpreter's ingenuity.[5]

To fill in the gaps, Warren, an ingenious interpreter, turns to police interrogation manuals, especially Fred E. Inbau and John E. Reid's *Criminal Interrogation and Confessions* (1962) and Charles E. O'Hara's *Fundamentals of Criminal Investigation* (1956), works that (in various editions) have had a combined circulation of over 44,000 copies. The tactics preached by these manuals are as chilling as one might imagine. As Warren notes, they recommend that interrogation take place in private, so that the suspect, isolated from all familiar surroundings, "be deprived of every psychological advantage"; that the interrogators assume from the outset that the suspect's guilt is a fact and that all they are after is an elaboration of a story the police already know; that interrogation create "an oppressive atmosphere of dogged persistence," that there be "no respite from the atmosphere of domination"; that interrogators use the "Mutt and Jeff," good-cop, bad-cop routine to scare the suspect, and suggest possible leniency if he cooperates; that they establish a context of dependency, so that the suspect feels he must throw himself on their mercy; that tricks be used, such as fake lineups with the accused identified by fictitious witnesses. The idea, says Warren, is to compel the suspect to confirm the "preconceived story the police seek to have him describe" (455). At this point, one must ask of the confession made: Whose story is it? If confession is in theory the most intimate and personal of statements by a subject, how can this story be supplied by a listener? In fact, most confessions by criminal suspects have traditionally taken the form of a statement written by the interrogators and then signed by the suspect.[6] As Warren concludes, the "interrogation environment is created for no other purpose than to subjugate the individual to the will of his examiner." From here, he argues the "intimate connection" between custodial interrogation and the Fifth Amendment privilege against self-incrimination.

I have only sketched how Warren uses the secrecy of interrogation to create a dramatic story of the closed room and the dramas of humiliation, deception, and coercion played out behind the locked door, convincing us that compulsion is "inherent" in custodial interrogation (458). He has effectively responded to Frankfurter's resigned complaint, in *Culombe v. Connecticut,* that "[w]hat actually happens to [suspects] behind the closed door is difficult if not impossible to ascertain" (367 U.S. 568, at 573–74). The closed room—in U.S. police stations, it is labeled the interview room—may remind us of the sealed Paris apartment of Edgar Allan Poe's "Murders in the Rue Morgue," the first detective story, the model for the genre, where this very closure activates the detective Dupin's interpretive method. The enclosed, self-contained space, from the English country house to the California villa, becomes a *topos* in detective fiction precisely because—like that *alcôve* where the young Sigmund Freud was instructed by his mentor to seek the secrets of hysteria—it appears to offer the inner sanctum of a hidden truth. And custodial police interrogation as we know it—as *Miranda* attempts to deal with it—historically is consubstantial with the rise of the detective story. There could be no cop stories before the nineteenth century because there were no police forces in the modern sense. Police interrogation at the station house did not take place much before the end of the nineteenth century. Earlier, other venues—such as the suspect's home or before a magistrate—were common, and the extension of the right against self-incrimination to the station house was unnecessary (a historical evolution that the dissents in *Miranda* ignore). The story of the closed room has its own historical precedents, especially in inquisitorial proceedings, but custodial interrogation by the police is very much a product of modern, urban crime and the social response to it. It is as if the pathological closed and isolated space of the interrogation room had been created to match the closed and isolated pathological space of the crime scene. Warren's creation of the story of the closed room, his opening to light its isolation and privacy and secrecy, his filling in the gaps in our knowledge, stands as an exemplary narrative. Where is voluntariness in such a story? What confession can be trusted?

Yet, since the purpose of police work is to convict suspects and thus protect society, one may feel some surprise, as well as admiration, at the creation of the counterconviction that suspects should be freed of the obligation to confess. That there is a right *not* to confess does not seem self-evident. It runs counter to standard morality, which censures concealment and values the confession of wrongdoing.[7] In many a routine case, confession is necessary to breach concealment and uncover the true story. Commonsensically, we might assume that the evidence against the accused produced from his own mouth is always the most reliable evidence we can have. When someone confesses, his judges may proceed to condemn him with a good conscience.

The Court's anxiety has a history, one that is intricated with religious practices of confession and with the ecclesiastical courts, reaching back at least to the Fourth Lateran Council of 1215, which defined the Christian faith, enjoined once-a-year confession on the faithful, and instituted a vast inquiry into heresy, including use of the oath of *de veritate dicenda,* holding those under suspicion to answer truthfully, under oath, any question that might be posed. As the Holy Office gained power in the fight against heretics, it developed the doctrine that confession to heresy was necessary to save the heretic's soul and preserve the purity of the Church: one had to stand condemned by one's own word—even if that word had to be extracted by the rack and the wheel and other ghastly techniques of torture.

Confession and inquisition in fact have close historical links. When the Fourth Lateran Council gave up "ordeals"—such divine proofs of guilt or innocence as putting one's hand into the fire—Continental Europe generally adopted rules of evidence, derived from Roman canon law, that said that in a capital case, only the testimony of two eyewitnesses or the defendant's confession constituted full proof, sufficient to condemn. Circumstantial evidence was only partial proof. If partial proofs—*indicia*—were abundant enough, there was justification for proceeding to seek full proof by way of torture in order to produce a confession. A confession made under torture was supposed to be fully repeated a day later without torture to be valid (but if not so repeated, the suspect could be tortured again until he agreed to make the "voluntary" confession).[8] In ordinary capital cases, confessions made under torture were also supposed to have their facts verified by independent means where possible.[9] In cases of religious inquisition—the inquiry into heretical beliefs—the matter being confessed to was entirely internal, making verification impossible. In cases of religious belief and deeply held personal conviction there could hence be no other source of convicting evidence than that produced by the defendant's own lips—however extracted from those lips.

In England, the High Commission, the ecclesiastical equivalent of the Star Chamber, imposed what was known as the oath ex officio, which, like the oath of the Inquisition, required that even in the absence of any specific charge one give a full accounting for one's beliefs. Taking the oath put the religious nonconformist—who, in Elizabethan England, could be either a Catholic or a Puritan—in a double bind. If one confessed to the charge of heretical belief, one was condemned. If one refused to confess, one was condemned for being in violation of the oath. It is in the context of such inquisitorial proceedings concerning matters of deeply held religious beliefs and personal conscience that the accused, with greater and greater frequency under Elizabeth and then under the Stuarts, began to put forward the defense summed up in the Latin phrase *nemo tenetur seipsum prodere:* "No one is required to bear witness against himself." This eventually became part of the Fifth Amendment to the Constitution.[10] It is originally a claim that there is a reserved domain, concerning matters of personal conscience and belief, on which persons cannot be required to speak in proceedings that could lead to their condemnation for that belief. Gradually, this right came to be established in English law, in some part thanks to the effort of lawyers associated with the Puritan cause to found the right in the Magna Carta—that is, to see it as entailed by the basic rights of free subjects—in a government where even monarch and church were constrained by the law. By 1609, Lord High Justice Sir Edward Coke could write:

> [T]he Ecclesiastical Judge cannot examine any man upon his oath, upon the intention and thought of his heart, for *cogitationis poenam nemo emeret* [no man may be punished for his thought]. And in cases where a man is to be examined upon his oath, he ought to be examined upon acts and words, and not of the intention or thought of his heart; and if any man should be examined upon any point of religion, he is not bound to answer the same; for in time of danger, *quis modus tutus erit* [how will he be safe] if everyone should be examined of his thoughts . . . for it hath been said in the proverb, *thought is free.*"[11]

This privilege, relating originally to ecclesiastical courts and to questions of religious belief, came to be recognized as a fundamental right of the accused in any accusatorial criminal proceeding.

It can be argued—as indeed both Justice Harlan and Justice White argue in their dissents in *Miranda*—that the privilege against self-incrimination and the rule against coerced confessions have separate origins and separate histories. Coerced confessions were originally barred because they were perceived to be unfairly obtained, thus unreliable and possibly false confessions. The privilege against self-incrimination, as I noted, arose essentially to protect beliefs and matters of conscience. Yet because the compulsion to self-incrimination could also produce confessions that were untrustworthy, and coerced confessions violated a suspect's right to refuse to answer under interrogation, there came to be an indissoluble connection between the exclusion of coerced confession and the privilege against self-incrimination.[12] If the trustworthiness of a confession seems the more pragmatic and perhaps useful test, voluntariness may be the more probative one, for it relates not only to the content of the confession (which in some cases can be verified from other sources) but also to how it was produced, its context. This test insists that the involuntary can never be accepted as trustworthy: to coerce a mental state or psychological disposition—the choice to confess—is somehow paradoxical, a forced voluntariness.[13] Above all, to compel confession may be an ethical violation, somehow an invasion of human dignity. The proposed procedural safeguards of *Miranda* touch on the relation of individual rights to the state's power.

In *Miranda,* Chief Justice Warren briefly evokes the history of the Fifth Amendment privilege as part of the search for "the proper scope of governmental power over the citizen" and concludes that "our accusatory system of criminal justice demands that the government seeking to punish an individual produce the evidence against him by its own independent labors, rather than by the cruel, simple expedient of compelling it from his own mouth" (460). Compulsion, inquisition, and torture lie in the background of the Court's suspicion of confession. As Abe Fortas, soon to be a Justice of the Supreme Court, eloquently summed it up: "*Mea culpa* belongs to a man and his God. It is a plea that cannot be exacted from free men by human authority. To require it is to insist that the state is the superior of the individuals who compose it, instead of their instrument."[14] The *Miranda* warnings, then, are to set the conditions in which the voluntary confessional narrative can unfold—or fail to unfold. The point, as Warren puts it, is that "a knowing and intelligent waiver of these rights [cannot] be assumed on a silent record" (498–99). A "silent record" is another gap attributable to the closed room. Henceforth, the record must speak of the accused's knowledge of the right not to say anything that might be self-incriminating.

The Court's debates about the contexts in which confession is allowable, in *Miranda* and other cases, and the continuing debate in legal scholarship about the scope and even the raison d'être of the privilege against self-incrimination may point, beyond issues of specific legal doctrine, to a more general problem in our thinking about confession. Consider that the law as we know it has elaborated as a most basic right of the accused the protection against involuntary confession, while, on the other hand, Western literature, from early in the romantic era onward, has made the confessional mode a crucial kind of self-expression, one that is supposed to bear a special stamp of sincerity and authenticity and to bear special witness to the truth of the individual personality. From Jean-Jacques Rousseau to Michel Leiris, from William Wordsworth to Philip Roth, the baring of one's innermost thoughts and desires has been held to be a business as necessary as it is risky. If psychoanalysis is perhaps the most characteristic development of modern thought in the human sciences, it, too, appears to be predicated on the confessional act, in a secular reinterpretation of auricular confession. Since the Council of Trent (1551), the Catholic Church has taught that confession, *exomologesis,* is of divine origin and necessary for spiritual salvation. And modern cultures have, in their literature and their therapies, adopted some version of this view. In a secularized world, the insistence has come to be placed on truth to oneself. And getting at this truth almost necessarily involves a confessional gesture, a claim to lay bare that which is most intimate in order to know oneself or to make oneself known.

Jean-Jacques Rousseau is the symbolic fountainhead here. The opening page of his *Confessions,* where he announces that he will present himself before his Creator on Judgment Day with this book in his hand, captures the transition between religious confession and the secular writing of one's intimate self into a book. "I have unveiled my inner being as you have seen it yourself," he announces to this "sovereign judge."[15] But readers of Rousseau have long been aware that the act of confessing does not offer so straightforward or unproblematic an access to the inner being as one might assume. The problem may not be one of error, in any simple sense: study of any autobiographical and confessional text can usually detect some errors of fact, but that does not necessarily invalidate the confession of the inner being, which has no referential verifiability other than the speech act that makes it known to us. But if that is the case, what is it that is being confessed to? In what sense is the confession true, if its apparent referent is false? What other kind of truth, what other place of truth, is involved? Herein lies the problem: What is the relation of the act of confessing to the reliability of what is confessed? If Rousseau and other writers in the modern confessional tradition are making voluntary confessions—in that no other person is coercing them to confess—can we therefore trust the fruits of confession? Indeed, what must we conclude about the very notion of voluntariness in confession when we look at the circumstances of the confessional speech act?

A good instance for making an approach to these questions is also a famous one: the episode of the "stolen ribbon" that closes book 2 of the *Confessions*. Briefly: Following the death of Madame de Vercellis, in whose household the young Rousseau has been a servant, a ribbon is found to be missing. It is discovered among Rousseau's things. Summoned publicly by the Comte de la Roque (acting as executor), Rousseau is asked where he got it. He accuses the young kitchen maid Marion of having given it to him. When she denies this calumny, Rousseau persists in his accusation, and the Comte de la Roque, uncertain where the truth lies, dismisses them both, with the comment that the conscience of the guilty one will avenge the innocent. This, says Rousseau, has happened every day since the incident. He goes on to imagine the future fate of Marion, dismissed under suspicion of theft, no doubt unable to find another place, condemned to a probable future of prostitution. Rousseau, on the other hand, has continued to suffer nighttime hallucinations in which he stands accused of the crime as if it happened only yesterday. He has never been able to confess the crime, even to his most intimate friends. The weight of the crime on his conscience was a key motive in his decision to write his confessions.

Thus far we seem to be close to Justice White's view that confession "may provide psychological relief and enhance the prospects for rehabilitation." But we may have some doubts about this result as we proceed. For now Rousseau moves from the narrative of what happened to the story of what he calls his *dispositions intérieures,* his "inner feelings" (86). And here he tells an entirely different story, one that stands in total contradiction to the external events. He tells us that malice was never further from his thoughts than in this "cruel moment." When he accused Marion, it is bizarre but true that his "friendship" for her was the cause. "She was present in my thoughts, I excused myself on the first object that came to hand." This seemingly random accusation is then specified: "I accused her of having done what I wanted to do and of having given me the ribbon since my intention was to give it to her." Thus we have a problem concerning desire, which thwarted in its intent, gives way to its apparent opposite, the wish to punish. If only his accusers had given him time to repent and the opportunity to confess privately, he would have told the truth. But the risk of being publicly declared a thief and liar was too strong for him to perform on the spot the confession he wanted to make—and now makes so many years later. Over those years, Rousseau says, he has been so persecuted that Marion has been well revenged. He concludes with the request that he be allowed never to speak of this incident again—a conclusion violated when he returns to the stolen ribbon in the fourth of his *Rêveries du promeneur solitaire.*

Rousseau's telling of the story of the stolen ribbon is a stunning and troubling performance. Not only does it represent the emblematic confession, where the failure to confess on the spot becomes the motive for the very act of confessing as an accounting for one's life, it also suggests that confession as a speech act accomplishes something other than the simple revelation of a truth. Confession here permits the staging of a scene of exposure, guilt, and retribution that is the very motive for confession. Paul de Man, in a classic essay on this episode, effectively underlines the issue: "What Rousseau *really* wanted is neither the ribbon nor Marion, but the public scene of exposure which he actually gets. . . . The more there is to expose, the more there is to be ashamed of; the more resistance to exposure, the more satisfying the scene, and especially, the more satisfying and eloquent the belated revelation, in the later narrative, of the inability to reveal."[16] In other words, this primal scene of exposure, shame, and guilt is absolutely necessary to the project of making a confession, and if the scene never occurred, one would have to invent something like it in order to motivate and perform the writing of the *Confessions.*

Qui s'accuse s'excuse, says the French proverb: Self-accusation is a form of self-excuse. As de Man suggests, the speech act of confession is double. In the terms of J. L. Austin's famous distinction, there is a constative aspect—the fault to which one confesses—and a performative aspect, precisely the elusive and troubling action of the statement "I confess."[17] When one says, "Bless me, Father, for I have sinned," the constative meaning is "I have sinned," while the performative meaning is "Absolve me of my sin." The confessional performance of guilt always has this double aspect. Because it does, it opens the possibility that the performative aspect will produce the constative, as the sin needed to permit the act of confession. The law is not without examples of signed confessions that have later been repudiated and sometimes discovered to have been false—as in Manchester, Vermont, in 1819—and there are no doubt other cases in which the truth never came to light.

How can someone make a false confession? Precisely because the false referentiality of confession may be secondary to the need to confess, a need produced by the coercion of interrogation or the subtler coercion of the need to stage a scene of exposure as the only propitiation of accusation, including self-accusation for being in a scene of exposure.[18] Or, as Talmudic law has recognized for millennia, confession may be the product of the death drive—which produces incriminating acts to assure punishment or even self-annihilation—and hence inherently suspect because it is in contradiction to the human instinct of self-preservation.[19] Or, as Freud would have it, unconscious guilt may produce crime to assure punishment as the only satisfaction of the guilt.[20] Guilt can in any event always be produced to meet the demand for confession, for there is always more than enough guilt to go around, and its concealment can itself be a powerful motive for confession. One might want to say that confession, even if compelled, is always in some sense "true" as a performative, indeed as a performance, but this does not guarantee that it is not false as a constative, as a relevant "fact."

Furthermore, the French proverb that I cited can be turned around: *Qui s'excuse s'accuse:* Self-excuse serves to incriminate one. "Excuses generate the very guilt they exonerate," writes de Man. And again: "there can never be enough guilt around to match the text-machine's infinite power to excuse." From which de Man concludes—using, I believe, the term "cognitive" where I would use Austin's "constative"—"Since guilt, in this description, is a cognitive and excuse a performative function of language, we are restating the disjunction of the performative from the cognitive: any speech act produces an excess of cognition, but it can never hope to know the process of its own production (the only thing worth knowing)."[21] That is, the performative aspect of the speech act is not itself the object of cognition.

To restate this in simpler terms: The confessional rehearsal or repetition of guilt is its own kind of performance, producing at the same time the excuse of guilt (by the fact of confessing it) and the accumulation of more guilt (by the act of confessing it) in a dynamic that is potentially infinite. The more one confesses, the more the guilt produced. The more the guilt produced, the more the confessional machine functions. The very act of confessing necessarily produces guilt in order to be functional. As a speech act, "I confess" implies and necessitates guilt, and if the guilt is not there in the referent, as an object of cognition, it is in the speech act itself, which simultaneously exonerates and inculpates. One typical way in which this doubleness of confession operates in criminal law is recorded in *Escobedo v. Illinois,* the predecessor case to *Miranda,* when the suspect Danny Escobedo is told that his associate Benedict DiGerlando has pinned the shooting on him. When Escobedo is taken to the room where DiGerlando is undergoing interrogation, he tells DiGerlando that DiGerlando is lying. Escobedo exclaims: "I didn't shoot

Manuel, you did it" (378 U.S. 478, at 483). Here Escobedo's attempt to exculpate himself involves an admission of direct knowledge of the shooting that inculpates him as at least an accomplice to the crime. By David Simon's detailed account of police interrogations in Baltimore, such self-incrimination through attempted self-exculpation would seem to be very common.[22] Rousseau's confession of the stolen ribbon is more complex and more akin to the sins of conscience aimed at by inquisitorial proceedings, yet he, too, may inculpate himself while ostensibly seeking exculpation.

Rousseau's example is different also, it may be claimed, because he *wants* to confess. Yet his voluntary confession comes under the compulsion of writing his *Confessions,* in a generic constraint to reveal all his guilty secrets; indeed, he could not confess without guilty secrets, which the act of confession would have to invent (and may in fact invent) if they did not already exist. Conversely, can we be sure that suspects in criminal cases do not want to confess, especially when they have been told, over days (and nights) of intensive interrogation that only by confessing can they be released from the obligation to confess—that their guilt is certain and its corroboration alone will release them from the extreme duress in which they find themselves? And that the refusal to confess is itself an admission of guilt?[23] Confession alone will bring release from the situation of accusation and allow reintegration with normal social existence and community. We come back to some of the deep-seated suspicions of confession that Justice White detected, I think correctly, in the majority opinion in *Miranda.* There is something inherently unstable and unreliable about the speech act of confession, about its meaning and its motives. Someone may, as in Rousseau's case, be confessing simultaneously to avoid punishment (to obtain absolution) and to assure punishment (to produce the scene of shame and guilt). Even without the oath de veritate dicenda, you may be damning yourself if you do confess or if you don't confess. Or you may be confessing to the wrong crime, that is, producing what you think your interrogators want in order to avoid confessing to something for which you feel more deeply guilty. Or, more generally, you may be confessing to something else, something other than what you think is the referent of your confession.

This brings us back to the question of voluntariness. In what sense can we say that a confession is voluntary? In the case of *Brewer v. Williams*—of which more below—Justice White, dissenting, writes: "Men usually intend to do what they do, and there is nothing in the record to support the proposition that respondent's decision to talk was anything but an exercise of his own free will" (430 U.S. 387, at 434). In another dissent in the same case, Chief Justice Burger states: "The human urge to confess wrongdoing is, of course, normal in all save hardened criminals, as psychiatrists and analysts have demonstrated" (420).[24] Although both White and

Burger disagree with the Court's conclusion that the suspect did not confess voluntarily, they offer somewhat different views of confession. For White, statements are utterances from which one can generally infer the intention to make them. Intention and utterance line up in an unambiguous manner. For Burger, the intention of the confessional statement is slightly displaced; it lies elsewhere, in the "urge to confess"—which may, as Rousseau's case so well demonstrates, be aberrant, the product of a need for exposure and punishment, and which thus may not fully coincide with White's kind of intentionality, a point that the two Justices do not confront.

Let me press harder on this question of the kind of voluntariness at issue in confession. To begin, here is a citation from Dean Wigmore concerning the decision whether to confess: "The situation is always one of choice between two alternatives—either one disagreeable, to be sure, but still subject to a choice. . . . All conscious verbal utterances are and must be voluntary; and that which may impel us to distrust one is not the circumstance that it is involuntary, but the circumstance that the choice of false confession is a natural one under the conditions" (3 J. Wigmore, *Evidence* § 824 [3rd ed. 1940]). This appears to confirm White's hardheaded doctrine that everything people say—if they are conscious and not under the influence of drugs or whatever—is necessarily voluntary, although it does leave open an important and troubling escape hatch: that circumstances may make the confessional utterance false rather than true.

Now here is a citation from Justice Jackson, dissenting in *Ashcraft v. Tennessee*, already mentioned in Justice Harlan's dissent in *Miranda*:

> It probably is the normal instinct to deny and conceal any shameful or guilty act. Even a "voluntary confession" is not likely to be the product of the same motives with which one may volunteer information that does not incriminate or concern him. The term "voluntary" confession does not mean voluntary in the sense of a confession to a priest merely to rid one's soul of a sense of guilt. "Voluntary confessions" in criminal law are the product of calculations of a different order, and usually proceed from a belief that further denial is useless and perhaps prejudicial. To speak of any confessions of crime made after arrest as being "voluntary" or "uncoerced" is somewhat inaccurate, although traditional.
>
> A confession is wholly and uncontestably voluntary only if a guilty person gives himself up to the law and becomes his own accuser. The Court bases its decision on the premise that custody and examination of a prisoner for thirty-six hours is "inherently coercive." Of course it is. And so is custody and detention for one hour. Arrest itself is inherently coercive, and so is detention. (322 U.S. 143, at 160 ff)

Jackson's dissent from the finding that Ashcraft's confession was coerced unfolds as a narrative of how Ashcraft dug a hole for himself during his interrogation: he attempted to implicate an accomplice but in a way that eventually pointed to his own guilt and obliged him to confess. Again we have inculpation by way of attempted exculpation.

Jackson's seems to me one of the most honest and accurate statements on confession from the Supreme Court, even though he uses it, in my view, to support the wrong conclusions. He effectively evacuates the issue of "voluntariness" in our usual acceptation of the term. He makes us understand that if we can say, with Wigmore and White, that all confessional statements are somehow intentional, in another sense they are all unintentional—or instead correspond to some intention other than that which we usually associate with intentional statements. To be put in a situation where one is made dependent on one's interrogators and asked to confess—pressured to confess—would always seem to create the possibility that the motive for the confessional statement will be different from that for normal intentional statements. The intentions will be aberrant, which, at worst, may make the confession false or at least a confession whose truth is not in its referent, a confession that is not constative but performative.

In *Brewer v. Williams* (1977), the suspect's confession and what produces it are particularly interesting. Robert Williams, the suspect—a recent escapee from a mental hospital—has surrendered to the police in Davenport, Iowa, on the advice of the Des Moines lawyer whom he has telephoned, and has been charged with abducting a nine-year-old girl in Des Moines. The Des Moines police set out to get Williams, and bring him back to Des Moines, but not before agreeing with the Des Moines lawyer, in an arrangement confirmed by a Davenport lawyer, that Williams will not be interrogated during the ride in the police car—a ride from which the Davenport lawyer is excluded. During the drive, Detective Leaming does refrain from an "interrogation" of Williams in the traditional sense. Instead, he makes what has come to be known as the Christian Burial Speech, addressing Williams (whom he knows to be a deeply religious person) as Reverend. "I want to give you something to think about while we're traveling down the road," Leaming says. And then:

> They are predicting several inches of snow for tonight, and I feel that you yourself are the only person that knows where this little girl's body is, that you yourself have only been there once, and if you get a snow on top of it you yourself may be unable to find it. And, since we will be going right past the area on the way into Des Moines, I feel that we could stop and locate the body, that the parents of this little girl should be entitled to a Christian burial for the little girl who was snatched away from them on Christmas [E]ve and murdered. . . . I do not want you to answer me. I don't want to discuss it any further. Just think about it as we're riding down the road. (430 U.S. 387, at 392-93)

Williams eventually directs the police to a service station where he claims to have left the girl's shoes, then to a rest area where he claims to have left a blanket in which the body was wrapped, and finally to the body itself.

No one sitting on this case doubts for a moment that Williams is guilty of a horrible crime. His confession is certainly reliable, validated by a corpse. The issue is whether that confession was obtained in violation of his rights. Williams had been warned of his right to remain silent and of his right to counsel, and his two lawyers had additionally obtained a promise from the police that he would not be interrogated, in absence of counsel, during the drive. Does Williams's confession, then, indicate a knowing waiver of his rights, making his confession voluntary, or an infringement of his rights, invalidating the confession? The Court, in another 5–4 split decision, reaches the conclusion that Williams's confession is invalid. It bases that decision not on *Miranda* but on the earlier case, *Massiah v. United States,* which established that the right to counsel guaranteed by the Sixth Amendment applied during pretrial interrogation. The use of *Massiah* rather than *Miranda* as precedent may represent a decision to take the simplest applicable rule and perhaps also to avoid the controversies that continue to swirl around the *Miranda* decision.[25]

Deciding whether Williams's confession was illegally obtained during interrogation in absence of counsel turns in part on judging whether the Christian Burial Speech was interrogation. To Chief Justice Burger, dissenting, an interrogative ought to be signaled by a question mark. "I find it most remarkable," he writes, "that a murder case should turn on judicial interpretation that a statement becomes a question simply because it is followed by an incriminating disclosure from the suspect" (419-20). Does a statement that elicits a response constitute a question? Burger characterizes Detective Leaming's speech as, not interrogation, but " 'statements' intended to prick the conscience of the accused." The majority, on the other hand, claims that the Christian Burial Speech is "tantamount to interrogation" (400). "There can be no serious doubts," Justice Stewart writes for the Court, "that Detective Leaming deliberately and designedly set out to elicit information from Williams just as surely as—and perhaps more effectively than—if he had formally interrogated him." The Christian Burial Speech is like the confession statement prepared by police interrogators for a suspect to sign: a confession written by another, to which, in this case, the suspect responds, not with a signature but with the revelation of a dead body. Justice Marshall, in his concurring opinion, characterizes Leaming's speech as a "charade," adding, with a citation from *Blackburn v. Alabama:* "The detective demonstrated once again 'that the efficiency of the rack and the thumbscrew can be matched, given the proper subject, by more sophisticated modes of "persuasion." ' " For Marshall, there is torture in the air, whereas for the dissenters, as Justice Blackmun puts it, "[p]ersons in custody frequently volunteer statements in response to stimuli other than interrogation" (439).

Blackmun's dissent contains a sentence that strikes me as slightly curious in a Supreme Court opinion and somehow characteristic of this strange case. He writes: "I am not persuaded that Leaming's observations and comments, made as the police car traversed the snowy and slippery miles between Davenport and Des Moines that winter afternoon, were an interrogation, direct or subtle, of Williams" (1260). That evocation of the police car negotiating the icy highway, with Leaming and Williams engaged in their weird and fateful dialogue, seems almost to suggest a classic situation of storytelling on a winter's afternoon.[26] There is a kind of dreamy atmosphere to it, as if we could never quite recapture the motives of telling and listening, never quite analyze the way that telling a story—as in the Christian Burial Speech—can elicit the profoundest, and most incriminating, responses from a listener. If Leaming's story is like Hamlet's "mousetrap," the play-within-the-play—"the play's the thing / Wherein I'll catch the conscience of the king"—who's to say whether such a play (Marshall's "charade") is innocent or not, for it simply reveals a preexisting guilt? Indeed, it leads to a dead body. And yet, is "pricking conscience" an innocent act? Or a violative one?

Brewer seems to me such an interesting and troubling case precisely because the motive of the confessional act, in that closed police car traversing the snowy and slippery miles, remains so obscure. Why does Williams confess? Should we inquire so closely into the why? In the absence of the rack and the thumbscrew, should we be suspicious of the charade, of the well-told story that pricks or traps its listener into self-implication, into signing-on to a confession prepared by another? Isn't this what many good stories attempt to do? Doesn't confessional literature of the type associated with Rousseau, with Dostoevsky, with Gide, want to elicit a counterconfession in which the reader admits to complicity? Yet in that case, whose story is it? Who is the author of the confession, Leaming or Williams? Hasn't the person who should be the listener to the story, Leaming, become its teller, and he who should be its teller, Williams, its listener? And what authority does the story then have? How can we authenticate a confession as voluntary when we know so little about the associated motives and intentions? And how can the law, which cannot remain within the ambiguities of literature, handle such elusive kinds of speech?

The Court has held, in a series of other cases, that it finds no problem with compelled evidence: a defendant may be compelled to surrender tax documents and bank records, to produce a handwriting sample, even to submit to a blood test.[27] In the case of the compelled blood test, *Schmerber v. California* (1966), Justice Brennan, writing for the Court, argues that the privilege against self-incrimination "protects an accused only from being compelled to testify against himself, or otherwise provide the State with evidence of a testimonial or communicative nature, and that the withdrawal of blood and use of the analysis in question did not involve compulsion to these ends" (384 U.S. 757, at 761). In dissent, Justice Black ripostes that the Court's finding that "compelling a person to give his blood to help the State convict him is not equivalent to compelling him to be a witness against himself strikes me as an extraordinary feat" (at 773). While one may be sympathetic to this view, as also to Justice Douglas's dissent on privacy grounds (citing *Griswold v. Connecticut*), Justice Brennan does, I believe, touch on a central distinguishing feature of Fifth Amendment history and jurisprudence: it is what defendants may do with their lips—what may issue from their mouths—that is considered worthy of special protection. It is as if the Court implicitly understood—without ever articulating the issue in this way—that the problem of confession, its voluntariness or its compulsion, concerns a speech act.

What I detect, in such cases as *Miranda* and *Brewer* and in the long, complex history of the right against self-incrimination, is the law's semiconscious struggle to come to terms with the difficult, layered, perplexing notion of the speech act that follows from the statement "I confess." Chief Justice Warren displays a certain awareness of this special aspect of confessions when, in *Miranda,* he notes of the Court's newly prescribed warnings: "[A] warning is a clear-cut fact" (at 469). If a warning is a "fact," it is so in the mode of a speech act: "I warn you that . . ." constitutes a performative, whatever the content of the warning. It is as if this performative were striving to do justice to the performative conditions of confession. Possibly some of the contentiousness and uncertainty of the debate about the Fifth Amendment protection could be illuminated, if not resolved, by fuller recognition that confession involves a special, and especially complex, form of speech act.

Speech acts, Austin tells us, can "misfire" if the "felicity conditions" are not right. For instance, if you consent to marriage before a priest who is really not a priest at all but your seducer's best friend in priest's clothing (something played out in a number of gothic novels), your "I do" has no standing. Yale Kamisar produces a hypothetical scenario for the law: The suspect asks for a priest in order to make confession and is sent a police officer disguised as a priest. What, then, is the status of the suspect's confession?[28] The outrageous example is not unrelated to *Brewer,* where Leaming addresses Williams as Reverend, although no one present merits that title. What are the felicity conditions in which the voluntary confession can be made and can be recognized as voluntary? What are the contexts in which Warren's "storytelling without fear" can go forward? Where confession is concerned, do these questions even make sense, or is the speech act so layered with contradictory intentions that one can never use the term "voluntary" in confidence and thus never be wholly sure that confession and its intention line up in any unambiguous way?

The Court has continued to assert that the acceptable confession must be the "product of a free and rational will," as Justice O'Connor states in *Miller v. Fenton* (474 U.S. 104 [1985], at 110). Yet as Justice Frankfurter recognized in *Culombe v. Connecticut*, "[t]he notion of 'voluntariness' is itself an amphibian. It purports at once to describe an internal psychic state and to characterize that state for legal purposes" (605). Frankfurter's opinion in that case offers a cautionary tale about why a traditional philosophical analysis of the problem of voluntariness, couched in terms of free will and responsibility, can never really reach the situation of confession and why *Miranda*, in its turn, encounters difficulties "by transforming an intractable metaphysical doctrine into a bureaucratically administrable test," as Louis Michael Seidman puts it.[29] Rules governing the conditions of confession may never be wholly adequate to the problem: They address only the context, not the nature, of confession. And they tend to create an infinite regress in thinking about the problem: What, for instance, will be the rules for a recognizing a "knowing waiver" of the right not to confess?

Robert Weisberg notes that in the wake of *Miranda* we still have "no coherent analysis of what it means to be autonomous in the face of the law, and we are left instead with shallow rationalizations about the psychology of volition"—essentially, with ideological rationalizations for a situation in which Supreme Court debates and the realities of the interview room have little in common. Citing David Simon's evidence, from his experience in Baltimore, that *Miranda* warnings do not prevent suspects from talking, Weisberg suggests that *Miranda* offers "a chance for some philosophical excursuses on why we have created this amazing ideological rationalization."[30] The sense of the individual, and of the individual's rights, implicit in our Constitution generally assumes that the individual is representative of an Enlightenment conception of man: an essentially rational choice maker with a free will. In a post-Freudian, post-Foucaultian age (to use shorthand), we know this conception is inadequate, yet we do not know what to substitute for it. The direction to be taken by those philosophical excursuses is unclear. But it may be fair to say that no philosophical excursus will ever quite reach the problem of confession unless it engages the nature of the confessional speech act.

As Abe Fortas seemed to suggest, in that eloquent line in which one hears an echo of Maimonides, confession may ultimately concern a truth of angels, not of men—or at least a truth whose use in the human arena is so fraught with complexities that it had better be set aside. A certain strain in modern literature, descending in direct line from Rousseau, has understood very well the disturbing power of the confession, whether autobiographical or fictional. Think of the self-abasing and self-aggrandizing confessional speeches of Dostoevsky's Karamazov or Raskolnikov or his Underground Man, the original instance of what Mikhail Bakhtin has called the dialogic because these monologues implicate the words and anticipated reactions of their listeners, so that listener, or reader, cannot escape scot-free from having listened to them. Think of a more recent instance, Albert Camus's *The Fall,* whose narrator tells his sordid tale to an unidentified listener in an Amsterdam bar precisely to pass on to that listener a taint of guilt, an implication in a story in which none of us can fully proclaim his or her innocence. Consider, finally, the complex version of confession presented in Jorge Luis Borges's story "The Shape of the Sword," where what appears to be the third-person recounting of the abject treachery of one Vincent Moon suddenly is revealed as the personal narrative of the speaker: "I am Vincent Moon," he concludes his narrative. "Now despise me."[31] Confession in this mode is serviceable less as a way to unburden one's own conscience than as a way to burden another's—in the manner of Leaming's Christian Burial Speech. The question, in these instances, is what to do with a confession received. What seems called for is a confession in return—which is what Rousseau challenges his reader to on the first page of his *Confessions.* This points toward a possible mass hysteria of confession—and the experience is not unknown—in which the excess of confessional discourse only makes it the more difficult to pin down the motive and the referent of the aberrant speech act. (One could think in this context of some of the troubling cases of mass child-abuse—alleged and rarely proved.) Given the obscurity of the motives for confession, that mode of discourse seems to be capable of producing both the deepest truth and the most damaging untruth.

Rousseau's desire to bare his soul entails an ethics and an aesthetics that he summarizes in his insistence that he is going to say everything, "*tout dire.*" "I have only one thing to fear in this enterprise," writes Rousseau; "that isn't to say too much or to say untruths; it's rather not to say everything, and to silence truths."[32] The enterprise of saying everything is not without its frightening aspects. One has only to think of Rousseau's deviant disciple, the Marquis de Sade, who pushes the tout dire to a kind of paroxysm, cudgeling his imagination to produce every "crime of love" that he can possibly invent, and detailing it all over hundreds of pages. The *One Hundred and Twenty Days of Sodom,* Sade's archetypal work, becomes a manic encyclopedia of perversity, of the need to speak the unspeakable, to confess to everything that society and repressed sexuality normally hold in check. What goes on in Sade's closed rooms suggests that the confessional urge, when unleashed, proliferates guilt and guilty pleasures that society prefers to censor.

We might think, finally, of the psychoanalytic model of confessional discourse, for it is perhaps our most sophisticated contemporary version of what it means to speak, against one's conscious intentions, a truth whose value is estimated by its difficulty. The patient with the psychoanalyst resembles a secularized version of the penitent with the priest—with this difference: that the patient does not know the "sin" to be "confessed" but only the disorders, the stumbling blocks, produced by material that has been repressed. The analyst, like the interrogator, must attempt to uncover what the analyst knows that the patient knows, but only unconsciously. In working toward the knowledge of this blocked knowledge, the analyst—relying, like both priest and interrogator, on a certain transferential bond with the patient— must attempt to elicit a confessional mode of discourse. But it is a strange mode, because the patient's "confessions" of truth must always be regarded with suspicion, as serving some other motive—guilt, revenge, self-justification, self-abasement. The real truth of the psychoanalytic situation is marked by resistances, by the patient's reluctance to articulate that truth, to come face to face with it. Much of analysis is usually directed to the resistances—that is, directed to the nonconfessional or the anticonfessional—on the assumption that this is where the truth is to be sought, the place that the unconscious has marked with its power of censorship.

Psychoanalysis in this manner recognizes that the speech act of confession is a dubious guide to the truth, which must instead be sought in the resistance to such speech, which itself may simply fulfill other purposes, be the confession to a kind of dependency on and propitiation of the analyst. The need to confess speaks *of* guilt, certainly, but it does not speak the guilt, does not locate that psychic configuration that needs discovery and healing. It is not the voluntary confession that interests the psychoanalyst, but the involuntary, that which, we can almost say, is coerced from the patient. For psychoanalysis, the claim of confession is necessarily of limited value and the object of suspicion, not a sure guide to the truth; and the test of voluntariness is an utterly misleading criterion. The true confession may lie most of all in the resistance to confession. Chief Justice Warren's "storytelling without fear" appears as a utopian construct.

The psychoanalytic understanding of confession is consonant with that enacted, rather than that proposed, by Rousseau—which is not surprising when one considers how much Freud owes to Rousseau. That is, psychoanalysis displays an awareness of the doubleness of the confessional act, the motivational discrepancy between the constative and performative aspects of confession, a suspicion that the referential matter of the confession—the sin or fault presented—is not necessarily the meaning or the truth of the confession, that which is intended by the speech act. In its understanding that speech, avowal, and, eventually, truth are transactional, transferential, dialogic, psychoanalysis warns us that the situations in which stories are told—the relative positions and the affective relations of tellers and listeners— can make all the difference.

Perhaps, then, the Supreme Court's difficulties in dealing with the concept and the act of confession have something to do with a semiconscious awareness of the problematic, double, perhaps even duplicitous nature of confession as a speech act. It may be that the only true confessions are involuntary, somehow coerced, if only by the fact that their truth is not there where it appears to be. So it is that confession may be inherently unreliable for purposes of the law, for the policing of society. The story of what goes on in that closed room, where interrogations lead to confessions, always leaves us uneasy, as do so many modern narratives proffered by "unreliable narrators," narratives, indeed, that give us no basis for judging what "reliability" might mean. In the case of confession, that unreliability can be contagious, for it suggests that the more the guilt confessed, the more the guilt to confess, because the act of confession produces further culpability.

As Jean-Baptiste Clamence, the confessional narrator of Camus's *The Fall,* puts it: "In any case, we can't affirm the innocence of anyone, while we can certainly affirm the guilt of everyone." For Clamence, this generalization of guilt becomes an explicit invitation to his listener to join in the confessional game:

> The more I accuse myself the more I have the right to judge you. Even better, I provoke you to judge yourself, which helps to comfort me. O my friend, we are strange and miserable creatures, and to the extent that we look back over our lives, we don't lack for occasions to be astonished and scandalized by ourselves. Try it. Be assured that I will listen to your own confession with a strong sense of fraternity.[33]

It is not certain that we want to join the game, that we want such a reduplication of confession, that we know what to do with it. Justice Harlan may unintentionally make the point when he says in *Miranda*—once again citing Justice Jackson: "This Court is forever adding new stories to the temples of constitutional law, and the temples have a way of collapsing when one story too many is added" (526). The pun on "stories" as architecture and as narrative is no doubt involuntary, but it suggests a perception of the uncontrollable proliferation of narratives produced by confession.

Paul Gewirtz

Victims and Voyeurs:
Two Narrative Problems
at the Criminal Trial

Law is all about human life, yet struggles to keep life at bay. This is especially true of the criminal trial. With the public typically ranking crime our country's most important problem, the criminal trial reflects and ignites large passions. Yet it usually seeks to exclude much of that passion from its stage as the trial proceeds with its structured process of legal proof and judgment.

Maintaining the boundary between the courtroom and ordinary life is a central part of what legal process is all about. Distinctive legal rules of procedure, jurisdiction, and evidence insist upon and define law's autonomous character—indeed, constitute the very basis of a court's authority. The mob may have their faces pressed hard against the courthouse windows, but the achievement of the trial is to keep those forces at bay, or at least to transmute their energy into a stylized formal ritual of proof and judgment.

But there is always a struggle between this idealized vision of law—which proclaims that law is and must be separate from politics, passion, and public resistance—and the relentless incursion of the tumult of ordinary life. This struggle was at the heart of the federal courts' most significant project of this century: the effort beginning with *Brown v. Board of Education* to desegregate American life, in which the courts have sought to disregard white resistance and yet have inescapably been forced to take account of it.[1] An analogous struggle is enacted on a daily basis in criminal courts throughout the country.

In the context of the criminal trial, the struggle is in large measure played out over narrative construction and reception—a struggle over what stories may be told at trial, over the way stories must be told and even listened to, over who should be the audience for a story. Storytelling must conform to certain distinctive legal rules of storytelling contained in the law of evidence and procedure. Seen in this way, in fact, the entire law of evidence, and much of the law of procedure, is really a law of narrative—a law of narrative transactions. Yet, for all the rules that seek to maintain the trial as a place separate and apart, there are unceasing pressures to let ordinary life in, to allow people to tell the stories they tell in ordinary life in the way they usually tell them.

In the narrative transactions of the criminal trial, two categories of insurgent participants pose the greatest challenge today, threatening to invade the criminal trial with their anger, fear, and ignorance, as well as their concern and curiosity. These are, first, crime victims, who through the modern "victims' rights movement" are pressing for an ever-larger but problematic role, and, second, the general public, which is terrified of crime and for that reason and others has become fascinated by criminal trials, and presses for involvement in new and rather alarming ways as both audience and participant.

These two categories of insurgent participants are my immediate subject. Beginning with the roles of crime victims, I first examine the growing use of "victim impact statements" at sentencing. I then consider the increasing presence of the general public as a voyeuristic audience for major criminal trials. Each has a place, I argue, in spite of serious risks. But my treatment of these interrelated issues of victim and public also reflects a broader underlying purpose, which is to augment our understanding of the criminal trial by examining it as a type of narrative and as a forum for narrative transactions.

Ideas about narrative and storytelling have become significant in legal scholarship in recent years, primarily as oppositional to traditional modes of legal argument and as a method of struggle by minorities, women, and other marginal groups.[2] In fact, though, narrative and storytelling pervade the law, from the competing narratives in trial court proceedings to the legal and historical narratives appearing in Supreme Court opinions. This essay should be seen as in part an effort to broaden the study of narrative in the law today. Thinking about the trial as narrative or storytelling can bring fresh attention to the communicative exchanges central to the trial, directing us to the fact that the trial is centrally an arena of speakers and listeners, that the trial's search for truth always proceeds by way of competing attempts to shape and present narratives for particular audiences, that the form of telling and the setting of listening affect everything, that telling and listening are complex transactions that jointly create meaning and significance. Recent legal scholarship has generally ignored these complexities of how narratives are constructed, presented, and gain their effect.

VICTIMS

THE VICTIM IN TRIAL NARRATIVES

The existence of a victim, of course, is what prompts the criminal trial. The earliest court proceedings in England denominated "criminal" were, in fact, private prosecutions brought by the victim directly.[3] But as the criminal process evolved, prosecution became a government function. The victim became a trigger and a witness for the prosecution, rather than the prosecution's director. Put another way, the victim was no longer the guiding narrator of the proceedings but became instead just one of many storytellers at trial. Today, criminal litigation against the alleged wrongdoer is controlled by a government prosecutor, not by the victim, and it is the government, not the victim, that decides which witnesses to present, guides the stories they tell, shapes opening and closing statements to the jury. Thus, the modern prosecution is not really a battle between the victim and the accused. A criminal prosecution claiming that Smith was robbed by defendant Jones is not captioned *Smith v. Jones* but is called *The State v. Jones* or *The People v. Jones*. The abstraction of the "state" calls the wrongdoer to account, displacing the victim because the wrong is seen as one against the community as much as any particular victim.

For many, substituting the state for the victim in prosecuting crime is a great achievement. It keeps at bay the immediate passions of an injured victim, especially unmediated revenge. It transforms a private vendetta into a public concern.[4] It depersonalizes law enforcement and underscores the public values at stake. Government prosecutors are guided by role norms that are supposed to make them more objective and public-spirited than the typical private lawyer—hence the motto inscribed in a rotunda in the U.S. Department of Justice: "The United States wins its point whenever justice is done."

There is much that is noble in this government role. But there is also a loss, or at least an asymmetry. The accused, after all, is represented by a lawyer devoted to his or her client's interests rather than "justice" and who thinks, in effect, that the defendant wins only when the jury votes not guilty. The professional prosecutor typically identifies with other law enforcement professionals and usually does not display the same personal association and identification with the victim that the defense lawyer displays for the defendant. The victim can be pushed to one side—

left in the dark about court dates, treated as an emotional annoyance by law enforcement bureaucrats, "victimized" a second time (as victims and their families often complain today). And the victim loses control of how his or her story is presented.

The place of the victim in the evolving courtroom narrative is most problematic in a murder case, where the victim is dead—dead and silent, unable to tell her or his own story. In many cases, in fact, victims are murdered *in order to* silence them.[5] The absence of the murder victim at trial can be a gaping absence, but it is still absence, and presence is almost always more vivid than absence. Thus, murder victims have a certain comparative disadvantage in the competing narratives of a trial. And they are at a disadvantage not simply because they are absent but because the plot of their life is over; we know how their story ends. Even if against our will, a murder trial inevitably draws us into the defendant's story simply because it remains incomplete and therefore invites us to supply imagined endings as the defendant's fate unfolds in court. By contrast, there is no suspense in courtroom narratives about the murder victim.

Murder victims are silenced in another respect. Because they cannot testify or be cross-examined, even their utterances and writings while they were alive may be excludable. Consider Judge Lance Ito's ruling on the admissibility of various pieces of evidence of O. J. Simpson's stalking and abuse of Nicole Brown Simpson in the notorious murder trial. The judge admitted evidence of O. J. Simpson's past behavior that living witnesses had observed; but he excluded evidence of what Nicole Brown Simpson herself had told others that O. J. Simpson was doing and excluded what she had written in her diary. What Nicole Brown Simpson told others was hearsay; because she was no longer alive, she could not be cross-examined about what she had said and written. The fact that there was no reason to doubt the truth of what Nicole Brown Simpson told others (or wrote), that what she said appeared to be distinctly reliable hearsay, was irrelevant. Evidence that tends to show that Nicole's husband had a motive to kill her becomes inadmissible *because* she was killed—because (on the prosecutor's theory of the case) her husband's alleged motive was a successful spur to action.[6]

Therefore, particularly in murder cases, where the victim is absent and silent, there is an understandable effort to make more present the life that was taken and to vocalize the suffering the murder caused. One is reminded here of an extreme case, the scene in Richard Wright's novel *Native Son* where the prosecutor actually wheels the dead and battered body of one of Bigger Thomas's victims into court to make her visible—a grotesque device that counters Bigger's grotesque device of trying to make his first victim literally invisible by incinerating her body in the family's furnace.[7] More realistically and currently, the prosecutors in the O. J.

Simpson case repeatedly showed the jury photographs and videotapes of the battered, bloodied bodies of the murder victims, not simply to establish technical facts about how they were murdered but precisely to balance the technical facts, and to insist on the vivid human particularity of the people whose lives had been extinguished. Similarly, the prosecutors played tapes of Nicole Brown Simpson's 911 phone calls to the police, not simply to give the jury some factual background for the murders (which a transcript of the phone calls could do) but to let them hear Nicole Brown Simpson's voice, let them hear her fear, to give her presence. And at the end of her closing argument to the jury, the prosecutor Marcia Clark replayed the 911 tapes and said: "Usually I feel I'm the only one left to speak for the victims. But Nicole and Ron are speaking to you."[8]

Others also try to fill the gap created by the victim's silence and absence in the narrative exchanges of the murder trial. Because murder victims can neither tell what happened to them nor witness their vindication, surviving family and friends usually try to fill those roles of storyteller and audience. Family and friends tell the victims' stories in an effort to keep the victims visible, as if to say, "We speak in place of those who cannot speak." And they sit prominently in the courtroom audience, as if to say to the other participants, "We are listening in place of those who cannot listen." Like victims themselves in nonmurder cases, survivors sometimes stand back from the criminal process with their own numbed silence; but like living victims, they commonly push with vocal sorrow and rage to be included. They, too, want a presence.

Modern law enforcement continues to struggle to find an appropriate place for victims and survivors in the criminal process without sacrificing the public purposes that structure and constrain the criminal trial. Indeed, no movement in criminal law has been more powerful in the past twenty years than the victims' rights movement, which has sought to enhance the place of the victim in the criminal trial process.[9] In significant part, this movement reflects the sense of many that the law had evolved too far in the direction of protecting the rights of defendants and had slighted the interests of victims. Thus, the contemporary victims' rights movement has successfully advocated not only that specific legal rules be modified to give the interests of crime victims greater weight (for example, definitions and proof rules in rape cases) but also that crime victims be assured of restitution, compensation, and counseling, that victims be consulted before plea bargains are finalized, and that victim impact evidence be considered at sentencing.[10]

VICTIM IMPACT EVIDENCE IN TRIAL NARRATIVES

The use of victim impact evidence in death penalty sentencing has been an explosive issue on the Supreme Court in recent years, and it is my focus here.[11] In 1987, in a case named *Booth v. Maryland*, 482 U.S. 496, a closely divided Court held that it is unconstitutional for prosecutors to use a victim impact statement (VIS) during capital sentencing.[12] But in a 1991 case, *Payne v. Tennessee*, 501 U.S. 808, a newly constituted Court overruled *Booth* and made most victim impact evidence admissible at capital sentencing—over angry and impassioned dissents.

Booth involved a brutal double murder of an elderly couple during a robbery in their home. The VIS in the case, given as an appendix to this chapter, is instructive about what such statements are like and what being a murder victim's survivor is like.[13] The VIS in this case was a document prepared by an employee of the state Division of Parole and Probation, who refers to herself as "the writer," and it was read to the jury by the prosecutor. The Supreme Court summarized the VIS as follows:

> The VIS in Booth's case was based on interviews with the Bronsteins' son, daughter, son-in-law, and granddaughter. Many of their comments emphasized the victims' outstanding personal qualities, and noted how deeply the Bronsteins would be missed. Other parts of the VIS described the emotional and personal problems the family members have faced as a result of the crimes. The son, for example, said that he suffers from lack of sleep and depression, and is "fearful for the first time in his life." He said that in his opinion, his parents were "butchered like animals." The daughter said she also suffers from lack of sleep, and that since the murders she has become withdrawn and distrustful. She stated that she can no longer watch violent movies or look at kitchen knives without being reminded of the murders. The daughter concluded that she could not forgive the murderer, and that such a person could "[n]ever be rehabilitated." Finally, the granddaughter described how the deaths had ruined the wedding of another close family member that took place a few days after the bodies were discovered. Both the ceremony and the reception were sad affairs, and instead of leaving for her honeymoon, the bride attended the victims' funeral. The VIS also noted that the granddaughter had received counseling for several months after the incident, but eventually had stopped because she concluded that "no one could help her."
>
> The DPP official who conducted the interviews concluded the VIS by writing: "It became increasingly apparent to the writer as she talked to the family members that the murder of Mr. and Mrs. Bronstein is still such a shocking, painful, and devastating memory to them that it permeates every aspect of their daily lives. It is doubtful that they will ever be able to fully recover from this tragedy and not be haunted by the memory of the brutal manner in which their loved ones were murdered and taken from them."[14]

As this summary indicates, the document contained three different kinds of victim impact evidence, all of which *Booth* deemed inadmissible in capital jury sentencing proceedings: (1) evidence about the impact of the crime on the victims and the victims' survivors; (2) evidence concerning the victims' particular characteristics;

and (3) survivors' personal opinions about the defendant and the appropriate sentence. I focus here on the first two categories of victim impact evidence, which are the two types of evidence that *Payne v. Tennessee,* in overturning *Booth,* has now held admissible.[15] Should these victim impact stories be excluded from sentencing—and, in any event, why are such stories so often perceived as problematic?

Introducing victim impact evidence at the proceeding on whether the defendant should live or die almost always increases the chance that the jury will impose a death sentence, so one basis for opposing such evidence is flat opposition to the death penalty itself. But this was not the rationale of the Supreme Court that excluded victim impact evidence in *Booth* (nor is it the rationale usually given, at least publicly, by critics who object to victim impact evidence). Rather, the *Booth* majority (like most other critics) argued that this evidence was irrelevant to whether the death penalty should be imposed and would distort and inflame the jury's judgment—thus "creat[ing] a constitutionally unacceptable risk that the jury may impose the death penalty in an arbitrary and capricious manner" in violation of the Constitution's prohibition on "cruel or unusual punishments."[16] But these arguments, for the most part, are weak.

Narrative Relevance   The *Booth* Court's main argument concerns relevance—a claim that evidence of the suffering of the victims' family and evidence of the victims' personal characteristics are irrelevant to the defendant's blameworthiness and thus irrelevant to the decision on whether this defendant should receive the death penalty. But even assuming that blameworthiness is the only measure of relevance in deciding whether to impose the death penalty, it is difficult to see why the defendant is not to blame for the suffering endured by the survivors of someone he has intentionally murdered. The *Booth* Court argues that the defendant may have had "no knowledge about the existence or characteristics of the victim's family" (482 U.S. at 504), but surely that does not mean the defendant is without blame or responsibility for that family's suffering. Precedent, as well as common sense, establishes that defendants are deemed blameworthy and responsible for the "probable consequences of their actions" and that acts done with the same state of mind may have different legal consequences depending on the actual harm caused.[17]

As Justice David Souter argues in his concurring opinion in *Payne,* which overruled *Booth,* "Every defendant . . . endowed with the mental competence for criminal responsibility" knows that a murder will predictably impose harms on survivors and that the life he takes is that of a unique human being.[18] Even Justice John Paul Stevens, who concurred in *Booth* and dissented in *Payne,* concedes this, and he is left to make the curious argument that particular "[e]vidence about who those survivors are and what harms and deprivations they have suffered is therefore *not necessary* to apprise the sentencer of any information that was actually foresee-able to the defendant." It would only "divert the jury's attention," he says.[19] But to the extent that predictable and foreseeable consequences of murder actually occur in a specific case, that particular evidence seems to be a highly relevant part of the reason for punishing a particular defendant more severely.

Justice Stevens embellishes his argument in *Payne* by making a distinction between what a legislature may do when setting general standards for sentencing and what a judge or jury may do in imposing an individual sentence: "The majority . . . fails to differentiate between legislative determinations and judicial sentencing. It is true that an evaluation of the harm caused by different kinds of wrongful conduct is a critical aspect in legislative definitions of offenses and determinations concerning sentencing guidelines. . . . But the majority cites no authority for the suggestion that unforeseeable and indirect harms to a victim's family are properly considered as aggravating evidence on a case-by-case basis."[20] It is hard to see, however, why there is any general problem with case-by-case judicial consider-ation of harm to survivors and, revealingly, Stevens fudges his objection by linking it to a claim that the particular harm to survivors is "unforseeable" or "indirect". The legislature punishes murder so severely at least in part *because* murder predictably imposes these harms. The actual occurrence of these predictable and foreseeable consequences of murder in a specific case seems to be a highly relevant part of the reason for punishing a particular defendant more severely. Certainly if relevant in legislatively setting the general parameters of punishment, it is relevant to the individual punishment decision. Indeed, the relevance of victim impact evidence to sentencing ultimately seems to be conceded even by the *Booth* majority, which is careful to emphasize that it is not holding that victim impact evidence must be excluded from *non*capital sentencing.[21]

One of the themes of the storytelling movement in law is relevant here. The account of the suffering of the victim's survivors in individual cases is a particular-ization of a generally foreseeable harm. Particularization, the theorists of storytell-ing remind us, invites empathetic concern in a way that abstractions and general rules do not, and encourages appreciation of complexity.[22] Indeed, something like that insight surely underlies the Supreme Court's constitutional rule that in death penalty sentencing *defendants* must be allowed to introduce any and all mitigating evidence—any and all particularized evidence about their background, upbringing, and so forth, that might lead a jury to conclude that a death sentence would not be appropriate.[23] Permitting similar particularization in victim impact evidence like-wise encourages empathetic concern for the victim and the victim's survivors, as well as a complex understanding of the defendant's crime.[24] To be sure, the defen-dant's story and the victim's or survivor's story are about different matters, but in the context of sentencing they can be seen as counterstories, which should both be available to the decisionmaker.[25] (Indeed, in the most literal sense, victim impact evidence consists of stories of victimized and silenced people, who are the usual concern of many in the storytelling movement.) If particularized storytelling should have a greater place in the law, does not the particularized story of the murder victim and the victim's survivors warrant that place?

In fact, however, many liberals who praise the place of stories in law believe that victim impact statements should be excluded from court. There are reasons to want these stories excluded—for example, opposition to any penalty-phase evidence that makes death sentences or longer prison terms more likely. But if this is the true reason, it makes something clear that is not always clear: For some in the storytelling movement, the point is not simply to strengthen the place of stories in law but to strengthen stories making particular political points; they are not really making a claim about the value of storytelling as an alternative way of knowing and persuading but rather a claim about the strategic value of *some* stories as an alternative way of promoting a particular substantive point of view.

One might perhaps distinguish here between the relevance of evidence about the harm suffered by the survivors (the first category) and the relevance of evidence of the victim's particular characteristics (the second category). On the one hand, the latter evidence can be seen as simply an extension of the first category, a particularization of the harm caused. This is how the *Payne* majority sees it—characterizing this evidence as simply "offering 'a glimpse of the life' which a defendant 'chose to extinguish,'" showing "each victim's 'uniqueness as an individual human being,'" making sure that the jury understands that the murdered person was a specific situated human being not just an abstract "victim."[26] But such evidence can be seen as not only a *particularization* of a life story but also a *valuation* of that particular life story. To the extent that this category of evidence makes an implicit or explicit claim that the life taken was comparatively more valuable than many other lives and that the death penalty is therefore more appropriate, it raises a distinctive moral problem.[27] But the relevance of impact evidence in at least the first category—evidence about the harm suffered by survivors—seems clear to me.

Narrative Presentation and Reception   Having said this, I nevertheless do think that there are grounds for concern about victim impact evidence—not based on the substance or relevance of the stories told but on the dynamics of presentation and reception of the stories. Those who focus on storytelling in law have generally focused on the substance of the stories told and the fact of their particularity but have not explored the dynamics of their transmission and reception, which have been themes of narrative theory in literary studies. Looking at victim impact evidence as a narrative transaction, however—narratives told and received in a certain way—highlights concerns about this evidence at least as serious as concerns about *what* they say.[28]

First, there is reason for concern about how victim impact evidence is received by its primary audience. Such evidence, which usually describes either the emotional responses of survivors or especially appealing characteristics of the murder victim, is likely to invite an emotional reaction from the jury that hears it.[29] Is the very fact that victim impact evidence would vividly remind the jury of the awful emotional reality of the crime's impact—one of the reasons such evidence seems relevant—also a reason for excluding it? The Supreme Court has often said, after all, that the decision of whether to impose the death penalty must turn on a "reasoned moral response . . . rather than an emotional one."[30] Indeed, more generally, a central part of the prevailing ideology of law is that it is a realm of reason, not emotion.[31]

Narrative theory insists on the importance of focusing on how stories are received, not simply on what they say[32]—all storytelling, after all, is transactional, with listeners affecting tellers as well as tellers affecting listeners. And the law, at least implicitly, is quite sophisticated about this. Judges instruct juries throughout the trial about how the jury should listen to what it hears—for example, that a given legal standard should provide the framework for listening to factual narratives, that certain evidence is admissible to prove X but not Y, that the jury should disregard certain evidence previously heard, not be swayed by passion or prejudice, and so forth. Theories of audience reception surely underlie these instructions.[33]

But the notion that evidence producing an emotional response should be inadmissible is indefensible. First, such a notion proves (and would exclude) far too much, because a high proportion of now-admissible evidence produces some emotional reaction in jurors. Both conservative and liberal members of the Supreme Court have been blatantly inconsistent about this, invoking the notion that law is reason, not emotion, only when it is convenient to do so. Justice Sandra Day O'Connor, for example, has insisted that death penalty sentencing must be a "reasoned moral response," not an "emotional response," as a reason for rejecting defendants' objections to jury instructions directing jurors not to be influenced by "sympathy."[34] But in *Payne v. Tennessee,* where prosecutors had introduced victim impact evidence that she conceded had "moved" the jurors, Justice O'Connor concluded that their emotional reactions were acceptable because the impact evidence "did not inflame their passion more than did the facts of the crime."[35] Liberals are inconsistent in the opposite way. Justice William Brennan, for example, joined *Booth v. Maryland,* which excluded victim impact evidence (as the defendant requested) and rested in part on the argument that the evidence was "emotionally charged" and that the death penalty decision had to be "based on reason rather than caprice or emotion."[36] But Brennan saw a place for emotion when, in his dissent in *Saffle v. Parks,* he agreed with the defendant that it was constitutional error for capital sentencing juries to be instructed not to be influenced by "sympathy"—even though Brennan seemed to acknowledge that sympathy is an "emotion" and is "fairly regarded as a synonym for 'compassion.'"[37]

The problem with the idea of excluding evidence that produces an emotional response is more fundamental, however, for the glib distinction between "reasoned" and "emotional" responses is far too simplistic.[38] This insight dates back at least to Plato.[39] But more recently, scholars from fields as diverse as philosophy, psychology, and neurobiology have demonstrated that emotions have a cognitive dimension and are connected to beliefs in various respects.[40] For example, emotions can open up ways of knowing and seeing and can therefore contribute to reasoning. (Fear and caring, for example, can make us attentive to more facts; sympathy may be part of properly assessing mitigation evidence in capital sentencing).[41] Indeed, reasons are constituted in part by emotion, and are modifiable by emotion. (Fear can be reduced by changing our beliefs; our general views about gay people can be changed by empathy we come to feel towards a gay relative.) Moreover, emotions can reveal beliefs that conscious thought conceals (grief sometimes does this). And emotions are often essential to the completion of a rational response (consider Michael Dukakis's answer during a campaign debate to a question about what he would think if his wife were raped and murdered, an answer that was so abstract and unfeeling as to suggest a not fully rational reaction).

This linkage and dialectic between emotion and reason is especially true of a jury sentencing decision. At the sentencing stage, the jury is not being asked to find a fact (Did the defendant do it?) but to make a judgment about an appropriate punishment. That judgment includes implementing retribution, which inevitably draws upon an emotional element.[42] In death penalty cases, that judgment also involves considering all of the defendant's mitigation evidence, which also brings into play the jury's sympathy and sense of mercy and surely involves nonrational elements. Similarly, considering victim impact evidence involves nonrational elements of sympathy and concern.[43]

This is not at all to deny that emotion can be a problem in the courtroom, but rather to affirm that it is inescapable and has an appropriate place. One should grant that emotion must be bounded if the court is to remain a place of law. But the issue is boundedness, not whether emotion has a place. By bounded emotion I mean in part that there must be a limit on certain types of emotional exchanges, such as those that are excessively inflammatory or those based on what we understand as prejudice. But, more important, I mean that emotional responses must be subjected to reasoned examination; the dialectic between reason and emotion should be explored. The trial setting facilitates this, for the lawyers on both sides are in a position to offer the jury reasoned argument about testimony, including emotional testimony. After victim impact evidence is presented, for example, the lawyers should be allowed to make reasoned arguments to the jury to encourage jurors to think about their emotional responses and test them through thought, and vice versa (both emotions and rational beliefs can be unreliable). The arguments will concern not only the significance of the victim impact evidence but also the weight that evidence should receive given the extraordinary nature of the death sentence, the relevant statutory standards governing application of the death penalty, and the defendant's mitigating evidence that seeks to generate a countervailing sympathy for the defendant.

These arguments can help to make the jurors more self-conscious about their reactions and can encourage reflection. The court can therefore reduce the likelihood of what Paul Brest calls in another context "*selective* sympathy and indifference," a particularly worrisome possibility here.[44] Some of the concern about victim impact evidence in death penalty cases surely rests upon the fact that in this context the main audience is a lay jury, not a professional judge, and we have concerns about jurors' capacity to reflect upon their emotional responses. But if the lawyers and the judge do their jobs, the emotional reactions produced by both the prosecutor's victim impact evidence and the defendant's mitigation evidence can be bounded and tested by reasoned argument—an activity that will not obliterate the emotional dimension but can cabin it and even deploy it to promote a more reasoned decision.

In response to the concern that victim impact evidence may introduce too much emotion into the jurors' sentencing decision, we might also consider some restrictions regarding the form of such evidence. The Maryland statute authorizing the use of victim impact evidence in *Booth* provided that such evidence could be presented in two different narrative forms: a government-prepared document could be read to the jury, or family members could be called to testify as to the information. These two forms of narrative may have very different effects on the jury, though, and concern about emotional effects might justify restrictions on live testimony by survivors.

Some differences between the forms of presenting victim impact evidence give each form advantages and disadvantages for the prosecutor or the defense. A VIS document can be shaped, structured, and polished to produce a desired effect. It also has the imprimatur of the "state" as author and therefore arguably gains narrative authority.[45] The judge can also review it in advance and order inflammatory material excised before the jury hears it. But, as a written document that is read, it will not have the human immediacy of live testimony from the victims' survivors, which allows their sadness and suffering to be observed, not just explained. And to the extent that the document reports on what others say, it may be unreliable. Live testimony, by contrast, is less shaped, because it must proceed by more fragmented questions and answers and by direct and cross examination, and in the end is less controllable by both the lawyers and the judge. But since the survivors will be testifying themselves, their evidence is likely to be much more emotionally charged than a VIS document. In the Wisconsin sentencing proceedings for Jeffrey Dahmer, for example, relatives of his murder victims gave live testimony; some testimony was so impassioned and angry that one surviving sister rushed at Dahmer and tried to attack him in front of the judge.[46]

If given a choice among these forms, prosecutors must decide what effect on the audience they wish to produce, as they must do in choosing how stories are told throughout the trial. The self-conscious trial lawyer becomes a theorist of narrative forms, and so does a self-conscious judge. A judge concerned about excessively emotional responses that victim impact evidence may unleash might consider requiring the prosecutor to present this evidence to the sentencing jury in the form of a VIS document instead of live survivor testimony. (The defense counsel in *Booth* himself requested that the victim impact evidence be presented through a government-prepared VIS document rather than through live witnesses precisely to reduce "the inflammatory effect of the information.")[47]

An obvious problem with this approach is that the defendant might be unable to directly challenge the victim/survivor statements in the document through cross-examination. But the defendant could be allowed to call the victim/survivors as witnesses and cross-examine them about their statements in the VIS; this system would limit prosecutors' ability to present victim impact evidence in its most vivid form but would allow defendants to decide whether the benefits from confronting live witnesses would outweigh the risk of generating too dramatic testimony.[48] In any event, it is settled constitutional law that the Sixth Amendment right to confront witnesses does not require the usual examination and cross-examination of live witnesses at the sentencing stage; sentencing judges all the time impose sentences based on written information in presentence reports that are not subject to cross-examination.[49] In short, judges seem to have the power to modulate the emotional effects of victim impact evidence by using narrative forms most suitable to this context—reducing, if not altogether eliminating, the problems of how this evidence is received.

Other problems with victim impact evidence concern the activity of storytelling itself, not the audience response. First, as the *Booth* majority noted, "in some cases . . . the family members may be less articulate in describing their feelings even though their sense of loss is equally severe."[50] This reminds us that every story needs to be constructed, requiring an ability and skill that exists unevenly in the population. The *Booth* majority goes further, arguing that this is a reason to deem expressions of grief inadmissible, since "the degree to which a family is . . . able to express its grief is irrelevant to the decision whether a defendant . . . should live or die."[51] In some sense the Court is right, just as it would be right to say that a family's ability to pay for the best lawyers in the world is irrelevant. But the fact that differing abilities may appear arbitrarily in the population does not make it arbitrary to distinguish among the different effects that those differing abilities help to produce. Moreover, as Justice White's dissent suggests, the *Booth* majority's argument proves too much. If courts were to exclude categories of testimony simply because some witnesses are less articulate than others, no category of oral testimony would be admissible.

A more serious narrative problem with victim impact evidence—though one that implicates no constitutional rights of the defendant—concerns the consequences of giving impact evidence on the survivors themselves. We have been assuming thus far that survivors are pushing to have their stories heard and that allowing victim impact evidence to be considered at the sentencing phase promotes the interests of the victims and the survivors. But surely the dynamic of survivor testimony is far more complicated. To tell the story of personal suffering requires the teller to relive that suffering, to retrieve it from repression, to reexpose wounds that may have started to heal. This may be beneficially therapeutic, but it may not be. For survivors to be asked to tell about the victim's particular characteristics in this context invites, moreover, a predictable selectivity in detail. Typically, if not universally, people have complex and conflicting feelings about family members. But how frequently does victim impact evidence after a family member's murder dwell on these complexities?

Participating in the sentencing process can also add to the survivors' sense of responsibility and can potentially add to the sense of guilt that survivors often feel.[52] It can create new conflicts. For example, survivors may not in fact want the defendant to receive the death penalty—they may be opposed to it on moral grounds or may think it recapitulates the violence they endured—but once included in the sentencing process, they may feel pressure to join in seeking the death penalty as an emblem of their outrage at the victim's murder. Where the survivors do favor seeking the death penalty, including them in the sentencing process may make them feel as if they have been given the responsibility to persuade the jury to recommend the death penalty. And if the jury that hears victim impact evidence does *not* recommend the death penalty, survivors may feel that they have let the victim down by not being adequately articulate in describing their suffering or by not describing the victim with sufficiently appealing particularity.[53] This may add to the sense of guilt that survivors often have simply because they have survived or because they think that somehow they could have saved the victim.[54]

Put more generally, storytelling is often a risky and anxious activity, for there is always the possibility that a story will not be told effectively. And the responsibility to tell victim impact stories, in particular, imposes that risk and anxiety on an already-vulnerable group of people. This may not deter victim rights advocates from seeking greater inclusion for victims and survivors at the criminal trial. But at the very least, it reminds us that storytelling is always consequential, to the tellers if not the listeners. And the consequences may not be what they at first seem.

VOYEURS

The victim is the subject of the trial, so the victim's place as at least a character in the criminal trial's narrative is definitional. This is not true of the general public, whose connection to the trial narrative is less definite. Indeed, there is considerable ambivalence about the general public's relationship to the trial; in some senses, it is an indispensable audience and participant, in other senses, a deeply distrusted one, always in danger of becoming a mob or "public opinion" that can assault and undermine legal processes. But whatever the ambivalence, the general public's increasing engagement with criminal trials is having important consequences.

Four benign aspects of the public's role stand out in traditional American ideas about the criminal trial. First, although the public is not the direct subject of the trial, the public is a direct object or target of the trial, for a central purpose of punishing particular individuals for breaking laws is to deter criminal behavior by others. Put another way, the public is a primary audience for the trial, although it has traditionally learned about the trial through the heavy filter of media accounts.

Second, the public is a watchdog. Its presence at criminal trials is thought to assure the sort of outside scrutiny that can help to prevent injustice. Indeed, it is for that reason that the Constitution has been interpreted to require that trials must almost always be open to members of the public and the media. Note that this constitutional requirement means only that the public and the media must be admitted insofar as courtroom space permits; not all members of the public have to be admitted, and (more important) there is no requirement that the media must be allowed to televise court proceedings, which would allow all members of the general public to see the trial for themselves. Representatives of the public must generally be allowed to attend criminal trials, not members of the public directly.

Third, what makes the criminal sanction unique is that it is said to be an expression of public morality, to embody the moral condemnation of the community. This means that a particular trial narrative is usually part of a broader social narrative, and the public is generally implicated in at least the latter. A related notion is that the trial is supposed to channel the retributive desires of the public; we can call this the public as voice. Once again, however, this public role (of community morality and retribution) is mediated and restricted. For one, at the legislative level public morality is expressed through general norms, not judgments about what particular individuals have done; indeed, the Constitution prohibits legislatures from adopting bills of attainder that punish particular individuals directly. In addition, at the trial itself, when a general norm is applied to particular behavior, public morality is expressed through a jury, a representative body that is supposedly screened for bias and restricted in what it may hear and how it may assess what it hears. (In origin, of course, the jury consisted of members of the community with direct knowledge of the offense.) Put another way, the general public is always kept at least one step removed from judgments in particular cases.

Fourth and last, the public is a constituent of trials. As a constituent, the public sees trials as an expression of public values. And when it follows trials, it bestows or withholds public confidence, and this can either weaken or strengthen the public's faith in its government.

In the past decade or two, the public has become more engaged as an audience for and participant in criminal trials than before. This may be part of a broader cultural interest in law—consider mass-market entertainment like *L.A. Law* and the John Grisham and Scott Turow best-sellers and the real-life increase in litigiousness. But the focus on the criminal trial is a distinct subset of this general public engagement. This engagement may result from a greater public fear about crime. In any event, it is a development that has been propelled and facilitated by the new technology of cameras in the courtroom and by Court TV, which have made the general public an immediate audience for many trials. Criminal trials have also received increasingly prominent coverage in the print media. There have been celebrated and notorious trials throughout U.S. history, of course. But nowadays there is almost always a trial that absorbs public attention, and the degree of absorption seems greater than ever before. Criminal court is always in session for the public audience. Over the past several years, day after day, some criminal trial or other has been treated by the media as a top national news story and received by the general public in that way—recall only William Kennedy Smith, Jeffrey Dahmer, Bernhard Goetz, the Menendez brothers, the Bobbitts, Heidi Fleiss, the police officers who arrested Rodney King, and, most recently and most flamboyantly, O. J. Simpson. Each trial is treated as a major cultural event and thus becomes one. These developments probably make the public better informed, as advocates of the televised coverage of criminal trials argue. But that characterization does not quite capture the broader cultural consequences of the public's greater involvement in trials.

These criminal trials have become a central moral arena for society. Because the criminal law intersects so many areas of U.S. society, the criminal trial is often the most prominent place where large moral issues are scrutinized—ranging from racial issues to assisted suicide. Criminal trials have always been a place for society to draw boundaries, but the trial has taken a more important cultural place in drawing these moral boundaries as other institutions that have traditionally engaged in moral line drawing, such as religion and the family, have declined in strength. The criminal trial has, moreover, become an arena in which social deviance is explored as well as defined—the twisted deviance of Susan Smith, the apparently brazen evil of the Menendez brothers.[55] The main dynamic at the trial is to support the norms of socially acceptable behavior by defining otherness, to mark off the ways the guilty defendant is different from the law-abiding public audience. But by providing the public with a close-up view of individuals on trial, by embedding the deviant act in circumstances that are often not themselves deviant, by allowing the full consideration of all the excuses offered up by defendants, the public also comes to experience the ways it is like, not simply different from, the criminal.

The criminal trial is also an important way for the public to confront its anger and fear concerning criminality, which have grown over the past several decades such that crime is now the public's number one concern. The point here is not simply that the result of a trial can satisfy the retributive urges of the general public, although it can surely do that. The form of the trial—its structure and formality—is itself part of that coming to terms. The trial structures social disorder and thus makes it less disturbing and even enjoyable. It is the sustained process of imposing legal order on criminal violence that reaffirms that life's disorder can be controlled. One of the cultural appeals of a television series like *Perry Mason,* a series that all but defined law for a generation of Americans, was the patterned closure of each program. The truth was always outed, the true criminal revealed; and the vindicated innocence of Perry Mason's client stood for the vindicated order that the legal process predictably imposed. The appeal of the classic detective story is similar, given its reiterated form: a puzzle of violence presented and ultimately solved (and solved through orderly reasoning). Real-life trials obviously do not have the neatness of the trials represented on *Perry Mason,* but they have some of its patterned quality—and, above all, they usually reach closure.

Not unrelated is that the criminal trial has become a source of entertainment. Part of the appeal of the criminal trial is that real people have been hurt and that a real defendant may be exposed and punished. But its reality does not interfere with—indeed, it arguably enhances—its entertainment value. The trial can have the organized combat of spectator sports, the emotional tumult of a soap opera, the heightened suspense of a thriller. When people say that the O. J. Simpson trial was a circus, part of what they surely mean is that it became, like a circus, a gaudy public entertainment. We see this more generally now that much of the media's coverage of "news" has blurred into "entertainment," with entertainment values now shaping what is covered, in what detail, and in what manner.

The trend toward a wide television audience for many criminal trials can be usefully considered alongside another recent development in television that rivals it in importance and to which I think it is linked—the rise of the *Oprah*-style television talk show. For both, the subject is usually some socially extreme behavior, behavior that tests or transgresses current boundaries of publicly acceptable conduct. The subjects are explored by considering the lives of actual people. And for both, the public audience to the spectacle and the exploration is critical.

At the center of *Oprah* and the trial is judgment. On *Oprah* the studio audience is invited to ask questions, but its critical function is to offer judgments of the behavior being displayed—and in articulating its judgments the studio audience is a stand-in for the audience at home, which is also invited to judge. But what is critically important when Oprah invites judgments is this: on *Oprah,* everyone's judgment has the same weight, every judgment is valid. To *feel* validates judgment. The implicit credo of *Oprah*'s audience is "I feel, therefore I may judge." The audience is endlessly valorized because Oprah treats its judgments so respectfully. And the cultural impact of *Oprah* is that it has increased the status of the ordinary person's judgment.

The widening coverage for criminal trials also invites public judgments. Part of the appeal of the trial for the public audience is that it invites these judgments: Did the defendant commit the crime? Should he be convicted? Is this or that witness lying? Are the lawyers doing a good job? And so forth. As the public has been allowed into the trial more and more as a direct audience, it has been encouraged more and more to make these judgments.

But surely there is a problem. Judgment at trial is carefully structured and circumscribed. Most things about the trial refute the idea that "I feel, therefore I may judge." Public judgment is rendered by an institution that represents the public— the jury—but it is a representative institution, whose members are screened and are expected to conform to distinctive and circumscribed role behavior. Only appropriately unbiased people are supposed to serve on juries and to judge. The jury may not hear everything, only evidence admitted in accordance with the restrictive law of evidence and procedure. Jurors must be a constant rather than intermittent audience. They may not be there one day and gone the next but must hear and consider everything that is admitted into evidence; and they must wait until the end of the trial, until they have heard all the evidence, to discuss the case with others and make their judgments. And the jury is expected to follow the instructions of the judge, instructions that reflect established legal rules.

The general public audience is restricted in none of these respects. It may be biased. It may be exposed to lots of evidence and argument that are inadmissible in court—indeed, the media that brings the public the trial itself also typically brings the public lots of additional evidence and argument. At the same time, the public is typically an intermittent audience and hears only part of the story. And the public is either ignorant of the legal instructions given to the jury or feels itself unrestrained by those instructions. Still—and this is the critical fact—the public feels itself entitled to pass judgment. "I feel, therefore I may judge."

I do not wish to romanticize the jury, which in some respects is infected with similar deficiencies, perhaps increasingly so. For example, the very idea of a jury as objective and unbiased is being replaced by the idea of a jury as a collection of representative biases. It was a major step forward when we moved from a jury system that was outrageously elitist and exclusionary to one that was supposed to be "a fair cross-section of the community." But the idea of "fair cross-section," which was initially a tool for reducing biases on juries, is today often used to legitimate biases as long as they are representative. Consultants are trying to make more scientific a process of picking a jury whose biases one side or the other likes—using the same techniques of polling and focus groups that politics uses. Moreover, there is at least anecdotal evidence of a disturbing increase in jury nullification—an increase in jurors' thinking that they are "the people" who therefore have the right to remake or disregard the law.[56]

But in spite of undoubted deficiencies in jury performance, the jury audience remains sharply differentiated from the public audience by pervasive restrictions on what it hears and how it behaves. And there is a real tension between these two main audiences of the trial. The jury decides, but the public separately decides on different evidence and in accordance with different criteria. What is disturbing is the public's increasing sense that it is either on a par with or superior to the jury. Before and during a trial, the public is constantly polled to see whether it thinks a notorious defendant is guilty or innocent, as if the facts to be developed at trial were incidental to understanding. Following a jury verdict, people on the street are interviewed about what they think, as if their judgment was adequately informed. Or they riot, as they did after the Rodney King verdict, and their rioting is seen to embody a superior truth to that determined by the jury. It matters not at all that the rioters may know next to nothing about the actual trial or about rules like the requirement of proof beyond reasonable doubt, and so forth. The trial becomes a mass political event, not a legal process—at least, for the public audience it is one thing, and for the jury audience it is another.

In a very real sense, there are now two trials: one for the jury and one for the public. Part of the trial directed to the public is really directed toward the jury, of course. Before the jury is picked in high-profile cases—indeed, from the moment of arrest—trial lawyers increasingly lay out their versions of the story to the public to affect the jury pool. One audience will become the other. Even after the jury is selected, the lawyers know that public opinion has a way of seeping into the courtroom—by influencing the lawyers, perhaps by influencing the judge, and maybe even by influencing the supposedly isolated jury. All the while, the lawyers may be polling or conducting focus groups in the community—with the general public treated as a proxy for the jury to test what arguments are likely to work in court.

But the trial participants address the general public for other reasons, both before and after the jury is chosen. They see the general public as an important audience in its own right. There is a separate trial for them. In part, this reflects the simple fact that "[t]he eagerness of a listener quickens the tongue of a narrator."[57] But the "narrators" also have a greater self-conscious awareness of the various roles the public audience can play. In addition, the defense is concerned about the defendant's public reputation, which is not necessarily defined by the jury verdict, and all the lawyers may be concerned about their own public reputations. They may do things in the courtroom, as well as outside, that cater to the broader public audience. The media may themselves help to run a separate "public" trial for the public's entertainment and their own financial gain.

We saw all of these things and much more in the O. J. Simpson murder trial, about which a few separate words seem appropriate. This most notorious and publicized criminal trial of our time was both wildly aberrational and yet utterly revealing about general trends—and, in any event, has become an inescapable touchstone for reflections about the criminal trial today. The grotesque spectacles outside the courtroom and in the media—and the public's insatiable appetite for the case's mixture of race, sex, violence, and celebrity—seriously damaged and debased the courtroom trial (which contained quite enough disturbing elements by itself). At every point there was a trial before the broader public at least as intense as the trial before the jury, and this broader public trial, magnified and distended by the media, profoundly affected what went on in the courtroom. Even intermittently attentive and poorly informed segments of the public felt justified in judging Simpson's guilt or innocence—and quite beyond whether Simpson was deemed guilty or innocent, vast segments of the public approached the trial as an occasion for cultural and sociological interpretation in which the defendant and victims were relatively minor details.

The jury's not-guilty verdict determined Simpson's courtroom fate. But his broader fate, as it seems to be playing out, is being determined by the court of public opinion, and much of the public has judged him a murderer (whether or not proven so beyond a reasonable doubt) and treats him like a pariah. The trial came to affect much more than Simpson's personal fate, however. It affected not only public attitudes about lawyers, the criminal justice system itself, and cameras in the courtroom but, most important of all, relations between the blacks and whites throughout the country.

Everything about the case took on heightened significance because of race. The defendant was a black sports hero and entertainer; the victims (a former wife he had repeatedly abused and a male friend of hers) were both white; the leading police department investigators on the case were white, and at least one of them was openly racist; the police department itself had a notorious history of racism; and the jury that acquitted was mostly black. The trial before the jury was punctuated by racial iconography, arguments, and codes; and the trial involving the public outside the courthouse, where constraints of the courtroom were inapplicable, became even more intensely race-focused. Judge Lance Ito, who presided at the trial, excluded certain odious evidence of police racism from jury consideration as irrelevant to its deliberations but let that evidence be aired in open court, apparently for the very purpose of having it heard by the general public. Throughout the trial, opinion polls and media interviews informed the public that it was sharply divided along racial lines about the defendant's guilt. And the public debated the racial significance of the case in the media and day-to-day life from the start.

The racial character of the case was intensified by the backdrop of powerful historical narratives about blacks and whites that were repeatedly used (sometimes unconsciously) to shape how the basic facts of the courtroom stories were perceived or to give those stories some wider symbolic meaning or resonance. For some blacks, for example, Simpson became a symbolic victim of the racism facing blacks throughout U.S. history, or at least a black hero whose fall would damage an entire race; for some, the trial became a test of whether a wealthy black celebrity could beat the system as wealthy whites often had before him, or whether black jurors would strike out against evidence of continuing white racism. For some whites, the evidence that a mainstream black celebrity who seemed so polished and likable might really be a brutal murderer reawakened atavistic fear and distrust of all blacks; or Simpson became the prototypical hustler using an irrelevant cry of racism to try to get away with murder; or his trial before a mostly black jury became a landmark test of blacks' capacity to wield public power and govern responsibly. The foregrounding of these wider possible meanings is what made the trial a traumatic event in our country's tortured history of race relations.

Significantly, the racial divisions fostered by the trial were not simply over Simpson's guilt or innocence but also over how the public reacted to the not-guilty verdict. After the verdict, the public audience judged both the defendant and the trial (including the witnesses and the jury), and then different segments of the public judged each other's reactions. These public reactions to the verdict revealed—and probably deepened—a huge racial divide in the country. Televised scenes of blacks jumping for joy at the verdict shocked many whites more than the verdict itself, for that audience reaction, suggesting a racial victory, revealed feelings and beliefs that a public opinion poll or a jury's secret vote could not. Many blacks, in turn, were angered at the aggressive disbelief many whites expressed about the verdict and its defenders, seeing that disbelief as a judgment that the mostly black jury and its defenders lacked the ability or willingness to voice the plain truth. The public audience for the trial became not simply listeners to racial narratives but authors of racial narratives as well. And in both of these roles, the public audience shaped the trial's enduring meaning far more than the jury could. In short, the second trial—the one before the public—largely displaced the first.

Nothing, of course, was typical about the Simpson case, and very little was admirable, including the disturbing jury verdict (reached after only three hours of deliberation) and the divisions fostered by the public verdicts. But the public's central role in the Simpson case, and its eventual overshadowing of the jury, is only an extreme and distorted instance of an increasingly common situation.

Indeed, as the general public pushes its way into the criminal trial, we are witnessing a phenomenon that seems connected to a broader cultural trend in American political life. Even as our political institutions have become more representative of America's diversity—just as the jury has become so—faith in representative institutions has declined. We are witnessing a rise in a commitment to direct democracy and a weakening belief in representative democracy. This movement, like that concerning criminal trials, is fueled by technology: C-SPAN, instantaneous public opinion polling, fax machines, talk radio, Internet, and so forth. But technology is simply facilitating what is a moral revolution. The people believe they have a right to decide not just at the end of the day, when elections are held and their representatives' achievements are assessed, but day by day, as issues receive legislative consideration. Political representatives themselves have lost either the faith or the courage to act as representatives. Daily they look to see what the public thinks, as if the public really was informed and knew how to assess its or the country's interests at every moment. This is a recipe for disaster: Representatives deliver policies that they know will not work but that satisfy some transient public mood; when the policies do not work, the public becomes further disenchanted with the representatives and demands even more direct input; that, in turn, usually produces even worse policies, and so forth. In such a climate, it becomes unthinkable—or at least terribly risky—to speak of expertise or the importance of representative democracy or to tell "the people" that they and their frequently confused contradictory desires are part of the problem.

In the case of politics, it can at least be said that our representatives have often failed in their roles, that they have not led strongly enough or taken even minimal chances in trying to handle the country's hard problems, that they have all too often been corrupt. But in the case of law and the courts, these points cannot be cited. The courts have generally done a good job, and they have been meticulous and fair in most of the high-profile cases that have galvanized the public in recent years. The media's and public's incursion into the courts is not the consequence of the courts' failures, even though it may rest in part on the public's increasing concerns about crime. To a large extent, it rests on a combination of voyeurs' prurient interests and the media's financial motivation. And to that extent, it reflects not a wholesome measure of informed critical scrutiny but destructive self-indulgence.

I am suggesting, in short, that the widening audience for the criminal trial can corrupt the storytellers at the trial. But that cannot be the judgment that ends my account. The reality of this wider audience's engagement cannot be wished away and is likely to endure. In part it will endure because it rests on another reality: crime and fear of crime *are* more central in people's lives these days. Neither reality—the public's great concern about crime or the public's closer observation of the criminal trial—can be ignored.

If the broader public audience sees the courts to be mishandling their tasks, the credibility of the courts and of law itself will be greatly hurt. The answer, of course, cannot be to allow public opinion to influence trial verdicts; that would destroy law in the name of saving it. But the courts' understandable concern about their authority, credibility, and effectiveness may justifiably lead them to take account of certain public attitudes when that does not destroy the integrity of law.

Here, then, I come back to the issue of victim impact evidence. Taking some account of public opinion, I believe, is one reason why victim impact evidence probably has a place at the capital murder trial (I discuss other reasons above and would not reach my overall conclusion without those reasons). In pressing for inclusion at trial, the victim and the victim's survivors are proxies for the general public, for people at large tend to see themselves as potential crime victims. To treat victim impact evidence as off-limits, especially when such particularized evidence about the defendant is within-limits, would be to say that what the public connects with most at the trial is inadmissible. If we wish to keep public confidence in the courts and public faith in law, and if we wish to allow the courts to continue to play their role of channeling public revenge, we cannot exclude too much of the reality of life—just as we cannot let too much in.

Justice Stevens ends his dissent in *Payne v. Tennessee* by ruefully suggesting that "the 'hydraulic pressure' of public opinion" may explain the result that the majority reaches:

> Given the current popularity of capital punishment in a crime-ridden society, the political appeal of arguments that assume that increasing the severity of sentences is the best cure for the cancer of crime, and the political strength of the 'victims' rights' movement, I recognize that today's decision will be greeted with enthusiasm by a large number of concerned and thoughtful citizens. The great tragedy of the decision, however, is the danger that the 'hydraulic pressure' of public opinion that Justice Holmes once described—and that properly influences the deliberations of democratic legislatures—has played a role not only in the Court's decision to hear this case, . . . but even in its resolution of the constitutional issue involved. Today is a sad day for a great institution.[58]

Justice Stevens's narrative is a counternarrative of explanation that seeks to undercut the majority's very different justification for its conclusion. He has accurately described the public climate and identified a real danger. But I think he greatly simplifies the matter of public opinion and judicial action. The place of public opinion cannot be dismissed so quickly, with "'a sad day' so easily proclaimed" because a great public institution may have tried to retain the confidence of its public audience. The hard reality, perhaps tragic, even if not sad, is that judicial narratives must be written with some attention to wider public narratives, and this may both threaten *and* sustain the greatness of our judicial institutions.

APPENDIX: VICTIM IMPACT STATEMENT READ TO THE PENALTY-PHASE JURY, IN *BOOTH V. MARYLAND*, 482 U.S. 496 (1987)

"Mr. and Mrs. Bronstein's son, daughter, son-in-law, and granddaughter were interviewed for purposes of the Victim Impact Statement. There are also four other grandchildren in the family. The victims' son reports that his parents had been married for fifty-three years and enjoyed a very close relationship, spending each day together. He states that his father had worked hard all his life and had been retired for eight years. He describes his mother as a woman who was young at heart and never seemed like an old lady. She taught herself to play bridge when she was in her seventies. The victims' son relates that his parents were amazing people who attended the senior citizens' center and made many devout friends. He indicates that he was very close to his parents, and that he talked to them every day. The victims' daughter also spent lots of time with them.

"The victims' son saw his parents alive for the last time on May 18th. They were having their lawn manicured and were excited by the onset of spring. He called them on the phone that evening and received no answer. He had made arrangements to pick Mr. Bronstein up on May 20th. They were both to be ushers in a granddaughter's wedding and were going to pick up their tuxedos. When he arrived at the house on May 20th he noticed that his parents' car wasn't there. A neighbor told him that he hadn't seen the car in several days and he knew something was wrong. He went to his parents' house and found them murdered. He called his sister crying and told her to come right over because something terrible had happened and their parents were both dead.

"The victims' daughter recalls that when she arrived at her parents' house, there were police officers and television crews everywhere. She felt numb and cold. She was not allowed to go into the house and so she went to a neighbor's home. There were people and reporters everywhere and all she could feel was cold. She called her older daughter and told her what had happened. She told her daughter to get her husband and then tell her younger daughter what had happened. The younger daughter was to be married two days later.

"The victims' granddaughter reports that just before she received the call from her mother she had telephoned her grandparents and received no answer. After her mother told her what happened she turned on the television and heard the news reports about it. The victims' son reports that his children first learned about their grandparents' death from the television reports.

"Since the Jewish religion dictates that birth and marriage are more important than death, the granddaughter's wedding had to proceed on May 22nd. She had been looking forward to it eagerly, but it was a sad occasion with people crying. The reception, which normally would have lasted for hours, was very brief. The next day, instead of going on her honeymoon, she attended her grandparents' funerals. The victims' son, who was an usher at the wedding, cannot remember being there or coming and going from his parents' funeral the next day. The victims' granddaughter, on the other hand, vividly remembers every detail of the days following her grandparents' death. Perhaps she described the impact of the tragedy most eloquently when she stated that it was a completely devastating and life altering experience.

"The victims' son states that he can only think of his parents in the context of how he found them that day, and he can feel their fear and horror. It was 4:00 P.M. when he discovered their bodies and this stands out in his mind. He is always aware of when 4:00 P.M. comes each day, even when he is not near a clock. He also wakes up at 4:00 A.M. each morning. The victims' son states that he suffers from lack of sleep. He is unable to drive on the streets that pass near his parents' home. He also avoids driving past his father's favorite restaurant, the supermarket where his parents shopped, etc. He is constantly reminded of his parents. He sees his father coming out of synagogues, sees his parents' car, and feels very sad whenever he sees old people. The victims' son feels that his parents were not killed, but were butchered like animals. He doesn't think anyone should be able to do something like that and get away with it. He is very angry and wishes he could sleep and not feel so depressed all the time. He is fearful for the first time in his life, putting all the lights on and checking the locks frequently. His children are scared for him and concerned for his health. They phone him several times a day. At the same time he takes a fearful approach to the whereabouts of his children. He also calls his sister every day. He states that he is frightened by his own reaction of what he would do if someone hurt him or a family member. He doesn't know if he'll ever be the same again.

"The victims' daughter and her husband didn't eat dinner for three days following the discovery of Mr. and Mrs. Bronstein's bodies. They cried together every day for four months and she still cries every day. She states that she doesn't sleep through a single night and thinks a part of her died too when her parents were killed. She reports that she doesn't find much joy in anything and her powers of concentration aren't good. She feels as if her brain is on overload. The victims' daughter relates that she had to clean out her parents' house and it took several weeks. She saw the bloody carpet, knowing that her parents had been there, and she felt like getting down on the rug and holding her mother. She wonders how this could have happened to her family because they're just ordinary people. The victims' daughter reports that she had become noticeably withdrawn and depressed at work and is now making an effort to be more outgoing. She notes that she is so emotionally tired because she doesn't sleep at night, that she has a tendency to fall asleep when she attends social events such as dinner parties or the symphony. The victims' daughter states that wherever she goes she sees and hears her parents. This happens every day. She cannot look at kitchen knives without being reminded of the murders and she is never away from it. She states that she can't watch movies with bodies or stabbings in it. She can't tolerate any reminder of violence. The victims' daughter relates that she used to be very trusting, but is not any longer. When the doorbell rings she tells her husband not to answer it. She is very suspicious of people and was never that way before.

"The victims' daughter attended the defendant's trial and that of the co-defendant because she felt someone should be there to represent her parents. She had never been told the exact details of her parents' death and had to listen to the medical examiner's report. After a certain point, her mind blocked out and she stopped hearing. She states that her parents were stabbed repeatedly with viciousness and she could never forgive anyone for killing them that way. She can't believe that anybody could do that to someone. The victims' daughter states that animals wouldn't do this. They didn't have to kill because there was no one to stop them from looting. Her father would have given them anything. The murders show the viciousness of the killers' anger. She doesn't feel that the people who did this could ever be rehabilitated and she doesn't want them to be able to do this again or put another family through this. She feels that the lives of her family members will never be the same again.

"The victims' granddaughter states that unless you experience something like this you can't understand how it feels. You are in a state of shock for several months and then a terrible depression sets in. You are so angry and feel such rage. She states that she only dwells on the image of their death when thinking of her grandparents. For a time she would become hysterical whenever she saw dead animals on the road. She is not able to drive near her grandparents' house and will never be able to go into their neighborhood again. The victims' granddaughter also has a tendency to turn on all the lights in her house. She goes into a panic if her husband is late coming home from work. She used to be an avid reader of murder mysteries, but will never be able to read them again. She has to turn off the radio or T.V. when reports of violence come on because they hit too close to home. When she gets a newspaper she reads the comics and throws the rest away. She states that it is the small everyday things that haunt her constantly and always will. She saw a counselor for several months but stopped because she felt that no one could help her.

"The victims' granddaughter states that the whole thing has been very hard on her sister too. Her wedding anniversary will always be bittersweet and tainted by the memory of what happened to her grandparents. This year on her anniversary she and her husband quietly went out of town. The victims' granddaughter finds that she is unable to look at her sister's wedding pictures. She also has a picture of her grandparents, but had to put it away because it was too painful to look at it.

"The victims' family members note that the trials of the suspects charged with these offenses have been delayed for over a year and the postponements have been very hard on the family emotionally. The victims' son notes that he keeps seeing news reports about his parents' murder which show their house and the police removing their bodies. This is a constant reminder to him. The family wants the whole thing to be over with and they would like to see swift and just punishment.

"As described by their family members, the Bronsteins were loving parents and grand-parents whose family was most important to them. Their funeral was the largest in the history of the Levinson Funeral Home and the family received over one thousand sympathy cards, some from total strangers. They attempted to answer each card personally. The family states that Mr. and Mrs. Bronstein were extremely good people who wouldn't hurt a fly. Because of their loss, a terrible void has been put into their lives and every day is still a strain just to get through. It became increasingly apparent to the writer as she talked to the family members that the murder of Mr. and Mrs. Bronstein is still such a shocking, painful, and devastating memory to them that it permeates every aspect of their daily lives. It is doubtful that they will ever be able to fully recover from this tragedy and not be haunted by the memory of the brutal manner in which their loved ones were murdered and taken from them."

Louis Michael Seidman

Some Stories About Confessions and Confessions About Stories

Here is a story. It is a story I tell my criminal justice students whenever we discuss the mystery of why we should have a Fifth Amendment privilege against self-incrimination and how anyone could believe that the privilege represents a sensible limit on state coercion.

Years ago I worked for the District of Columbia Public Defender Service. It became apparent to me after a while that the alibis my clients offered took a standard form. Invariably, at the time of the murder or robbery or burglary, they were at home watching television with their girlfriend and their mother. The cross-examination that the prosecutor used to destroy this alibi also took a standard form. What was frustrating was that even though prosecutors used the same trick each time, it always worked. Suppose the robbery occurred at 3:00 P.M. on August 9. The prosecutor would get up and say, "Now Mr. X, you claim that at 3:00 P.M. on August 9 you were at home watching television with your mother and your girlfriend. Would you care to tell the jury where you were at 3:00 P.M. on August 8?"

Then my client was sunk. Either he had to claim (implausibly) that he could remember where he was at every minute of every day of his life, or he had to explain (implausibly) why it was that he remembered his whereabouts on August 9 but not August 8.

One day I was representing an armed robbery defendant who offered the standard alibi: he was at home watching television with his wife and his mother at the time of the robbery. The prosecutor, who seemed even more pompous and supercilious than usual, began the standard cross-examination, and I sat back with the calm resignation that is the one benefit that comes with having seen disaster played out many times before.

But this time something totally unexpected happened. After the prosecutor asked his first few questions, my client suddenly stood up, straightened himself to his full height, and said in words that will live as long as the English language is spoken, "Fuck this shit!"

Then he returned to the counsel table and refused to participate any further in the proceedings.

He was convicted. If you want to know more details of the story, you can still reach him care of the Lorton Reformatory. But in a deeper sense, he was a truly free man. They had his body, but they couldn't touch his soul.

Here is a story about the story. This one is an excluded story—the kind of follow-up story that a law professor hopes no student will raise in class.

It is bizarre to treat my client's behavior as an argument for the self-incrimination clause, because what my client did was not protected by the self-incrimination clause. Many courts have held that although criminal defendants have a right to remain silent and a right to testify, they do not have a right to choose both options—to testify and then to refuse to participate in cross-examination.[1] So, in fact, the law does not protect what my client did, and he could have been held in contempt for it.

Here is a paradoxical story about the story. To the extent that this is a story about the triumph of human will over state coercion, the story resonates only because my client was not protected by the Fifth Amendment. My client was able to resist state coercion only because there was state coercion to resist. If he had had a Fifth Amendment right to terminate his testimony, I could no longer claim that his exercise of that right marked a triumph for human freedom.

Here is a skeptical story about the story. My client was hardly a hero. He was a vicious armed robber who deserved to be locked up. The notion that his decision amounted to an assertion of untrammeled will is absurd. His actions were part of a pattern of antisocial behavior, of thumbing his nose at legitimate authority—behavior that was hardly free. Instead, it was entirely determined by his childhood, his social class, and deeply seated psychological malfunctioning.

Here is a confession. The story I told you—it never happened, or at least it never happened to me. I have some dim recollection from my Public Defender Service days that it may have happened to someone else, but I am not certain of this. I may also have made the whole thing up. In any case, I have been telling my students for years that it happened to me because I hoped to impress them with my real-world experience and because the punch line sounds better if I say that the story happened to me.

Here is a confession about the confession. My confession may sound as though I am coming clean, as though I am being brutally honest and telling you what actually happened. But I am not doing anything of the kind. The confession is just another mask, a mask over the first mask. It is designed to impress the audience with how clever I am—with my understanding of what I take to be the central point of both Paul Gewirtz's and Peter Brooks's essays. That point is that ultimately there is nothing but masks on top of masks and frames within frames. We are fascinated by confessions because they seem to offer an escape from the problem of intersubjectivity, because people who confess offer a window into their true self. But confessions are dangerous because they present the illusion of escape when there is no escape: confessions are always just another mask.

Similarly, it is said that the rules of evidence are designed to allow juries to get at the truth. What they provide, instead, is a particular frame that produces a particular truth. If you choose another frame, you get another truth.

So my confession is just another frame, just another stance that takes us no closer to reality.

Here is a confession about my confession about my confession. You may have thought that I was coming clean just now. If you did, you were wrong.

Here is a final story. When I was a child, television was also in its infancy, and Dave Garroway (the original host of the *Today* show) was in his laid-back prime. I remember a live shot of Garroway standing in front of a television watching himself on the television. (A little later, George Burns on the *Burns and Allen Show* would turn on the *Burns and Allen Show* to find out what Gracie was up to.)

"Dave Garroway here," Garroway said from within the endless electronic frames. But which "here" was here?

How fascinating to look at infinitely smaller images of Dave Garroway. How easy to get sucked into that endless vortex. One thing was certain: When you were sucked in, you ended up looking at a very small portion of the television screen.

I think that Dave Garroway eventually went mad.

Elaine Scarry

Speech Acts in Criminal Cases

Discussions about the place of narrative in the law often depend on a set of overt oppositions. One is numerical: the particularity or singularity of the story is juxta-posed to an alternative form of discourse that is understood to be numerically expansive, even universal. The second is material: the story is taken to be closer to concrete lived reality and to bodily events than is its alternative, which is thought of as abstract and empty of material content. The third is cognitive: the story draws on our capacity for empathy and emotion; its alternative relies on rational argument and debate.

The integrity of any one pair of opposites is strong enough that we recognize the validity of the opposition, even when it is presented telegraphically. It is because there is a coherence to these claims that the assertion of them can stop short of full articulation. Thus we even encounter the odd phenomenon that Robert Weisberg has complained about, the dead-end announcement that "X is a story" as though that in itself tells us what we need to know about X and proves, without elaboration, that X is something valuable.[1]

The sequence of oppositions becomes problematic when the three are taken as a triptych: the first member of any one pair is understood as opposite to the second member not only of its own pair but of any other pair. Because a nonstory may be numerically expansive, for instance, and because a nonstory may be nonmaterial, we sometimes assume that the numerically expansive must be nonmaterial. But this is often untrue. Body counts, for example, are a form of language that rides as close to concrete bodily events as stories do (sometimes even closer). Again, because a nonstory (whether a principle, a statistic, an argument) may be numerically expansive and because a nonstory may rely on rational argument, we wrongly assume that the numerically expansive must somehow be antagonistic to empathy. But it is probably more useful to recognize two forms of compassion: individual compassion and what in public health is called statistical compassion.[2] Thus we may say that former President Reagan had a great deal of individual compassion (he responded to stories on *Sixty Minutes* with immediate feeling and action) but lacked statistical compassion (he could not hear in a set of figures about wages or housing the concrete realities embedded there). Another person might have a stronger capacity for statistical compassion than for narrative compassion. Our educational aspirations ought to include both.

At present, more public resources seem to be directed toward developing our capacity for narrative compassion than for statistical compassion. Whereas a story tends to be about a small number of people,[3] the number to whom the story can be addressed is vast; and, conversely, whereas principles and statistics and rational argument often seem to be numerically expansive, we seem, rightly or wrongly, to assume that their audience is small. Public discourse—television, newspapers, radio—thrives on narrative. Given two subjects to report, one of which can be told in story form and the other of which requires some alternative kind of discourse (argument, numerical analysis), the first is usually covered and the second ignored.[4]

I have so far been describing the way we talk about stories by setting them in opposition to an alternative form of discourse.[5] But we often stay within the category of narrative and talk about an opposition, or competition, between stories. "Whose story gets told?" has become a frequently posed question in the past decade. A third form of opposition may be between a story and the absence of a story. Although all three forms of opposition are present in the essays by Paul Gewirtz and Peter Brooks,[6] it is this third one that is key.

Together, the essays by Peter Brooks and Paul Gewirtz give us an extraordinarily stark portrait of the criminal case. A particular case may, by the time it is completed, have many volumes of spoken text and a large array of speakers. But Brooks and Gewirtz ask us to concentrate exclusively on the principal participants, the defendant and the victim, on their own relatively minimal acts of speaking, and the relation between their speech acts and the punishment that follows.

Each major speech act by the state in a criminal case comes to define the defendant. Each becomes a verb that acts on the defendant. An accusation is made and the defendant becomes the accused. A verdict is reached and the defendant becomes the verdicted, or, as we more often say, the convicted. A sentence is announced and the defendant is sentenced. To be sentenced, to be physically punished, is to be directly acted on by a verbal sentence, a connection that calls to mind the etymological kinship between "sentence" and "sentience." The sentence is inscribed into the defendant's body.

What part do the two principal actors have in shaping the sentence that imposes the injury? Peter Brooks looks at the defendant's own speech act, the confession, its effect on the court's sentence, and hence the eventual inscription of the defendant's voice into the defendant's own body. Paul Gewirtz looks at the victim's speech act (or, if the victim is dead, the victim's family's), the victim impact statement, its effect on sentencing, and hence the way the victim's voice is inscribed into the body of the defendant. Thus the stark quality of the portrait they together give: it is as though sentences directly spoken by the two major participants record themselves bodily without going through the intervening institutions of court and district attorney. Robert Cover stresses the distance between literary stories and legal stories, noting that the literary story rarely etches itself into material reality, whereas the legal story potentially always does.[7] But Cover is speaking of the trial as a whole, of the court's words, which, through a sequence of mediating agents, impose an act of violence on the defendant. In concentrating on the confession and the victim impact statement, these mediating institutional elements seem for a few moments to disappear.

On one level, then, the two portraits present the adversarial system in its purest form: the whole elaborate apparatus of the court, with its secondary and tertiary events, suddenly falls out of focus, and we see before us only the two principal combatants. But on a second level, each portrait entails the erasure of the adversarial system: the defendant's speech and the victim's speech seem like rips or tears in the legal fabric out through which the legal frame itself can suddenly disappear.

The confession, after all, may eliminate the need for dispute and adjudication. And this should make us worry. If the adversarial profession has gone a long way toward eliminating or discouraging confession, it has gone a long way toward eliminating or discouraging a phenomenon the existence of which would eliminate the adversarial profession. Its advocacy is not unselfinterested. Lawyers do, of course, have wholly honorable grounds for objecting to coerced confession. The hidden room to which Chief Justice Warren refers in *Miranda*—what Peter Brooks calls the story of the closed room—is so starkly incompatible with the law that if the only way to close off such a possibility were to eliminate all speech on the defendant's part, this might seem a necessary outcome. But is silencing the defendant the only way to eliminate coerced confession?

Those who would eliminate all genres of confession move by a series of many half steps so that all forms of first-person description on the part of the defendant eventually come to be understood as submerged or disguised forms of the hidden room. Taking O. J. Simpson or any other accused murderer into a hidden room would be impermissible and without question a reason for disallowing any confession. But suppose that someone dropped off in the person's cell a copy of Augustine's *Confessions* or Rousseau's *Confessions?* Or suppose it could be shown that at some time long ago in the person's early education, he or she had been asked to read these books? Peter Brooks brilliantly critiques the law for the series of half steps it takes to invalidate first-person speech but them himself provides a more radical version, making us worry that our culture itself, by everywhere honoring openness and honesty, acts on us as coercively as the physical and psychological torments inflicted in a hidden room.

Although each of the many half steps seems coherent in isolation, we should worry about arriving at a final position where (1) a suspect comes to be understood as someone inherently incompetent to confess or (2) the accused comes to be understood as someone incompetent to confirm or deny—or in any way advise us about the accuracy of—the accusation.

The retraction of first-person speech from the legal subject is likely to seem even more troubling when placed side by side with the medical subject. Patients, like criminal defendants, are often perceived as people incapable of giving a first-person report; they are unreliable narrators whose stories should be gotten away from, or around, as quickly as possible so that the medical professional may get to the hard data of x-rays and blood tests, even though many problems are known not to show up there. The fact that the prohibition (or discouragement) of self-description occurs in both the legal and the medical fields makes one wish to inquire more carefully into the motives of the two professions.

But the full gravity of the outcome is visible even if we look at the law alone. Is there any way to disallow one form of first-person speech while allowing another form? If the defendant is not allowed to affirm his guilt (whether by confession or by entering a guilty plea), is it logically possible to maintain his option of asserting his innocence? Isn't the person's power to dissent from the conclusions that the court has arrived at in accusing him and putting him on trial severely impaired by the erasure of his option of consenting to an accusation of guilt? The only position available to him would be maintaining his innocence, thereby (in the instance where the person is guilty) requiring him to lie about his act, to abstain from accepting any responsibility until the state instructed him as the result of a guilty verdict, to do so (that is, not as the result of his own deliberations but wholly as a result of the court's). There is no question that the defendant's stature as moral agent would be greatly impaired. And what about persons who really are innocent? Will not their repeated declarations of innocence sound vacant when uttered against the uniform white noise of innocent pleas?

It seems, then, logically impossible to maintain an asymmetry in which persons may affirm their innocence but not affirm their guilt; the deniability of a crime is eliminated if the act of acknowledging it is disallowed. But let us, for a moment, grant what seems impossible and imagine the asymmetry surviving. Would this outcome be benign? Would it be to the defendant's advantage? It can be argued that the asymmetry would increase the death penalty (or whatever penalty is the maximum allowable in a given place) and increase it from two directions: the direction of the now-eliminated guilty plea and the direction of the innocent plea.

Historically, confessions have worked to diminish the number of cases in which the defendant is put to death. This is not to sentimentalize or soften the realities of the prisoner's speech act. Although the confession often reduces the sentence from the death penalty to imprisonment, imprisonment is itself a grave outcome and one that might not have happened without the confession. Furthermore, confession does sometimes lead to the death penalty. There is a genre of cases in which the maximum penalty is warranted if there has been a previous conviction, and the previous conviction has in some instances entailed a case in which the defendant has confessed.[8] The defendant's own utterances may thus eventually contribute to his or her own execution. But these facts qualify without changing the overarching frame. Confession more often than not reduces the death penalty; eliminating confession would therefore deprive defendants of having the means, through their own good faith, of moderating the punishment downward.

The increase in the number of death penalties would also come from the direction of the innocent plea. In a world that permits both the guilty plea and the innocent plea, the person will be in one of four positions: he may confess his guilt and be telling the truth; he may confess his guilt and be lying; he may maintain his innocence and be telling the truth; he may maintain his innocence and be lying. In the asymmetrical world that we are imagining, the first two positions have been eliminated and the defendant may only be in the third or fourth position. In the fourth position—the one in which the defendant perjures himself—he may increase the severity of his punishment. In an array of states—Illinois, Alaska, California, Wisconsin, and others—perjury has been cited as a reason for enhancing the sentence.[9] The asymmetrical situation, then, in which one form of first-person utterance is disallowed and the other is permitted works to the defendant's disadvantage (as well as everyone else's): the defendant has now lost the power to confess, which in former times worked to reduce the sentence, and still retains the power to perjure himself or herself, which now, as in former times, may work to increase the sentence.

First-person utterances by the defendant should continue to be allowed, even though confessions of guilt require a society's constant scrutiny to sort out lawful from unlawful ways of inviting confession. What, now, about the first-person speech of the victim, the question to which Paul Gewirtz directs our attention?

Our starting place here resembles our starting place when we looked at the defendant. One might fairly complain that the victim impact statement at the moment of sentencing works to eliminate the adversarial system because—as Paul Gewirtz acknowledges in one ghostly passage—there is no cross-examination.[10] This is an extremely odd feature of the speech act. True, the verdict has already been reached and thus contestation may seem over. Yet it is precisely because one question—the severity of the punishment—still remains open that the victim (or the victim's relative) is making a statement. The cases under consideration are not ones in which the issue is limited to number of years in jail but in which the death penalty itself is in question. The victim's words have, in the most literal way, the possibility of inscribing themselves in material reality. Yet they are unchallengeable: they can neither be shown to be false nor, through rigorous testing by the other side, be confirmed in their accuracy.

The oddness of the situation can be appreciated by juxtaposing the victim impact statement in the criminal case with a victim's description of pain and suffering in a civil tort case. The latter victim may be subjected to elaborate cross-examination (which may work to discredit or, instead, to verify the truth of the injured person's words). Nothing about either the criminal or the civil situation makes the truth in the one more difficult to test than the truth in the other; in both cases, the statements made by the injured person can be challenged by witnesses for the defense, and in both, the defense may determine that the injured person's statements are unimpeachable and unchallengeable. Furthermore, if there is a missing cross-examination in either the civil case or the criminal case, one would expect the aberration to come in the civil case, for a much weaker standard of evidence is needed there. To find for the plaintiff in a civil case requires only that on balance the evidence favors that side. In a criminal case, in contrast, a verdict of guilt requires certainty beyond a reasonable doubt. This difference corresponds to the difference in the degree of harm that the verdict can bring to the defendant: in the civil case, money is usually at issue; in the criminal case, a person's imprisonment and possibly life itself are in question.

Earlier I argued that because the defendant's confession diminishes the need for lawyerly dispute, one ought to be suspicious of lawyers who urge that confession be disallowed. Since the victim impact statement also takes place outside the adversarial system, it might seem that—to be consistent—one ought to be suspicious of lawyers urging its elimination.[11] But eliminating adversarialness when it is the accused's own speech act and eliminating adversarialness when it is the accuser's seem to be radically different propositions. In the moments immediately prior to sentencing, the court must maintain the ethical rule that holds throughout all other parts of the criminal trial, the rule "that penal and criminal statutes be strictly construed against the state and in favor of the accused."[12]

The argument I wish to make is not that the victim impact statement ought to have as counterpart a challenge from the defense (although this would be less objectionable than a missing cross-examination) but rather that the victim impact statement in death penalty cases (and probably in all cases) ought to be eliminated altogether.

There are four main problems with the victim impact statement. The first is that it is inconsistent across persons. If the person injured has no ability to articulate the scale of personal hurt or if the person is an orphan with no relatives to be outraged by the crime, the severity of the punishment will be less than for a crime committed against a victim who is articulate or who has many siblings or who has a sibling with extraordinary standing in the community. Is this inconsistency tolerable? Paul Gewirtz rightly points out that all parts of the criminal case are riddled with this kind of inconsistency. His observation is important enough that this first objection to victim impact statements is the weakest of the four. But Gewirtz's observations do not wholly eliminate the objection. A criminal case tries to even out many of the inconsistencies that occur in a civil case. For example, because the plaintiff in the criminal case is not the injured person but the state itself, the attorney who speaks on the injured person's behalf comes from the district attorney's office regardless of whether the victim is rich or poor, famous or unknown; the attorney is supported not by the stature of the victim's family, which varies from case to case, but by the unchanging stature of the state. It is possible, of course, that the district attorney's office will choose to put its most brilliant prosecutor on a case simply because the status of victim or perpetrator encourages wide coverage in the press. But there is a key difference between inconsistencies that the structure of the trial is designed, but fails, to eliminate and inconsistencies that are actually promoted by structural features of the trial. The victim impact statement falls into the second category. By countenancing the idea that the injured person's own speech act should help to shape the court's sentence, it countenances the idea that injury to those without the power of speech will be regarded as less offensive to the community. Far from simply failing to guarantee equal treatment, it actively encourages inequality.

A second argument against the victim impact statement is that it backloads what should be frontloaded. Let us suppose that after reaching a verdict that the person accused of carrying out a certain act has indeed carried out that act, the jury or judge now begins to deliberate about whether that particular act should be considered lawful or unlawful. Hearing how awful the injury is might indeed make it clear that the act should be judged unlawful. Imagine now that the court tries to decide whether this unlawful act is a misdemeanor or a felony. Again, a description of the horrors to which the victim has been subjected might make it perfectly clear that the act is felonious. But why are we waiting until the end of the trial to determine that the act is unlawful and felonious? Shouldn't we have contemplated what injuries we will hold to be unlawful and felonious before any one particular trial even begins? And isn't the severity of the felony and hence the severity of the punishment also something that should be decided by thinking about human injuries in general (antecedent to their actual occurrence) rather than in a particular case? Of course, the appropriate punishment may actually be not a single act but a small choice of acts among several that fall into a narrow spectrum of punishments, and the features of the criminal (such as previous conviction record) may help to determine which punishment is most appropriate. But should the personal features and opinions of the victim determine this?

The third argument parallels the second, for it, too, can be summarized by saying the victim impact statement backloads what should be frontloaded; but whereas before we were talking about the correct moment to think about the legal status of the crime, we are now thinking about the appropriate moment at which to think about the cultural status of the crime. The entire phenomenon of the victim impact statement seems to have come into being to compensate for the grotesque under-representation of the injured person's point of view in our culture. The visual and verbal imagery of our culture is dedicated to narratives that glamorize the criminal; films and television depict bodies being injured only to startle, surprise, and entertain us, not to initiate us into the heartache of what this might, in real life, be like for the person hurt. No wonder, then, that for anyone to imagine a severe punishment for a terrible crime requires an eleventh-hour meditation on how horrible such an injury really is. But is this the solution—to ignore the victim and then, at five minutes to midnight, try to make up for it by last ditch attention to the problem set into a trial in a way that dismantles the basic ethical rules of the legal proceeding? Shouldn't we instead conclude that it is our cultural images that need to be changed, that we ought to carry around in our heads a more realistic (less coarse) assessment of how awful crimes are so that we can recognize our own aversion to them before we find ourselves sitting on a jury, scratching our heads, trying to figure out whether a given injury is acceptable or unacceptable?

The fourth problem with the victim impact statement is the feature noted at the opening of the analysis: it literally permits the victim's words to shape the court's sentence and hence comes close to inscribing the victim's first-person speech into the body of the punished criminal. The phrase "victim impact statement"—though lamentable as a piece of jargon—has the virtue of announcing its effects clearly, for it is a verbal act (a statement) that not only summarizes the impact of the crime on the victim but itself impacts on, inscribes itself into, the final act of the court. Paul Gewirtz divides victim impact statements into three categories—(1) the impact of the crime on the victim and the victim's survivors, (2) the personal characteristics of the victim, and (3) the victim's personal opinion about the severity of the sentence—and ingeniously imagines that the three can be held securely separate from one another, so that the first two features can be maintained while erasing the third, scandalously inappropriate one. But even if this outcome were achievable, it would not eliminate the objectionable quality of the victim impact statement. The first three arguments above are directed almost as much against features 1 and 2 as against the more overtly problematic 3. But is it really possible to decouple 1 and 2 from 3?

On close inspection, the three categories seem always to collapse into one another. The victim impact statement is usually introduced to seek the more severe of any two punishments: the personal features of the victim and the injury all "speak" the victim's opinion that the punishment should be harsh. Is there any feature of the victim named in court in these final moments that does not urge the death penalty? Any recitation of the victim's suffering that does not urge the death penalty? It may well be that such a crime should in fact be punished with death; but if so, the responsibility for the execution should rest on the judgment of the state and community, not on the opinion of the victim or the victim's family. If the victim or victim's family had suffered a crime that was ordinarily punished by the death penalty in their community and if the victim or family wished that the criminal be shown leniency, their recommendation should count only as heavily as that of every other member of the community. They, like anyone else in the community, should have the option, for example, of writing to the governor requesting mercy. But at no point should the state's action in punishing, or abstaining from punishing, be a transcription of the wishes or opinions or recommendations of the individual who has been hurt.

I have been arguing here that we ought to sustain our belief in the capacity of individuals to make true confessions and return (as in *Booth v. Maryland* and *South Carolina v. Gathers*) to prohibiting victim impact statements in death penalty cases. I have therefore taken an asymmetrical position on the appropriateness of first-person speech by the defendant and the victim. Because the defendant is the person who will be punished, the fact that his or her own speech may help to shape that punishment seems appropriate.[13] If confession is permissible but not coercible, a person who has committed a crime has the option of becoming a contributory agent to his or her own punishment or, alternatively, the option to let the state be the sole agent. The victim, in contrast, ought not to have a direct hand in shaping the punishment. Victims ought to have restored to them the power of first-person speech in cultural narratives so that the community at large comes to be better educated about the nature of crime and can recall why it is that such acts are held to be illegal, felonious, and worthy of rigorous punishment. But the power of first-person speech should not be given to the victim at the moment of sentencing. Throughout the trial, the state's own speech has replaced the victim's; even the name of the case indicates that the whole community has been injured when any one person suffers a criminal violation. That magnification and shared communal responsibility ought to be maintained through the final seconds of the trial.

Part IV

The Rhetoric of the Judicial Opinion

John Hollander

Legal Rhetoric

The title of this chapter is meant to be provocative rather than provoking. It could easily refer to what many laymen consider to be bad, windy, evasive, false, self-protecting, unnecessarily hermetic, self-congratulating, and somehow phony things that lawyers might say. It can apply to what is unjustly felt to be a fussy, hermetic, dubiously exclusionary, and semantically unjustifiable technical vocabulary; or it can more legitimately apply to extralegal pleading—on behalf of the profession, its practices, or one's own personal practice of those practices—in the court of some sort of public opinion. But if so employed, the phrase would have to be considered—just in that sense of the words—lay rhetoric, a bit of nonprofessional jargon. I do not mean to consider what is meant by this most common use of the term at all, but rather some more general questions arising from other and more important uses of it. In particular, I will consider some of the questions of authority and persuasion that lie at the heart of classical and modern rhetoric. I shall certainly touch on the rhetoric of *stare decisis,* as well as on some other, less obvious questions about the texts of judicial opinions. But before going any further, let us remind ourselves of how the word "rhetoric" has generally been used.

The Word

I. A Kind or Aspect of Human Discourse

a. A lot of hot air: inane spoken language usurping the place either of silence or of meaningful discourse and indicating some sort of moral fault in the speaker (and perhaps even in the audience), either because the speaker has nothing to say, or wishes to evade the truth. Colloquially, "bullshit."

b. Oratory generally, whether pejoratively considered or not. This might also include the notion of language palpably calling attention to its own linguistic resources; and language that seems merely to decorate or else to underscore emotionally—in either the speaker or the audience—a point being made.

c. A narrower use in literary criticism, for example, William Butler Yeats on forceful writing that is nevertheless to be contrasted with true poetry: "Out of men's quarrels with others they make rhetoric; out of quarrels with themselves, poetry."

d. An older term for a sort of archaic curriculum in the art of writing.[1]

II. The Theory of the Effective Uses of the Arts of Language and Thereby an Analysis of Some Aspects of Human Discourse

e. A classical subject: The art of persuasion (the subject of written treatises by Aristotle, Quintilian, Cicero, and so forth). How to persuade other people to do things without resorting to physical force. How to win cases in law courts, get people to vote for you, argue a point in the Senate, move listeners by public praise or blame. Classical treatises on the art of rhetoric themselves constitute a theoretical study or discipline, which we might classify as

f. A kind of macrolinguistic theory—on the one hand, like both logic and grammar; on the other hand, much more comprehensive, dealing with larger units of utterance and possibly containing elements of both logic and grammar in its analysis. Classical rhetoric dealt with questions that would in modern times be parceled out among linguistics, philosophy, psychology, and other more recently institutionalized intellectual disciplines, such as stylistics and some branches of literary critical theory and practice.

    1. Medieval and Renaissance adaptations of classical rhetoric. These become a theory of writing, and the persuasion was not direct but indirect—upon a reader, not a listener—and the end is not to get the reader to act publicly in a certain way but rather to get the reader to feel or believe something about (a) the author and (b) what has been said. Renaissance rhetoricians were literary critics and theorists, for the most part, and their powers of persuasion were directed toward acts of interpretation and internalized judgment rather than toward the elicitation of a desired verdict or vote. (This change occurred in the context of a slowly developing condition of authorial authority, as it were, and authenticity, these notions being involved with one another as they emerged during the Renaissance and the era of printed books.)[2]

    2. Various modern versions of nonliterary, classical rhetorics, such as a theory of advertising; about half of what might be in some lawyer's handbook

called, for example, *The Practical Litigator;* a theory of political speech writing and delivery; a good part of the contents of some other book called *Practical Leadership,* for example; the subject of the coaching sessions that an experienced classroom teacher might have with his or her trainee, and so on. I am leaving out one other obvious possible group of examples to which I shall shortly return.

3. Certain thinking in other contemporary fields. Those who might be thought of as rhetorical theorists include, in literature, Kenneth Burke; in philosophy, J. L. Austin and his follower John Searle—speech-act theory having to do with certain classes of utterances, in certain situations, which bring about, rather than refer to, a new state of fact, for example, "You're out!" (if you are an official umpire: if not, not) or "Guilty!" (if you are the designated chief juror of a duly constituted jury) or, I suppose, "He's dead" (if you are a licensed medical practitioner, but not "You're dead," which, if understood by the subject of the sentence, could not be quite true: this is a trivial, but not really a frivolous, case)—even, in sociology, Erving Goffman.[3]

We might further remark here that in one of these cases, that of the jury, we would have to distinguish between the rhetoric of the arguments—of the case as presented considered as a rhetorical performance—and the illocutionary rhetoric of the jury's verdict. That such verdicts have been traditionally phrased as what the jury had "found"—rather than what they had made (invention claimed as discovery)—is of additional, but very specialized, rhetorical interest. One might also observe that a good part of the content of classical rhetoric had to do with analyzing the relations between what Austin would call the illocutionary and the perlocutionary force of a particular performative utterance or speech act. In general, we might ask how the law considers word as deed. This has vast ramifications, I think, in the area concerning how the law considers words to be deeds and construes utterances as acts. (In contracts, and in torts, it might be imagined that the complex rhetoricity of a verbal act would figure very differently: one could do better in defending oneself against a charge of conditional assault by claiming that one had only been pretending than one could do in trying to wriggle out of a contract.)

It may be instructive at this point to examine the analytic elements and concepts of classical rhetoric. Aristotle takes as his basic element not so much a particular speech or speech act as what he calls a *pistis,* or "argument" (his translators often use the word "proof," but that has no connection with a logical or mathematical or inductive "proof," nor even, in the older senses of the word, with a test, or experiment, or, generally, experience. Consider, for instance, "The proof of the pudding is in the eating"—which does *not* mean we are to exclaim "Q.E.D." instead of "delicious" when at dessert time—or, more interestingly, "The exception proves the rule.") Speeches themselves, Aristotle divides into three types:

forensic (proving guilt or innocence, for example)

deliberative (on public policy, for example)

epideictic (praise or blame, for example, and best suited, according to Aristotle, to the written word)

More interestingly, he distinguishes among three modes or types of pistis, saying that "the [proofs] furnished by the speech are of three kinds. The first depends upon the *ēthos* [character] of the speaker, the second upon putting the speaker into a certain frame of mind, the third upon the [content of] the speech itself, insofar as it [rationally] convinces, or seems to convince."[4] These are the moves (for so we might call them) of *ēthos, pathos,* and *logos*—arguments, verbal routines, or whatever appeals to three different elements of the hearer's consciousness.

Ēthos works on the hearer's sense of the speaker's various possible kinds of authority, status as speaker, relationship to the listener, and so on.

Pathos works at the hearer's emotions.

Logos depends on the truth, logic, consistency, of the argument itself.

The Aristotelian triad of ēthos, pathos, and logos can be illustrated in the analysis of ordinary speech (and as such has legal interest with regard to matters of paraphrase, of the framing of indirect discourse ("What did he say?" "He said that . . ."). So, for example, the following exchange:

A: What time is it, please?

B: [looks at watch, smiles] It's almost 2:30.

Logos (the required information), pathos (the pleasant delivery of the information), and ēthos (the manifest consultation of an authority, the watch) are all clearly and simply served. The last two have a particular quality that doesn't guarantee the watch is not slow, but they might give grounds for A's belief that B isn't lying or dangerously, rather than helpfully, approximating. On the other hand, B might scowl and mutter, "Well, if you must know it's 2:30," radically modulating the pathos, or, as pleasantly as in the first instance, answer, "Oh, I dunno; 2:30, maybe?" somewhat diminishing the grounds of his or her authority to answer the question satisfactorily—a matter of ēthos.

To understand a spoken or written statement in ordinary language means in part to be able to distinguish among these realms (although it must be said that in poetry, just as form seems to be part of content, so ēthos and pathos become part of the matter, the argument, the logos, and a good reader will see, feel, and understand how this can be true). You may snarl, whisper, giggle, or sing that today is Thursday, but whether it is or not remains independent of what I feel on hearing you. If, in the first instance, A responds to B's pleasant answer by saying, "Well, to hell with you, too!" or "Don't condescend" or "You're wounding me by trying to minimize my otherness," we would have to think that there was something crazy or boringly frivolous about A, unless, perhaps, this occurred in a unique situation in which many large public clocks, visible to both parties, were all in loose agreement that it was between 12:28 and 12:31. B might well wonder why A had asked in the first place, perhaps concluding that some protest might indeed be called for.

Although for classical rhetoricians the significant unit of utterance is the "speech," we may throughout these observations substitute a more flexible notion of "routine" or "move." The classical purpose of deploying the arts of language was to persuade. But as I observed, this concept of persuasion, particularly when it became associated with the art of writing, expanded to include other modes of influence, such as getting someone to realize something or to perceive it. Consider, for example, this situation: You and I are viewing a not-too-distant mountain.

I: Oh, see that wonderful red-and-white-striped rock!

YOU: Where? I don't see it.

I: Well, do you see the lone pine halfway up the east face?

YOU: Yes.

I: Then take that as a center, and drop a diagonal down from it toward four o'clock; halfway down to the bottom you'll–

YOU: Oh, there it is! Not wonderful, but OK.

Now: given how close to each other we are standing and our distance from the mountain, the parallax is such that for you to have "noticed" the rock after having virtually stared straight at it would require no measurable ocular movement at all. The epistemologist will be concerned with what sort of event might be said to have occurred in the natural world that led you to say "Oh, there it is!" The rhetorician will want to consider the nature and structure of exactly what I said to you that led you to say it. And indeed, this sort of thing might be considered a branch of heuristic rhetoric, or the art of teaching.

On the other hand, purely rhetorical activities can produce the acutely measurable bodily changes "in pain, hunger, fear and rage," as the great physiologist Walter B. Cannon listed them in the title of his 1915 study, and although he noticeably omitted sexual excitation from the brief list in his famous title, one has only to observe that printed language on a page can be literally arousing. Tears and laughter are produced more often in rhetorical situations than by irritants or tickling. To tell a joke to someone is to exercise a powerful rhetorical tyranny, with frequently violent neuromuscular effects arising from the sudden and sometimes repeated onset of laughter.

It may not be surprising in this regard, by the way, to discover that, among all of Aristotle's writings, it is primarily in his treatise on rhetoric that he lists, and discusses in detail, the various emotions, distinguishing among anger, contempt, spite, insolence, mildness, love, friendship, fear, shame, benevolence, pity, virtuous indignation, envy, emulation, and so forth. It is as the targets of arguments of pathos, or emotion, that emotions must be carefully mapped.[5]

The Roman rhetoricians following Aristotle, like Quintilian, Cicero, and the author of a treatise called the *Rhetorica ad herrenium,* divided the whole subject matter of rhetorical analysis into five parts, a division that remained traditional through the sixteenth century, until rhetoricians were by and large concerned with literature. As will be seen, this division reflected an interest in the sources and manifestations, not of knowledge per se, but of what could be the substance of a persuasive oral performance. The traditional parts of rhetoric were, then:

invention—where conceptual material comes from; the *topoi,* or places, and the paradigms and structures in which subject matter occurs.

arrangement.

style—for example, distinctions among High, Middle, and Low rhetorical styles and their appropriateness to various situations. This was called the matter of decorum and had nothing to do with good manners but rather with what would work, appropriateness being primarily a matter of effectiveness.

memory—an important subject. The art of memory was concerned with providing conceptual models for what we would call—using our own metaphors—storage and retrieval. Classical and Renaissance rhetoric employed the model not of a filing system (which those of us over a certain age all implicitly use—alphabetization of names and such) nor of a personal computer (which will be happening more and more—consider how the colloquial idiom "call it up" now suggests, not a spell, which summons up a hiding or lurking presence, but a simple keyboard procedure). A conventional system assigned matters to be remembered—names, lists—positions around a table or in a room. Memory art then involved visualizing the room and seeing the various elements as topoi, or actual places—hence some of our modern senses of "topic."

delivery—not wholly unlike what a contemporary, Chomskyan model of language acquisition might call performance, but not in any musical or theatrical sense.

Style and delivery both involved careful deployment of linguistic resources, and it is under these rubrics that so much of what became the purely literary theory of Renaissance and later rhetoric was discussed: literal and figurative language; the various tropes, or ways of being nonliteral, such as metaphor, metonymy, irony, allegory, rhetorical questioning, and so forth; as well as the various schemes, or ways of playing around with linguistic patterns that did not involve words used in other than literal senses, such as syntactical repetitions like anaphora or—as in modern languages—rhyme (for instance, "Rhyming makes these lines more dense / But doesn't make them change their sense"). When it comes to the rhetoric of literary texts—poems, in particular—trope becomes not so much a matter of effective ornament and gesture in *elocutio,* or delivery, as something that lies at the heart of *inventio* itself. Since literature is figurative by design and intention, both the will to figuration and the germ of the literary utterance, its imaginative deep structure or whatever, propound tropes.

And here arises the matter of metaphor and the law, considered from a rhetorical, rather than from a strictly logical, point of view. Any consideration of law and literature would have to find this subject of great interest. Traditionally considered have been such matters as the training at the Inns of Court of so many seventeenth-century English poets—John Donne being the foremost of these, perhaps—who were masters of metaphoric deployment, as well as of forms of argument and pleading and, in particular, of strained conceits and comparisons. One can easily imagine a "metaphysical" poetic conceit, whether in verse or in prose, that would propound a likeness—say, of an infant and the church—not because of an implied sanctity that they shared but because of their common anomalous personhood in law. The language of common sense would find the conceit crazy.

Metaphor, analogy, likeness, are all connected. Rhetorically speaking, a simile is an assertion that a likeness exists (whereas metaphor assumes or implies the foundation of that likeness and moves forward with it). A grounded simile is one in which the properties constructing the likeness are specified: "A dolphin is like a seal in that they are both marine mammals" or, to cite the unanswered riddle that so intrigued Alice at the Mad Tea-Party, "A raven is like a writing-desk" (in that the English words designating them both start with the phoneme /r/, even though inscribed differently). In neither case can we deny the truth of the assertion, for both engage matters of undisputed fact; we can only acknowledge that the likeness has been legitimately drawn. Even in a weak case, where the grounding seems trivial, we can at best groan and say, "Well, I guess so." (To acknowledge the high probability of such responses, we might rewrite "X is like Y" as "X may be compared to Y without fear of dismissal, catcalls, groans at the triviality of the univocal ground, or any other denial, not that the likeness *could* be invoked, but that it shouldn't have been and that it was very bad discursive manners to do so.)

But there can obviously be similes that are simply false: "A raven is like a writing-desk in that they are both marine mammals" has no authority to assert the likeness because the grounding is factually false. To invert the micronarrative structure of a simile by asking "What property X likens A to B?" is to ask a riddle. It should be observed that an ungrounded simile, "X is like Y," remains logically in suspension and, in fact, functions like a riddle and like a metaphor: we cannot assert, "No, it isn't," as we could in a falsely grounded simile—except in a kind of rhetorical joking.

The law is always constructing analogies and similes, going so far as to invent new kinds of grounding for them. In a process that poststructuralist literary theory has delighted to pounce on, what has been *constructed* is perceived to have been properly *construed* (from the same Latin word, and undifferentiated in French). When nice distinctions are involved, it is often the role of rhetorical persuasion—albeit operating in what was for Aristotle the highest mode of logos, or rational substance—to convince others that the analogy "holds," as we might put it, or at least "holds for" a particular instance. Logic would also have to hold throughout such an argument, but its domain would still be rhetorical, though not in a popular sense that would regard proofs of pathos alone as defining rhetoric.

This matter of figurative language in legal discourse could be looked at in another way, with respect to trope or metaphor in a general sense, rather than in terms of formally framed simile or analogy. I may perform some small act; then, moving a few feet away, I perform the identical act. (I am assuming our joint pragmatic grasp of identity here: if I can repeat an act in the same place at a differenttime, then I should be able to repeat it elsewhere as well.) The act is the same. Butthe second time, across a state line, the act will enter a web of metaphors calledstatutes—as metaphorically strong as statues, though breakable with different consequences—just as it might enter a little allegory in a poetic text. In the poem of thelaw, the act would come under the criminal code of the second state but not of thefirst. Literally, it would be the same act; only figuratively—its commission hasbeen interdicted and metaphorically designated a crime—is it different.[6]

We might say that poetry, theology, and law all involve systems of tropes.[7] The law draws its great strength from its enforceability. If a poet says to the laws of the state of Connecticut, "You are nothing but a pack of tropes"—unlike Alice, who tells her trial scene in Wonderland, "You're nothing but a pack of cards," at which they all fly up into the air in a grand display of fifty-two pickup—the poet will get short shrift. The law would reply at best, "I daresay," and, if the circumstances called for it, invite the poet to deconstruct the bars of his or her holding cell. In short, the law wouldn't give a tinker's damn (and in fact, if it was generous enough to be instructive, could claim that it would be delighted to rewrite all statutes as pure imperatives, removing any entities upsetting to the narrowest nominalist). Poetry, on the other hand, gets its strength from its absolute prima facie acknowledgment that its entities are metaphors. Theology, the weak sister in this matter, insists that its entities are literal and factual; it is only under theocratic circumstances that such insistence is enforceable in a quasi-legal pattern. (But theology is the part of religion that appeals to intellectuals, and were religion to depend on that, rather than the terrors of annihilation at death or the general fear of standing free as a member of no sect or church, then religion might vanish.)

In the writing of opinions, obiter dicta provide an interesting question for rhetorical analysis, particularly, perhaps, because the doctrine of stare decisis does not cover them; their persuasive role may be fruitfully problematic. Dissenting opinions are not formally to be considered obiter dicta with respect to majority ones; their entire rhetorical basis is shifted slightly, and their points cannot constitute formal precedent, even as the very range and targets of their persuasion are fundamentally different. In some ways, dissenting opinions are more like moral essays, or theoretical analyses, or literary criticism, than they are like effectively instrumental opinions. At this point I shall not go into the vast question of the inference of judicial intention from judicial text but only observe that it implies considerable rhetorical analysis. A celebrated instance would be that of the phrase "all deliberate speed" in *Brown v. Board of Education,* with its complex history (if only in the nineteenth century) in poetic as well as legal language. It was a rhetorical consideration that Paul Gewirtz, in writing of the phrase, engaged when he observed that style was "in this case, inseparable from substance."[8] On the other hand, consider familiar moves in the writing of opinion by which the author will suddenly, and apparently pointedly, lapse into a homely or popular mode of diction, usually to embrace a homely or fashionably popular exemplary phrase. We might say that the mere lapse itself is a rhetorical move at the level of elocution: it induces a kind of rhythmic change, analogous to, say, the sudden introduction of a sentence fragment, without a verb, perhaps, into a texture woven of complex, periodic sentences. As if one were suddenly speaking. Rather than writing. It is as if this not only operated aesthetically on the attention but rhetorically in the realm of pathos (to the degree that the author might want to make the reader relax, smile, or even giggle) and thereby, perhaps, of ēthos: The essential humanity, good humor, sincerity, or whatever of the writer would be claimed by what was a sort of stage aside.

One might imagine, for example, that in some matter of contract law or in a question of contingent responsibility or right, a judge might add, "It takes two to tango." The phrase itself comes from a pop song of 1952 known widely in a celebrated performance by Pearl Bailey; by now, it could seem to many only a proverbial phrase. The song took a self-evident truism and allegorized it. A nice rhetorical point might distinguish between an audience who knew the song and an audience who knew only the phrase. As a matter of fact, I have found some thirty federal opinions of the last twenty-five years that cite the phrase, quote a citation of it in previous opinions, or misquote it. A few examples: "It takes two to tango, in courts as well as on the ballroom floor" (*Grenada Steel Indus. v. Alabama Oxygen Co.*, 695 F.2d 883 [1983]); or, concerning a labor dispute, "There is scarcely a situation proving so much the old saw that it 'takes two to tango'" (*Cooper v. General Dynamics*, 533 F.2d 163 [1976]); or, with grotesquely mispointed wit, "[I]t takes at least two to tango for conspiracy purposes" (*U.S. v. Villasenor*, 894 F.2d 1422 [1990]); or, more forthrightly and pointedly (in a conspiracy question), "This is a situation where it takes more than two to tango" (*Gant v. Aliquippa Borough*, 612 F. Supp. 1139 [1985]).

More generally, we should have to ask of such an allusion whether the move involved the realm of logos as well—Was the tag line (which might, in another century, have been a tag in Latin from Horace or Virgil) pointedly and enlighteningly used? Did it helpfully sum up a longer formulation, perhaps with some final bit of clarification? Was there, perhaps also, an implication that common sense, the truisms enshrined in proverb and folklore, is a kind of quasi precedent—that they have an authority and relevance in the realm of writing, rather than in the strictly constructed realm of judicial authority?

This is one of the problems of legal rhetoric that make it uniquely interesting— the precise placing of the rhetorical role of precedent in framing the discourse of opinion, in particular. Most nonlegal writing is not procedurally binding, although there are indeed many counterinstances, where the precedents must by nature be very recent. This is especially true in verbal games, such as the discourse of bidding in contract bridge or in public auctions. In these instances, precedents are to be observed and applied strictly and narrowly. (N: "Three no-trump." E: "Two hearts." Everybody: "WHAT???" E: "Obviously, N was joking"—this won't do; even as E's joke, it was an aside and not a bid.) Good conversation, however, can frequently involve a free play on interpretation of the forces of any particular precedent and, in addition, the flexible nature of precedence itself. It is in this that what could be thought of as the poetics of prolonged conversation might consist. In science, precedent is both optimally rigid and clearly and simply open to the revisions demanded by new data. One might say that in a model's fragility lies its very strength. As a lay rhetorician, I can only surmise that the issue of interpretation with respect to a precedent or even a statute might itself be open to interpretation along at least two logical or epistemological axes: Is it the precedent with respect to the statute that is being construed, or is it the accident of the particular case with respect to a quasi-rigid, quasi-statutory principle? Or both? In any event, the citing of a precedent in literature or even in conversation, could be considered a rhetorical move of ēthos or pathos. In law, it is so substantive a question as to constitute a move of logos.

This foregrounds again the matter of authority as opposed to persuasion; it seems to parallel a rhetorically constructed difference between the various roles of ēthos-logos-pathos in pleading before a jury, in the framing of an appeal, and, particularly, in the writing of an opinion. It would seem that there are several layers of authority to be considered: the duly constituted authority of being a judge, of what sort, of what appropriate jurisdiction, and so forth. This might be said to confer the right to try, under the circumstances of the case, to persuade, either a yet higher court or, if the buck stops here, subsequent duly constituted opinion. More generally, persuasion—say, that a particular analogy holds in a particular case, an instance mentioned previously—operates in argument as well as in the writing of opinion. And because stare decisis gives precedent itself a certain kind of authority, it provides no issue for the rhetoric of persuasion.

The performative rhetoric of the concluding judicial phrase, "It is so ordered," presents no metaphysical questions begged by its idiom, as in the case of a jury being said to "find" a verdict (as in having searched through the Book of Just Verdicts and found the one in question inscribed there). But the extension of the phrase is still of interest here: Is the "it" simply part of a passive construction, as in the purely empirical statement "It has been so ordered [that is, in the past] that X be dealt with as Y"? Clearly not: "It is [hereby, herewith] so ordered" makes no such claim to fact. But the "it" becomes more problematic: Does it apply to the whole of the opinion, to all of its language, to its obiter dicta and its various versions of "It takes two to tango"? Clearly not; but to identify its antecedent still makes logical demands on the grammatical analysis. This kind of problem comes from a sort of deconstruction of current idiom (rather than from the hidden metaphor in semantic change, say) that is extremely relevant to the analysis of literary—especially poetic—language. It engages not so much the stances and moves of an agent persuading a listener or reader as that rhetorical microcosm of the interaction, what I. A. Richards called the interanimation of words. A question remains about its applicability to the language of legal discourse. And, although apparently trivial and certainly minute, that question may stand for the problematic efficacy and utility of the linguistic, stylistic, and overall rhetorical analysis—a paralegal analysis, perhaps, at best—of that quasi-literary genre, the judicial opinion.

Sanford Levinson

The Rhetoric of the Judicial Opinion

Judicial opinions are rhetorical performances. The critic who essays an assessment of any performance, whether dramatic or judicial, must be aware, among other things, of the particular role assigned to the actor, the likely audience for the performance, and the effects sought by the performer.[1] In the case of the judicial opinion especially (but not exclusively), these effects include, among other things, persuading the audience and demonstrating a certain authority over it, which, as we shall see, are not at all the same thing.[2]

SETTING THE STAGE

Can one meaningfully discuss the rhetoric of the judicial opinion without specifying, at the very least, the cultural stage upon which the judge is acting and the role he or she is playing? Is there, for example, any good reason to believe that the opinions of the U.S. Supreme Court, United States district courts, state courts, Indian tribal courts, and British, Italian, and Chinese courts (at all levels), not to mention Islamic and other religious courts, share many common characteristics, even if the examination is synchronic? And would it not be even more remarkable if any of these significant commonalities, assuming that any emerged, survived further diachronic scrutiny?

Consider, for example, one extremely important aspect of judicial opinions, the official attribution of authorship. The present practice in the U.S. Supreme Court is to state, in most opinions, that Justice X has written "the opinion of the Court." On occasion, there is no opinion of the Court, only a result constituted by the votes of the Justices, accompanied, however, by individual opinions signed by the Justices.[3] This represents a perhaps unintended reversion to traditional English practice, in which each individual Law Lord issues an opinion and professional lawyers are left with the task of integrating the various views into "the holding of the case." It is quite rare for the Supreme Court to issue only a per curiam opinion lacking any indication of specific authorship.[4] Other judicial systems, however, suppress completely any such explicit authorship, preferring instead to speak only as "the court."[5] What difference might any of this make?

One obvious implication of the suppression of individual authorship is that the contingencies of judicial membership on the Court are irrelevant; the law is instantiated as the product of a truly impersonal institutional judgment. Concomitantly, assignment of individual responsibility invites the onlooker to become all too aware of the importance of assignment practices within the Court because of the potentially different styles and approaches associated with the particular members of the Court. Similar considerations can obviously be raised by the decision whether to allow dissents and whether to disclose who is dissenting and for what reasons, as opposed to a simple indication that there was dissent, although one does not know from whom or why. We can infer that these basic rhetorical practices differ both synchronically and diachronically within and among legal systems and that one might well attend to the importance of such differences for the enterprise of the rule of law and the popular legitimacy of judicial decisions.

Indeed, curiosity about the meaning of the "rule of law" underlies much of my interest in judicial rhetoric. One of my few expectations regarding judicial opinions, for example, is that they will almost always be written in a tone of impersonality suggesting that the legal materials themselves, rather than the personal desires of the judge, required the result in question.[6] Consider Felix Frankfurter's assertion that "when the issue demands judicial determination, it is not the personal notion of judges . . . which must prevail."[7] Should Frankfurter's rhetoric be typical, that would be no small point; one of the central myths of most legal systems, I suspect, is that they are indeed a rule of law instead of the rule of the particular men and women who were, as part of the ruling political coalition, selected for appointment—or, as in many U.S. states, elected—to the judiciary.

I also wonder if it is a general feature of judicial opinions—or only of the U.S. ones that I am most familiar with—that, like the legal briefs they resemble in so many ways, they adopt a tone of overweening confidence.[8] I am always struck when opposing views are airily dismissed as, in one of my favorite judicial phrases, "without merit." How often does one find a judicial opinion that frankly says that the question is an exceedingly close one, with much to be said on both (or all) sides, even if one must at the end decide and thus jump, even if with only a 51 percent certainty level, toward a given resolution that results in what, from the loser's perspective, is a 100 percent loss? Few judges—even such a renowned skeptic as Holmes—have made their reputation by confessing (at least in print) how close they were to deciding a case in the opposite direction. As Robert Ferguson has written, "The only thing the judge never admits in the moment of decision is freedom of choice. [The opinion] must instead appear as if forced to the inevitable conclusion."[9] Not the least reason to avoid such confession, of course, is the likelihood that it would make the losing side even less likely to view its fate as simply the operation of the impersonal "rule of law." What some might regard as touching evidence of the judge's own human ambivalence and modesty in the face of complexity would for others be evidence instead of the terrifying arbitrariness that underlies much of the legal system, even in its judicial (as distinguished from legislative) aspects where, presumably, the rule-of-law ideology would be strongest.

Consider in this context the mordant comment of Judge Richard Posner, who writes that "[j]udges are not comfortable writing opinions to the effect that 'We have very little sense of what is going on in this case—the record is poorly developed, and the lawyers are lousy—and we have no confidence that we have got it right—we know we're groping in the dark—but we're paid to decide cases, and here goes,' though that is the actual character of many appellate cases that are decided with a published opinion."[10] He then footnotes a "famous acknowledgment" from one of Learned Hand's opinions: "The fact that we are ourselves not agreed cautions us that we should not be too sure of our conclusion; and obviously the really important matter is that the question should reach the Supreme Court as soon as possible."[11] What makes Hand's comment so citable, however, is precisely that it is so exceptional. Far more typical are the disdainful dismissals of opponents as barely competent, if that, should they not share one's own view as to what the law requires.[12]

PLAYING A PART: RHETORIC AND ROLE

I want to disclaim the kind of knowledge necessary to discuss something called *the* judicial opinion. Such knowledge as I have about judicial opinions is decidedly "local knowledge," as Clifford Geertz might put it, based on the study of the law emanating from (or rhetorically linked to) the Constitution of the United States. This is, to put it mildly, but one small branch (or genre) of one legal system. No doubt someone whose expertise was different, even within the U.S. legal system, would stress different aspects of judicial opinions than the ones on which I shall be concentrating.[13]

But establishing the genre only begins our inquiry, for it is also necessary to determine at what institutional level our presumed judicial author is operating. That is, what role has our judge undertaken, and how might the rhetorical scripts of various roles differ in interesting ways? Consider, for example, the difference it might make whether we are analyzing the rhetoric of opinions of the U.S. Supreme Court or, instead, the rhetoric of opinions issued by what the Constitution labels "inferior courts." One would find, I believe, strikingly different rhetorics.

In two notable books, my colleague Philip Bobbitt has argued that constitutional law talk is constituted by a distinctive rhetorical discourse, what J. M. Balkin and I have termed a constitutional grammar.[14] Such law talk is composed, according to Bobbitt, of six "modalities" of argument. Three of them—textual, historical, and structural modes of argument—relate to the fact that (at least part of) the Constitution is written. A fourth, doctrinal argument, takes explicit cognizance of the role of courts in providing interpretations, for doctrinalists (unlike, say, textualists or historicists) concentrate on the prior considerations of similar issues by predecessor judges rather than, say, the unadorned text of the Constitution or the thought of James Madison. A fifth modality, prudentialism, involves looking unabashedly at the consequences of a particular outcome and, presumably, shaping the decision accordingly. Bobbitt's sixth category, ethical argument, is by far the most controversial, in both its descriptive and its normative aspects. For him, ethical argument is at least quasi-textual, bearing a strong family resemblance to Justice Douglas's "penumbras and emanations" instantiated in *Griswold v. Connecticut;*[15] for me, it is far closer to a socioanthropological "fundamental values" notion based on grasping the deep structures that constitute us as a specific social order. The central point, so far as Bobbitt is concerned, is that ethical argument is not the equivalent of recourse to natural law or some other foundational system but instead a derivation from the ethos of a constitutional order.

There is much that is valuable about Bobbitt's approach, as well as much that is worth debating. He seems, for example, to believe that he has identified the particular discursive practices—the modalities of argument—that allow one to identify something as a judicial-legal opinion about the Constitution rather than, say, a political theory or public policy discussion of some of the relevant issues presented in a case. His approach has difficulty handling a judicial opinion—a writing signed by a judge acting in his or her official capacity—that indeed reads just like a standard-form discussion of political theory or public policy. At this point what appears to be an empirical enquiry—that is, if we read thousands of judicial opinions, what, if any rhetorical regularities do we find?—suddenly becomes transformed into a normative one: What criteria do we use to divide the universe of signed writings into "authentic" judicial opinions, on the one hand, and, on the other, what a devotee of J. L. Austin might call misfires or attempted judicial opinions that, even though signed by judges, are not acceptable examples of the genre? (Interestingly enough, even a misfire might have legal consequences if the judge's writing, whatever its deficiencies, contains an order that is disobeyed only at one's peril.)[16]

Whatever else may be said about Bobbitt's claims, it is essential to recognize that the judges whom he focuses on are playing the equivalent of the Palace, that is, the Supreme Court. Justices are the stars of the judicial theater; as such, they have the juiciest parts with the greatest opportunity to show the range of their talents.[17] There is no doubt that Bobbitt's schema helps us to understand the constitutional discourse of opinions written by members of the U.S. Supreme Court (or similarly supreme state courts engaged in interpreting their own constitutions). In these opinions one will indeed see a full panoply of interpretive modalities; doctrinal arguments are met, often angrily, with textual or historical counterthrusts, and one or other Justice angrily accuses his or her colleagues of irresponsibly ignoring the consequences for our polity of the abstract legalisms embraced.[18]

But if one leaves the judicial equivalent of Broadway for a look at the provinces, one finds strikingly different discursive practices. Even at the federal level of the judiciary, anyone looking through the *Federal Reporter* or the *Federal Supplement* "could be pardoned for thinking that doctrinalism—the analysis of precedent, especially those of 'superior' courts—is the privileged modality."[19] The reason for this emphasis on doctrinalism and the sheer frequency of the kind of case crunching reminiscent of the most traditional form of legal education is (deceptively) simple: As the very term suggests, "inferior courts" are most often viewed as part of a command structure in which superior courts—and ultimately the Supreme Court—give the orders that the lower courts are required, whether contentedly or sullenly, to enforce.[20] Or perhaps, to stick with the dramaturgical metaphor, the Supreme Court should be viewed as writing the lines that the actors within the legal system are required to read.

It is by focusing on the task of these inferior actors that one sees most exposed the fault lines in regard to the pretensions of the law as a system of reasoned deliberation, as contrasted with one or another form of brute positivism. Whatever one's views may be about the performance of the Supreme Court, about which I shall have more to say presently, it is impossible, once one adds into the analysis the role of the inferior court, to adopt Mary Ann Glendon's hymn to "[r]eason, now and always, the life of the law," unless we emphasize, like Lord Coke, the truly "artificial reason" that is the law and its deviance from what ordinary people might think is suggested by the rhetoric of appeals to "reason."[21]

Whatever may be the status of the U.S. Supreme Court as a forum for republican dialogue and the play of reason, the formal status of any inferior court is decidedly different.[22] The Supreme Court, for example, has made it clear that it rejects in toto Andrew Jackson's altogether-plausible assertion that the analyses of the Court "have only such influence as the force of their reasoning may deserve."[23] Consider, for example, the Supreme Court's reaction to a Fourth Circuit decision that held constitutionally "cruel and unusual" a forty-year sentence that was imposed for possessing with intent to distribute, and distributing, nine ounces of marijuana.[24] The Supreme Court treated the Fourth Circuit's opinion as fit for a per curiam reversal inasmuch as it purportedly ignored an earlier 5–4 decision in *Rummell v. Estelle*.[25] According to the Supreme Court, "[T]he Court of Appeals could be viewed as having ignored, consciously or unconsciously, the hierarchy of the federal court system created by the Constitution and Congress." Needless to say, this was intolerable, at least from the Supreme Court's perspective. The Court fired the heaviest of rhetorical guns—adopting the dictionary definition of "rhetorical" as "marked by or tending to use bombast":[26] "[U]nless we wish anarchy to prevail within the federal judicial system, a precedent of this Court must be followed by the lower federal courts *no matter how misguided the judges of those courts may think it to be*."[27] The Supreme Court appears to believe that judges take their oaths to obey not the Constitution but the Court itself.[28]

This emphasis on the actual institutional stage occupied by the judge enables me to offer answers to two of the questions I aimed to address: "How do arguments from precedent make their effect . . . and what may they conceal?"* They make their effect primarily by an appeal to hierarchy, or, less elegantly, power.[29] After all, what makes precedent interesting as a theory of decisionmaking is precisely that it calls upon decisionmakers to follow what they otherwise believe to be even grievous mistakes. As Jeremy Bentham put it, "The deference that is due to the determination of former judgments is not due to their wisdom, but to their authority."[30] Or, as the district judge for whom I clerked many years ago put it when withdrawing an order that had granted relief to a person who claimed that he was the victim of an illegal search by the police, "In deference to the superior force and authority, though not to the principles [of a controlling new decision], I find it my duty to save the state an unnecessary appeal and to reverse the prior order."[31]

*The panel for which this chapter was originally prepared was entitled "The Rhetoric of the Judicial Opinion," and the program included these questions: "How do judicial opinions gain their authority and persuasiveness? How do arguments from precedent make their effect? How are they supplemented and what may they conceal?" This chapter should thus be understood as an answer to these questions.

Indeed, only when one is, in some genuine sense, unhappy about the outcome and would have decided otherwise had the precedent not been deemed "controlling" can precedent really be said to have effect. This may, as Frederick Schauer has suggested, be an attribute of *any* rule following insofar as it requires that one adopt a suboptimal outcome in the instant case because of the perceived benefits of adhering to a standard practice.[32] *All* rules within a system of positive law require, at least on occasion, the subordination of "wisdom" to "authority." Judge-made rules do not differ, as a logical matter, from legislatively created ones, at least from the perspective of actors beneath the respective judges or legislators in the institutional hierarchy. What distinguishes the felt obligation to follow a legislative command from a similar obligation to obey a judicial ruling is, as the adjectives suggest, only the source of the rule generating the obligation.

In any event, it is essential to focus on particular courts rather than on some generalized judiciary when discussing the role played by precedent in judicial rhetoric. Only such specification sensitizes us to the important analytical distinction between what might be termed horizontal and vertical precedent.[33] The only question facing the Supreme Court, when it operates in its doctrinal mode, is what respect it wishes to pay prior decisions by a predecessor Court on its own horizontal plane.

It is an analytical truth that there is no court superior to the "supreme" court within a given legal system. Hierarchy is still involved insofar as one views past decisionmakers as in some sense possessing power over their successors. It is clear, however, that the Court—whatever its sometime obeisance to horizontal precedent, as in the 1992 decision in *Planned Parenthood v. Casey*—also has for at least 150 years provided itself with escape hatches when precedents seemed too confining. Whatever presumptions operate in favor of precedents, they are in fact rebuttable, which means that they can be overridden in the name of some other important value. That, for the Supreme Court, is not anarchy but rather, presumably, the law working itself pure. What evokes the fulmination of the Court is any challenge to its vertical position atop the judiciary, not a challenge to the sanctity of precedent per se.

Because of the fixation by most constitutional scholars on the decisions and practices of the Supreme Court alone, academic ink is spilled almost exclusively over cases like *Casey* rather than instances of vertical precedent. I think, however, that the vertical domain is not only equally interesting as a theoretical matter but practically speaking of far more import. After all, most ordinary citizens receive their law from these courts rather than from the absent, often-mysterious entity far off in Washington, D.C.

Demands by the Supreme Court directed to inferior courts to adhere to its own precedents only barely conceal, if at all, the rather obvious role of raw power in constituting constitutional meaning. For true doctrinalists, the quality of reasoning is like Mae West's view of goodness: it has "nothing to do with" explaining one's success in the world, including the claim of judicial opinions to authority. As Richard Posner (who with Guido Calabresi is surely among the most intellectually distinguished of any currently sitting federal judges) has put it, "Judicial decisions are authoritative because they emanate from a politically accredited source rather than because they are agreed to be correct by individuals in whom the community reposes an absolute epistemic trust."[35] I am not sure what importance Posner places on "absolute" trust; it should surely be enough that many of us would place more comparative epistemic trust—including trust in what constitutes correct interpretations of the Constitution—in practically anyone besides certain members of the current Supreme Court and, quite probably, even a majority of that august body. I presume that few of us would join Horace Greeley in saying that "with every respect for those Judicial dignitaries, . . . I would rather trust a dog with my dinner," but I suspect that the sentiment has been widely shared at one time or another by many who are reading this essay.[36]

After all, it was Dean Calabresi himself who with delicious flamboyance pronounced: "I despise the current Supreme Court and find its aggressive, willful, statist behavior disgusting."[37] Yet the truly important point relative to the present discussion is that this expression of disgust presumably does not entail for now Judge Calabresi, a member of the U.S. Court of Appeals for the Second Circuit, the conclusion "and therefore I will not consider myself bound by its terrible decisions that mock our constitutional aspirations to protect the most vulnerable among us from the depredations of complacent, powerful elites who want to use the state apparatus only to further their own misbegotten ends." That statement would surely have kept him permanently at Yale, whereas his more limited statement, however hostile to the Supreme Court, can presumably be dismissed as irrelevant. The U.S. Senate that confirmed him presumably considered him an honorable man and potential judge, which in this context means, at least in part, that the Senators perceived in him a willingness to assume the role of a loyal satrap of his hierarchical betters.[38]

This emphasis on hierarchy—and on the presuppositions of legal positivism more generally—also enables us to understand what to some nonlawyers might be a certain peculiarity in the question "How do judicial opinions gain their authority *and* persuasiveness?" Surely the (naive) scientist, for example, might believe that a scientific paper gains its authority precisely from its ability to persuade its readers. That is, "authority" comes from a capacity to "persuade," and "persuasion" in turn leads one to deem the persuader an "authority." Even the landmark work of Thomas S. Kuhn, so devastating to some naive models of the scientific enterprise, can easily enough be assimilated into this understanding insofar as it can be interpreted as focusing on the socially constructed nature of systems of persuasion. Kuhn does not describe, for example, a duty of "inferior" scientists to accept without significant question the commands of those above them in a defined hierarchical structure even as he notes the various ideological and incentive systems that might explain why inferiors are hesitant to trust their own doubts regarding the views of their more famous superiors. To be told, moreover, that one is putting one's career in jeopardy by challenging some well-placed figure—and thus, as a prudential matter, one might properly be cautious in doing so—is altogether different from being told that one has a moral obligation to adhere to settled ways.[39] The phrasing of the question posed above may indirectly recognize Posner's basic insight that persuasiveness may have nothing to do with authority in a positive law system organized hierarchically. Or, to be more exact, "authority" can, at least on occasion, be contrasted with "persuasiveness" rather than considered a synonym. Indeed, the first dictionary definition for "authority" is precisely "the *power* to judge, act or command." Only down the page do we find "authority" as "persuasive force."[40] There is a world of difference between these two notions of authority.

This difference is illuminated in a number of cases in which state supreme courts have proffered interpretations of the language of state constitutions which is basically identical to the language of the federal Constitution that are nonetheless different from the interpretations proffered by the U.S. Supreme Court.[41] That is, the latter court may indeed be authoritative in its construction of the national Constitution, at least for inferior courts; but it has no such authority to offer ultimate constructions of state constitutions, even if the language is identical.

PERSUADING THE JUDICIAL AUDIENCE

That authority as force differs from authority as persuasion should not blind us to the extent that they are also intertwined. I am reminded of Richard Neustadt's emphasis, in his classic study *Presidential Power,* on President Truman's description of Eisenhower's likely frustrations in the presidency: "'He'll sit here,' Truman would remark (tapping his desk for emphasis), 'and he'll say, "Do this! Do that!" *And nothing will happen.* Poor Ike—it won't be a bit like the Army. He'll find it very frustrating.'" And, indeed, according to Neustadt, that turned out to be the case. He quotes a 1958 comment by one of Eisenhower's aides: "The President still feels that when he's decided something, that *ought* to be the end of it . . . and when it bounces back undone or done wrong, he tends to react with shocked surprise."[42] As Neustadt put it, formal legal "powers are no guarantee of power." Those with such powers do "not obtain results by giving orders—or not, at any rate, merely by giving orders. [Their] *power* is the power to persuade."[43] To again quote Harry Truman: "I sit here all day trying to persuade people to do the things they ought to have sense enough to do without my persuading them. . . . That's all the powers of the President amount to."[44]

Even if one discounts this reduction of presidential power to little more than that of a law school deanship—after all, Robert Cover would have instantly pointed out that political officials like the president and judges can send people to their deaths—it is an important corrective to the confusion of formal power with empirically available power.[45] Judges must always be concerned with persuading as well as with invoking their formal authority to order.

This naturally brings us, then, to the first of the standard dictionary definitions of "rhetoric": "the study of the *effective* use of language."[46] The notion of effectiveness inevitably raises the question of the audience whom the language is supposed to affect. Any well-trained lawyer knows that language is almost never directed to the world at large, but rather to specific readers whose persuasion is deemed crucial to attaining the lawyer's ends.

Consider what even political liberals would write in a brief to be submitted to the current Supreme Court as against what would have been said in, say, 1968; one would expect much greater reference in briefs circa 1968 to the Court's role in instantiating the fundamental values that underlie the American vision of equal justice under law. Today's briefs would be markedly different. In Bobbitt's terms, liberals today are likely to be our leading doctrinalists, desperately trying to save the cases identified with the Warren (more properly, Brennan) Court from the evisceration so obviously desired by several members, perhaps even a majority, of the current Court. Today's brief would happily cite the O'Connor-Souter-Kennedy opinion in *Casey* and join in its embrace of the values of institutional stability and adherence to precedent even in the face of what many would find withering critique.[47] Similarly, it would be contemporary conservatives who would most emulate Robert Jackson, Hugo Black, the William J. Brennan of the 1960s, and other great New Deal and post–New Deal judges who were properly disdainful of these values at an earlier constitutional moment. For them, precedent took a decided second place to plain text—Justice Black often emphasized that the words "no law" in the First Amendment mean that *no* law abridging freedom of speech is legitimate—or to invocations of the deepest aspirations of our polity.

There is, presumably, no disagreement with the proposition that only the most foolish lawyers would ignore the audience when writing their briefs. Why would one expect or even desire anything different when some of those lawyers become judges? This requires us, among other things, to identify the probable audiences for judicial opinions. There are, to be sure, many candidates. Consider, for example, the description of Judge Augustus Hand's "intended audience [as] not the bench, bar, or university world in general, but the particular lawyer who was about to lose the case and the particular trial judge whose judgment was being reviewed and perhaps reversed."[48] One wonders how often the losing lawyers or judges ended up agreeing that they deserved their fate, although, presumably the real point was the assurance provided by Hand that their views were taken seriously even if they did not prevail. Whether or not they changed their mind, they should have felt that their dignity as human beings was respected—no small achievement.

One wonders how many contemporary federal judges would adopt Hand's view of his model audience. I would expect an inverse correlation between the "height" of the judge within the hierarchy and any genuine concern about the feelings of the specific losing party. I would, therefore, be astonished if Justices of the Supreme Court took care to speak to the losing party unless that conveniently accorded with their other rhetorical interests. It would be far less surprising if such considerations were prominent in regard to those judges likely to come into contact with the losers in a given case, such as federal district judges. Federal circuit court judges presumably fall in between.

No sensible judge can believe that the world is composed only of persons who await their orders and will thereafter move with alacrity to comply with them. The judge must therefore always be sensitive to the task of eliciting cooperation from those who would otherwise prefer to go their own way. Only an awareness of intended audience—and an appreciation for the de facto limited power of courts—enables us to understand what is surely one of the most famous judicial opinions of the twentieth century, Chief Justice Warren's opinion for a unanimous Court in *Brown v. Board of Education*.[49] There are many things one might say about that opinion, which was much criticized at the time and thereafter. I confess that I find it remarkably unilluminating about the history of American racial relations. There is fleeting reference to discrimination against African Americans, but none whatsoever to who were the discriminators and how a sociopolitical regime had been constructed on the premise of what has been termed a herrenvolk democracy. If one role of the Supreme Court is truly to educate its audience about the background circumstances of a case and the relation of those circumstances to the outcome, then *Brown* must be pronounced a failure.[50] It is difficult to teach *Brown* to a generation of students who no longer have a specific understanding of the political context that enables them to read between the lines of the otherwise bland opinion.

But the central point is that Chief Justice Warren made a deliberate decision to write the way he did. Why did he reject the opportunity to truly try to educate the public about the ravages of racial segregation or to arouse a truly righteous anger against the oppression that had characterized, at that time, well over three centuries of American history? The answer is provided by Warren himself, who wrote his colleagues, on May 7, 1954, that "the opinions [in *Brown* and the companion case of *Bolling v. Sharpe*] should be short, readable by the lay public, non-rhetorical, unemotional and, above all, non-accusatory."[51] According to Barrett Prettyman, who was clerking for Robert Jackson during that fateful term and who had been asked by Jackson what he thought of the opinion, Warren succeeded admirably. Although Prettyman indicated that he wished the opinion "had more law in it," he praised its "genius" in being "so simple and unobtrusive. [Warren] had come from political life and had a keen sense of what you could say in this opinion without getting everybody's back up. His opinion took the sting off the decision, it wasn't accusatory, and it didn't pretend that the Fourteenth Amendment was more helpful than the history suggested."[52]

It is, I think, not at all irrelevant that Warren was a remarkably successful politician, three times governor of California and a vice presidential candidate in the race that Thomas Dewey was supposed to win in 1948. He knew the importance of not getting everybody's back up when embarking on important political campaigns, even if the cost was a certain candor or cogency of argument. He was concerned, altogether properly, not to antagonize needlessly the editorial writers of the great Southern newspapers, who would have to translate the decision for their readers, and the politicians, who would presumably have to take the lead in advising compliance with the decision (whatever that would turn out to mean).

Warren was properly concerned as well with a very different audience—his fellow Justices, from whom he sought a unanimous vote. The marginal cost of even one dissent was, no doubt, perceived as extremely high. Imagine the headlines throughout the South had the Kentuckian Justice Reed, a former solicitor general of the United States, adopted the tone of the contemporary Antonin Scalia or, less anachronistically but equally dangerously, the tone of Reed's predecessors, like Holmes and Stone, who relentlessly pointed out that courts ought not deem themselves uniquely equipped to govern the United States. That would have been an unequivocal disaster.

Reed was none too happy with the decision, according to his law clerk, although "[f]or the good of the country, he put aside his own basis for dissent." But this was not a freewill offering by Reed. According to the clerk, he extracted from Warren a pledge that implementation of the decision would be slow enough to allow the gradual dismantling of segregation rather than a too-rapid wrenching of traditional Southern mores.[53] And, no doubt, he would not have tolerated an "accusatory" opinion. We do not know whether Warren was "persuaded" that this was the best understanding of the Constitution or that Reed had enough power to compel its adoption given the importance of a united front. What we know is that probably the most politically savvy Chief Justice in our history found it advisable to make the choices he did, which should certainly teach us much about how one constructs a judicial opinion (as distinguished, perhaps, from simply deciding who ought to win or lose a specific case), at least in circumstances like those facing the Court in *Brown*.

Brown is, to be sure, exceptional, but one must never overlook, even in cases far less freighted with public controversy, the importance of institutional factors and their influence on the shaping of judicial rhetoric. As Felix Frankfurter once said, "When you have to have at least five people to agree on something, they can't have that comprehensive completeness of candor which is open to a single man, giving his own reasons untrammeled by what anybody else may do or not do."[54] And even the slightest perusal of Justice Brennan's papers reveals a Justice who was willing to subordinate his own "best view of the law" or most felicitous expression of his point of view to the far more important task of gaining a fifth vote.[55]

But getting the agreement of five people is only the very first stage in an extraordinarily complex process of bringing about changes in behavior in the world beyond the courthouse. The same costs in candor (or persuasiveness in an academic sense) that must be paid to gain the fifth (or, as in *Brown*, the ninth) vote may be paid even more often to gain the assent of the so-called inferior judges and the even more remote public officials and bureaucratic underlings whose behavior must ultimately be affected if desired changes are to occur. As Walter Murphy pointed out thirty years ago, there are "elements of judicial strategy" built into any opinion of the Supreme Court.[56]

Not the least difficulty of making sense of Supreme Court opinions comes from the obvious fact that they expect at least their more important opinions to be read by multiple audiences. Some audiences are professional, including the lawyers in the given case, judges who must ostensibly enforce the wider "law of the land" purportedly contained within the resolution of the case, legal academics who parse opinions, and hapless law students who are assigned them. But some, as already suggested, are decidedly nonprofessional, including members of the Congress and state legislatures, newspaper reporters, and even, on occasion, editorial writers. Indeed, Joseph Goldstein has argued in his important book *The Intelligible Constitution* that the primary audience for opinions of the Supreme Court should be We the People. The primary task of the Court therefore is "to maintain the Constitution as something comprehensible to the People," and he therefore condemns Frankfurter's and Brennan's easy toleration of less than full candor and explicitness in the writing of opinions.[57]

Whatever one's views as to the primary audience of a court, there are additional audiences, and I am sure that it is impossible to write persuasively to all of these audiences. Judges presumably pick and choose their primary audience, depending on the case. Whatever one's theory of audience, incidentally, I suspect that few judges conceive their primary audience as legal academics, even though the law clerks who are, alas, increasingly responsible for writing opinions may believe that is true. Perhaps the most unattractive trait of legal academics is to overlook this obvious fact and to delight in exposing the "stupid" opinions of those nominated by the president and confirmed by the Senate, rather than recognizing that these opinions often—though not always—can be explained by reference to the fact that the judge, even if not the clerk, has another motivation than the desire to gain an A from those who teach at Harvard or Yale or those who write law review articles for elite law journals.

PERSUADING THE AUDIENCE FOR JUDICIAL OPINIONS

Courts write to audiences, then, but are these actual audiences or only intended, hoped-for audiences? Who actually reads judicial opinions? While preparing this chapter, I asked several of my fellow legal-academic specialists if they necessarily read all of the Supreme Court's opinions even in constitutional law (let alone statutory opinions). I found few indeed who admitted to going through the advance sheets with any great diligence. Just as fewer judges appear to be reading the work produced by legal academics, so do more academics, particularly at elite schools, appear ever less interested in reading the opinions written by judges (or, more to the point, their clerks).[58] One reason is simple: How often do academics expect to find in the pages even of the federal reports what would count within the university community as first-rate discussion of serious problems? Even those with first-rate minds, like Posner and Calabresi, are surely better (and more efficiently) confronted in their academic writings than in most of their opinions, especially if they are opinions of the Court that may have required just the sort of evasions suggested by Holmes and Frankfurter.

In any event, one wonders who the actual audiences for judicial opinions are. How often do any of us (that is, those who teach constitutional law at elite law schools) read opinions of any other court besides the Supreme Court (and, as already suggested, how seriously do we pore over the Court's handiwork)? I can recall no more than a dozen federal court opinions that I read in the past year, and I can think of only three state court decisions that I read in the same period. I do not have the impression that my ignorance of the overwhelming majority of the judicial opinions produced by U.S. appellate courts even in my area of purported expertise is at all unusual.

What does authority or persuasiveness mean in the absence of an audience? How can an opinion "gain" either one, if few people read it? If we were discussing, for example, how academic articles gain their authority and persuasiveness, we would, among other things, discuss such obvious factors as the venue of publication and the actual number of readers (and their social locations), in addition to the rhetorical mechanics within the articles. To be sure, one can always discover hitherto unknown articles (or opinions) and praise their persuasiveness and make claims for their authority—that is a standard ploy of the ambitious academic seeking to disrupt the existing canon and thus, not at all coincidentally, to dislodge those who have made their mark by identification with that canon—but it seems that we might want to describe such pieces as potentially authoritative or persuasive rather than actually possessing those attributes, at least if we are social analysts.

Let us assume that an opinion is read by a relevant audience: How does it persuade? This is, to put it mildly, no easy question to answer, not least because of difficulties attached to the very notion of persuasion. Before one can discuss the attributes of persuasiveness, one must first, after all, be persuaded. How does one determine when this has occurred? Does "being persuaded," for example, phenomenologically mean that one changes one's mind about something that one considers important and has previously reflected upon in a reasonably systematic way? This is, to be sure, a very strong notion of persuasion—or test of the persuasiveness of an opinion. Perhaps it is too strong. Thus we might ask only if a piece of writing leads us to adopt views about matters we have not previously considered or do not regard as particularly important. It should be clear, however, that the word "persuasion" loses any very helpful meaning if it can be used in reference to hearing or reading arguments that we have already adopted. The most persuasive writing would then be that which builds on one's own work! Still, I think we would all regard as odd the statement that someone was persuaded by reading her own statements in someone else's article, even if it is the case psychologically that the display of good sense by an author in favorably quoting our own work leads us to trust that author in other parts of the article dealing with matters about which we in fact know little.

I assume that all of us, at least on occasion, do find ourselves passing the strongest test of persuasion—that is, changing our mind after reading something even about a matter about which we consider ourselves very knowledgeable. Assuming this is our test, the next question is how often, if ever, is the agent of such change a judicial opinion? Speaking for myself, I can recall no occasion in recent years where that has occurred, even though I can easily cite academic articles that have jarred my accepted notions in just the way described.[59] I do not think that my experience is unique. I have discovered, in speaking with colleagues in the academy, that almost none can cite a judicial opinion that persuaded them in this strong sense.

But the asking of such questions ineluctably leads to a change of emphasis in this discussion. Up to now I have been offering more or less detached comments about the attributes of authority and persuasiveness. My stance has been "externalist": I have been discussing how it is that opinions make their way into the consciousness of an audience—and perhaps cause that audience to do something, even if only change their mind, as distinguished from causing measurable changes in behavior. Appropriately, I have drawn my arguments, or speculations, from sociology, political science, and other disciplines that look upon law from afar. But I conclude these remarks by shifting to a more "internal" perspective, in which I will try to answer a question that I have used as part of the final examination in my first-year course in constitutional law.

I have several times asked students to select the opinion assigned during the course that was most persuasive in the specific sense of offering the most truly satisfactory model of legal analysis. It is always interesting to read the students' answers, and I have often been quite happy that I did not have to answer my own question. But the time has come to do that, even though I hope that I will not be graded too harshly on my answer.

I am currently inclined to view as the most truly intellectually satisfying—and thus at least in some sense persuasive—opinion in our two-hundred-year constitutional history that of Robert Jackson in *Youngstown Sheet and Tube Company v. Sawyer.*[60] Why do I think so, especially given that the result—that President Truman has no authority to seize Youngstown's mills—is reached and defended in no fewer than four other opinions, including ones by such giants as Black and Frankfurter? Moreover, Jackson's opinion gained no other adherents, so, as a formal matter, there is no evidence that he persuaded even a single one of his colleagues. Yet for me it is one of the few opinions that make me proud to be a constitutional lawyer. Can I explain this?

The answer, for me, is (deceptively) easy: Jackson's opinion is the best example I know of what might be termed a self-consciously postrealist encounter with the nature of legal judgment. He therefore speaks both to and from the jurisprudential world that I inhabit, which is not the case with most opinions, where the judicial voice seems eager to avoid recognition of the post-Holmesian sea change in legal consciousness. Jackson, who perhaps not coincidentally is the last Justice to have been without the benefit of formal legal education, was every bit as aware of the intellectual consequences of legal realism as, say, his colleague William O. Douglas or his New Deal compatriots Jerome Frank and Thurman Arnold. Jackson was thus well aware of the limitations of ordinary legal materials in providing answers to the difficult problems presented by President Truman's attempt, from his perspective, to protect the interests of those Americans (and others) risking their lives on the Korean Peninsula in what many (including Chief Justice Vinson in dissent) viewed as the first battle of World War III. Instead, Jackson begins his opinion by referring to his own experiences as attorney general and solicitor general in the Roosevelt administration, and he goes on to admit that "[w]hile an interval of detached reflection may temper teachings of that experience, they probably are a more realistic influence on my views than the conventional materials of judicial decision which seem unduly to accentuate doctrine and legal fiction."[61] Not for him is the facile identification of "the rule of law with the law of rules" or the retreat to any other kind of sterile formalism.[62] It is just such sterility that characterizes the opinion for the Court written by Justice Black, which basically relies on an abstract civics-book approach to separation of powers while avoiding any mention of the facts of post–World War II life that might lead one either, like Vinson, to acquiesce in or, like Jackson, to be fearful of exertions of presidential power. For me, Jackson provides a magnificent, inspiring example of how a serious person wrestles with the difficult problem of preserving some notion of liberal democracy in a modern world full of horrendous threats and "emergencies" calling for vigorous response.

I ascribe almost no importance to the famous tripartite analysis that Jackson offers of presidential power, even though it appears in most casebooks—and is surely underlined by most students—as the heart of the opinion. To ask whether Congress has explicitly authorized, remained silent, or explicitly prohibited some presidential action is at best to begin analysis, certainly not to complete it. Jackson himself makes no claims at all that it provides any neat algorithm. It is an aid to reflection rather than a substitute for the ultimate duty of the judge to make a decision under almost terrifying conditions of uncertainty.

What leads me to call the opinion great is precisely the interplay of persona and analysis that is revealed—or, I suppose, constructed—by the rhetoric of the opinion. I would, incidentally, be extraordinarily disappointed to find out that Jackson did not write the opinion himself, that the signature does not, at least in the case, attest to the authorship. It is vitally important that the voice really is that of Robert Jackson, not a clerk who has been told to mimic his master's voice. Indeed, it may be that the decision of Jackson to write so much in his own voice, including reference to his autobiography, is what explains the fact that none of his colleagues joined the opinion.[63]

James Boyd White is our guide here insofar as he, more than any other contemporary writer, has emphasized the subordination of propositional argument—teachable techniques of analysis—to the mysteries of individual character in evaluating judicial handiwork.[64] I was, in the pages of the *Yale Law Journal*, critical of some of White's arguments.[65] Without recanting in toto—it is hard to imagine a world as lacking in propositional argument as White sometimes seems to suggest—I think it important to acknowledge the sense in which White is deeply correct.

There is no escaping the extent to which the rule of law in each and every truly important case—a case involving the kinds of issues that can worry serious adults—instantiates the characterological dispositions of the judges who write (or otherwise accept responsibility for) the opinions, in addition to whatever proficiency in legal grammar might be required to identify them as playing the adjudication game.

I trust Jackson's opinion in *Youngstown* because I find Jackson a person worthy of trust, even as his capacity to write such opinions as *Youngstown* or, almost a decade earlier, *West Virginia Board of Education v. Barnette* is part of the evidence of what makes him trustworthy.[66] There is an element of circularity in the argument; whether it is a vicious circle is up to the reader to decide.

This ascription of trustworthiness is, to be sure, not unqualified. I strongly disagree with Jackson's opinion in *Dennis v. United States,* which supported the shameful suppression of the civil liberties of Communists.[67] There, Jackson's experience as the primary prosecutor at the Nuremberg Tribunal, which emphasized the Nazi conspiracy, undoubtedly made him too quick to accept claims about the necessity of cracking down on American Communists. So something more is involved than identifying an author and deciding whether one generally admires him or her. That "something more" we like to call the persuasiveness of the arguments made, and requires reference to the formal structures of argument, which are not lacking in any of Jackson's opinions (or, indeed, in the opinions of any halfway-competent judge).

This latter point being conceded, I insist that it is naive to pretend that those formal structures determine persuasiveness; were that the case, one would expect *every* (competent) reader to be persuaded, although we know that wholesale conversion does not happen, as demonstrated most dramatically by dissenting judges who castigate majorities with ill-concealed contempt for their proficiency, or lack thereof, in basic legal analysis. One might resist this conclusion, saying instead that certain statements just *are* persuasive; those who disagree are, therefore, incompetent, deluded, or malicious. I rarely find this argument plausible. We must recognize that assertions that a particular opinion is persuasive often tell us as much about the commitments of the person who is persuaded as it does about the abstract qualities of the argument itself.

CODA

In thinking about opinions as rhetorical performances and about the conditions under which they are persuasive, I have been led back to the remarkable insights of Erving Goffman, who casts bright illumination on the conditions of contemporary life. In a brilliant lecture entitled, suitably enough, "The Lecture," Goffman captured what I think is the deepest aspect of our topic. Can we believe—have faith in—the possibility of nonarbitrary order in the world? To take either formal lectures or judicial opinions seriously is to resist capitulating to the fear that the world is chaotic, that it includes the particular chaos that is manifest (and seemingly uncorrectable) injustice. I therefore conclude with Goffman's own conclusion to his lecture on lecturing, although I invite the reader to substitute, as appropriate, the image of the author of the judicial opinion wherever Goffman refers to "the lecturers."

> The lecturer and the audience join in affirming a single proposition. They join in affirming that organized talking can reflect, express, delineate, portray—if not come to grips with—the real world, and that, finally, there is a real, structured, somewhat unitary world out there to comprehend. . . . And here, surely, we have the lecturer's real contract. Whatever his substantive domain, whatever his school of thought, . . . he signs the same agreement and he serves the same cause: to protect us from the wind, to stand up and seriously project the assumption that through lecturing, a meaningful part of the world can be conveyed, and that the talker can have access to a picture worth conveying.

> It is in this sense that every lecturer, merely by presuming to lecture before an audience, is a functionary of the cognitive establishment. . . .

> Those who . . . speak must claim some kind of intellectual authority in speaking, and however valid or invalid their claim to a specialized authority, their speaking presupposes and supports the notion of intellectual authority in general: that through the statements of a lecturer we can be informed about the world. Give some thought to the possibility that this shared presupposition is only that, and that after a speech, the speaker and the audience rightfully return to the flickering, cross-purposed, messy irresolution of their unknowable circumstances.[68]

Pierre N. Leval

Judicial Opinions as Literature

I am a judge. I know nothing of the theories of narrative and of literary criticism of law. I wondered why I was invited to contribute to this volume. Because we are discussing stories, it occurred to me that a clue might lie in a story—a story told in one of the greatest paintings of all time, Rembrandt's *Anatomy Lesson*. Close your eyes and pull it up on the screen of your mind's eye. Learned doctors crowd around a table in rapt attention, disputing over the body parts of a cadaver laid out in front of them. Like many paintings, this one tells a story by freezing on a single frame. One wonders what happened next. Did they all break for lunch? It has always amused me to speculate that in the next frame the corpse suddenly joins in the discussion of his parts. What reaction among the doctors? At first, of course, astonishment and wonder. But these are serious and accomplished doctors, engaged in the study of anatomy, not necromancy. After a flurry of astonishment, they refocus their attention on his limbs and organs and ignore the comments of the corpse. He is, after all, only a corpse and they are learned doctors. What has he to tell them about anatomy—even his own? This Rembrandt masterpiece led me to understand why I was invited to contribute. A judge was invited to play the role of the corpse. It is an experiment to see if, after he has spoken for four or five minutes, anyone is still listening.

I will use the occasion to object to a movement that tells judges we should consider our opinions literature and invest them with the power of literary and dramatic rhetoric. At the start, I recognize that rhetoric is inevitably present in every judicial opinion—indeed, in every episode of verbal communication. It would be impossible, even if it were desirable, to banish rhetoric from opinion writing. When I use that term in this discussion, I am referring to literary devices that quest after persuasive power or beauty.

I have no doubt that judges' opinions are a form of literature. I do not dispute that they are poorly written and capable of great improvement. I acknowledge that rhetorical skill can improve them and, in very rare instances, in the work, for example, of Hand, Holmes, and Cardozo, has done so.

You might then ask, "Where's the harm?" I suggest that the potential for harm is real and considerable. The objectives and duties of the judicial opinion are far different from those of polemics, poetry, and the narrative forms of literature; the employment of their rhetorical techniques of suggestion and evocation will more likely be at the expense of, than in the service of, the opinion's capacity to achieve its goals. Pursuit of literary techniques is more likely to undermine than to reinforce the success of the opinion in meeting its judicial obligations.

The function of the published opinion—the dynamic instrument of the common-law system—is (as a consequence of deciding the dispute between the parties) to instruct in the meaning of the rules of law, indeed, in many cases to declare rules of law. Opinions thus perform a function, which has much in common with the function of statutes.

For obvious reasons, we would be cautious in applying the rhetoric of literature to the writing of statutes. For the same reasons and others, I suggest that great caution is warranted in applying it to creating judicial opinions.

What are the essential tasks of the opinion? (1) To analyze the problem and its solution clearly and logically and (2) to state the holding clearly, with clear explanation (including recitation of pertinent facts) of the reasons supporting it. The opinion is performative, and the performance of its task depends on clear analysis and clear transmission of its message.

The suggestion is sometimes made that this is a naive fantasy, that the law has no neutral content capable of objective analysis, and that the decision of each case is merely a product of the judge or jurors' perception of their own role or status in relation to the story being told. Although I cannot argue that such a model is never operative, I would contend it is seriously exaggerated. More important, assuming that it holds some truth, each judge's duty is constantly to combat it—constantly to seek to ensure that the law is administered fairly and evenhandedly.

The deliberate adoption of rhetorical devices to strengthen the persuasive power of an opinion very likely conceals either a failure to perform the analysis or a failure to clarify the resulting rules. If an explanation is not sufficiently compelling, the reason may well be that there are flaws in the reasoning—flaws that may be masked by literary device. Rhetoric, including reliance on emotional stories, seduces the speaker, as well as the audience. Using it risks blinding judges to the merits that a thorough analysis would yield and risks tempting them to short-circuit their laborious duties. I quote Harlon Dalton's powerful statement in his essay in this volume: "When a story is well told, I park my analytic faculties."

Am I saying that this is inevitable—that literary rhetoric is incompatible with responsible decisionmaking? Of course not. I do say that judges risk sacrificing clarity of thought and expression for elegance or power.

I recognize that the problem was not created by the law and literature movement. Judges have long felt an inclination to resort to rhetorical forms of persuasion for a variety of reasons. For one, they have perceived that their opinions can be important events in public political debate. Furthermore, because courts do not command armies to enforce their decrees, persuading the people of the justice of their decisions is important to the preservation of the courts' role in government. These, I acknowledge, are valuable uses of rhetoric.

High court judges, who frequently deal with momentous issues in society, see themselves brushing up against immortality; the discussion of such weighty issues as freedom of speech and rejection of invidious discrimination invites them to spurn the vulgar tongue and use sonorous forms that will resonate in history. That sonorous rhetoric often replaces intelligent thought.

So judges employ rhetoric. Like politicians, they sense the value of the sound bite. Long, complicated sentences do not play well on Main Street. Therefore, judges, including the greatest of them, have devised quotable quips:

"[P]eople, not land or trees or pastures, vote."[1]

After saying that only "hard core" pornography is unprotected, "I shall not today attempt further to define [it] . . . ; and perhaps I could never succeed. . . . But I know it when I see it, and the motion picture involved in this case is not that."[2]

"Property does not have rights. People have rights."[3]

"The Fourteenth Amendment does not enact Mr. Herbert Spencer's *Social Statics*."[4]

We have seen, furthermore, long narrations on the history of the flag and the history of baseball (with quoted poetry and anthem), offered to seduce or entertain but immaterial to the reasons for the decision of the case, and a rhapsodic celebration of the beauty of the wilderness, with its woodpecker, coyote, bear, and lemming, making *some* legal point at the end but leaving us to guess in bewilderment what the legal point was.[5]

No doubt there are examples of admirable rhetoric. But does anyone who has studied law doubt that for every case in which impressive rhetoric strengthens the opinion we can find a thousand where a self-conscious literary device conceals shallow reasoning—where epigram substitutes for analysis?

The Holmes example that I gave—that the "Fourteenth Amendment does not enact Mr. Herbert Spencer's *Social Statics*"—is sometimes cited as a masterpiece of judicial rhetoric. It seems to me to be an aphorism that detracted from, rather than added to, the clear understanding of the question under debate (which was whether a statute regulating hours of labor was consistent with due process). If we agree with Justice Holmes that the Constitution does not enact Herbert Spencer's text, as indeed we must, where does that take us? Does that mean we should agree with his view of the case? Q.E.D.?

Justice Stewart's refusal to even try to define the boundary line that places pornography outside the protection of the First Amendment is cited with admiration in law and literature studies for its blunt candor. However beguilingly candid, it seems to me a flip abdication of duty. Even if we know that we cannot find a *logical* dividing line, a judge's obligation is to try to define the line in the best possible way. Snappy one-liners underlining the impossibility of the task may be memorable, but they are not helpful.

The proposition that rights belong to people, not to property, was completely irrelevant to whether 28 U.S.C. § 1343 gives the federal courts jurisdiction over suits involving property rights, as well as those involving personal rights, and was perhaps wrong to boot.

I offer as a counterexample Henry Friendly. I clerked for HJF. Not a quotable judge. Not a maker of aphorisms. In his near thirty years on the bench, during which he delivered authoritative guidance on virtually every subject that came under his scrutiny, I doubt that anyone can find an instance of a rhetorical device used to make an issue seem simpler, or a solution more satisfactory, than in fact it was. We may well disagree with him from time to time, but we cannot accuse him of three-card monte. His efforts to persuade were by painstaking analysis, even when it taxed the limits of the reader's endurance.

Here is an example of such an analysis of a complex problem of the *Palsgraf–Wagon Mound* type.[6]

We see no reason why an actor engaging in conduct which entails a large risk of small damage and a small risk of other and greater damage, of the same general sort, from the same forces, and to the same class of persons should be relieved of responsibility for the latter simply because the chance of its occurrence, if viewed alone, may not have been large enough to require the exercise of care. By hypothesis, the risk of the lesser harm was sufficient to render his disregard of it actionable; the existence of a less likely additional risk that the very forces against whose action he was required to guard would produce other and greater damage than could have been reasonably anticipated should inculpate him further rather than limit his liability.[7]

Dizzying? Without question. But it was not written to entertain. And there is not a superfluous or inexact word in it.

Without question, we judges have serious shortcomings as writers of opinions. There is much that professors of literature can teach us: to use simple direct language, to avoid euphemisms, and to face the facts and problems head on; to avoid relying on cant and shibboleths; to test the rules we proclaim against less congenial hypothetical facts and to avoid careless, overbroad generalizations.

But they should not tempt us to the role of the Bourgeois Gentilhomme and the discovery that we write in prose, or tell us that our opinions are literature, or try to teach us to become prose stylists. First of all, they will fail. If that were all, well enough. But it is not. In all but the rare cases, our efforts to distinguish ourselves as stylists will be at the sacrifice of the integrity of our opinions.

Have I indulged in the sins of rhetoric and overstated the case? Are there instances, especially on the docket of the Supreme Court, where rhetoric serves a valuable function? Of course.

The Supreme Court inevitably is mired in politics. At times its decisions will cause pain or hardship to a substantial segment of the population. Without doubt the Court is justified in using the crafts of language to convey its compassion for such hardship and to *sell* the importance of the reasons that make a decision necessary. Often Supreme Court cases are directly political in that they involve a clash of competing social values with no way, through logic or legal authority, to justify the decision on which of the competing values will prevail. Without question there is justification for the Court to use the power of the written word to help persuade the populace that such decisions are responsible and just.

But make no mistake. However justified, the practice is always dangerous. Such rhetoric deceives the speaker along with the audience. It should not be invoked without good reason and without redoubled care to ensure that the rhetoric is not offered in the place of sound judicial analysis.

Sic dicit mortuus.

So saith the corpse.

J. M. Balkin

A Night in the Topics:
The Reason of Legal Rhetoric
and the Rhetoric of Legal Reason

An ironic feature of the current revival of interest in rhetoric and narrative in American legal scholarship has been its relative neglect of the classical tradition of rhetoric.[1] This neglect is ironic for three reasons. First, the classical tradition of rhetoric was not understood as something foreign to law and therefore a possible subject of "interdisciplinary" study. On the contrary, the art of rhetoric was seen as organically related to the practice of law.[2] Indeed, what we would today regard as legal education was to a significant degree education in rhetoric.[3] Second, many of the problems that fuel our contemporary interest in rhetoric—the importance of pathos or emotion, the significance of personal testimony and narrative, and the role of metaphor, figure, and fiction in shaping the persuasive impact of an argument and in assisting or misleading the audience—were all subjects of intense practical and scholarly concern in the ancient world.

   Third and most important, the neglect of the classical tradition has led to a neglect of the substantive connections between rhetoric and reason. A familiar view of rhetoric holds that it is concerned primarily with style rather than substance, with persuasion rather than discovery of the better argument, with emotion rather than reason, with dazzling effect rather than rigorous analysis. Hence the dangers of rhetoric are the dangers of misplaced sentiment, fuzzy thinking, passion overbearing reason, and susceptibility to deceit and chicanery. Even the defenders of rhetoric have sometimes bought into the opposition between rhetoric and reason, assuming that the value of rhetoric and narrative lie in their ability to provide some alternative to sterile logic or to respond to some deficit in legal reasoning.

Yet those who identify rhetoric primarily with ornament, passion, specious argument, and deceit, and even those who defend rhetoric as a desirable alternative or supplement to legal reasoning, fail to do justice to the signal importance of rhetoric in the ancient world as a means for public deliberation about public issues under conditions of uncertainty. Despite Plato's famous criticisms of rhetoric as mere flattery, the ancient world well understood that rhetoric had a substantive as well as a stylistic dimension; hence, the common association of rhetoric with the merely stylistic aspects of deliberation is entirely misleading. In this chapter I want to focus on the substantive aspects of rhetoric and show how they remain central to the contemporary work of lawyers, judges, and students of the law.

RHETORIC AS THE STUDY OF INVENTION

In the classical tradition, the study of rhetoric was composed of five canons, each involving the mastery of a particular skill. Given the epithets usually hurled at rhetoric, one might think that the first canon would be the development of style, but this is not so. The first canon of rhetoric is invention (*inventione* in Latin, *heurisis* in Greek).[4] The skill of invention is concerned with discovering and formulating arguments on any subject, opinions on the resolution of any problem, or reasons for or against any proposed course of action. Thus, despite the usual associations between rhetoric and ornament, the art of invention is inherently a substantive art. Moreover it is essentially pragmatic in orientation, because it is directed to the solution of difficulties placed before the student.

The primacy of the skill of invention in the canons of rhetoric makes perfect sense. Before engaging in stylistic flourishes, one must have arguments upon which to hang them. To say something well, one must first have something to say. Indeed, having something to say is often the most difficult task that faces any orator or deliberator, whether ancient or modern.

Classical rhetoricians approached the problem of invention through the use of *topoi,* or "topics." Topics are things to talk about. The Greek word *topos* literally means "place." The spatial metaphor of place has a number of interlocking meanings and evocations. First, topics are places from which one can argue. Second, topics are "commonplaces," that is, concepts, subjects, or maxims that are widely shared in the culture or are associated with the wisdom that has been distilled into common sense. Third, topics are like pigeonholes or boxes into which situations and events can be placed, that is, located, categorized, and organized in their proper places. Fourth, Aristotle suggested that topics correspond to places in the mind from which different arguments might be fetched.[5] Finally, just as things appear different from different places, one can think of topics as a perspective or as a way of looking at things.[6]

The point of identifying topics, making lists of them, and committing them to memory was to have at one's immediate disposal a checklist of things to talk about no matter what subject one was presented with and no matter what problem of analysis one faced. Thus, a frequent practice of rhetoricians was the composition and organization of catalogs of topics, which could be memorized and employed by the student. In theory, one could mechanically employ a catalog of topics like a checklist to solve a problem or form an opinion, but in practice, the student of rhetoric hoped to internalize the different topics so that they became like second nature.

Let me give a simple example of how one might use the classical topoi. An example of a topic is "part and whole." Suppose one is asked to give a speech about a particular subject, say, elephants. One can apply the topic to this subject in several ways. First, one can discuss the various parts of an elephant and their relation to the whole. Conversely, one can discuss the relation of the elephant to the larger units of which it might form a part: a herd of elephants, the species of elephants, the category of all mammals, the class of all animals, and so on indefinitely. Although this particular topic does not produce very elaborate arguments, it may act as a spur to further invention, and it does give the speaker a number of directions in which to improvise and analyze. And this is the whole point of the topical approach: to use topics to spur imagination and organize analysis. A contemporary version of this technique is the journalist's injunction to ask "who, what, when, where, why, and how" in composing a story.

The topic of part and whole is so general and abstract that it can apply to almost any subject matter. Aristotle called such topics "general topics." He distinguished them from "special topics," which were relevant to a particular subject matter, a specific body of knowledge, or a professional practice.[7] Medicine has special topics, as does law. Indeed, as we will see presently, any theoretical enterprise tends to develop its own set of special topics as soon as it creates its own set of distinctive concepts and approaches. Metaphorically speaking, special topics have more meat on their bones than do general topics: they tend to direct analysis and argument more clearly, and they tend to have more substantive consequences. The trade-off is that they are relevant to many fewer types of problems and situations.

Aristotle wrote a famous treatise on topics in which he tried to give a systematic philosophical discussion of what he regarded as the essential general topics. Unfortunately, Aristotle's *Topics* is pitched at such a high level of abstraction that it is virtually useless for an advocate. By contrast, Cicero wrote his *Topics* and his earlier treatise *De inventione* for the benefit of advocates. Not surprisingly, many of Cicero's topics—as well as his examples—intersect with the legal categories of his time. This connection is not accidental; indeed, it is exemplary of the important connections between the topical approach and the demands of legal practice. Cicero's goal in providing a topic catalog was to enable an advocate to do two things. The first was to analyze a factual situation as a legal problem; the second was to devise arguments for interpreting the law and applying it to a case in one way rather than another.

These tasks have been the bread and butter of lawyers' work from Cicero's day to our own. Thus, it is not surprising that when scholars like Chaim Perelman in Belgium and Theodor Viehweg in Germany sought to revive the classical tradition in rhetoric, they focused on the canon of invention and, in particular, on the topics.[8] For example, large parts of Perelman's *New Rhetoric* read very much like an old-fashioned topic catalog.[9] Viehweg and his followers in the Mainz school made a name for themselves by insisting that legal analysis is a form of topical reasoning.[10] Viehweg's argument was especially controversial in Germany, because the civil code creates the appearance of a systematic, deductive structure. In fact, Viehweg's point is much easier to see in a common-law jurisdiction like the United States, in which the topical structure of argument is laid bare in the development of doctrine through precedent.[11]

Like these scholars, I also believe that there is a deep connection between legal reasoning and rhetoric, and I also believe that the key to understanding this connection lies in an understanding of how topics assist the reasoning process.

Topics are heuristics; they provide a roadmap, or starting point, for the discussion of problems and the resolution of difficulties. They are both a method of problem recognition and a means of problem solution. Invention uses topics to identify and analyze difficulties placed before an actor.[12] Hence invention and topical reasoning are essentially pragmatic in nature, for they are directed to the solving of problems about what to do.

When one is stuck for something to say, one turns to a catalog of arguments or approaches. When one wants to know how to solve a problem, one turns to a checklist or a troubleshooting guide. The catalog of arguments and the troubleshooting guide are both examples of topical reasoning: they offer a ready-made path to pursue, a place from which to begin one's investigations. Although they do not predetermine the result of the investigation, they shape the nature of the inquiry, just as the place from which one begins a journey shapes the subsequent development of the journey.

Put more generally, people attempting to solve a problem need a preexisting framework to get started. They need a way of characterizing a problem and a way of approaching the problem once it is identified. The most convenient way to do this is through a set of intellectual tools that can be readily adapted to a number of problems and that lie readily to hand. The need for preexisting tools and frameworks does not undermine the creativity of the process but informs and enables it, in the same way that all invention and improvisation require materials to build on. In like fashion, topics undergird invention and discovery; they are commonly shared tools of understanding (hence "commonplaces") that simultaneously frame problems and assist in their solution.

No tool is perfect for all occasions, and sometimes the intellectual tools one is bequeathed may be only awkwardly adapted to the problem at hand. Indeed, because intellectual tools are used both for solving a problem and for recognizing that a problem exists in the first place, a badly adapted or limited set of topics may lead one to overlook important features of a situation, just as a troubleshooting checklist that is too brief may lead one to miss the most important problem that needs to be resolved. Thus, the value of a system of topics lies in their comprehensiveness and adaptability, as well as their being ready to hand.

We can think about much of the work of legal analysis by judges, lawyers, and students of law as a kind of problem solving.[13] When I say that the work of legal reasoning is problem solving, I do not merely mean the solution of intellectual puzzles. After all, trying to decide on the right thing to do, the most persuasive argument before a tribunal, or the proper advice to offer a client is also a quest for a solution to a difficulty. In any case, the idea of lawyers as problem solvers is a familiar one. Lawyers analyze legal problems, form legal opinions, interpret statutes, reconcile and distinguish cases, offer policy justifications for doctrines, predict the actions of legal decisionmakers, advise clients, and develop persuasive arguments for legal positions. These different activities, these different forms of problem solving, are not in all respects identical, but they are interrelated. For example, when we try to justify a particular rule of law to another person, we must find arguments that justify it, and to do this we ourselves must analyze the situation and determine the most plausible arguments for and against the position that we are taking. So the tasks of persuasion and analysis go hand in hand. One should also note that the tasks of legal analysis for the advocate, the judge, and the law student may differ because of their differing roles and purposes. Nevertheless, those tasks, too are interrelated.

When we think about what lawyers and judges do as the identification and solution of problems, we begin to see how lawyers actually use topics and topical styles of reasoning in many different aspects of their work, how topics help lawyers, judges, and law students perform the various tasks of legal analysis and argument.

To vary Holmes's famous maxim, we begin to see that the life of law has not been logic—it has been problem solving.

At the same time, this highly pragmatic description of legal reasoning is fully consistent with the techniques of deduction and logical inference. Deduction is an important feature of legal reasoning, but deduction is always in need of premises. Invention is the means by which premises can be produced so that deduction can proceed. Deduction is formal, and form is always in need of substance. Topics help provide that substance. Thus, topical reasoning is not necessarily opposed to deductive reasoning; it is often its aid and ally.

USING TOPICS IN LEGAL ANALYSIS

To show how topics work in legal analysis, I am going to draw a connection between what I am calling topical argument and an area of legal theory that has come to be known as legal semiotics. As its name implies, legal semiotics is the study of the law as a system of signs and methods of signification. The variety of legal semiotics that I am concerned with, however, is generally associated with the American critical legal studies movement and the newly emerging category of postmodern jurisprudence. It studies and classifies the recurring forms of argument used to justify legal doctrines. The practice of justification involves two interrelated tasks. The first is offering arguments for why the law should adopt one rule rather than another. The second is discovering policy justifications that underlie existing legal rules and arguing for extensions or applications of these rules on the grounds that they are most consistent with the principles and policies undergirding the law.[14] Legal semioticians like Duncan Kennedy, Jeremy Paul, Jamie Boyle, and myself argue that lawyers tend to justify legal positions in terms of recurring categories of arguments.[15] Moreover, there are standard pro and con responses for each form of argument that can be applied repeatedly in many different doctrinal settings.

In tort law, for example, a standard defendant's argument is "No liability without fault." A standard plaintiff's rejoinder is "As between two innocents, let the person who caused the damage pay."[16] In this case, the defendant talks about fault, while the plaintiff emphasizes causal responsibility. But the plaintiff can also argue that the defendant was at fault ("One who is at fault should be liable"), and the defendant can also deny causal responsibility ("No liability without causation"). Thus, there are fault-based and causation-based arguments for both sides. These stereotypical arguments recur constantly in tort law; indeed, they normally appear whenever a choice between two possible rules would change a tort defendant's responsibility (or potential liability) toward a plaintiff.

Consider the famous case of *Vosburg v. Putney,* in which the defendant, a young schoolboy, playfully kicked his classmate in the leg.[17] Because of a preexisting condition the plaintiff unexpectedly developed a serious disease in the leg that eventually resulted in his becoming permanently disabled. The issue before the court was whether the defendant had to pay all of the damages caused by the kick, no matter how unforeseeable, or only those reasonably foreseeable from the defendant's perspective. This is a classic situation in which the rule of law chosen affects the defendant's potential responsibility toward the plaintiff, hence the standard tort law arguments apply.

The defendant might make the following arguments (among many others).

1. The defendant gave the plaintiff a harmless kick on the leg. He did nothing wrong, or if he did some wrong, it was completely out of proportion to the damages that resulted. It is unjust to impose enormous and burdensome damages on the defendant because of an unforeseeable freak accident. (No liability without fault.)
2. Moreover, the real cause of the unfortunate accident was the plaintiff's preexisting condition. (No liability without causation.)

The plaintiff can respond in kind.

1. The defendant kicked the plaintiff without his consent and therefore acted wrongfully. (One who is at fault should be liable.)
2. Moreover, even if the defendant was without moral fault, the plaintiff was also entirely innocent. The plaintiff was no less injured because the defendant meant no harm. Someone must bear the loss from this accident, and it is better that the loss fall on the person who occasioned it. (As between two innocents, let the person who caused the damage pay.)

In this example I have arranged the plaintiff's and defendant's arguments so that they directly respond to each other. The plaintiff argues fault, the defendant denies fault. The defendant denies casual responsibility, the plaintiff asserts it. In real life, of course, the plaintiff might respond by changing the subject. When the defendant pleads lack of fault, the plaintiff might assert the defendant's causal responsibility, or the plaintiff's rights, or the bad consequences that would flow from the defendant's proposed rule, and so on, because the defendant's fault-based argument might be more plausible than any fault-based argument that the plaintiff can think of. Thus, each type of argument is formally available to both sides, but not all formally available arguments within the rhetorical system are equally strong or equally plausible.

With sufficient time and patience, one can go through the whole of tort law and catalog the various kinds of policy arguments that lawyers and legal academics make, showing the typical pro and con responses made by plaintiffs' and defendants' counsel. I have done this for a number of fields of law (tort, contract, criminal law).[18] This collection of recurring argument forms has considerable practical significance for lawyers as well as students of the law. If students know the basic forms of policy argument, they can apply them to virtually any tort law issue that comes before them. Moreover, if they are asked to defend or justify a particular rule of law, they have at their fingertips a list of available arguments of justification that can be invoked at a moment's notice. Finally, because they can generate an opponent's likely arguments as well as their own, they can more easily generate counterarguments and fine-tune their original claims for maximum force and plausibility. After teaching the law of torts in this fashion for over a decade, I can report that all of these benefits do accrue to law students when they learn to master the recurring forms of legal justification.

The point I wish to emphasize here, however, should by now be obvious from the description of legal semiotics just offered. *The recurring forms of argument that are the subject of legal semiotics are topics in the classical sense.* The plaintiff's argument that one who is at fault should pay and the defendant's rejoinder that there should be no liability without fault are two opposed versions of the same basic topic, which is fault. Similarly, causal responsibility, harm, action (versus inaction), and intention are all topics relevant to tort law issues. Each topic gives both the plaintiff and the defendant something to talk about, a starting point for analysis of the situation. Each is a source for the invention of new arguments. Each can give rise to subtopics—for instance, the idea of foreseeability as an articulation of the concept of fault. Finally, each can be combined with other topics to produce increasingly complicated and sophisticated forms of argument.

Legal semiotics has generally been concerned with one of the central tasks of legal analysis and argument—the justification and application of legal doctrines. But my point is more general: what is true of the work of justification is also true of other tasks of legal analysis. We can find topics and topical reasoning employed in other kinds of legal reasoning and legal problem solving.

Take, for example, the interpretation of statutes. It is not accidental that Duncan Kennedy's original formulation of legal semiotics was inspired by Karl Llewellyn's famous article on statutory construction.[19] Llewellyn listed many of the familiar canons of statutory construction and showed how they could be lined up in pro and con fashion. For each canon of interpretation, Llewellyn argued, there was a contrasting canon that argued in the opposite direction. Llewellyn's argument has often been viewed as showing the indeterminacy and hence uselessness of reasoning by canons. But a better interpretation of what Llewellyn demonstrated can be stated in terms of topics.

Canons of statutory interpretation are topics for discussion of the meaning of statutes and their reconciliation with other statutes (including the Constitution). Canons of interpretation are starting points, like a troubleshooter's checklist, that give the interpreter a way in to the discussion of statutory and constitutional problems.[20] Like the topic of fault in tort law, canons of interpretation are necessarily general and cannot determine the scope of their own extension. Nor can they be dispositive in every case, even though they may be persuasive in any particular case. Indeed, the problems for canons of interpretation arise precisely when too much is demanded of them. It is at that point that they produce a sterile formalism that inhibits imagination rather than stimulates it. If we begin to think of canons of interpretation as heuristics rather than formulas, as methods of getting started in the discussion of problems rather than solutions in themselves, we will better understand both their usefulness for generations of lawyers and their inherent limitations.

Precedental argument also makes use of topics, but in a slightly different way. To begin with, there are familiar techniques of doctrinal manipulation, which Llewellyn also cataloged in his *Common Law Tradition*.[21] With a little practice, one can learn the relatively standard ways in which lawyers distinguish and connect cases, broaden and narrow precedents, distinguish and construct lines of authority. These techniques become second nature to lawyers, and Llewellyn merely took it upon himself to categorize and classify the techniques that he found in the common law. Thus, the common-law tradition of which Llewellyn spoke is not simply a tradition of precedents; it is a tradition of intellectual tools and approaches that can be brought to bear on legal problems even as they help to construct the very nature of these problems. Lawyers sometimes call these techniques "craft." Whatever term we use to describe it, this craft consists in significant part in the use and mastery of topics whose very existence helps constitute our shared legal culture.

The various techniques of precedental manipulation can form a topic catalog of their own. Yet topics are already built into the structure of precedents. Doctrinal categories and distinctions are topics woven into the fabric of the law.

As I noted previously, topics are places; they are places where one can place things. They are intellectual pigeonholes for the organization of experience. Legal doctrines and distinctions are also pigeonholes of this kind. Legal doctrines constitute laws, but for this reason they simultaneously become a template for the organization of legal experience and a framework for the discussion of legal problems. Thus, legal doctrine has a dual nature, both as authority and as topos. Because legal doctrines and distinctions are backed by the authority of the state, they help constitute what a legal problem is in a given legal culture.

The structure of the law school exam provides an excellent example of the topical nature of legal doctrines. Most law school exams are organized around the skill of issue spotting. Students are presented with an elaborate factual situation; they are then asked to discuss the probable legal consequences of the hypothetical and the best legal arguments on both sides. The exam is, of course, a quintessential exercise in problem solving. It requires students to recognize a factual situation as a legal problem and argue for the best application of legal categories. Yet students cannot do this unless they understand the basic doctrinal pigeonholes relevant to the problem. They must have ready to hand a set of distinctions and a framework of doctrines that allow them to characterize the problem and set in motion their discussion of the legal consequences.

A student's legal analysis has three interrelated components. First, it involves pattern and problem recognition. Second, it demands arguments about the best match between different possible patterns and the facts at hand. Third, it requires a reinterpretation and redescription of the facts in light of the available doctrinal pigeonholes. Law students work with legal materials backed up by the authority of the state, but this does not change the fundamentally problem-solving nature of their task. On the contrary, it is precisely the authoritative nature of the materials that determines the kind of problem being set before them.

In sum, the topical structure of law is built into its nature as law. Every doctrinal category or distinction can function as a special topic for the formulation and discussion of legal problems. What looks like the development of doctrine from one perspective can be seen as the use of topics from another. We can redescribe the techniques of precedental manipulation, reconciliation, subordination, distinction, and exclusion in this light. Precedental argument involves the use of preexisting topics or the creation of new ones. For example, a new topic is created when a salient factual difference is made the basis for a doctrinal distinction that will control the application of the law in succeeding cases. More generally, whenever law creates a new distinction or a new category, it also creates a new topic for the analysis and resolution of legal problems.

I am not arguing that the legal categories we find in statutes and legal decisions are nothing more than rhetorical topics. I am merely pointing out that they can and do function as topics. Conversely, I am not arguing that doctrinal categories and distinctions are the only topics involved in legal analysis and reasoning. Many scholars argue that principles and policies underlying legal doctrines should be considered part of legal analysis and reasoning even if they are not explicitly codified in doctrinal materials. These principles and policies are the particular concern of legal semiotics. As the previous discussion of legal semiotics shows, these principles and policies are organized into recurring forms of argument that also function as topics. So the claim that legal reasoning has a topical structure is entirely consistent with an expansive view about the materials of the law that includes not only statutes and legal decisions but also principles and policies.[22]

STUDYING LEGAL CULTURE THROUGH THE TOPICS

Why should we be interested in topics today? There are at least three different sets of reasons: practical, sociological, and critical.

First, thinking about law in terms of topics has practical value for both lawyers and law students. Obviously, learning doctrine involves learning the topics contained within it. However, it is equally useful to understand and recognize the recurring forms of policy argument. Knowing the standard forms of legal justification helps advocates to discover new arguments and to frame existing ones more persuasively, particularly because they can figure out what arguments an opponent is likely to make. Moreover, knowing the common topics of justification not only helps advocates to justify existing legal doctrines and persuasively argue for their proper extension and application but also enables advocates to criticize legal doctrines. Recognizing that legal doctrines have recurring forms of justification helps lawyers to discover hitherto-unacknowledged tensions between the justifications for existing doctrines in the same area of law or in different areas. Practicing this skill can sharpen lawyers' critical faculties, stimulate legal creativity, and advance the critical refinement of legal doctrines.

Because of its practical advantages, the systematic study of the topics of legal justification is an excellent way to approach the study of law and can easily form part of the first-year curriculum. I have taught my first-year torts classes in precisely this way. I require students both to master doctrine and to recognize and practice recurring policy arguments in order to discuss and debate problems in the law of accidents. The study of the law through topics was an important part of legal education in antiquity, and perhaps it could be so again.

Second, the study of legal topics is the study of legal culture. Recall that one of the meanings of the word "topoi" was "commonplaces." The study of topics is the study of the commonplaces that bind together a practice of reasoned argument. It is the study of a shared social practice of argumentation and thus the study of a shared form of social life. Legal topics are shared tools of understanding that characterize legal practice. Some legal topics are shared because they involve categories and distinctions woven into the fabric of positive law that has binding force on a community. Other topics—for example, those that concern underlying legal justifications—are shared by the members of a community whether or not they are explicitly written into positive law. The recurring topics of policy justification—

like fault, causal responsibility, and efficiency—show the fundamental acceptance within the legal community (and the larger community outside it) of certain basic ideas through which disputes will be framed and debated.

As common tools of legal understanding, topics offer us a glimpse into the background assumptions that we share in understanding and dealing with legal problems. We can study changes in legal culture by noting the entry of new topics into legal discourse. We can tell that our background culture is changing when the topics we use to formulate and discuss legal problems change. A good example is the rise of economic analysis in the legal academy. Many law professors now routinely employ such concepts as efficiency maximization, the Coase theorem, transaction costs, and agency problems. These concepts, borrowed from economics, become new topics for the framing, recognition, and discussion of legal problems. Other interdisciplinary movements, such as critical legal studies, feminism, and critical race theory, have also introduced new ways of thinking about law and, with them, new topics.[23] These new frameworks for problem solving have led in turn to the recognition of problems not previously recognized as such. Thus, we can think of each new jurisprudential movement as an attempt to inscribe new rhetorics and new topics into the language of law and legal justification.

It may seem surprising at first to think about law and economics as a body of topics. But any systematic body of study, including social science, will necessarily develop its own set of special topics and thus produce its own substantive rhetorical categories. The fact that these concepts may act as rhetorical topics in no way undermines their usefulness. To the contrary, it is precisely because they are useful for framing and solving many different kinds of problems that they function as topics. Once again we must free ourselves from the pernicious confusion of rhetoric with mere style or deception. Rhetoric, in the form of topics, undergirds the substantive reason of the law.

If a legal culture is defined by its characteristic topics, then different legal cultures may be distinguished by differences in their commonplaces for argument. For example, the self-conscious adoption of sophisticated economic concepts has occurred much more slowly and in more limited or specialized areas in legal practice than in the world of the legal academy. The increasing divergence in the topics employed in legal practice and in the legal academy is yet another a sign of the increasing divergence between these two subparts of legal culture.

Finally, in addition to practical and sociological reasons, we should study the topics for critical reasons. Focusing our attention on recurring topics in legal discourse helps us critically examine the ways we talk about and hence think about legal problems.

To begin with, we can study the kinds of arguments that people with different interests or social positions tend to make and the different ways they tend to characterize situations and evaluate them. For example, we can compare how causal responsibility is characterized in products liability cases as opposed to cases involving freedom of speech.[24] We can examine how members of different political and social groups tend to frame questions of benefit and burden, equal or differential treatment, fault, causal nexus, or personal responsibility. Much critical race theory and feminist legal theory has been implicitly concerned with these questions.[25]

We can also study how the tools of understanding we use to frame and discuss legal questions might limit the way we understand and evaluate the social world. As heuristics for analysis, topics both empower and limit our legal imaginations. Just as no tool is equally good for every purpose, no set of topics is equally useful for recognizing and addressing all problems. Confining ourselves to one set of topics may lead to an impoverished conception of the situation, which serves the interests of neither truth nor justice. When we are limited in the topics we employ, we limit not only our legal imaginations but our ability to recognize our own limitations. As the old saying goes, When all that you have is a hammer, everything starts to look like a nail.

To be critical about legal topics, we need to play various topical approaches off against each other; for example, we might play off the language of efficiency and transaction cost reduction against the language of moral responsibility and desert. That is because we can often see the limitations of topics only by means of other topics that we bring to bear. A critical approach to legal topics also suggests the continual need to borrow new topics from areas of social life outside legal discourse. In fact, we do this all the time: we constantly borrow topics from other areas of life and fashion them to the needs of legal problems. And when we import these topics, we also subtly change the nature of legal argument and legal analysis. Thus, the critical approach to the study of topics reminds us that the boundary between legal topics and other topics is always permeable, even if at any point in time there are some special topics that are distinctly legal.

Like any other form of ideological analysis, the critical study of topics is potentially self-referential. It involves recognizing limitations and problems in the legal discourse we are studying. Yet the discourse in which we examine legal discourse can also be understood in terms of its own recurring topics, its own distinctive modes of problem recognition and solution. The ways we classify and criticize existing topics may therefore have their own limitations. So when we study the rhetoric of the law critically, we do not abandon topics or escape rhetoric. We do not finally engage in some more authentic or pure form of discourse that cannot itself be studied and criticized rhetorically. Nevertheless, this recognition does not make the task of critical analysis or critical reflection impossible. It merely helps us to see the conditions under which it occurs. This brings me back to my central theme: the use of the rhetorical art of invention is not a hindrance to reason but part of its modus operandi.

Topics are key elements in any pragmatic—that is, action oriented—approach to knowledge. I believe, in fact, that there are deep connections between a topical approach to legal reasoning and the recent revival of legal pragmatism, although I cannot discuss the matter fully here. What I do hope to have shown is how rhetorical invention through topics is fully integrated into the substantive reason of the law. The familiar opposition between rhetoric and reason misunderstands their appropriate relation, for rhetoric does not take the reason of the law on holiday, but to its true home in the topics.

Reva B. Siegel

In the Eyes of the Law: Reflections on the Authority of Legal Discourse

How do judicial opinions gain their authority? Sanford Levinson invites us to consider the following paradox: judicial opinions gain authority by persuasion *and* by force. To illustrate this dynamic, Levinson directs our attention to certain distinguishing features of the judicial opinion.

To begin with, the authority of the judicial opinion flows from the ascribed authority of its author. Only judges who have been duly appointed can write opinions that bind litigants before them. As important, a judge's opinion functions as precedent that controls the decisions of "inferior courts" (by exercise of "vertical" authority) as well as future decisions of the judge and the judge's successors (by exercise of "horizontal" authority).[1] Considered from this standpoint, the judge's exercise of authority bears much in common with the exercise of brute force. It operates on the model of command and control, like a sovereign ordering us to do something we wouldn't otherwise do by the light of our reason. Thus, the judge of an appellate court is bound to follow the law as interpreted by the Supreme Court, even if she would interpret it differently. And, under doctrines of *stare decisis,* the Supreme Court is bound to follow its own precedent, even if the Court would decide the question differently if presented with it as an issue of first impression.

Levinson draws our attention to these features of the legal system precisely because they are at odds with conventional assumptions about the legal system. We do not ordinarily view the rule of law as a system of command and control. Nor would it be wholly accurate to do so. In diverse ways, law draws its authority from the gentler forces of reason. Judges do not merely issue orders; they write opinions giving reasons to justify their orders. Indeed, much of the rhetoric of the judicial opinion is designed to persuade the reader that the opinion does not merely reflect the judge's personal opinion or wishes but is instead a faithful account of "what the law requires." In this society, we say that we live under a government of laws, not men; we *expect* judges to write opinions that will persuade us, time and again, that this is so. And judges oblige us. Given our legal culture, this rhetorical strategy makes sense. Judges do not have forces at their disposal to enforce the orders they give; they must persuade those whom they would order to comply.

Thus, Levinson argues, judicial opinions derive their power from two kinds of authority. Judicial opinions have authority both because they command and because they persuade. While this framework casts light on some distinguishing features of the judicial opinion, I would like to consider certain features of the framework itself. Levinson counterposes authority-as-command and authority-as-persuasion, brute force and reason, as antithetical social phenomena. But much current critical theory—often loosely dubbed postmodernist—suggests that power and knowledge are mutually constitutive.[2] Considered from this vantage point, power and knowledge may be intimately intertwined, working to reinforce each other in ways that easily escape notice.

This essay will explore some ways in which judicial opinions exert authority that do not conform to the dichotomous understanding of power and knowledge on which Levinson's account rests. As I will show, we are not always conscious of how legal discourse exerts authority in our lives, for the simple reason that we understand important aspects of our social universe through the language of the law. Because the language of the law structures fundamental aspects of our social experience, it plays a more pervasive and less perceptible role in ordering social relationships than Levinson suggests.

We might begin our analysis of legal discourse with John Hollander's observation that "poetry, theology, and law all involve systems of tropes." In a striking passage of his essay, Hollander invites us to consider the following proposition. An act, for example, sodomy, performed in state A may be a crime when it is performed in state B because "the act will enter a web of metaphors called statutes. . . . Literally, it would be the same act; only figuratively—its commission has been interdicted and metaphorically designated a crime—is it different."[3]

In this account, the law operates upon a substratum of "literal" or physical reality, adding figurative meaning to it; thus, in Hollander's example, the language of the law ensnares a simple physical act and transforms it into a "crime." But the language of the law plays a greater role in structuring social experience than this account suggests. *Many of the acts law regulates do not exist apart from the language that defines them.* Consider the example of rape: the physical act of sexual penetration is a rape only in circumstances where there is no "consent." As we attempt to determine whether A has injured B, we sometimes ask whether A reasonably believes that B "consented," or, in other circumstances, what A "intended" to do to B, or, in yet other circumstances, whether A proximately "caused" B's predicament or took B's "property." It is through tropes such as consent, intent, causation, and property that we define certain physical acts as legally cognizable injuries. Such tropes play an important role in deliberations about how the law should respond to some event that has happened. But often "what happens" occurs in a domain of social meaning inseparable from language itself. Was the man denied a job because of his qualifications or because of race? Was an invitation to participate in this conference distributed on the basis of qualifications or race? In this society the distinction matters terribly. Yet in such cases can we determine what happened outside language? The language of the law mediates our understanding of social relationships: a boss may grope his secretary; her capacity to utter the words "sexual harassment" pushes back.

Sometimes law is self-conscious about its own lingual resources and the power to order social relations they entail, as in the case of tropes it denominates legal fictions. Under the Fourteenth Amendment, a corporation is a "person" but the unborn are not. The personhood of corporations is a clear case of a legal fiction, but what about *Roe v. Wade*'s declaration that "the word 'person,' as used in the Fourteenth Amendment, does not include the unborn"?[4] When we say that "the state has an interest in protecting potential life" is this just a fancy way of saying that the state has an interest in compelling women who are resisting motherhood to bring a pregnancy to term? Most would immediately reply that the state's interest in protecting potential life has nothing to do with making pregnant women act like good mothers should. Does *that* make the state's interest in protecting potential life a legal fiction?[5] Consider another example. The doctrine of marital unity is classically understood as a legal fiction, to wit: "In the eyes of the law, husband and wife are one."[6] Today, by contrast, courts construing common law and the Constitution tell us that husband and wife are "equal" in the eyes of the law.[7] What does it mean to say that husband and wife are equal in the eyes of the law? Is this relationship also a legal fiction? Along similar lines, we might ask: How do we know when we are in the "private sphere"—the place where work and battery are regulated, not as work or battery, but as love? Are husband and wife equal in the eyes of the law *there*?

While it is conventionally assumed that the category of legal fictions is sparsely populated by a few quaint counterfactuals, it seems instead that the category of legal fictions is quite large—the figural terrain on which we fight some of the major social conflicts of our day.

Owen Fiss recently offered me an ad hoc definition of a legal fiction as something that can't possibly be true.[8] But this definition does little to restrict the class of assertions that might count as legal fictions. For by what criterion of truth are we to test claims about social meaning of the sort law is always making? When we are discussing assertions about consent, intent, causation, property, personhood, the structure of marriage, or the scope of the private sphere, correspondence with empirical reality is not sufficient—and coherence theories of truth do not lift us out of the domain of the figural. "Legal fiction" may itself be a figure of speech that naturalizes the rich variety of ways that the language of the law constructs the social world we inhabit.

From this standpoint, it is easier to appreciate some of the more subtle ways in which the language of the law exerts authority. Tropes such as property, personhood, marriage, equality, and privacy structure important dimensions of our social experience, both individual and collective. In this conceptual field, where social facts are inseparable from social values, where the descriptive is entangled with the normative, and knowledge is entwined with power, the language of the law organizes social relationships, exerting authority in ways that often escape our notice.

To explore one instance of this dynamic, we might consider how the concept of citizenship shapes understandings of race relations in the United States. In the aftermath of the Civil War, when the Supreme Court upheld Jim Crow laws in *Plessy v. Ferguson,* Justice Harlan wrote a dissenting opinion arguing that the Constitution does not distinguish citizens by race.[9] A passage in that dissent has since become orthodoxy on the question:

> The white race deems itself to be the dominant race in this country. And so it is, in prestige, in achievements, in education, in wealth and power. So, I doubt not, will it continue to be for all time, if it remains true to its great heritage and holds fast to the principles of constitutional liberty. *But in the view of the Constitution, in the eye of the law, there is in this country no superior, dominant, ruling class of citizens. There is no caste here. Our Constitution is color-blind, and neither knows nor tolerates classes among citizens.* In respect of civil rights, all citizens are equal before the law. The humblest is the peer of the most powerful. The law regards man as man, and takes no account of his surroundings or of his color when his civil rights as guaranteed by the supreme law of the land are involved.[10]

Let us consider the familiar language of Justice Harlan's dissent a bit more closely. What or where is "in the eye of the law"—the social standpoint from which it can be claimed that "there is in this country no superior, dominant, ruling class of citizens"? Was this proposition a legal fiction in 1896? Is it in 1995? Quite plainly, in 1896 Justice Harlan was advancing a counterfactual—a vision of the Constitution at odds with the regime of apartheid upheld in *Plessy*. But the color-blind constitution that Harlan exhorted his Brethren to embrace was counterfactual in yet a deeper sense: Harlan argued that law should refuse to recognize the regime of racial caste that in fact prevailed in American society. He advocated a radical separation in legal and social discourses about race as the foundational feature of a postslavery jurisprudence. Harlan did not suggest that adopting a color-blind constitutional regime would cause social relationships to evolve toward the norm espoused by law and so lead to a classless society. To the contrary, when Harlan asserted that "[o]ur Constitution is color-blind," he was proposing that law blind itself to the *continuing* racial stratification of American society, assuring his readers that the white race "is [and] will . . . continue to be for all time" the "dominant race in this country, . . . in prestige, in achievement, in education, in wealth and in power."

In 1896, Justice Harlan argued that the nation should disestablish racial hierarchy in formal political discourse, but not in social fact. To accomplish this, he proposed a new mode of talking about citizenship centered on the trope of color blindness. Considered from this vantage point, the trope of color blindness is of ambiguous political valence: although Harlan advanced the discourse of color blindness as a basis for criticizing the regime of segregation upheld in *Plessy,* he also demonstrated how the discourse of color blindness might be used to legitimate diverse manifestations of racial hierarchy in American society. As Harlan explained it, by modifying the rule structure and rhetoric of citizenship, the nation could repudiate a regime of racial caste *in the eyes of the law* while continuing a regime of racial caste in social fact.

What is the sociopolitical logic of color-blindness talk today? When I read Justice Harlan's dissent with my first-year constitutional law class, the group unanimously endorsed it as a correct understanding of the equal protection clause but immediately divided over its meaning. Few students were willing to read Harlan too "literally." Surely, they argued, when Justice Harlan endorsed color blindness, he advocated legal formalism in the service of social change. Yet scarcely anyone in the class had the patience to consider whether color-blind constitutionalism in fact promoted the elimination of racial caste. Instead, as properly socialized members of our legal culture, the students predictably launched into a debate over affirmative action. For them, the discourse of color blindness was *about* affirmative action.[11]

But how, we might ask ourselves, has this passage in a dissenting opinion from the late nineteenth century come to have such specialized racial meaning today—central in the disposition of the Court's most recent affirmative action case[12]—while seemingly irrelevant to the welfare reform debate prompted by the proposed Personal Responsibility Act of 1995?[13] In the decades after World War II, the color-blindness trope was invoked for the purpose of disestablishing a regime of caste. Today, by a process that Jack Balkin has termed ideological drift, its redistributive valence has switched, and it is invoked as a *constraint* on caste-disestablishing reform with equal moral fervor (along with civil rights idiom like "quotas" and "special rights").[14] But this is not all. The color-blindness trope invites us to scrutinize affirmative action while allowing the race talk of the Personal Responsibility Act to proceed with impunity, if not equal moral fervor:[15] today one can ardently endorse color blindness while heartily denouncing the "lazy welfare queen." In short, the ascendancy of the color-blindness trope marks a shift in the rule structure and justificatory discourse of racial status. In 1995 it is no longer constitutionally acceptable to distribute entitlements explicitly by race, but it is acceptable to distribute entitlements by racially coded norms.[16] "Welfare" is one of those racially coded norms.[17] This is the thinly veiled racial text of current political orthodoxy, which calls for imposing deep cuts in "welfare" while protecting social security payments and the deduction for home mortgages.

To repeat my question: Just where is "in the eye of the law"—the social standpoint from which it can be claimed that *"there is in this country no superior, dominant, ruling class of citizens. . . . Our Constitution is color-blind"*? As we have seen, the discourse of color blindness today supports an explosive conversation about race, about protecting the entitlements of white citizens from redistribution to people of color.[18] Contemporary proponents of color blindness can advance their arguments against racial redistribution with all the moral fervor of the crusade against Jim Crow and with considerably less candor than Justice Harlan, who at least was forthright about the regime of racial stratification that such constitutional formalism could support.[19] Indeed, it is striking testimony to the power of color-blindness talk that its contemporary proponents generally need not address these matters. Color blindness is a coherent and self-contained symbolic discourse, of such ethical and constitutional legitimacy that its proponents are rarely called upon to justify the assertion that color blindness is racial equality or to substantiate the claim that color blindness will bring about racial equality.

Indeed, Justice O'Connor made neither of these claims when she justified her commitment to color blindness in the recent case of *J.E.B. v. Alabama ex rel. T.B.* In *J.E.B.,* the Court held that the use of gender-based peremptory strikes during jury selection violates the equal protection clause, following its decision in *Batson v.*

Kentucky, which outlawed peremptory strikes based on race.[20] Justice O'Connor explained why she found gender-based peremptory strikes violative of the equal protection clause:

> We know that like race, gender matters. A plethora of studies make clear that in rape cases, for example, female jurors are somewhat more likely to vote to convict than male jurors. . . . Moreover, though there have been no similarly definitive studies regarding, for example, sexual harassment, child custody, or spousal or child abuse, one need not be a sexist to share the intuition that in certain cases a person's gender and resulting life experience will be relevant to his or her view of the case. . . .
>
> Today's decision severely limits a litigant's ability to act on this intuition, for the import of our holding is that any correlation between a juror's gender and attitudes is irrelevant as a matter of constitutional law. But to say that gender makes no difference as a matter of law is not to say that gender makes no difference as a matter of fact. I previously have said with regard to *Batson: "That the Court will not tolerate prosecutors' racially discriminatory use of the peremptory challenge, in effect, is a special rule of relevance, a statement about what this Nation stands for, rather than a statement of fact."*[21]

From the 1890s to the 1990s, this disjunction in legal and social discourses about race has created an imaginary domain in which America has projected a vision of citizenship never realized in social practice. But how does this ritualized renunciation of social knowledge create a domain of symbolic meaning in which we believe ourselves capable of transcending the gap between what this nation *is* and what it *stands for?* And why does this turn from social experience create a social experience of law as that which has the power to redeem the social experience of American life—even as we recognize that it is law *in just this symbolic sense* that legitimates the distributive inequities it is always summoning us to transcend? In the figure of color blindness, or blind justice, the aspirational and legitimating functions of law fuse in maddening consort. It is on this figural terrain—where we fight some of the major social conflicts of our time—that we must reckon with the authority of legal discourse, both as it is expressed in the judicial opinion and as it circulates in everyday conversation of the sort conventionally referred to as "outside" law.

Catharine A. MacKinnon

Law's Stories as Reality and Politics

Requested to reflect upon this conference as a whole, I hazard that it coheres around appropriating reality—reality, that vexed, even beleaguered notion. Law's way of taking in the world grounds it as a distinctively potent form of text. Case law has always started with stories called the facts. It is the sense that the facts have not felt real enough, that something has gone missing in them or was struggling to break through them, that has called law's embrace of reality into question and impelled the specific movement back toward the world that has taken the form of narrative.

The lack of felt verisimilitude in the law has arisen not only in going from thick to thin—in other vocabularies, from specific to general, from particular to universal, from concrete to abstract, from case to rule. Nor has the urgency behind the shift toward narrative as a form arisen only to avoid abstracting trauma or, to extrapolate Elaine Scarry's phrase, to reverse a movement from the one to the many.[1] Storytelling entered legal discussion at a prior moment: upon realizing that the analytic-argumentative engine has been running on particulars that have not been particular enough, and on submerged or entirely absent specifics. Legislation has been predicated on elided voices, the common law marching majestically by unbringable cases. In the absence of women, children, people of color, and working people, the legal mill has been working on grist that is too thin to begin with. To adapt Lévi-Strauss's terms, the raw of the law, not only its cooking, has been a problem.

As a practitioner of narrative, the first thing I do when I take an appeal is redo the account of the facts. In the form in which a case comes to me, the story is never right: never points to what happened directly enough, never shows the injury or embodies the theory sharply enough. Usually, the facts are constructed to concede most of what matters to the result. As such, in David Rosen's terms, it also seldom resonates with the client.[2] This same sense of an imposed unreality to be broken through, of prefabricated concepts to be remade from the ground up through the more real account emerging, has given birth to legal storytelling.

Conceptually, stories start over to put back in what has been left out. But there is more to their politics than that. As Paul Gewirtz delicately put it, there has been a relation between storytelling as method and a particular point of view.[3] The systematically exluded accounts, the pervasively silenced voices, have been of certain people: the unequal. Equality movements have noticed the elision; the legal claim for equality has given the world as reconstituted by stories some standing in the yet-to-be reconstructed legal system. Thus Robert Ferguson's oral Gabriel, movingly resurrected,[4] embodies the politics of subordinated communities denied literacy.

Social inequality, Alan Dershowitz, is not random;[5] it is determinate as well as cumulative and systematic. Stories are persuasive that rely on its teleology. Most men who batter women do not kill them—that would be a third to a half of American women murdered by male intimates[6]—but few murdered battered women are probably killed by anyone other than their batterers.[7] (Fewer still are the innocent battering husbands of murdered wives who drive around with her DNA all over the inside of their cars.) Considering the controversy over whether the Holocaust, an extreme in inequality, occurred, Jean-François Lyotard observed that reality is the plaintiff's problem.[8] The one who was hurt and seeks accountability must provide the account. In other words, if you are the one whose ending needs to be changed, you need to show that what got you there is both determinate and contingent enough to have been different.

It is thus not coincidence that storytelling—bearing witness, giving account as we know and practice it—took shape within civil rights movements. Since 1968 the women's liberation movement has contributed distinctively to this tradition through its speakouts and consciousness-raising. Women produced their analysis of women's condition in this form because there was no choice. It was women's experience, most crucially of sexual abuse, that had been left out of account. Existing concepts denied it—they still do—so it came out as story, howling and broken. These original victim impact statements had the narrative structure of machine language: and then he, and then he, and then he.

This process and its products—nerves exposed, inelegant by comparison with glossy abstractions—was, and continues to be, stigmatized and denigrated in the hierarchy of public discourse. It is actually a bit startling to find what we do called narrative and given some dignity, even literary cachet. Women's accounts have been more commonly called anecdotes, impressions, although they are at the very least testimony and, as such, evidence. Regarding a paper on sexual harassment—a legal concept that did not exist in the early 1970s—an editor of the *Yale Law Journal* told me that the legal argument was terrific, but all those personal accounts at the beginning "just did not add all that much." Take them out, you have a law review article. And why don't the accounts of real prostituted women have the credibility and literary gravity of Rousseau's fantasies of Marion?[9]

Much of the contemporary storytelling impulse has sprung from resistance to the claim of exclusivity of the single dominant version of social reality, as Martha Minow's Verona story appealingly illustrates.[10] Enlightenment "truth" accordingly took considerable heat in this conference for flattening reality's many dimensions. It is an old point. Capturing multiplicity, nuance, situatedness, perspectivity, storytelling teaches a new version of the old rule: now at least two realities must inhabit any account. Reality lies in interpretation; in postmodernity, where no one actually lives, interpretations are infinite.

It is time to ask whether this is all there is to this movement in reality appropriation. Are all stories equal so long as they are stories? Will "Rashomon" lurk in the underbrush, nineteenth-century objective/subjective epistemic regresses inhabiting our method forever? Is the most pointed contribution of narrative to law its challenge to the singleness of the dominant version—or is it to the domination of that version, hence its likely falsity, or at least its interestedness? Or has the shift in form masked an abdication of content? Maybe only one thing *did* happen, just not the one we were told. The Jews *were* allowed to stay in Verona. Further, if the whole story has not been told before, the principles that have been predicated on the assumption that the story *was* whole cannot be unbiased principles. But in telling stories and stopping there, have we abandoned principle for counterpoint, our claim of right for the jester's place at court?

The contribution of narrative to law, this conference showed, so far centers on defiance of canon. Daniel Farber and Martha Minow report it; Harlon Dalton and Richard Delgado exemplify it.[11] Storytelling has opened up legal discussion, giving it sweep of gesture, depth, ambiguity, connection, vaulting it toward literature. The breath of human life animates stories as it never did facts; a human face is envisaged in them. Empathy is encouraged, which victims of inequality could use. But there is no magic to the story form as such. Perpetrators of inequality—often at just the point of being held accountable for what they have done to their victims— claim that they, too, have stories, and they do. Stories can support accountability and tell a reality that dominant concepts have not accommodated. They have been a vehicle for the down and out. But the form itself is no guarantee of a view from the outside or the bottom. Stories break stereotypes, but stereotypes are also stories, and stories can be full of them. Do not mistake form for content, as abstracting narrative as method away from its origins in the critique of inequality that substantively impelled it does. Disembodied and decontextualized stories are also stories.

Even when accounts remain rooted in a critique of hierarchy, storytelling has real dangers. One of these is accepting a place at the margin. Storytelling as method originated in powerlessness and can bring a fear of power with it. Instead of telling power it is wrong, tell it a story. No offense. Avoid finger pointing. Power and powerlessness can both be right. Storytelling can be ingratiating when it cedes reality to power this way while presenting itself as just another version, a grace note. Storytelling can be a strategy for survival when one dare not argue. But it can ask too little. Dominant narratives are not called stories. They are called reality.

Further along the same lines, storytelling hazards entertainment. The point of storytelling is to make law more real, but because a story is a story, it can also be less real. When story becomes fantasy, the account passes into a different order of experience in which reality is hidden, distanced, occluded, or denied. The comments of Louis Michael Seidman provide an excellent example of this.[12]

A related risk is excess credibility, resulting from Harlon Dalton's suspension of critical faculties.[13] Sometimes the audience is having too good a time, particularly when the story tells power what it wants to hear. Freud, invoked several times here, was all story—many mythological, many, it turns out, false.[14] Stories can be powerful, evocative, resonant, death-defyingly influential, yet cover up the most relevant possible facts, such as, in Freud's case, the realities of child abuse. How do you counter the appeal of a story that power wants to believe? A story on the other side, of which there are many, has not been enough. This brings us full circle to the point where there is much to be said for data. As to child abuse, we have it.[15] Freud did not. Of course, the basis for the data is women's accounts of their abuse as children, which remain largely unbelieved and overwhelmingly not acted upon, while the baseless stories of Freud continue to ground much psychology and policy. The issue remains not form but content, specifically the politics of content.

Lies are the ultimate risk of storytelling as method. This may be embarrassingly non-postmodern, but reality exists. Of this the law, at least, has no doubt. Something happened or will be found to have happened. You can still be tried for perjury even though there supposedly is no truth. You can still be sued for libel, so somewhere reality exists to be falsified. Janet Malcolm's side bars preserve jurors' illusions, offering fact finding by imagination.[16] But each side's story cannot be simply assumed equally spoiled by the law's masks or equally dependent on an excluded reality for its power. Malcolm offers the joy of the half-imagined fact, the justice of the good read.[17] Seidman's text itself offers a series of such masks, a series of self-contained side bars, lying as commentary.[18] Fiction can be closer to reality than nonfiction, or it can be lying as art.

Storytelling in law is regressive when it promotes the notion that there is no such thing as "what happened" in a society that is still determinately unequal and a legal universe that will find that inequality or not. No one who seeks change can afford to pretend that they live in Gertrude Stein's Oakland, where there is no there there.

It is my view that the major conflicts of our time are over the real and only secondarily over versions of it and methods for apprehending it. The struggle over reality is conducted through contending versions and debates over verification. For instance, the discussion of pornography and prostitution can be seen as a debate in two stories. In story 1, a woman wakes up in the morning and decides, Today is my lucky day. I can choose whether to become a brain surgeon or whether to go find a pimp and spread my legs for a camera. In story 2, a girl is sexually abused at home, runs to the street thinking nothing can be worse, is picked up by a pimp, is molested, raped, beaten, starved, drugged, threatened, and sold for sex. Story 1 is a story of choice, equality, liberation; story 2 is a story of force, inequality, slavery. As story, there is no way to distinguish between them. The fact that most women in the industry were sexually abused as children, entered it as children, are desperately poor, report massive violence against them, and say they want to leave but cannot[19] supports story 2, but all this is extrinsic to the narrative form. Story 1 is fantasy, entertainment, lie—it is propaganda—but its support for power makes the real story of story 2 into just another story. Storytelling as method requires only the story form for validation. Pimps and tricks have stories, too. Story as method is thus located at a critical expansion joint in discourse as well as in a position to ensure that it gets nowhere.

Narrative's future in scholarship is an open one. More discussion comparing first-person narrative with other personae would further its growth. Lawyers usually work in stories not their own. Sometimes this is representation in the legal sense; sometimes it is representation in the aesthetic sense; sometimes it is using other people in the everyday sense. Judicial authorship, too, varies in voice, including across cultures. In Canada, even judges writing for the majority will use "I"; the first-person singular never appears in majority opinions in the power-obsessed, objectivity-sensitive United States.

Analysis of first-person accounts could give us a tighter grip on the crucial issue of credibility, a consideration begun in Robert Ferguson's essay and continued in Peter Brooks's. What is it about stories as such that makes them so believable? The observation that narrative has more persuasive force than statistics could productively be furthered in this context. As one who bursts into tears at columns of figures, I have no idea why 85 percent of federal workers can be known to be sexually harassed for a decade,[20] but not until one of them embodies the experience on national television does sexual harassment in the federal work force become real in some sense. I want to know. Why is it not real that 38 percent of girls are sexually abused before they reach the age of majority?[21] Why the stories behind facts like these are not taken as real when presented as data is the other side of why narrative has a peculiar capacity to make them real. This may be especially true in individualistic cultures, where biography is imagined to be singular. Yet no narrative has yet made child sexual abuse real to the degree that it happens, either.

In this connection, one form of narrative, the example, needs to be theorized within and beyond the common law. What does "case by case" really mean? What is the point and function and consequence of moving onto that level and back? What *is* an example? In connecting one particular with another, John Hollander briefly opened an important discussion of the relation between metaphor and knowledge[22]: What is it that allows us to see some things as similar to other things, to know one through knowing another? Crucial growth in human rights has occurred through this process; through seeing racism as a metaphor for inequality, as well as a prime instance of it, inequalities on other grounds have been exposed and understood as well. Pursuit of law's poetics could deepen understanding of this feature and its function in the legal process.

Finally, close analysis of specific rhetorics like legal fictions may serve to unmask law's devices for legitimacy. My favorite candidate for this role is the "I so regret to do this" of the judicial opinion, which goes far beyond the example of a hypothetical Calabresi that Sanford Levinson offered.[23] This ubiquitous trope of bench in extremis serves up the source of authority as "not me," such that the more you hate to do what you are doing, the more authoritative you become. Operating by compulsion behind a figleaf of moral regret apparently transforms atrocity into principle. The most egregious cases, like *Collin v. Smith,* in which the Nazis were permitted to march in Skokie because the First Amendment was said to require it, lean heavily on this, as in "[W]e feel compelled once again to express our repugnance. . . . Indeed, it is a source of extreme regret . . ."[24] Why is legitimacy enhanced by revulsion? Why does caving in to power validate? Perhaps it hides the power that law does have—to intervene or not, to equalize power or not, not to slide down any slope that it doesn't want to (or that may not exist)—behind the resigned pose of passivity of *ich kann nicht anders.* Analysis of such specific rhetorics, engagingly shown by "It takes two to tango,"[25] could help expose how law imposes itself on a world whose stories are never quite the same again.

Notes

PAUL GEWIRTZ, "NARRATIVE AND RHETORIC IN THE LAW"

1. One sees a similar turn to literature in the field of philosophy. I have in mind here especially the work of Martha Nussbaum and Charles Taylor.
2. Richard Delgado, "Storytelling for Oppositionists and Others: A Plea for Narrative," 87 Mich. L. Rev. 2411 (1989). Delgado spoke at the conference that led to this book but was committed to publishing his essay elsewhere.
3. It is worth recalling here Lionel Trilling's once-famous "Introduction" to *The Liberal Imagination* (1950), which makes a case for reading literature that anticipates many recent arguments by scholars of "storytelling" concerning the limits of general rules and the unique contributions of literary narratives in their particularity and complexity.
4. Consider just the eliciting of the client's story. Far from being a one-way transmission from a client-teller to the lawyer-listener, the usual process by which the client initially tells his story to the lawyer is extremely interactive. A lawyer not only asks questions but asks them from a perspective and with a purpose. The meeting of lawyer and client is a meeting of two cultures. The lawyer asks questions knowing the legal significance of various factual possibilities. The lawyer tries to bring out details that may have little significance in the client's experience and understanding of the events in question but which the lawyer knows to have legal significance. The lawyer may also help to shape the client's recollection—or at least the formulation of that recollection—in light of those legal meanings. Far from being passive listeners, then, lawyers are active responders and collaborators, always aware of the argumentative possibilities within the emerging story and always aware of their need to retell the story themselves somewhere down the road.

    Nor does the client simply tell the lawyer a full-blown story. The client may start out as an incompetent storyteller, forgetting details or not knowing their significance. Or the client may be a deceptive storyteller, concealing things from the lawyer or delaying their telling until after the lawyer discusses possible strategies.

5. In analyzing this relational complexity—as well as other aspects of legal narratives—it is useful to distinguish among three things: the lawyer's strategy of performance; the lawyer's psychology; and the lawyer's ethical obligations.

As performer to a decisionmaking audience, the lawyer typically identifies with the client's story. A jury, for example, typically thinks the lawyer knows the truth about the client's position, and so the lawyer seeks to convey total conviction in retelling the client's story at trial.

With the lawyer's psychology, there are two poles and a range between them: identifying with the client's cause and making it in some sense the lawyer's own versus maintaining an attitude of detachment and independence. Most lawyers realize that they cannot effectively represent a client if they do not maintain sufficient detachment to see the weaknesses in the client's story and to imagine how things look from many different perspectives; on the other hand, many, if not most, lawyers find themselves increasingly identifying (and believing in) a client's case over the course of a representation.

Ethically speaking, the lawyer must negotiate the twin ideals of zealously representing the client's interests and meeting public obligations as an officer of the court. The question here is whether there are limits on what stories a lawyer may properly present in court. Must lawyers vouch for the truth of the stories they narrate? May lawyers present stories they know to be false? A story they believe (but do not know) to be false? If lawyers are required to believe in what they narrate, can unpopular or apparently guilty defendants get the trial and zealous representation to which legal norms say they are entitled? If lawyers may narrate without sponsoring a narrative's truthfulness, can we expect the adversary system to produce a truthful result in the end? (This question of whether there are "ethical" limits on the stories that a lawyer may properly present in court is just a piece of the much broader problem of limits on the kinds of stories that may be told at trial—the explicit subject of the third group of essays in this volume.)

6. This is not to disagree with Daniel Farber and Suzanna Sherry, whose essay in this volume argues that storytelling scholars and critical legal scholars share some common ground—most important, a belief that the sources of legal meaning emphasized in traditional accounts are very frequently indeterminate.

MARTHA MINOW, "STORIES IN LAW"

I thank my parents and siblings, who have always taught me that stories are the best way to make a point; Vicky Spelman, Avi Soifer, Cass Sunstein, Charles Fried, and Lucie White for helpful conversations; and Joe Singer and Mira Singer, who love stories.

1. See Kathryn Abrams, "Hearing the Call of Stories," 79 Cal. L. Rev. 971 (1991); Randall Kennedy, "Racial Critiques of Legal Academia," 102 Harv. L. Rev. 1745 (1989); Daniel A. Farber and Suzanna Sherry, "Telling Stories Out of School: An Essay on Legal Narratives," 45 Stan. L. Rev. 807 (1993); Jane Baron, "Resistance to Stories," 67 S. Cal. L. Rev. 255 (1994); Angela P. Harris, "Foreword: The Jurisprudence of Reconstruction," 82 Cal. L. Rev. 741 (1994).

2. Board of Education of Kiryas Joel Village School District v. Louis Grumet, 114 S.Ct. 2481 (1994). My paper, presented as the Harris Lecture at Indiana University and forthcoming in the *Indiana Law Review,* is "The Constitution and the Subgroup Question"; an earlier version was presented as the Beatrice K. Schneiderman Social Action Series lecture at Kehilath Anshe Maarav-Isaiah Israel, Chicago.

3. Naomi W. Cohen, *Jews in Christian America: The Pursuit of Religious Equality* 11 (1992).

4. Morton Borden, *Jews, Turks, and Infidels* 110 (1984).

5. Jerome R. Mintz, *Hasidic People: A Place in the New World* 29 (1992).

6. Aguilar v. Felton, 473 U.S. 402 (1985); Wolman v. Walter, 433 U.S. 229 (1977).

7. Brief for Petitioner, Board of Educ. of Kiryas Joel Village School Dist. v. Louis Grumet and Albert W. Hawk, on writ of certiorari to the New York Court of Appeals, No. 93–517, at 6 (quoting Affidavit of Hannah Flegenheimer).

8. Id., at 11, Petitioner Appendix 115a–1171.
9. Exhibit 6 to Brief of Amicus, Committee for the Well-Being of Kiryas Joel, Board of Educ. of the Kiryas Joel Village School Dist. v. Louis Grumet and Albert Hawk, on writ of certiorari to the New York Court of Appeals, No. 95–517.
10. Id.
11. Mintz, at 313–148.
12. 114 S.Ct. 2481, 2487–2490 (Opinion of Souter, part II-A) (relying on Larkin v. Grendel's Den, Inc., 459 U.S. 116).
13. Lemon v. Kurtzman, 403 U.S. 602 (1971).
14. Cass Sunstein's comments were especially helpful to me as I formulated these thoughts.
15. This question reflects my assumption that state neutrality is impossible in at least some cases pitting subgroups in the society against one another. I defend this assumption elsewhere. See Minow, "Constitution and the Subgroup Question"; Martha Minow, *Making All the Difference* (1990).
16. Martha Minow, "Rights for the Next Generation," 9 Harv. Women's L.J. 1 (1986) (arguing for conceptions of children's interests); Martha Minow and Richard Weissbourd, "Social Movements for Children," 122 Daedalus 1 (Winter 1993) (same); Robert Cover, "The Supreme Court, 1982 Term—Foreword: *Nomos* and Narrative," 97 Harv. L. Rev. 4 (1983) (emphasizing the significance of local origins of meaning neglected by contemporary constitutional adjudication).
17. Minow, "Constitution and the Subgroup Question."
18. Bollenbach v. Board of Education of Monroe-Woodbury Central School District, 659 F. Supp. 1450 (SDNY 1987).
19. Mintz, at 310.
20. Indeed, I suggest that this willingness to forgo sex segregation is a sign of the Satmar's good-faith deference to public norms in the public school system, justified internally in the community, however, by reference to an interpretation of Talmudic law. Minow, "Constitution and the Subgroup Question."
21. I mean to suggest here that a storyteller should seek out contrasting stories, rather than wait for them to present themselves. Too often the stories that go unheard are those of people with minimal access to power or resources to make themselves heard.
22. Martha Minow, "Surviving Victim Talk," 40 UCLA L. Rev. 1411 (1993).
23. Seyla Benhabib, "Hannah Arendt and the Redemptive Power of Narrative," in Lewis P. Hinchman and Sandra K. Hinchman, *Hannah Arendt: Critical Essays* 111 (1994).
24. Hannah Arendt, *The Origins of Totalitarianism* (3d enlarged ed. 1973); Arendt, *Eichmann in Jerusalem: A Report on the Banality of Evil* (rev. ed. 1965); Arendt, *Men in Dark Times* (1968).
25. David Luban, "Explaining Dark Times: Hannah Arendt's Theory of Theory," in Hinchman, at 79; Melvyn A. Hill, "The Fictions of Mankind and the Stories of Men," in *Hannah Arendt: The Recovery of the Public World* 275 (Melvyn A. Hill ed. 1979).
26. Luban, at 101. See also Hanna Pitkin, *Wittgenstein and Justice,* at 242 (1972, 1993).
27. Arendt, *Human Condition* 38–39.
28. Hill, at 283.
29. Benhabib.
30. See id., at 114.
31. Id., at 131.
32. Id., at 122–23.
33. See id., at 123.
34. See Hill, at 284.
35. See Benhabib, at 119, 121.
36. Hill, at 284.
37. See id., at 291.
38. Id., at 275–76.
39. See James Boyd White, *Heracles' Bow: Essays on the Rhetoric and Poetics of Law* (1985) (stories

construct worlds of meaning). See also Baron, at 252–53; Alasdair MacIntrye's *After Virtue* (1981) (a similar theme but is more explicitly nostalgic for a past world of coherence); Martha Nussbaum, *Love's Knowledge* (1990) (style itself makes a statement, and the style of literature expresses more fully how to live than linear philosophic argument can; conceptions of the good life are embedded in the very structure of imaginative works of literature, including the tensions and contrasting levels of attention).

40. Benhabib, at 124, 130.

41. Benhabib, at 122, 126. Perhaps the process of telling stories conveyed for Arendt even more basically the adoption of the role of judge for the storyteller: "Story telling reveals meaning without committing the error of defining it . . . it brings about consent and reconciliation with things as they really are, and . . . we may even trust it to contain eventually by implication that last word which we expect from the 'day of judgment'" (Arendt, *Men in Dark Times,* 108). The point is not that each story is true but that it is faithful to the reality of what happened and thereby lends meaning to it; imagining other people's perspectives would be crucial to storytelling in Arendt's sense—see Hill, at 292, 297.

42. Benhabib, at 126.

43. Id., at 121.

44. See Nancy Hartsock, *Money, Sex, and Power: Toward a Feminist Historical Materialism* 254 (1983) (discussing Hannah Arendt).

45. It would be interesting to explore whether stories are more arresting when other modes of speech and analysis are dominant, but the long-standing place of stories in, for example, rabbinic tradition, suggests that stories can compel even against the backdrop of other analyses.

46. Arendt specifically argued that modern anti-Semitism is more pernicious than the traditional Christian doctrine that blamed Jews for crimes committed against Jesus, because in Christianity one can atone for one's crime by conversion, penance, or denunciation of one's associates. Modern anti-Semitism, "which erupts when Jews en masse begin to enter 'society,' without fully becoming its members," treats Jewishness as an undefinable essence that cannot change. The individual Jew loses an account-able self and instead becomes a specimen of the species Jew. Benhabib, at 117.

47. See Michael Walzer, "The Communitarian Critique of Liberalism," 18 Political Theory 6 (1990) (arguing that the United States is in no danger of becoming a community, given people's geographic mobility, divorce rates, class membership mobility, and political party shifts).

48. Compare Elizabeth Janeway, *Powers of the Weak* (1980).

49. Would these values be more dominant if storytelling itself became the dominant mode of academic discourse?

DANIEL A. FARBER AND SUZANNA SHERRY, "LEGAL STORYTELLING AND CONSTITUTIONAL LAW"

We would like to thank the participants at the Yale conference and at faculty workshops at the University of Southern California and Southern Methodist University for their helpful comments. We also thank Ann Coughlin and Paul Edelman.

1. See sources cited in notes 20, 44, 56, 61, and 69, infra.

2. We will use the term "critical legal theory" to refer to critical legal studies (CLS), radical (or "domi-nance") feminism, and critical race theory (CRT).

3. See the next section for a discussion of the indeterminacy thesis.

4. We have not found a clear articulation of this thesis in the critical literature. Alex Johnson has noted in passing that both the storytelling movement and CRT "reject neutral principles and the process pursuant to which those principles are deduced." Alex M. Johnson, Jr., "Defending the Use of Narrative and Giving Content to the Voice of Color: Rejecting the Imposition of Process Theory in Legal Scholar-ship," 79 Iowa L. Rev. 803, 824 (1994).

5. Stronger forms of indeterminacy, of the kind associated—at least in the law school world—with deconstruction, would make this move more problematic.

6. David Kairys, "Law and Politics," 52 Geo. Wash. L. Rev. 243, 244, 247 (1984) (footnote omitted).

7. For a sampling of recent scholarship on this subject and references to earlier work, see Jules Coleman and Brian Leiter, "Determinacy, Objectivity, and Authority," 142 U. Penn. L. Rev. 549 (1993); J. M. Balkin, "Review Essay: Ideology as Constraint," 43 Stan. L. Rev. 1133 (1991); Ken Kress, "Legal Indeterminacy," 17 Cal. L. Rev. 283 (1989).

8. Lawrence B. Solum, "On the Indeterminacy Crisis: Critiquing Critical Dogma," 54 U. Chi. L. Rev. 462 (1987). We will be making use of Solum's description of the indeterminacy thesis, rather than his critique. Based on our own review of the critical literature, we believe that he has provided a fair summary of the CLS position.

9. Id. at 465–66.

10. Conceivably, people are nevertheless persuaded by particular legal arguments because they are unaware that they would find contrary arguments equally valid. One might think that at least individuals like judges, who are continually exposed to legal arguments, would eventually become aware of this reality. In any event, from the viewpoint of those seeking social change, this is a dismal scenario, because it seems unlikely that the oppressed can match the gladiators of the powerful in this rhetorical struggle.

11. Some might say that this range contains all cases that would ever be litigated; others might identify a subset of cases, such as Supreme Court decisions. Mark V. Tushnet, "Following the Rules Laid Down: A Critique of Interpretivism and Neutral Principles," 96 Harv. L. Rev. 781, 806–18 (1983).

12. See generally Ronald Dworkin, *Taking Rights Seriously* 31–39 (1977).

13. Duncan Kennedy, "Cost-Benefit Analysis of Entitlement Problems: A Critique," 33 Stan. L. Rev. 387 (1981); Jay M. Feinman, "Critical Approaches to Contract Law," 30 UCLA L. Rev. 829, 847 (1983).

14. Richard Delgado, "Norms and Normal Science: Toward a Critique of Normativity in Legal Thought," 139 U. Penn. L. Rev. 933, 962 (1991); Pierre Schlag, "Values," 6 Yale J.L. & Humanities 219, 277 (1994).

15. Joseph William Singer, "The Player and the Cards: Nihilism and Legal Theory," 94 Yale L.J. 1, 21 (1984) (noting "controversial political and moral commitments" as an additional factor); Robert W. Gordon, "Critical Legal Studies Symposium: Critical Legal Histories," 36 Stan. L. Rev. 57, 125 (1984); Clare Dalton, "An Essay in the Deconstruction of Contract Doctrine," 94 Yale L.J. 997, 1010 (1985); Tushnet, supra note 11, at 823; Steven L. Winter, "Indeterminacy and Incommensurability in Constitutional Law," 78 Cal. L. Rev. 1441, 1463 (1990); see also id. at 1473 (cultural constructs and stabilized matrices).

16. Ludwig Wittgenstein, *Philosophical Investigations* ¶¶ 139–201 (G.E.M. Anscombe trans. 3d ed. 1958). See also Saul A. Kripke, *Wittgenstein on Rules and Private Language* (1982). This difficulty is particularly acute given the critical view that this is our normal, possibly our universal, situation.

17. By "nonpropositional" we mean essentially that language is not being used to make an assertion that can be judged as either true or false; for example, fiction, poetry, and (by a small expansion) visual images cannot be so judged.

18. Joseph William Singer, "Persuasion," 87 Mich. L. Rev. 2442, 2455 (1989).

19. Some of the best-known examples of storytelling do not seem to gain their effect from narrative in the sense of one thing following another. Patricia Williams's Benetton story, for instance, provides a visual image of a black woman with her faced pressed against a store window, facing a derisive young white salesclerk. This could as well be a photograph.

20. Lucinda M. Finley, "Breaking Women's Silence in Law: The Dilemma of the Gendered Nature of Legal Reasoning," 64 Notre Dame L. Rev. 886, 903 (1989) ("things that just cannot be said"); see also Kathryn Abrams, "Hearing the Call of Stories," 79 Cal. L. Rev. 971, 1028 (1991) ("The entire point of the feminist epistemology reflected in narrative is to argue that there are forms of knowledge that may not be generated or validated by scientific objectivity, through which we may nonetheless learn critical things about ourselves and our world."); id. at 1049 (sometimes translation may be impossible in the absence of stories); Richard Delgado, "Storytelling for Oppositionists and Others: A Plea for Narra-

tive," 87 Mich. L. Rev. 2411, 2415 (1989) (stories' "graphic qualit[ies] can stir imagination in ways in which more conventional discourse cannot"); Lynne N. Henderson, "Legality and Empathy," 85 Mich. L. Rev. 1574, 1577 (1987) ("more meanings will be available to legal discourse" using the language of empathy rather than that of rationality); id. at 1575 (legal language cannot talk about emotion or experience); Mary I. Coombs, "Outsider Scholarship: The Law Review Stories," 63 U. Colo. L. Rev. 683, 695 (1992) ("explode"); Henderson, supra, at 1576 ("received"); Jane B. Baron, "Intention, Interpretation, and Stories," 42 Duke L.J. 630, 631 (1992) ("disrupt"); Delgado, supra, at 2414 ("shatter"). Coombs, supra, at 697 ("seduce"). Compare William N. Eskridge, Jr., "Gaylegal Narratives," 46 Stan. L. Rev. 607 (1994) ("disruptive" effect of stories); Abrams, supra, at 1003 ("flash"); see also id. at 1023–24; id., supra, at 1002 ("resonate"); Mari J. Matsuda, "Looking to the Bottom: Critical Legal Studies and Reparations," 22 Harv. C.R.-C.L. L. Rev. 323, 324 (1987) ("seen"); Delgado, supra, at 2437 ("therapy"). Delgado has become less optimistic about the efficacy of stories.

21. Gerald P. Lopez, "Lay Lawyering," 32 UCLA L. Rev. 1, 10 (1984); Abrams, supra note 20, at 976; see also id. at 1028–44; id. at 1036 (discussing feminist scholars' rejection of "scientific rationality"); Finley, supra note 20, at 893–94; see also Delgado, supra note 20, at 2415 (stories "offer a respite from the linear, coercive discourse that characterizes much legal writing"); Matsuda, supra note 20, at 359; Robin West, "Jurisprudence and Gender," 55 U.Chi. L. Rev. 1, 64 (1988).

22. Steven L. Winter, "The Cognitive Dimension of the Agon Between Legal Power and Narrative Meaning," 87 Mich. L. Rev. 2225, 2228 (1989).

23. Jane B. Baron, "Resistance to Stories," 67 S. Cal. L. Rev. 255, 255–57, 277–85 (1994); see also Mari J. Matsuda, "When the First Quail Calls: Multiple Consciousness as Jurisprudential Method," 11 Wom. Rts. L. Rep. 7, 8 (1989) (outsider scholars "reject the artificial bifurcation of thought and feeling"); Martha L. Minow and Elizabeth V. Spelman, "Passion for Justice," 10 Cardozo L. Rev. 37, 47–48 (1988) (criticizing distinction between reason and emotion).

24. Delgado, supra note 20, at 2413.

25. Thomas Ross, "The Rhetorical Tapestry of Race: White Innocence and Black Abstraction," 32 Wm. & Mary L. Rev. 1, 40 (1990).

26. See e.g., Matsuda, supra note 20, at 335 (transformation); Coombs, supra note 20, at 715; Ross, supra note 25, at 2; Winter, supra note 22, at 2228; Jerome McCristal Culp, Jr., "Autobiography and Legal Scholarship and Teaching: Finding the Me in the Legal Academy," 77 Va. L. Rev. 539, 543 (1991); see also id. at 559 (narratives used in teaching should "change what our students see as reality"); Baron, supra note 23, at 261 (construction); Richard Delgado, "Shadowboxing: An Essay on Power," 77 Cornell L. Rev. 813, 818 (1992); Eskridge, supra note 20, at 607, passim; see also Delgado, supra note 20, at 2414 (stories "can open new windows into reality, showing us that there are possibilities for life other than the ones we live").

27. For some recent contributions to this debate, see Carlin Meyer, "Sex, Sin, and Women's Liberation: Against Porn-Suppression," 72 Tex. L. Rev. 1097 (1994); Marianne Wesson, "Girls Should Bring Lawsuits Everywhere . . . Nothing Will Be Corrupted: Pornography as Speech and Product," 60 U. Chi. L. Rev. 845 (1993).

28. For background on the ordinance, see Paul Brest and Ann Vandenberg, "Politics, Feminism, and the Constitution: The Anti-Pornography Movement in Minneapolis," 39 Stan. L. Rev. 607 (1987); David P. Bryden, "Between Two Constitutions: Feminism and Pornography," 2 Const. Comm. 147 (1985).

29. We will utilize MacKinnon's latest book, *Only Words* (1993), as a succinct synthesis of her views. MacKinnon's views on the role of language in constructing reality—specifically, the role of pornography in constructing sexuality and gender—are explored in Jeanne L. Schroeder, "The Taming of the Shrew: The Liberal Attempt to Mainstream Radical Feminist Theory," 5 Yale J. L. & Fem. 123, 127–28, 137–38, 140, 144, 151, 156 (1992).

30. MacKinnon, supra note 29, at 106.

31. Id. at 13 (emphasis in original).

32. Id. at 30–31 (emphasis in original).

33. Id. at 24.

34. Id. at 16–17, 62, 108; MacKinnon quotes a Yiddish proverb: "[A] stiff prick turns the mind to shit." Id. at 17. Pornography results in rape because of a conditioning process, not because rapists are persuaded by ideas or even inflamed by emotions. Id. at 16. Because of MacKinnon's reliance on conditioning as the cause of behavior, the term "mindset" might be more accurately replaced with "culturally conditioned propensities toward behavioral responses." We do not regard the distinction as significant for present purposes, although it does raise interesting philosophical issues.

35. Id. at 99.

36. Id. at 104.

37. We are once again fortunate in being able to make use of a recent work that provides a concise synthesis of this argument, Mari J. Matsuda et al., *Words That Wound: Critical Race Theory, Assaultive Speech, and the First Amendment* (1993). For a brief bibliography of the hate speech debate, see Daniel A. Farber, "Foreword: Hate Speech After *R.A.V.*," 18 Wm. Mitchell L. Rev. 889, 902 (1992).

38. Matsuda et al., supra note 37, at 62, 129, 136.

39. Id. at 68, 74, 91, 92, 93, 95.

40. Id. at 77.

41. Id. at 49.

42. Charles B. Lawrence III, "The Id, the Ego, and Equal Protection: Reckoning with Unconscious Racism," 39 Stan. L. Rev. 317, 343 (1987). Compare Delgado's recent efforts to explain the mindsets of civil libertarians. Richard Delgado, "Foreword: Essays on Hate Speech," 82 Cal. L. Rev. 847 (1994). See also John E. Morrison, "Colorblindness, Individuality, and Merit: An Analysis of the Rhetoric Against Affirmative Action," 79 Iowa L. Rev. 313 (1994).

43. Readers may notice a contradiction here. To the extent that the advocates of storytelling believe in the ability of their stories to counter the dominant racist stories and change the prevailing mindset, they should not need to advocate governmentally imposed limits on even malign stories. The demand for regulation of hate speech–often, in practice, made by the same scholars who praise or engage in storytelling–is an implicit confession that stories from the bottom are unlikely to be successful in changing the prevailing mindset. Nevertheless, critical theorists place their faith, however weak and wavering, in the noncognitive aspects of storytelling rather than in traditional rational argument. That those most uncertain in their faith are most likely to seek coercive measures to back it up is a not uncommon human paradox.

44. Delgado, supra note 26, at 818; Delgado, supra note 20, passim; Baron, supra note 23, at 266; Richard Delgado, "On Telling Stories in School: A Reply to Farber and Sherry," 46 Vand. L. Rev. 665, 670 (1993).

45. Lawrence, supra note 42.

46. Lawrence, supra note 42, at 322, 331–35.

47. Id. at 337–38 (footnotes omitted).

48. Id. at 339.

49. Matsuda et al., supra note 38, at 68.

50. Brown v. Board of Education, 347 U.S. 483 (1954).

51. Lawrence, supra note 42, at 362–63.

52. Washington v. Davis, 426 U.S. 229 (1976).

53. See, e.g., Robin West, *Progressive Constitutionalism: Reconstructing the Fourteenth Amendment,* 34, 37, 58 (1994).

54. Lawrence, supra note 42, at 356. Compare with O'Connor's "message of endorsement" test for establishment clause cases.

55. Lawrence, supra note 42, at 358.

56. See Daniel A. Farber and Suzanna Sherry, "Telling Stories Out of School: An Essay on Legal

Narratives," 45 Stan. L. Rev. 807 (1993); Mark V. Tushnet, "The Degradation of Constitutional Discourse," 81 Geo. L.J. 251 (1992); Toni M. Massaro, "Empathy, Legal Storytelling, and the Rule of Law: New Words, Old Wounds?" 87 Mich. L. Rev. 2099 (1989).

57. J. Peter Byrne, "Academic Freedom: A 'Special Concern of the First Amendment,'" 99 Yale L.J. 251, 269–71 (1989).

58. G. Edward White, "Felix Frankfurter, the Old Boy Network, and the New Deal: The Placement of Elite Lawyers in Public Service in the 1930's," in *Intervention and Detachment: Essays in Legal History and Jurisprudence* 149, 155 (1994); Rodney Smolla, "Academic Freedom, Hate Speech, and the Idea of a University," in *Freedom and Tenure in the Academy* 195, 216 (William van Alstyne ed. 1993) ("island"); Robert C. Post, "Racist Speech, Democracy, and the First Amendment," 32 Wm. & Mary L. Rev. 267, 324 (1991); see also J. Peter Byrne, "Racial Insults and Free Speech Within the University," 79 Geo. L.J. 399, 419 (1991) ("the commitment to forms of thought and expression conducive to truth and coherence lies at the core of academic values"); Edward L. Rubin, "The Practice and Discourse of Legal Scholarship," 86 Mich. L. Rev. 1835, 1846 (1988); Byrne, supra note 57, at 258 ("basis of reason"). See also id. at 261 ("The structures of academic discourse can be justified because they facilitate the rational pursuit of truth").

59. For the classic statement of this paradigm of law, see Herbert Wechsler, "Toward Neutral Principles of Constitutional Law," 73 Harv. L. Rev. 1 (1959). See also John Hart Ely, *Democracy and Distrust: A Theory of Judicial Review* (1980); Philip Bobbitt, *Constitutional Fate: Theory of the Constitution* (1982); Bobbitt, *Constitutional Interpretation* (1991). There is some evidence that this view still prevails outside legal academia. See Michael E. Solimine and Susan E. Wheatley, "Rethinking Feminist Judging," 70 Indiana L.J. 891, 909–10 & n.136 (1995).

60. Brown v. Board of Education, 347 U.S. 483 (1954); Gideon v. Wainwright, 372 U.S. 335 (1963); INS v. Chadha, 462 U.S. 919 (1983); TVA v. Hill, 437 U.S. 153 (1978). In *Gideon,* an indigent drifter's criminal appeal established the constitutional right to government-financed defense counsel, contrary to Supreme Court precedent. In *Chadha,* an immigrant's effort to fight deportation resulted in the invalidation of a major tool of post–New Deal government, the legislative veto. Jagdish Chadha apparently now works at a video store in Washington. See Jessica Korn, *The Myth of the Legislative Veto* (unpublished manuscript). In *TVA v. Hill,* construction of a hundred-million-dollar dam was halted by the Court to save an obscure endangered species of fish. The opinion by Chief Justice Burger (no environmentalist) closes with an invocation of the ideal of the rule of law. 437 U.S. at 195.

61. See Farber and Sherry, supra note 56, at 849–53; Matthew W. Finkin, "Reflections on Labor Law Scholarship and Its Discontents: The Reveries of Monsieur Verog," 46 U. Miami L. Rev. 1101, 1138–43, 1147 (1992); Tushnet, supra note 56, at 251 (favoring "objective stance," which seems to depend on reasoned argument); see also Edward L. Rubin, "On Beyond Truth: A Theory for Evaluating Legal Scholarship," 80 Cal. L. Rev. 889, 954 (1992) (suggesting that storytelling is not a distinctive sub-discipline because it does not have "an interlinked set of consciously articulated procedures that generate research"). But see Anne Coughlin, "Regulating the Self: Autobiographical Performances in Outsider Scholarship," 81 Va. L. Rev. 1229 (1995) (criticizing storytellers for using a narrative structure that implicitly reenacts the liberal perspective).

62. Larry Alexander, "What We Do, and Why We Do It," 45 Stan. L. Rev. 1885, 1890–96 (1993); see also Solimine and Wheatley, supra note 59 (criticizing feminist jurisprudence for abandoning the traditional model of rationality); Henry Louis Gates, Jr., "Let Them Talk: Why Civil Liberties Pose No Threat to Civil Rights," New Republic, September 20 & 27, 1993, at 37, 47.

63. This division between emotive and rational uses of language does not completely describe the jurisprudential landscape. As Nadine Strossen notes, some proponents of hate speech regulations (especially the narrower regulations) would deny racist speech constitutional protection precisely because it is emotive rather than rational. Strossen herself finds the emotive aspects of speech well worth protecting. Nadine Strossen, "Regulating Racist Speech on Campus: A Modest Proposal?" 1990 Duke L.J. 484,

547–49; see also Byrne, supra note 58 (universities should be able to prohibit nonrational, but not rational, racist insults).

64. Post, supra note 58, at 282. The term is John Rawls's, but, as Post recognizes, the idea permeates traditional democratic theory. Id.; Carlin Meyer, "Sex, Sin, and Women's Liberation: Against Porn-Suppression," 72 Tex. L. Rev. 1097, 1197 (1994). She also points out that at least some of the advocates of suppressing pornography have a "one-dimensional view of representation," which holds that "what an image *depicts*, it *urges*." Id. at 1142 (emphasis in original); Burt Neuborne, "Ghosts in the Attic: Idealized Pluralism, Community and Hate Speech," 27 Harv. C.R.-C.L. L. Rev. 371, 394–399 (1992).

65. See Daniel A. Farber, "Free Speech Without Romance: Public Choice and the First Amendment," 105 Harv. L. Rev. 554 (1991).

66. Gates makes this point, noting in opposition that "things like reason, argument and moral suasion did play a significant role in changing attitudes toward 'race relations.'" Gates, supra note 62, at 48.

67. See Tushnet, supra note 56; Gary Peller, "The Discourse of Constitutional Degradation," 81 Geo. L.J. 313 (1992); Mark V. Tushnet, "Reply," 81 Geo. L.J. 343 (1992).

68. We hope to address this question at least briefly in a forthcoming book.

69. See Jim Chen, "Unloving," 80 Iowa L. Rev. 145 (1994); Daniel A. Farber and Suzanna Sherry, "The 200,000 Cards of Dimitri Yurasov: Further Reflections on Scholarship and Truth," 46 Stan. L. Rev. 647 (1994). Many of the storytellers have also used conventional scholarly methods of scholarship in their writings.

70. See Michael Brint and William Weaver, eds., *Pragmatism in Law and Society* (1991) (collecting papers by legal scholars such as Posner, Dworkin, and Minow, as well as work by pragmatist philosophers such as Richard Rorty and Hilary Putnam).

71. Ludwig Wittgenstein, *Tractatus Logico-philosophicus* (1961).

ROBERT WEISBERG, "PROCLAIMING TRIALS AS NARRATIVES"

This chapter is drawn from a monograph, *Literary Criticisms of Law* (coauthor Guyora Binder of the Law School, State University of New York at Buffalo), to be published by Princeton University Press in 1996.

1. Robert Gordon, Historicism in Legal Scholarship, 90 Yale L.J. 1117 (1981).

2. Id. at 1124–37.

3. For example, David Luban, Difference Made Legal: The Court and Dr. King, 87 Mich. L. Rev. 2152 (1989).

4. Robin West, *Narrativity, Authority, and the Law* 345 (1993).

5. Charles Beard, *An Economic Interpretation of the Constitution of the United States* (1941).

6. Douglas Hay, Property, Authority and the Criminal Law, in Hay et al., eds., *Albion's Fatal Tree: Crime and Society in Eighteenth-Century England* 17 (1975).

7. Morton Horwitz, *The Transformation of American Law, 1790–1860* (1977).

8. For example, Wayne C. Booth, *The Company We Keep: An Ethics of Fiction* (1988).

9. Richard Sherwin, A Matter of Voice and Plot: Belief and Suspicion in Legal Storytelling, 87 Mich. L. Rev. 543, 551 (1988).

10. See John Searle, *Speech Acts: An Essay in the Philosophy of Language* (1969).

11. Even a dramatic and expensive trial that ends in a defense victory–like the William Kennedy Smith rape trial–may prove this point. As seen on Court Television, the defense attorney Roy Black performed a witheringly straightforward, unemotional, distinctly nondramatic cross-examination and closing argument in that case to win a quick victory. See Susan Estrich, Palm Beach Stories, 11 J. of Law and Philosophy 5 (1992).

12. A representative sampling appears in Symposium: Legal Storytelling, 87 Mich. L. Rev. 2073 ff. (1989).

13. Thomas Kuhn, *The Structure of Scientific Revolutions* (1962).

14. David Ray Papke, Neo-Marxists, Nietzscheans, and New Critics: The Voices of Contemporary Law and Literature Discourse, 1985 A.B. F. Res. J. 883.

15. Isabel Marcus, Locked In and Locked Out: Reflections on the History of Divorce Law Reform in New York State, 37 Buffalo L. Rev. 375 (1988).

16. Northrop Frye, *An Anatomy of Criticism* (1957).

17. Steven Winter, The Cognitive Dimension of the Agon Between Legal Practice and Narrative Meaning, 87 Mich. L. Rev. 2225 (1989).

18. William James, *Pragmatism: A New Name for Some Old Ways of Thinking* (1907).

19. Wayne C. Booth, supra note 8, at 13–17.

20. Kim Scheppele, Foreword: Telling Stories, 87 Mich. L. Rev. 2073, 2083–98 (1989).

21. Mark Kelman, *Critical Legal Studies* 86–113 (1987).

22. Kim Scheppele, Just the Facts, Ma'am: Sexualized Violence, Evidentiary Habits, and the Revision of Truth, 37 N. Y. L. Rev. 123, 145–72 (1992).

23. Alan Dershowitz, Life Is Not a Dramatic Narrative, in this volume.

24. Id.

25. State v. Williams, 4 Wash. App. 908, 484 P.2d 1167 (1971).

26. Jack Getman, Voices, 66 Tex. L. Rev. 577 (1988).

27. For example, Anthony Alfieri, Speaking Out of Turn: The Story of Josephine V., 4 Geo. J. Legal Ethics 619 (1991); Alfieri, Disabled Clients, Disabling Lawyers, 43 Hastings L. Rev. 769 (1992).

28. Christopher Gilkerson, Poverty Law Narratives: The Critical Practice and Theory of Receiving and Translating Client Stories, 43 Hastings L. Rev. 861 (1992).

29. Id. at 864–73.

30. Anthony Alfieri, Reconstructive Poverty Law Practice: Learning Lessons of Client Narrative, 100 Yale L.J. 2107, 2131–45 (1991).

31. Id. at 2127–30.

32. Lucie White, Subordination, Rhetorical Survival Skills, and Sunday Shoes: Notes on the Hearing of Mrs. G., 38 Buff. L. Rev. 1 (1990).

33. Id. at 21–32.

34. Id. at 48–49.

35. Id. at 52.

36. Goldberg v. Kelly, 397 U.S. 254 (1970).

37. Lucie White, supra note 32, at 54.

38. See Simon's own poverty narrative in William Simon, Lawyer Advice and Client Autonomy: Mrs. Jones's Case, 50 Md. L. Rev. 213 (1991).

39. Id. at 217–20.

40. See examples discussed in Daniel Farber and Suzanna Sherry, Telling Stories Out of School: An Essay on Legal Narratives, 45 Stan. L. Rev. 807, 814–19 (1993).

41. For example, Richard Delgado, When a Story Is Just a Story: Does Voice Really Matter? 76 Va. L. Rev. 95 (1990); Delgado, Storytelling for Oppositionists and Others: A Plea for Narrative, 87 Mich. L. Rev. 2411 (1989); Alex M. Johnson, Jr., The New Voice of Color, 100 Yale L. J. 2007 (1991).

42. Lawrence Stone, *The Past and the Present Revisited* 72–96 (1987).

43. Id. at 76–78.

44. Id. at 78–79.

45. Id. at 81.

46. Id. at 94–96.

47. Hayden White, *The Content of the Form: Narrative Discourse and Historical Representation* 1–25(1987).

48. Id. at xi.

49. Id. at 11–14.

50. See G. W. H. Hegel, *Lectures on the Philosophy of History* 60–63 (J. Sibree trans. 1956).

51. Id. at 14–17.

52. Homi Bhaba, *Nations and Narration* 1 (1990).

53. Id. at 1–7, 291–322.

54. Id. at 292; see id. at 292–97.

55. Id. at 293–97.

56. Robert A. Ferguson, Story and Transcription in the Trial of John Brown, 6 Yale J. L. & the Humanities 37 (1994).

57. Id. at 38.

58. Id. at 40–43.

59. David Brion Davis, *The Slave Power Conspiracy and the Paranoid Style* (1969).

60. Id. at 18 ff.

61. Id. at 24–27.

62. Id. at 21–31.

63. Id. at 71–76.

64. Robert A. Ferguson, supra note 56, at 44.

65. For Ferguson's comparison, id. at 46.

66. Id. at 55–62.

67. Id. at 70–73.

68. Id. at 73, quoting Roland Barthes, *Image, Music, Text* 79 (Stephen Heath trans. 1977).

ROBERT A. FERGUSON, "UNTOLD STORIES IN THE LAW"

1. See W. Lance Bennett and Martha S. Feldman, "Storytelling in the Courtroom," *Reconstructing Reality in the Courtroom: Justice and Judgment in American Culture* (New Brunswick, N.J.: Rutgers University Press, 1981), pp. 3–18; and David Ray Papke, *Narrative and the Legal Discourse: A Reader in Storytelling and the Law* (Liverpool, Eng.: Deborath Charles, 1991). For an excellent practical demonstration of how notions of storytelling apply to courtroom narratives, see Karen Halttunen, " 'Domestic Differences': Competing Narratives of Womanhood in the Murder Trial of Lucretia Chapman," in Shirley Samuels, ed., *The Culture of Sentiment: Race, Gender and Sentimentality in Nineteenth-Century America* (Oxford: Oxford University Press, 1992), pp. 39–57, 286–89. In the words of Bennett and Feldman, "[T]he criminal trial is organized around storytelling." "The story is an everyday form of communication that enables a diverse cast of courtroom characters to follow the development of a case and reason about the issues in it. Despite the maze of legal jargon, lawyers' mysterious tactics, and obscure court procedures, any criminal case can be reduced to the simple form of story. Through the use of broadly shared techniques of telling and interpreting stories, the actors in a trial present, organize, and analyze the evidence that bears on the alleged illegal activity."

2. Peter Brooks, *Reading for the Plot: Design and Intention in Narrative* (New York: Knopf, 1984), pp. 3–7, 37–38.

3. Perhaps the best quick summary of this point comes in Hayden White's explanation that the world does not just "present itself to perception in the form of well-made stories, with central subjects, proper beginnings, middles, and ends." Someone must create a narrative or story based upon modes of perception and presuppositions that are value laden. Hayden White, "The Value of Narrativity in the Representation of Reality," in W. J. T. Mitchell, ed., *On Narrative* (Chicago: University of Chicago Press, 1981), p. 23.

4. Rape trials provide perhaps the clearest example of this phenomenon of stereotyping in contemporary American culture. For a good treatment of the subject, one that discusses both courtroom and popular narratives, see Helen Benedict, *Virgin or Vamp: How the Press Covers Sex Crimes* (New York: Oxford University Press, 1992).

5. Theophilus Parsons, Jr., *Memoir of Theophilus Parsons, Chief Justice of the Supreme Judicial Court of Massachusetts; with Notices of Some of His Contemporaries* (Boston: Ticknor and Fields, 1859), pp. 218–19. For the frequently applied epithet "the giant of the law in Massachusetts" and its signifi-

cance, see pp. 156–57, 166, 206–8. Parsons's high status came not just from his legendary displays of learning both as a lawyer and then as a judge but also from his prominent role in eighteenth-century republican constitutional theory. *The Essex Result,* a pamphlet published by Parsons based on the Essex County Convention's opposition to the Massachusetts Constitution of 1778, became a fundamental source in the formation of both the Massachusetts Constitution of 1780 and the Federal Constitution of 1787.

6. The vocabulary for each of the imputed defenses named in this paragraph can be found in Charles J. Sykes, *A Nation of Victims: The Decay of American Character* (New York: St. Martin's, 1992), pp. 11, 118, 127–30, 148, 154.

7. Sykes describes relevant cases in all four categories in *A Nation of Victims.*

8. For recent analyses of the generic implications of courtroom narrative, particularly the move from the execution sermon to the sentimental account, the gothic tale, the criminal docudrama, and the melodrama, see Daniel A. Cohen, *Pillars of Salt, Monuments of Grace: New England Crime Literature and the Origins of American Popular Culture, 1674–1860* (Oxford: Oxford University Press, 1993); and Karen Halttunen, "Early American Murder Narratives: The Birth of Horror," in Richard Wightman Fox and T. J. Jackson Lears, eds., *The Power of Culture: Critical Essays in American History* (Chicago: University of Chicago Press, 1993), pp. 67-101. For the emergence of the romance as a genre in courtroom narratives, see Robert A. Ferguson, "Story and Transcription in the Trial of John Brown," *Yale Journal of Law and the Humanities,* 6 (Winter 1994), 37–73.

9. Clifford Geertz, "Common Sense as a Cultural System," in Geertz, *Local Knowledge: Further Essays in Interpretive Anthropology* (New York: Basic Books, 1983), pp. 73–93. See, in particular, pp. 75–76, 84–85. Among other things, Geertz argues that "common sense is not what the mind cleared of cant spontaneously apprehends; it is what the mind filled with presuppositions . . . concludes."

10. Robert Sutcliff, *Travels in Some Parts of North America, in the Years 1804, 1805, and 1806* (York, Eng.: C. Peacock, 1811), p. 50.

11. James Monroe to Joseph Cabell, February 8, 1828, quoted in Douglas R. Egerton, *Gabriel's Rebellion: The Virginia Slave Conspiracies of 1800 and 1802* (Chapel Hill: University of North Carolina Press, 1993), p. 112; James Monroe to Thomas Jefferson, September 15, 1800, in Stanislaus Murray Hamilton, ed., *The Writings of James Monroe* (New York: G. P. Putnam's Sons, 1900), 3:208–9; and Thomas Jefferson to James Monroe, September 20, 1800, in Paul Leicester Ford, ed., *The Writings of Thomas Jefferson* (New York: G. P. Putnam's Sons, 1896), 7:457–58. Monroe describes how he "made a display of our force and measures of defence with the view to intimidate those people." Jefferson, in response, recommends caution while agreeing with the need for "some severities," and he wonders "whether these people can ever be permitted to go at large among us with safety." For the most accurate record of the executions and other punishments administered by the Henrico County slave courts after the slave rebellion of 1800, see Philip J. Schwartz, *Twice Condemned: Slaves and the Criminal Laws of Virginia, 1705–1865* (Baton Rouge: Louisiana State University Press, 1988), pp. 324–27.

12. All of these measures are described at some length in Egerton, *Gabriel's Rebellion,* pp. 88, 141, 164–68.

13. Daniel Sisson, *The American Revolution of 1800* (New York: Knopf, 1974).

14. Sigmund Freud, *Civilization and Its Discontents,* in James Strachey, ed., *The Standard Edition of the Complete Psychological Works of Sigmund Freud* (London: Hogarth Press, 1961), 21:141, 95–97, 60, 69–70.

15. Freud, "The Uncanny," in Strachey, ed., *Standard Edition of the Works of Freud,* 17:219–20, 241, 245.

16. Mary Douglas, *How Institutions Think* (Syracuse, N.Y.: Syracuse University Press, 1986), pp. 69–70, 76, 90.

17. "The Trial of Gabriel," "Confessions of Ben Alias Ben Woolfolk," and "The Trial of Gilbert, the Property of Wm. Young," in H. W. Flournoy, ed., *Calendar of Virginia State Papers and Other Manuscripts from January 1, 1799, to December 31, 1807; Preserved in the Capitol at Richmond,* vol. 9 (Richmond: Virginia State Library, 1890), pp. 164–65, 150–53. All trial records of the slave rebellion

are contained in this source, pp. 140–74, hereinafter cited as "Gabriel Rebellion," in *Calender of Virginia State Papers.*

18. Sutcliff, *Travels in Some Parts of North America*, p. 50.

19. Arthur Lee, "Address on Slavery," *Virginia Gazette*, March 19, 1767. Other Virginians were so outraged by this essay that the publisher of the *Virginia Gazette* refused to publish a sequel to it.

20. Thomas Jefferson, "Query XVIII: Manners," in Jefferson, *Notes on the State of Virginia*, ed. William Peden (Chapel Hill: University of North Carolina Press, 1955), pp. 162–63; and Thomas Jefferson to John Holmes, April 22, 1820, in Merrill D. Peterson, ed., *Thomas Jefferson: Writings* (New York: Library of America, 1984), p. 1434. This is the famous "fire bell in the night" letter over the Missouri question, which, in Jefferson's words, "filled me with terror." In private correspondence with confidants, Jefferson could be even blunter and more alarmed. Speaking of the potential rebelliousness of Virginia slaves in 1797, he wrote, "[I]f something is not done, & soon done, we shall be the murderers of our own children [for] the revolutionary storm, now sweeping the globe, will be upon us." Thomas Jefferson to St. George Tucker, August 28, 1797, in Ford, ed., *Writings of Thomas Jefferson*, 7:168.

21. "Only one term sums up all the qualities that enable a speculation to become established and then to escape oblivion; that is the principle of coherence. . . . [I]t needs to be compatible with the prevailing political values, which are themselves naturalized." Douglas, *How Institutions Think*, p. 90.

22. George Earlie Shankle, *State Names, Flags, Seals, Songs, Birds, Flowers, and Other Symbols* (New York: H. W. Wilson, 1934), pp. 215–18. See also Benjamin F. Shearer and Barbara S. Shearer, *State Names, Seals, Flags, and Symbols: A Historical Guide* (Westport, Conn.: Greenwood Press, 1987), pp. 59, 30.

23. John Locke, chapter 4 of *An Essay Concerning the True Original, Extent, and End of Civil Government* (1690), in Peter Laslett, ed., *Two Treatises of Government*, 2d critical ed. (Cambridge: Cambridge University Press, 1967), p. 302.

24. Freud, "The Uncanny," pp. 220–25, 241. "For this uncanny is in reality nothing new or alien, but something which is familiar and old-established in the mind and which has become alienated from it only through the process of repression." For a general analysis of the prevalence of the uncanny in patterns of American thought, see Priscilla Wald, *Constituting Americans: Cultural Anxiety and Narrative Form* (Durham, N.C.: Duke University Press, 1995).

25. Lee, "Address on Slavery." In parallel fashion, Jefferson writes that "these liberties are of the gift of God," but he finds "physical and moral" differences between the races that are "fixed in nature" and that suggest of blacks that "their inferiority is not the effect merely of their condition of life." "I advance it therefore as a suspicion only," he concludes, "that the blacks, whether originally a distinct race, or made distinct by time and circumstances, are inferior to the whites in the endowments both of body and mind." Thomas Jefferson, *Notes on the State of Virginia*, pp. 163, 138–43.

26. Racist theories of delay receive more and more elaborate formulation from later Southern writers. The underlying goal is always to stretch out the timing for any prospective revolution. By 1832, for example, Thomas Roderick Dew could write in the *American Quarterly Review*, "[I]s it an evil of yesterday's origin? . . . No, we have to deal with an evil which is the growth of centuries and of tens of centuries." Hence, revolution *now* is an unnatural act. The black revolutionary in Dew's construct becomes a Frankenstein monster to be held in place indefinitely. "In dealing with a negro," Dew claims, "we must remember that we are dealing with a being possessing the form and strength of a man, but the intellect only of a child. To turn him loose in the manhood of his passions, but in the infancy of his uninstructed reason, would be to raise up a creature resembling the splendid fiction of a recent romance; the hero of which constructs a human form with all the physical capabilities of a man, and with the thews and sinews of a giant, but being unable to impart to the work of his hands a perception of right and wrong, he finds too late that he has only created a more than mortal power of doing mischief, and himself recoils from the monster which he has made." For this and other elaborate defenses of the Southern slave system against the prospect of revolution, see Drew Gilpin Faust, ed., *The Ideology of*

Slavery: Proslavery Thought in the Antebellum South, 1830–1860. (Baton Rouge: Louisiana State University Press, 1981), pp. 60 ff.

27. Most variations on the theme of a minority founding father defuse the logic of rebellion. Typically, Venture Smith (Broteer Furro) is portrayed as "a Franklin and a Washington, in a state of nature" only after he has been safely "enfeebled and depressed by slavery" and "broken by hardships and infirmities of age." Venture Smith, *A Narrative of the Life and Adventures of Venture, a Native of Africa, but Resident Above Sixty Years in the United States of America* (1798; rpt., Middletown, Conn.: J. S. Stewart, 1897), p. 2. Queequeg, in *Moby-Dick,* is "George Washington cannibalistically developed," but, again, the description carefully casts its subject in repose rather than in one of Queequeg's many moments of prowess or physical power. Herman Melville, *Moby-Dick; or, the Whale,* ed. Charles Feidelson, Jr. (New York: Bobbs-Merrill, 1964), p. 82.

28. For the many, detailed references at the trial to the military organization of the slave conspirators, see "Gabriel Rebellion," in *Calendar of Virginia State Papers,* pp. 141, 144–45, 146, 151–53, 159–60, 164–65, 168, 170–71. For John Randolph's conclusion, supported by others, that the "execution of [Gabriel's] purpose was frustrated only by a heavy fall of rain which made the water courses impassable," see Egerton, *Gabriel's Rebellion,* p. 77. Randolph was impressed and shaken by the martial vigor and discipline that he observed in the defendants at trial. "The accused have exhibited a spirit, which, if it becomes general, must deluge the Southern country in blood," he wrote when they were executed. "They manifested a sense of their rights, and contempt of danger, and a thirst for revenge which portend the most unhappy consequences." John Randolph to Joseph H. Nicholson, September 26, 1800, quoted in William Cabell Bruce, *John Randolph of Roanoke, 1773–1833* (New York: G. P. Putnam's Sons, 1922), 2:250–51.

29. George Washington, "To the President of Congress, Cambridge, February 9, 1776," "General Orders, January 1, 1776," and "To the President of Congress, September 24, 1776," in William B. Allen, ed., *George Washington: A Collection* (Indianapolis: Liberty Classics, 1988), pp. 63, 56, 80. See also George F. Scheer and Hugh F. Rankin, eds., *Rebels and Redcoats: The American Revolution Through the Eyes of Those Who Fought and Lived It* (New York: World Publishing Co., 1957), pp. 304–5; and James Thomas Flexner, *Washington: The Indispensable Man* (Boston: Little, Brown, 1969), pp. 37, 68–69.

30. Thomas Jefferson to Dr. Walter Jones, January 2, 1814, in Peterson, ed., *Thomas Jefferson: Writings,* pp. 1318–19.

31. Washington's Last Will and Testament, written in his own hand, is dated July 9, 1799, and he clearly meant to give the emancipation provision a special prominence; it appears on the first page in just the fourth paragraph of a document of more than five thousand words, preceding all other bequests with the exception of those to Martha Washington, "my dearly loved wife." See Allen, ed., *George Washington: A Collection,* pp. 667–79.

32. Sutcliff, *Travels in Some Parts of North America,* p. 50.

33. Claude Lévi-Strauss, *The Savage Mind* (Chicago: University of Chicago Press, 1962), p. 32.

34. Douglas, *How Institutions Think,* p. 102.

35. For the long record of legal repression of slavery issues in the United States, see Robert M. Cover, *Justice Accused: Antislavery and the Judicial Process* (New Haven: Yale University Press, 1975).

36. Patricia Williams, *The Alchemy of Race and Rights* (Cambridge: Harvard University Press, 1991), pp. 119–20, 191; see also pp. 4, 129, 183, 191. In perhaps the best concise expression of the burden she feels, Williams makes it clear that breaking silence in the face of discrimination takes courage and requires the help of others. Caught in such a situation, she writes: "I think that the hard work of a nonracist sensibility is the boundary crossing, from safe circle into wilderness; the testing of boundary, the consecration of sacrilege. It is the willingness to spoil a good party and break an encompassing circle, to travel from the safe to the unsafe" (p. 129).

37. James Monroe to Colonel Thomas Newton, October 5, 1800, in Hamilton, ed., *Writings of James Monroe,* 3:213.

38. These are the words of Mrs. Prices John, one of the slave conspirators, during the trial of Gabriel's second in command, Jack Bowler, who lost the election that Gabriel won "by the far greater number" of votes taken. "Gabriel Rebellion," in *Calendar of Virginia State Papers*, p. 159.

39. Freud, "The Uncanny," p. 249.

40. Herman Melville, *Benito Cereno*, in Harrison Hayford, Alma A. MacDougall, and G. Thomas Tanselle, eds., *The Piazza Tales and Other Prose Pieces, 1839–1860*, in *The Writings of Herman Melville* (Evanston, Ill.: Northwestern University Press and the Newberry Library, 1987), 9:47–117, 116, 112. For the most complete treatment of *Benito Cereno* and slave rebellions, see Eric J. Sundquist, *To Wake the Nations: Race in the Making of American Literature* (Cambridge: Harvard University Press, 1993), pp. 135–89. See also Susan Weiner, " 'Benito Cereno' and the Failure of Law," *Arizona Quarterly*, 47 (Summer 1991), 1–28; and, more generally, Carolyn L. Karcher, *Shadow over the Promised Land: Slavery, Race, and Violence in Melville's America* (Baton Rouge: Louisiana State University Press, 1980).

41. William Styron, *The Confessions of Nat Turner* (New York: Random House, 1966). For a summary of negative reactions, particularly from African Americans, see John Henrik Clarke, ed., *William Styron's Nat Turner: Ten Black Writers Respond* (Boston: Beacon Press, 1968).

42. Clarke, ed., *William Styron's Nat Turner*, x. Clarke adds that "our Nat is still waiting." For some attempts to find him, see John B. Duff and Peter M. Mitchell, eds., *The Nat Turner Rebellion: The Historical Event and the Modern Controversy* (New York: Harper and Row, 1971); Eric Foner, ed., *Nat Turner: Great Lives Observed* (Englewood Cliffs, N.J.: Prentice-Hall, 1971); Henry Irving Tragle, *The Southampton Slave Revolt of 1831: A Compilation of Source Material* (Amherst: University of Massachusetts Press, 1971); and Albert E. Stone, *The Return of Nat Turner: History, Literature, and Cultural Politics in Sixties America* (Athens: University of Georgia Press, 1992).

43. Arna Bontemps, *Black Thunder* (1936; rpt., Boston: Beacon Press, 1968), vii.

44. This point is aptly expressed in writings by Nathaniel Hawthorne. "What is there so ponderous in evil," he asks in *The House of the Seven Gables*, "that a thumb's bigness of it should outweigh the mass of things not evil, which were heaped into the other scale! This scale and balance system is a favorite one with people of Judge Pyncheon's brotherhood." Millicent Bell, ed., *Nathaniel Hawthorne: Novels* (New York: Library of America, 1983), p. 551.

45. In the peroration to *Soul on Ice*, written in prison, Eldridge Cleaver seeks to speak with "the new voice," "the voice of the Black Man," away from the "obsequious whine of a cringing slave," away from the "unctuous supplications of the sleek Black Bourgeoise," away from even the "bullying bellow of the rude Free Slave." To do so he actively invokes the spirits of black rebels past, Toussaint L'Ouverture, Gabriel Prosser, Nat Turner, and Denmark Vesey. They are part of a larger promise: "[W]e shall have our manhood. We shall have it or the earth will be leveled by our attempts to gain it." Cleaver, *Soul on Ice* (New York: McGraw-Hill, 1968), pp. 205, 208, 61.

46. Melville, *Benito Cereno*, 9:98.

47. "Gabriel Rebellion," in *Calendar of Virginia State Papers*, pp. 153, 164.

ALAN M. DERSHOWITZ, "LIFE IS NOT A DRAMATIC NARRATIVE"

1. Alan M. Dershowitz, *The Advocate's Devil* 24–25 (1995). This fictional account is based on an actual case I won with the help of this argument. In real life, my son, Elon—then in college and today a film producer—came up with the Chekhov analysis.

2. *Anton Tchekhov: Literary and Theatrical Reminiscences* 23 (S. S. Koteliansky, ed. and trans., 1974).

3. Initially attributed to the ancient Greeks, Cosmos is the idea that everything in the universe, from the motions of the planets to the workings of the human mind, can be explained by science or reason. *Dictionary of the History of Ideas* 4:46–51 (Philip P. Weiner, ed., 1973).

4. Compare Rabbi Adin Steinsaltz, *The Talmud: The Steinsaltz Edition: A Reference Guide* 6 (1989) ("Points already made are not repeated without reason.").

5. See e.g., Sigmund Freud, *The Interpretation of Dreams* 32 (Brill translation, 1994).

6. See e.g., Robert Bork, *The Tempting of America* 145 (1990). Even a quick reading of some carelessly written, confusing and even mistaken provisions of our hastily drafted Constitution and Bill of Rights should dispel any notion of divinity in its very human authors. For example, the Seventh Amendment provides for trial by jury in "suits at common law, where the value in controversy shall exceed twenty dollars." I can just imagine the framers looking down at our crowded courts from constitutional heaven and moaning, "Did we say twenty dollars? Damn, we meant the *value* of twenty dollars taking inflation into account. We didn't want every two-bit case in front of a jury. Why didn't we write it more carefully!"

7. Stephen J. Gould, *Wonderful Life* (1989).

8. The "naturalistic fallacy" refers to G. E. Moore's discussion of the analytical flaw whereby a person "is *either* confusing Good with a natural *or* metaphysical property *or* holding it to be identical with such a property or making an inference *based* on such a confusion." Casmir Levy, "G. E. Moore on the Naturalistic Fallacy," in *G. E. Moore—Essays in Retrospect* 297 (Alice Ambrose and Morris Lazerowitz, eds., 1970) (emphasis added). Egregious examples of such thinking include statements by Patrick Buchanan that AIDS is "nature's form of retribution" against "unnatural acts" and by Rabbi Eliezer Shach that the Holocaust was caused by Jews eating pork. Buchanan, "AIDS Is Retribution," *Newsday,* February 28, 1992, *Star Tribune,* December 28, 1990.

9. Jean-Paul Sartre, *Nausea* 39–40 (Lloyd Alexander, trans., 1964).

10. This is not to discount the power of science as a predictive tool in many areas, including human behavior. Among the most difficult predictive tasks, however, is to identify correctly, without too many false positives, which individuals will engage in relatively rare conduct.

11. A Production Code enforced by the Motion Picture Producers and Distributors of America in the 1930s dictated that "the sympathy of the audience shall never be thrown to the side of crime, wrong doing, evil or sin." Raymond Moley, *The Hayes Office* 98–99 (1945) (emphasis omitted). Since then, movie audiences have grown used to seeing crime always followed by punishment.

A wonderful parody of the classic Chekhov canon appears in the film *Hot Shots!* (1991).

DEAD MEAT: Mary! Mary! (embrace) Have you come to watch me fly?

MARY: There was a meltdown at the plant so they gave me the afternoon off.

DEAD MEAT: Aw, terrific! (black cat runs across their path)

MARY: Oh good news! We just closed escrow on our little dream house.

DEAD MEAT: Wonderful! When do we move in?

MARY: Tuesday. I've got the kids stripping the asbestos off the pipes right now.

DEAD MEAT: Aw, that's great. (walks under a ladder) Things just couldn't be better for us. I'm so blessed.

MARY: Oh—your life insurance forms came for you to sign. (drops her mirror from her purse and it shatters) Oh, my mirror!

DEAD MEAT: (pen doesn't work) Huh.

MARY: I'll get another pen.

DEAD MEAT: No need. I'll sign it when I get back.

MARY: Well, you know best.

DEAD MEAT: Honey, you know that global warming problem? I've discovered how we can reverse it.

MARY: Tell me!

DEAD MEAT: No, not now lovey bumpers. There'll be plenty of time for that later. And my investigation into the assassination of JFK . . .

MARY: You found the evidence you were looking for?!?

DEAD MEAT: Yes, I have proof. It's right here in my pocket. It's big, honey. It's really big. It goes all the way to the White House.

MARY: Do you want me to hold it for you?

DEAD MEAT: Naw. It will be safe right here. I'm in a jet. What could go wrong?

MARY: Oh Dead Meat . . . We just couldn't be any more perfectly happy. (they blow kisses at each other.)

Dead Meat's airplane then crashes.

12. Another parody is recounted in James Gleick's biography of Richard Feynman: "He had developed pointed ways of illustrating the slippage that occurred when experimenters allowed themselves to be less than rigorously skeptical or failed to appreciate the power of coincidence. He described a common experience: an experimenter notices a peculiar result after many trials—rats in a maze, for example, turn alternately right, left, right, and left. The experimenter calculates the odds against something so extraordinary and decides it cannot have been an accident. Feynman would say: 'I had the most remarkable experience. . . . While coming in here I saw license plate ANZ 912. Calculate for me, please, the odds that of all the license plates . . .' And he would tell a story from his days in the fraternity at MIT, with a surprise ending.

"'I was upstairs typewriting a theme on something about philosophy. And I was completely engrossed, not thinking of anything but the theme, when all of a sudden in a most mysterious fashion there swept through my mind the idea: my grandmother has died. Now of course I exaggerate slightly, as you should in all such stories. I just sort of half got the idea for a minute. . . . Immediately after that the telephone rang downstairs. I remember this distinctly for the reason you will now hear. . . . It was for somebody else. My grandmother was perfectly healthy and there's nothing to it. Now what we have to do is to accumulate a large number of these to fight the few cases when it could happen.'" Gleick, *Genius: The Life and Science of Richard Feynman* 374 (1992).

13. In this chapter I focus on the narrative as traditionally employed in classic literature. The works of Mamet, Beckett, Pirandello, Proust, Robbes-Grillet, Duras, and others often employ narratives that are much more reflective of the randomness of life.

14. Alan Cowell, "German Scholar Unmasked as Former SS Officer," New York Times, June 1, 1995.

15. See 3 *The Interpreter's Bible* 1196–97 (George Arthur Buttrick et al., eds., 1954).

16. If the concept of "law" begins with human laws of behavior, such as "Thou shalt not murder," one might think that science borrowed this concept of laws and metaphorically applied it to natural phenomena, as with the laws of thermodynamics. In reality, the laws of science predate human laws, and the latter are borrowed from the former. In some languages, there are distinct words for human and scientific "laws."

17. Richard K. Sherwin, "Law Frames: Historical Truth and Narrative Necessity in a Criminal Case," 47 Stan. L. Rev 39 (1994) (demonstrating the tendency in the legal search for truth to oversimplify complex situations to meet the demands of the modern mind for consistency and certainty).

18. The issue is complex. It is probably true that a significant percentage of women who end up murdered by an unknown assailant were murdered by spouses or lovers who had previously abused them. But it is also probably true that a significant percentage of murdered women were murdered by spouses or lovers who did *not* abuse them. The question is the relative saliency of the relationship (spouse, lover) or of the act (battering).

19. See State v. White, 271 N.C. 391, 395, 156 S.E.2d 721, 724 (1967).

20. A related misuse of narrative would be for a prosecutor to introduce evidence in a rape case that a defendant viewed pornography. In some feminist narratives, the viewing of pornography is followed by rape or, retrospectively, rapists admit that they were viewers of pornography. In the Dworkin-MacKinnon narrative, readers expect that the story of the viewer of pornography will end with him becoming a rapist. In real life, the story is far more likely to go something like this: "John started with *Playboy* as a

child, then he moved up to *Penthouse,* and soon he was watching hard-core videos. Eventually, he became an accountant with a wife and three kids." Such boringly realistic narratives are never told, although they reflect the statistical reality that the vast majority of pornography viewers are and remain law-abiding citizens. Indeed, whenever I read agenda-driven narratives, I suspect selective editing. But such narratives are difficult for scholars to challenge without questioning the accuracy or integrity of the storyteller. See "Scientists Deplore Flight from Reason," *New York Times,* June 6, 1995, at C1.

21. See Amos Tversky and Daniel Kahneman, "Judgment Under Uncertainty: Heuristics and Biases," 185 *Science* 1124 (1974), reprinted in *Judgment Under Uncertainty: Heuristics and Biases* (Daniel Kahneman et al., eds., 1982).

22. Even Chekhov acknowledges the often-unrealistic nature of his canon: "Shtcheglov-Leontyev blames me for finishing the story with the words, 'There's no making out anything in this world.' He thinks a writer who is a good psychologist ought to be able to make it out—that is what he is a psychologist for. But I don't agree with him. It is time that writers, especially those who are artists, recognized that there is no making out anything in this world, as once Socrates recognized it, and Voltaire, too. The mob thinks it knows and understands everything; and the more stupid it is the wider it imagines its outlook to be. And if a writer whom the mob believes in has the courage to say that he does not understand anything of what he sees, that alone will be something gained in the realm of thought and a great step in advance." Anton Chekhov, Letter to A. S. Suvorin, May 30, 1888, in *Letters of Anton Chekhov to His Family and Friends* 84, 89 (Constance Garnett, trans, 1920).

PETER BROOKS, "STORYTELLING WITHOUT FEAR?"

For helpful advice and comments on this essay, I would like to thank several friends and colleagues who read and criticized earlier drafts: Akhil Amar, Owen Fiss, Juliet Mitchell, Louis Michael Seidman, Robert Weisberg, and Paul Gewirtz. Coteaching a course on narrative in law and literature with Paul Gewirtz has proved an incomparable learning experience.

1. These essentials of the narrative are presented on the title page of the most recent recounting of the case, by John Spargo, *The Return of Russell Colvin* (Bennington, Vt.: Bennington Historical Museum and Art Gallery, 1945). See also Leonard Sargent, *The Trial, Confessions and Conviction of Jesse and Stephen Boorn, for the Murder of Russell Colvin, and the Return of the Man Supposed to Have Been Murdered* (Manchester, Vt.: Journal Book and Job Office, 1873). Sargent, later lieutenant governor of Vermont, was one counsel for the defense at the trial.

2. On the "prophylactic standards," see *Michigan v. Tucker,* 417 U.S. 433 (1974).

3. Frankfurter's plurality opinion in *Culombe v. Connecticut* is characterized as a "treatise" by Chief Justice Earl Warren, concurring, who points out that the opinion is going to offer very little helpful guidance to police officers (thus necessitating the *Miranda* decision). *Culombe,* 367 U.S. 568, at 636.

4. The Court retreated from some of the implications of *Miranda* in subsequent cases—for example, *Harris v. New York* (1971), *Michigan v. Tucker* (1974), *Rhode Island v. Innis* (1980), *New York v. Quarles* (1984)—but the substance of *Miranda* can nonetheless be said to have remained in place. The most thoughtful discussion of the issues raised by *Miranda* that I have seen is by Louis Michael Seidman, in *"Brown* and *Miranda,"* 80 *California Law Review* 673 (May 1992), who considers whether *Miranda* should be considered a "rejection of liberal individualism" or a "victory of liberal individualism," effectively bringing out the contradictions that inhabit the decision. See also the penetrating comments of Robert Weisberg, in "Criminal Law, Criminology, and the Small World of Legal Scholars," 63 *University of Colorado Law Review* 521 (1992). For a wealth of additional detail about the *Miranda* case, see Liva Baker, *Miranda: Crime, Law and Politics* (New York: Atheneum, 1983).

5. See Wolfgang Iser, *The Implied Reader [Der Implizite Leser]* (Baltimore, Md.: Johns Hopkins University Press, 1984). Note that Justice Harlan in dissent objects to Warren's extrapolation of the story of the closed room from police interrogation manuals, which he characterizes as "merely writings in this field by professors and some police officers" (499).

6. In *Escobedo v. Illinois* (378 U.S. 483), we learn that the police summoned "an experienced lawyer who was assigned to the Homicide Division to take 'statements from some defendants and some prisoners that they had in custody.'" The lawyer "'took' petitioner's statement by asking carefully framed questions apparently designed to assure the admissibility into evidence of the resulting answers."

7. See Henry J. Friendly: "[W]hile the other privileges accord with notions of decent conduct generally accepted in life outside the court room, the privilege against self-incrimination defies them. No parent would teach such a doctrine to his children; the lesson parents preach is that while a misdeed, even a serious one, will generally be forgiven, a failure to make a clean breast of it will not be. Every hour of the day people are being asked to explain their conduct to parents, employers and teachers. Those who are questioned consider themselves to be morally bound to respond, and the questioners believe it proper to take action if they do not." "The Fifth Amendment Tomorrow: The Case for Constitutional Change," 37 *University of Cincinnati Law Review* 680 (1968). Friendly's comment elides the difference between confessing to benevolent authorities and confession to the police, who are not about to forgive a misdeed—as he partially acknowledges in a footnote. But he makes the important point that the Fifth Amendment privilege is counterintuitive to everyday morality.

8. I follow here largely the work of Edward Peters, *Inquisition* (New York: Free Press, 1988), 65 ff.; and John H. Langbein, *Torture and the Law of Proof* (Chicago: University of Chicago Press, 1977), 3–17. See also Nicolau Eymerich and Francisco Peña, *Le Manuel des inquisiteurs,* trans. and ed. Louis Sala-Molins (Paris: Mouton, 1973). Eymerich, a Dominican from Catalonia, composed the *Directorium inquisitorium* in Avignon in 1376; it was printed in 1503. Peña's recompilation and updating of the *Directorium* was published in Rome in 1585.

9. See Langbein, *Torture and the Law of Proof,* 9.

10. The most useful study of the history of the right against self-incrimination is the magisterial book by Leonard W. Levy, *Origins of the Fifth Amendment,* 2d ed. (1968; New York: Macmillan, 1986). Some of Levy's historical arguments have been challenged; see R. H. Helmholz, "Origins of the Privilege Against Self-Incrimination: The Role of the European *ius commune,*" 65 *New York University Law Review* 962 (1990).

11. *Coke's Rep.* 9, at 10 (1609), 77 *Eng. Rep.* 1421, 1422, cited in Levy, *Origins,* 246.

12. See Levy's discussion of this point in *Origins,* 328.

13. For a probing analysis of this issue, see Louis Michael Seidman, "Rubashov's Question: Self-Incrimination and the Problem of Coerced Preferences," 2 *Yale Journal of Law and the Humanities* 149 (1990). Seidman argues, in part in reference to the permissible compulsion of *United States v. Doe,* 465 U.S. 605 (1984), in which the defendant was forced to sign a "consent decree": "The point is not that the government *ought not* to coerce such statements [regarding internal mental states]. Rather, the government *cannot* coerce such statements because the application of coercive pressure makes them something other than statements regarding internal mental states" (158). I will argue later that this may be correct, but the statements may in that case hold another kind of confessional truth. I am not convinced that a preference theory of the Fifth Amendment privilege can wholly respond to the root objections to compelled confessions, which seem to me to be ethical. In this context, see the appropriately skeptical remarks of Robert Weisberg: "The jurisprudence of the Fifth Amendment directly raises the question raised indirectly by searches and seizures: What image of the autonomous human being do we believe in?" (538). And: "We have no coherent analysis of what it means to be autonomous in the face of the law, and we are left instead with shallow rationalizations about the psychology of volition, abetted in the Sixth Amendment area by hilarious rationalizations about the effects of the invisible formalities of state prosecution on the volition of a poor wretch of a subject." "Criminal Law, Criminology, and the Small World of Legal Scholars," 63 *University of Colorado Law Review* 538–39 (1992).

14. Abe Fortas, "The Fifth Amendment: *Nemo tenetur seipsum prodere,*" 25 Cleveland Bar Association, *Journal* 91 (1954), at 98–100, passim, cited in Levy, *Origins,* 431.

15. Jean-Jacques Rousseau, *Confessions: Autres textes autobiographiques,* ed. Bernard Gagnebin and Marcel Raymond (Paris: Pléiade, 1962), 5. The translations from Rousseau are my own.

16. Paul de Man, *Allegories of Reading* (New Haven: Yale University Press, 1979), 285.

17. J. L. Austin, *How to Do Things with Words* (Cambridge: Harvard University Press, 1962).

18. This is consonant with the psychoanalytic model of confession developed by Theodor Reik in *The Compulsion to Confess* (New York: Farrar, Straus and Cudahy, 1959). For Reik, confession expresses a desire for punishment, and to the extent that it is made to a father-figure—a representative of the superego—it is perfectly consonant with the dependency model of police interrogation. Reik says of the confession that takes the form of "acting out" in psychoanalysis: "This confession is often not an end in itself. It has the meaning of an appeal to the parents or their substitutes, which is what makes necessary the addition of a concluding sentence: 'Please consider those weaknesses! Just because this is how I am, you must forgive me! Punish me, but love me again!' Thus the confession becomes an eloquent plea for absolution" (208).

19. Consider the Talmudic rule that in a criminal case, a person can be condemned only on the testimony of two witnesses and that a person's own confession, even if voluntarily given, cannot be admitted as evidence. According to Maimonides' commentary: "It is a scriptural decree that the court shall not put a man to death or flog him on his own admission [of guilt]. . . . For it is possible that he was confused in mind when he made the confession. Perhaps he was one of those who are in misery, bitter in soul, who long for death, thrust the sword into their bellies or cast themselves down from the roofs. Perhaps this was the reason that prompted him to confess to a crime he had not committed, in order that he be put to death. To sum up the matter, the principle that no man is to be declared guilty on his own admission is a divine decree." *The Code of Maimonides, book 14: The Book of Judges,* trans. Abraham M. Hershman (New Haven: Yale University Press, 1949), 52–53, cited in Levy, *Origins,* 438. As Levy pertinently comments, in this view "confession was a form of suicide, which was sinful and violative of the instinct of self-preservation."

20. See Sigmund Freud, "Some Character-Types Met With in Psychoanalytic Work," *Standard Edition of the Complete Psychological Works* (London: Hogarth Press, 1953–74), 14:332–33.

21. De Man, *Allegories of Reading,* 299–300.

22. See David Simon, *Homicide: A Year on the Killing Streets* (Boston: Houghton Mifflin, 1991), 200 ff. See also Stephen J. Schulhofer on the fact that the *Miranda* warnings have not significantly reduced the number of confessions: "Nonetheless, suspects agree to talk without the need for pressure or deception (often because they think they can talk their way out of trouble)." "Reconsidering *Miranda*," *Occasional Papers from the Law School, the University of Chicago* (Buffalo, N.Y.: William S. Hein, 1987), 23. The attempt to talk their way out of trouble often involves unwitting confessions to incriminating knowledge.

23. Schulhofer quotes the pre-*Miranda* edition of Inbau and Reid's *Criminal Interrogation and Confession* (1962), in which the interrogator is instructed to say to the suspect: "Joe, you have the right to remain silent. That's your privilege. . . . But let me ask you this. Suppose you were in my shoes and I were in yours . . . and I told you, 'I don't want to answer any of your questions.' You'd think I had something to hide." "Reconsidering *Miranda*," 14 n.14.

24. Burger refers his reader here to Reik's *Compulsion to Confess* without, I think, understanding the full implications of Reik's argument, which suggests that the need to confess may have little to do with the crime committed. Indeed, in his "Postscript" to "Freud's View on Capital Punishment" (a contribution to a 1926 symposium to which Reik gave a statement based on a conversation with Freud), Reik argues, along the lines of "Criminals from a Sense of Guilt," that crime may be the result of guilt, rather than vice versa: "Freud has shown that, in the criminals at whom criminal legislation is really directed, a powerful unconscious feeling of guilt exists even before the deed. . . . It is hence not the consequence of the deed, but its motive. . . . As a result, punishment, according to accepted views, the most effective deterrent against crime, becomes, under certain psychological extremely common conditions in our culture, the most dangerous unconscious stimulus for crime because it serves the gratification of the unconscious feeling of guilt, which presses toward a forbidden act" (473–74). This under-

standing of the relation of guilt, crime, and punishment is fully consonant with what we have seen in Rousseau.

Technically, *Brewer v. Williams* is not a voluntariness case because it was decided on Sixth Amendment, not Fifth Amendment, doctrine, but it does turn on whether Williams voluntarily waived his right to counsel (for which there is a special set of rules).

25. Yale Kamisar, in *Police Interrogations and Confessions* (Ann Arbor: University of Michigan Press, 1980), argues that *Brewer* should have been decided as a *Miranda*-doctrine case, not a *Massiah*-doctrine case. The question of whether Williams voluntarily waived his right to counsel points to a continuing difficulty in *Miranda* doctrine: How can we know if a waiver is voluntary? If counsel is necessary to avoid unwitting self-incrimination, isn't counsel necessary knowingly to waive the right to counsel? Let us note that the statement "I waive [my right to . . .]" is another performative.

26. See Italo Calvino, *If on a Winter's Night a Traveller [Se una notte d'inverno un viaggiatore]*, trans. William Weaver (New York: Harcourt Brace Jovanovich, 1981).

27. See, e.g., *United States v. Doe*, 465 U.S. 605 (1984), on tax records, and *Gilbert v. California*, 388 U.S. 263 (1967), on handwriting samples. See also *New York v. Quarles* 467 U.S. 649 (1984), where Justice O'Connor, concurring in part and dissenting in part, claims: "Only the introduction of a defendant's own *testimony* is proscribed by the Fifth Amendment's mandate that no person 'shall be compelled to be a witness against himself.' That mandate does not protect an accused from being compelled to surrender *nontestimonial* evidence against himself" (at 666). I have benefited here from reading an essay by Akhil Reed Amar and Renée B. Lettow, "Fifth Amendment First Principles: The Self-Incrimination Clause" 93 *Mich. L. Rev.* 857 (1995).

28. Kamisar, *Police Interrogations*, 187. One finds versions of this hypothetical in cases involving jailhouse informants.

29. Seidman, "*Brown* and *Miranda*," 719. Seidman also characterizes Frankfurter's opinion in *Culombe* as a "disaster." For a critical examination of the philosophical analysis of the problem, see Joseph D. Grano, "Voluntariness, Free Will, and the Law of Confessions," 65 *Virginia Law Review* 859 (1979). Kamisar argues in *Police Interrogations* that "trustworthiness" is a better test than "voluntariness," although it, too, presents problems.

30. Weisberg, "Criminal Law, Criminology, and the Small World of Legal Scholars," 538–40.

31. Jorge Luis Borges, "The Shape of the Sword," trans. D. A. Yerby, in Borges, *Labyrinths* (New York: New Directions, 1954), 71.

32. Rousseau, *Confessions*, 175.

33. Albert Camus, *La chute* (1956; Paris: Le Livre de Poche, 1968), 119, 152. The translations are my own.

PAUL GEWIRTZ, "VICTIMS AND VOYEURS"

This essay (indeed, this book and the symposium on which it is based) is an outgrowth of a seminar on narrative in law and literature that I have co-taught several times with Peter Brooks. I am immeasurably grateful to him not simply for comments on the ideas in this essay but also for our entire collaborative enterprise, which has opened up a wealth of new understandings and been such a pleasure for me.

1. See Paul Gewirtz, "Remedies and Resistance," 92 Yale L. J. 585 (1983).

2. See, e.g., Richard Delgado, "Storytelling for Oppositionists and Others: A Plea for Narrative," 87 Mich. L. Rev. 2411 (1989); Kathryn Abrams, "Hearing the Call of Stories," 79 Cal. L. Rev. 971 (1991); William N. Eskridge, "Gaylegal Narratives," 46 Stan. L. Rev. 607 (1994); Kim L. Scheppele, "Foreword: Telling Stories," 87 *Mich. L. Rev.* 2073 (1989); Mari J. Matsuda, "Looking to the Bottom: Critical Legal Studies and Reparations," 22 Harv. C.R.-C.L. L. Rev. 323 (1987); Jane B. Baron, "Resistance to Stories," 67 S. Cal. L. Rev. 255 (1994); Patricia J. Williams, *The Alchemy of Race and Rights* (1991); Derrick Bell, *And We Are Not Saved: The Elusive Quest for Racial Justice* (1989). Critiques of some of this scholarship include Daniel A. Farber and Suzanna Sherry, "Telling Stories

Out of School: An Essay on Legal Narratives," 45 Stan. L. Rev. 807 (1993); and Randall Kennedy, "Racial Critiques of Legal Academia," 102 Harv. L. Rev. 1745 (1989).

3. See John H. Langbein, "Origins of Public Prosecution at Criminal Law," 17 Am. J. Legal History 313 (1973). See also Comment, "The Victim's Veto: A Way to Increase Victim Impact in Criminal Case Dispositions," 77 Cal. L. Rev. 417 (1989).

4. The central myth about the birth of law in Western literature, Aeschylus' *Oresteia,* is an account of a transformation from a system of blood revenge to a public process of adjudicating crimes. See Paul Gewirtz, "Aeschylus' Law," 101 Harv. L. Rev. 1043 (1988).

5. See, e.g., Booth v. Maryland, 482 U.S. 496, 498 (1987), discussed infra. There, an elderly couple was murdered in the course of a robbery because the robber "knew that [they] could identify him."

6. To be sure, Judge Ito did rule admissible a considerable amount of evidence about O. J. Simpson's prior abuse of his wife. So it might be said that he simply excluded evidence that was not necessary for the prosecution and that was most questionable as a matter of evidence law (and, if admitted, would make a conviction most vulnerable to reversal on appeal). There is truth to this, but the excluded evidence would have significantly added to the cumulative weight of O. J. Simpson's prior abuse. And it is the cumulative evidence of abuse that arguably demonstrated the degree and intensity of his obsessiveness for control and therefore made more plausible the argument that it could ultimately escalate to murder. In any event, the excluded evidence does underscore the various ways in which victims are silenced at trial—silenced by their murderers, but also by legal rules that reinforce that silence.

7. Richard Wright, *Native Son* 305–8 (Perennial Library ed. 1966).

8. "A Haunting End to O.J. Trial," San Francisco Examiner, September 30, 1995, p. 1.

9. For discussions of the modern victims' rights movement in criminal law, see, e.g., George Fletcher, *With Justice for Some* (1995); Andrew Karmen, *Crime Victims: An Introduction to Victimology* (1984); Robert Elias, *The Politics of Victimization* (1986); President's Task Force on Victims of Crime, *Final Report* (1982); U.S. Department of Justice, *Four Years Later: A Report on the President's Task Force on Victims of Crime* (1986); Martha Minow, "Surviving Victim Talk," 40 UCLA L. Rev. 1411 (1993); Lynne Henderson, "The Wrongs of Victims' Rights," 37 Stan. L. Rev. 937 (1985); Donald Hall, "Victims' Voices in Criminal Court: The Need for Restraint," 28 Am. Crim. L. Rev. 233 (1991); Josephine Gittler, "Expanding the Role of the Victim in a Criminal Action: An Overview of Issues and Problems," 11 Pepp. L. Rev. 117 (1984); LeRoy Lamborn, "Victim Participation in the Criminal Justice Process: The Proposals for a Constitutional Amendment," 34 Wayne L. Rev. 125 (1987); Abraham Goldstein, "Defining the Role of the Victim in Criminal Prosecution," 52 Miss. L. Rev. 515 (1982).

On the history and theory of victimhood more generally, see Joseph Amato, *Victims and Values: A History and Theory of Suffering* (1990); Charles Sykes, *A Nation of Victims: The Decay of the American Character* (1992); and William Ryan, *Blaming the Victim* (1971).

10. Representative samples of items on the victims' rights agenda are contained in the Federal Victim and Witness Protection Act, 18 U.S.C. §§ 1512–15, 3664, and the Federal Victims of Crime Act of 1984, 42 U.S.C. §§ 10601–4 (Supp. 1991).

11. In addition to the more general literature on the victims' rights movement cited at note 9 supra, writings specifically on victim impact statements include Carole A. Mansur, "*Payne v. Tennessee:* The Effect of Victim Harm at Capital Sentencing Trials and the Resurgence of Victim Impact Statements," 27 N. E. L. Rev. 713 (1993); Angela P. Harris, "The Jurisprudence of Victimhood," 1991 Sup. Ct. Rev. 77; Vivian Berger, "Payne and Suffering: A Personal Reflection and a Victim-Centered Critique," 20 Fla. St. L. Rev. 21 (1992); Victor Vital, "*Payne v. Tennessee:* The Use of Victim Impact Evidence at Capital Sentencing Trials," 19 Thur. Mar. L. Rev. 497 (1994); Dina R. Hellerstein, "The Victim Impact Statement: Reform or Reprisal?" 27 Am. Crim. L. Rev. 391 (1989).

12. *Booth* was followed in South Carolina v. Gathers, 490 U.S. 805 (1989).

13. Interestingly, one of the things we learn from the VIS is that a sizable part of the pain of being a victim or

survivor is telling and listening to stories about the murder, hearing about the murder on television, watching details about the murder at the trial. Several of the survivors became unable to listen to further stories about the crime or, for that matter, stories about other crimes. One "can't watch movies with bodies or stabbings in it." Another can't watch television news stories about violence. A granddaughter who had previously been an "avid reader of murder mysteries" can't read them anymore. As we learn, however, survivors are unable to escape the worst stories about the murder, the stories they tell themselves. Most of the survivors describe reenacting the crime or its discovery in their imagination again and again; the narrative refuses to conclude, rewinding and replaying endlessly.

14. *Booth,* 482 U.S. at 499–500 (1987) (citations omitted).
15. Evidence in the third category—survivors' personal opinions about the defendant and the appropriate sentence—raises different issues, is relatively uncommon, and is the sort of witness "opinion evidence" that is typically inadmissible. All of the six Justices who voted in Payne v. Tennessee to overturn *Booth*'s exclusion of the first two categories of evidence were careful not to approve admitting this category of evidence. Payne v. Tennessee, 501 U.S. 808, 830 n.2 (1991); id. at 835 n.1 (Souter, J., with whom Justice Kennedy joins, concurring).
16. *Booth,* 482 U.S. at 503. Legal rules about the use of victim impact statements can be seen and evaluated like any other problem of evidence in criminal trials. But the legal status of such evidence is a special problem for at least three reasons: it has become an issue of constitutional law (the law of evidence is mostly common law or statutory law); it concerns evidence used at sentencing rather than at the guilt phase of a trial; and the leading cases all concern its use in the context of death penalty sentencing. Nevertheless, the issues posed by victim impact statements can be divided into the two questions typically considered when deciding whether certain evidence should be admissible at trial, and the Supreme Court has at least implicitly addressed these two questions in analyzing the status of victim impact statements under the Constitution. First, is the evidence relevant to some issue being decided at trial? Second, assuming that the evidence has relevant probative value, is it likely to have a "prejudicial effect" that outweighs its usefulness—most typically, is the evidence likely to distort the search for truth more than enlighten it? These are both socially contingent inquiries that may change over time. Many kinds of stories have historically been excluded from trial as irrelevant because of what we would now call a failure to define the contested issue properly or a blindness to some reliable connection between the story and the contested issue. The idea of prejudice is also socially contingent. Over the years, as social and political attitudes have changed, the prior sexual behavior of defendants or victims, for example, has been deemed either relevant or irrelevant to the proof of certain crimes, and at times unduly prejudicial (and thus excludable) and at times not.
17. *Payne,* 501 U.S. at 818–19; South Carolina v. Gathers, 490 U.S. 805, 818–20 (1989) (O'Connor, J., dissenting); *Booth,* 482 U.S. at 516–17 (White, J., dissenting). In a pre-*Booth* capital case, Tison v. Arizona, 481 U.S. 137 (1987), the Court held that the Eighth Amendment did not bar imposing the death penalty on two brothers who had assisted their father in an armed prison breakout and a related kidnapping and robbery that resulted in several murders, even though the brothers themselves had not taken "any act which [they] desired to, or [were] substantially certain would, cause death." Id. at 150. As Justice O'Connor subsequently argued in *Gathers,* 490 U.S. at 818, 819, "What was critical to the defendants' eligibility for the death penalty in *Tison* was the harm they helped bring about" and their "reckless indifference to human life," regardless of whether they had the intent to kill. Indeed, as Justice White argued in his dissent in *Booth,* it is common in the law for punishment to turn on the harm caused, "irrespective of the offender's specific intent to cause such harm." "[S]omeone who drove his car recklessly through a stoplight and unintentionally killed a pedestrian merits significantly more punishment than someone who drove his car recklessly through the same stoplight at a time when no pedestrians were there to be hit." *Booth,* 482 U.S. at 516.

The argument that different levels of punishment may be appropriate where there are different consequences, despite the fact that the punished people have the same state of mind, is bolstered by important recent philosophical writing on "moral luck." This work has challenged the notion that the moral statue of an action is dependent solely on factors under the actor's control, and suggests that the luck of unintended consequences (or of personality or intentions) can affect an action's moral status. See Thomas Nagel, "Moral Luck," in *Mortal Questions* 24 (1979); Bernard Williams, "Moral Luck," in *Moral Luck* 20 (1981); Martha C. Nussbaum, *The Fragility of Goodness* 336–40 (1986). The notion being challenged—that luck cannot affect one's moral status—has its classic expression in the work of Immanuel Kant. See, e.g., *Groundwork of the Metaphysics of Morals* (H. J. Paton, trans., 1964) (1785) 62.

18. *Payne,* 501 U.S. at 838 (Souter, J., concurring).

19. Id. at 865 (Stevens, J., dissenting) (emphasis added and citation omitted).

20. Id. at 861.

21. *Booth,* 482 U.S. at 507–9 n.10 & n.12. For reasons related to but distinct from those that lead me to disagree with Justice Stevens's arguments, I am not persuaded by Elaine Scarry's argument that one problem with allowing victim impact evidence at sentencing is that it "backloads what should be front-loaded." Scarry, "Speech Acts in Criminal Cases," in this volume. Why should the "severity of the punishment . . . be decided by thinking about human injuries in general (antecedent to their actual occurence) rather than in a particular case," as Scarry believes? True, predictable sorts of harms are properly considered "antecedently" at the legislative stage in deciding whether certain kinds of acts constitute crimes at all, what crimes they constitute, and what the possible penalties should be; and, true, evidence about these harms may feed into the guilt or innocence decision at a trial establishing whether a particular defendant has committed a crime, of what type, and with what range of possible punishments. But why shouldn't harms—the actual harms—be considered at the sentencing stage, too, in setting a defendant's penalty? Similarly, it is surely right to include the point of view of crime victims in our cultural images about crime—but why not in assessing the sentencing consequences of a particular criminal act as well? Different sorts of public deliberations about crime have different functions and purposes, but the harms suffered by victims may be relevant to all of them, albeit in somewhat different forms for each. So, too, there is nothing illogical or wrongheaded about having one stage of a criminal trial focus on one set of issues (say, Did the defendant do it?) and a later stage focus on different issues (Do the equities, including actual victim harm, warrant a more or less severe sentence?). I certainly agree with Scarry's most important point: that victims should not "determine" the appropriate punishment, which is a matter for judge and jury. But this does not mean that partic-ularized victim evidence about a crime's actual harms should be excluded from the deliberations about the sentence.

22. See articles cited in note 2 supra and my introductory essay in this volume.

23. For example, Eddings v. Oklahoma, 455 U.S. 104 (1982).

24. The dissenters in *Booth* and the majority in *Payne* argue that it is only fair to allow evidence about particular characteristics of the murder victim because the Constitution has been interpreted to allow capital defendants to introduce any evidence about their particular characteristics that might lead a jury to decide to mitigate the punishment. It is true, as Justice Stevens says in his *Payne* dissent, that our law often embraces rules "weighted in the defendant's favor" (the requirement of proof beyond reasonable doubt; rules regarding evidence of the defendant's character and reputation). 501 U.S. at 860. But the question is, Why should there be a weighting or asymmetry in this context? If information about the defendant's particular characteristics is thought helpful at sentencing, why isn't the same true of information about the victim's particular characteristics?

25. As Martha Minow writes in her essay in this volume, "The biggest check on selectivity problems in storytelling lies in the availability of another story." Minow, "Stories in Law."

26. *Payne,* 501 U.S. at 823–24 (citations and emphases omitted).

27. Many people do believe that some lives are more valuable than others—although they would probably prefer to say that some lives contribute more to human betterment than other lives, so their loss imposes more harm on the community. But many others believe such a position is repellent. The majority in

Booth suggests, albeit in a footnote, that "our system of justice does not tolerate" the notion that "defendants whose victims were assets to their community are more deserving of punishment than those whose victims are perceived to be less worthy." 482 U.S. at 506 n.8. The majority in *Payne* tries to avoid this issue by insisting that evidence of the victim's particular characteristics "is not offered to encourage comparative judgments of this kind. . . . It is designed to show instead *each* victim's 'uniqueness as an individual human being,' whatever the jury might think the loss to the community resulting from his death might be." 501 U.S. at 823. The question is whether the jury will distinguish between this particularization and a comparative valuation (and whether, if pushed, the *Payne* majority would say the jury has to).

Justice White's dissent in *Booth* took on the majority more directly, arguing that the state may, "if it chooses, include as a sentencing consideration the particularized harm that an individual's murder causes to the rest of society." This is apparently a willingness to allow stronger punishments to be imposed on defendants whose victims are perceived to be greater assets to the community. 482 U.S. at 517. (White points to federal statutes that authorize death sentences for the murder of only certain specified public officials, such as the president, although those statutes can be seen as authorizing greater punishments when a killing is an attack on the state as well as an individual victim.) As noted in the text, the Court majority in Payne v. Tennessee tries to avoid White's argument. However, in other legal contexts, such as civil wrongful death actions, juries are invited to make different-sized damage awards based on the relative harm caused by the loss of the life in question or some similar valuation.

28. I do not address in the text one aspect of this that the *Booth* opinion discusses: that evidence about the victim and survivors may lead the defendant to want to rebut this evidence, producing a minitrial about the victim and victim's family that consumes time and distracts attention from the defendant and the crime. 482 U.S. at 506–7. Telling a story often prompts others to tell a story, and this is especially true in our adversarial system, where virtually no utterance by one side goes unanswered by the other. But the argument about distraction begs the question here, which is whether victim evidence is indeed a distraction from relevant matters or is itself one of the relevant matters. That issue I have discussed in the text above. The length of court time that such matters take up is essentially a management issue that courts are well equipped to handle—indeed, they handle such issues on a daily basis. The fear of distraction is largely chimerical. Indeed, in *Booth* itself there was no distraction problem, for victim impact evidence was presented through the reading of a compact document rather than through the more time-consuming presentation of live witnesses, and there was no defense rebuttal.

29. *Booth,* 482 U.S. at 508–9 ("[T]he formal presentation of this information by the State can serve no other purpose than to inflame the jury and divert it from deciding the case on the relevant evidence concerning the crime and the defendant. As we have noted, any decision to impose the death sentence must 'be, and appear to be, based on reason rather than caprice or emotion.' . . . The admission of these emotionally charged opinions as to what conclusions the jury should draw from the evidence clearly is inconsistent with the reasoned decisionmaking we require in capital cases.") (citations omitted); *Payne,* 501 U.S. at 856 (Stevens, J., dissenting) (victim impact evidence "serves no purpose other than to encourage jurors to decide in favor of death rather than life on the basis of their emotions rather than their reason"); cf. id. at 831–32 (O'Connor, J., concurring) (observing that jurors were "moved by this testimony" about the survivors' emotional suffering, and acknowledging "the possibility that this evidence may, in some cases, be unduly inflammatory," but concluding that this does not justify a prophylactic, Constitution-based rule that this evidence may never be admitted, because "unduly inflammatory" evidence that renders the proceedings "fundamentally unfair" may be excluded under the due process clause of the Fourteenth Amendment); cf. id at 836 (Souter, J., concurring) ("Evidence about the victim and survivors, and any jury argument predicated on it, can of course be so inflammatory as to risk a verdict impermissibly based on passion, not deliberation."). See also "Victim Justice," *New Republic* (April 17, 1995), 9.

30. Saffle v. Parks, 494 U.S. 484, 491 (1990) (refusing to strike down an instruction at the penalty phase of a capital trial telling the jury to avoid any influence of sympathy). See also id. at 493 ("It would be very

difficult to reconcile a rule allowing the fate of a defendant to turn on the vagaries of particular jurors' emotional sensitivities with our long-standing recognition that, above all, capital sentencing must be reliable, accurate, and nonarbitrary."); id. at 495 ("The objectives of fairness and accuracy are more likely to be threatened than promoted by a rule allowing the sentence to turn not on whether the defendant, in the eyes of the community, is morally deserving of the death sentence, but on whether the defendant can strike an emotional chord in a juror."); California v. Brown, 479 U.S. 538, 545 (1987) (O'Connor, J., concurring) (in the course of upholding a judge's instruction to a capital sentencing jury that it should not be swayed by "mere sympathy," affirming that the death penalty decision must be a "reasoned moral response," not an "emotional response").

31. See Gewirtz, supra note 4.

32. For example, Peter Brooks, *Reading for the Plot* 216–37 (Vintage ed. 1985); Mikhail Bakhtin, *The Dialogic Imagination* 259 (Michael Holquist ed. 1981).

33. It would be fascinating to examine various "model instructions" that judges use and try to excavate theories of audience reception that underlie them, including the basic assumption that a judge's instructions can significantly affect how the jury processes what it hears.

34. California v. Brown, 479 U.S. 538, 545 (O'Connor, J., concurring).

35. *Payne,* 501 U.S. at 832 (O'Connor, J., concurring). See also note 29 supra.

36. *Booth,* 482 U.S. at 508.

37. Saffle v. Parks, 494 U.S. at 513–14 (Brennan, J., dissenting).

38. I develop some of these points at greater length in "On 'I Know It When I See It,'" 105 Yale L. J. 1023 (1996).

39. See Anthony Kronman, "Leontius' Tale," in this volume.

40. See, e.g., *Explaining Emotions* (Amelie Rorty, ed., 1980); Ronald de Sousa, *The Rationality of Emotion* (1987); Martha C. Nussbaum, *Love's Knowledge* (1990); Antonio R. Damasio, *Descartes' Error: Emotion, Reason, and the Human Brain* (1994); Robert Solomon, *A Passion for Justice: Emotions and the Origins of the Social Contract* (1990).

41. Cases like California v. Brown and Saffle v. Parks, upholding anti-sympathy jury instructions, fail to acknowledge this last point, however. See note 30 supra.

42. See Samuel Pillsbury, "Emotional Justice: Moralizing the Passions of Criminal Punishment," 74 Corn. L. Rev. 655 (1989).

43. See Williams v. Chrans, 945 F.2d 926, 947 (7th Cir. 1991) ("we must recognize that the state should not be required to present victim impact evidence . . . devoid of all passion.").

44. Paul Brest, "Foreword: In Defense of the Antidiscrimination Principle," 90 Harv. L. Rev. 1, 6–9 (1976) (emphasis added). The problem of selective sympathy can undoubtedly surface in the context of victim impact evidence. Specifically, evidence about the victim's particular characteristics might evoke sympathy only for victims who come from a juror's own racial, ethnic, or class background. See Harris, supra note 11. This problem is not peculiar to victim impact evidence. It arises just as much in the context of the defendant's mitigation evidence, where there is a risk that jurors will react sympathetically only to mitigating circumstances that resonate with their own backgrounds. (This is one concern that the Supreme Court has said justifies the use of anti-sympathy instructions at trials. See notes 30 and 41 supra.) It also arises during the guilt phase of trial, where there is always the possibility that jurors' assessments of witnesses' credibility will rest upon selective identification with certain witnesses that is rooted in nonrational factors. Thus, the risk of selective sympathy—which, in my judgment, is not only one of the most serious problems with victim impact evidence but a serious problem in the criminal justice system more generally—cannot be a basis for excluding victim impact evidence in particular. It can, however, be the basis for efforts by lawyers and judges to make jurors more aware of their possible biases.

45. As noted, in the *Booth* case the vis read to the jury was prepared by a government official, "the writer" in the vis. Using indirect discourse, she retells the stories that the victims' family members have told her. But the writer also reacts to what she has recounted ("Perhaps [the victims' granddaughter] de-

scribed the impact of the tragedy most eloquently when she stated that . . ."; "It became increasingly apparent to the writer as she talked to the family members that . . ."). So we are made aware of the shaping voice of a narrator, and what the survivors are reported as saying gains weight because this calm official narrator stands behind them. And because this official narrator tells usher response to what the survivors have told her, we the audience—and, more important, the audience of jurors—are pointed to an "appropriate" response and thus encouraged to respond in the same way.

46. ABC *World News Tonight,* February 17, 1992.
47. *Booth,* 482 U.S. at 501.
48. Such a system would appear to satisfy Elaine Scarry's concern that statements by victims or survivors must be "challengeable" and able to "be shown to be false." Scarry, "Speech Acts in Criminal Cases," in this volume.
49. See Williams v. New York, 337 U.S. 241 (1949).
50. *Booth,* 482 U.S. at 505.
51. *Booth,* 482 U.S. at 505. As a threshold matter, there must be a story to construct and a storyteller to do the constructing—and some murder victims may leave no survivors. Making victim impact evidence part of the capital sentencing process may make the defendant's likelihood of receiving a death sentence turn on the presence or absence or survivor storytellers. Narratological questions to one side, the fairness of such a situation implicates matters discussed above.
52. See Berger, supra note 11.
53. Testimony during the guilt phase of the trial can create some of this anxiety, but at that stage, survivor witnesses typically testify to relatively objective facts—very different from the accounts of subjective suffering or the heavily shaped victim portraiture in victim impact evidence.
54. See, e.g., Dean Kilpatrick and Randy Otto, "Constitutionally Guaranteed Participation in Criminal Proceedings for Victims: Potential Effects on Psychological Functioning," 34 Wayne L. Rev. 7 (1987).
55. The highest visibility cases over the past several years have certain common subject matter and themes. Most involve a riveting role reversal, as when a celebrity or member of some respectable elite is accused of being base (Kennedy Smith, Simpson, the Menendez brothers, Fleiss and her clientele, the Rodney King police). Most involve either matters of sex (Kennedy Smith, Dahmer, the Bobbitts, Fleiss, Simpson) or race (Simpson, Rodney King). Only a few—Susan Smith's killing of her children, for example—rivet precisely because of the emergence of horrifying deviance out of utter ordinariness (although here, too, the notoriety developed out of a major role reversal: the pleading mother revealed to be the hunted murderer).
56. "Color Blinded? Race Seems to Play an Increasing Role in Many Jury Verdicts," Wall Street Journal, October 4, 1995, p. 1.
57. Charlotte Brontë, *Jane Eyre,* chapter 19.
58. *Payne,* 501 U.S. at 867 (Stevens, J., dissenting) (citation omitted).

LOUIS MICHAEL SEIDMAN, "SOME STORIES ABOUT CONFESSIONS AND CONFESSIONS ABOUT STORIES"

I thank Lisa Heinzerling and Gerry Spann for their help in preparing these comments.

1. See e.g., United States v. Panza, 612 F. 2d 432 (9th Cir. 1979) (upholding right of trial judge to strike defendant's testimony if defendant refuses to answer prosecutor's questions). For a famous application of the rule, see United States v. Hearst, 563 F. 2d 1331 (9th Cir. 1977) (defendant's testimony that she acted under duress when she committed bank robbery waived Fifth Amendment privilege with respect to cross-examination concerning later period).

This rule helps to explain a line of Supreme Court authority that is otherwise baffling. In Jenkins v. Anderson, 447 U.S. 231 (1980), the Court held that a defendant who took the stand could be impeached by his pre-arrest silence. See also Harris v. New York, 401 U.S. 222 (1971) (permitting impeachment with *Miranda*-bad statements after defendant takes the stand); Fletcher v. Weir, 455 U.S. 603 (1982) (permitting impeachment with post-arrest, pre-*Miranda* warning silence). These decisions seem inconsistent with Griffin v. California, 380 U.S. 609 (1965), where the Court held that adverse comment to a jury on the defendant's silence during trial violated the Fifth Amendment because it tended to compel speech. The decisions are reconcilable so long as one accepts the proposition that a defendant who chooses to take the stand waives the right not to be compelled to participate in cross-examination. If compelled testimony can be produced at the trial itself, it would seem to follow that testimony compelled at an earlier point (by penalizing silence, for example) is permissible as well.

ELAINE SCARRY, "SPEECH ACTS IN CRIMINAL CASES"

1. Robert Weisberg, "Proclaiming Trials as Narratives: Premises and Pretenses," in this volume.
2. This term originated among physicians at the Department of Public Health at Cornell Medical. It was invented by Walsh McDermott.
3. Storytellers like Zola, Dickens, and Tolstoy, with their vast arrays of characters, are being left out of account here.
4. A government can keep information secret simply by making sure that the subject is never presented in a story form. On what I call mimetic deliberation—the habit of a citizenry to tell stories rather than to deliberate political and philosophic issues, see Elaine Scarry, "Watching and Authorizing the Gulf War," in *Media Spectacles,* ed. Margorie Garber and Rebecca Walkowitz (New York: Routledge, 1993), 51–62.
5. Many of the chapters in this book are structured around these oppositions.
6. Paul Gewirtz, "Victims and Voyeurs: Two Narrative Problems at the Criminal Trial," and Peter Brooks, "Storytelling Without Fear? Confession in Law and Literature," both in this volume. The opposition between empathy and reason, for example, is explicitly addressed in the late sections of Paul Gewirtz's essay.
7. Robert Cover, "Bonds of Constitutional Interpretation: Of the Word, the Deed, and the Role," 20 *Ga. L. Rev.* (1986), 815. Cover calls attention to the oddity of the fact that nothing internal to a verbal statement registers the degree to which it will, or will not, take effect in the material world: "The sentence of death is the most profound act of sentencing that a judge may encounter. . . . But the grammar of the judicial utterance is as simple as that of any other criminal sentence."
8. See, e.g., McCrae v. State, 395 So. 2d 1145 (Fla. 1980); Tanner v. State, 502 So. 2d 1008 (Fla. App. D2); Jackson v. State, 502 So. 2d 409 (Fla. 1986); Commonwealth v. Travaglia, 502 Pa. 474 (1983); and Thompson v. State, 492 N.E.2d 264 (Ind. 1986).
9. See, e.g., Fox v. State, 569 P.2d 1335 (Alaska 1977); Davis v. State, 635 P.2d 481 (Alaska Ct. App. 1981); People v. Redmond, 29 Cal. 3d 904; People v. Jones, 52 Ill. 2d 247, 287 N.E.2d 680 (1980); State v. Schilz, 50 Wis. 2d 395, 184 N.W.2d 134 (1971, a case in which perjury and confession are conflated); and Lange v. State, 54 Wis. 2d 569, 196 N.W.2d 680. Sometimes the enhancement entails not just an increment in a stationary form of punishment (for example, an increase in the number of years imprisoned) but a shift in the kind of punishment (for example, imprisonment rather than probation, as in State v. Carsten, 264 N.W.2d 707 [S.D. 1978]). A number of these cases explicitly seek to differentiate their use of false speech as a ground for increasing the severity of the sentence from a court's use of a defendant's nonspeech or silence or refusal of self-incrimination as a grounds for increasing the punishment (see also United States v. Dunnigan, 113 S. Ct. 1111 [U.S. 1993]). In many of the cases, the judge describes the act or agent of perjury in language that underscores the speech act: "boldfaced liar" in *Schilz,* for example; "organized perjury" in *Lange.*
10. In the brief history of victim impact statements (in cases involving the death penalty and in those involving less severe sentences), there has often been no cross-examination. The court in *Booth v. Maryland* (482 U.S. 496 [1987] at 506) went beyond historical observation in arguing that victim impact statements were not only historically unchallenged but logically unchallengeable. A wise defendant will abstain from challenging the victim because that challenge will be seen as an attempt to

divert the court by putting the victim on trial and so will work to the disadvantage of the defendant. The dissent in *Booth* disagreed that victim impact statements are unchallengeable, yet indirectly confirmed the majority opinion by observing that the "petitioner introduced no . . . rebuttal evidence, probably because he considered, wisely, that it was not in his best interest to do so" (at 518). The majority in *Payne v. Tennessee* similarly disagreed with the *Booth* court's assessment of unchallengeability, yet acknowledged that "it might not be prudent for the defense to rebut" (501 U.S. 808 [1991] at 812).

11. Of course, the two are not symmetrical: the defendant's confession may eliminate contestation and adjudication on both sides. In contrast, the absence of cross-examination in the victim impact statement diminishes only the defense lawyer's chance to be adversarial, not the prosecutor's, and does so only in this one segment of the trial.

12. This sentence or a close equivalent is cited in hundreds of criminal cases, state statutes, and codes, where it is variously referred to as a "well-established" or "universally recognized" "rule" or "doctrine" or "principle" or "maxim" of either "statutory construction" or "common-law pleading." The structural features of the trial (innocent until proven guilty; guilty beyond a reasonable doubt) follow this same weighting against the state and for the defendant. Gewirtz questions whether there exists a logical basis for this asymmetrical weighting in favor of defendants. The answer is yes. Social contract theory imagines society as a place where (in contrast to the state of nature) we give up our opportunity to injure one another. Contractual society aspires to be injury-free. This means that in those exceptional situations where the prohibition on injuring is lifted, the most rigorous forms of scrutiny and procedures for consent must first be gone through. It is not accidental that Locke's *Second Treatise of Government* again and again names two practices—punishment and war—in its discussions of consent. These two are singled out precisely because they are situations of willfully inflicted injury. All bias must be against going to war and against inflicting punishment unless a rigorous deliberative process has been gone through that explicitly permits the lifting of the general prohibition against injuring.

13. The defendant's speech may determine whether the defendant comes to be punished at all, and may either increase or decrease the severity of the penalty.

JOHN HOLLANDER, "LEGAL RHETORIC"

1. For example, Hugh Blair's *Lectures on Rhetoric and Belles Lettres* (London, 1983).

2. An excellent introduction to classical and modern rhetoric and their conceptual and historical relations is that of Edward P. J. Corbett, *Classical Rhetoric for the Modern Student* (New York, 1971).

3. See Erving Goffman, *The Presentation of Self in Everyday Life* (New York, 1959), *Interaction Ritual* (New York, 1967), and, particularly, *Forms of Talk* (Philadelphia, 1981).

4. Aristotle, *The "Art" of Rhetoric*, trans. J. H. Freese (Loeb Edition, 1957), I.ii. 3.

5. Ibid., II.i–xvii. Aristotle's discussion of the role of narrative is in II.xvi.

6. Another question suggests itself here: What might a general theory of how the law treats word as deed look like? Coming from outside legal scholarship, I do not know how this might apply to a contract: Is it an agreement with both substance of its own as agreement in the abstract and a linguistic form, or representation, or clothing, or expression, or whatever? Or does the contract consist only of language and a sense that the agreement was an inference from or interpretation of that language? Is the matter of word and deed quite different with respect, say, to contracts and torts? Here, (1) "I agree to do X with the promise that . . ." is opposed to (2) "I'll kill you if you play that thing again!" Who would say that (1) is "mere rhetoric"? Might I be believed if I said in the case of (2) that I didn't really mean it or was only pretending?

7. A recently fashionable source of the seemingly outrageous view that all discourse is somehow metaphoric is Nietzsche's essay "On Truth and Falsity in an Extra-Moral Sense." For a particularly interesting discussion of law and metaphoric language, see Owen Barfield, "Poetic Diction and Legal Fiction," in Max Black, ed., *The Importance of Language* (New York, 1962), 51–71.

8. Paul Gewirtz, "Remedies and Resistance," *Yale Law Journal* 92:585 (1983) 610. Also see the entry on "all deliberate speed" in Fred R. Shapiro, ed., *The Oxford Dictionary of Legal Quotations* (New York, 1993).

SANFORD LEVINSON, "THE RHETORIC OF THE JUDICIAL OPINION"

I am grateful to J. M. Balkin, Betty Sue Flowers, Lewis LaRue, Hans Linde, Richard Posner, and Scot Powe for their reactions to an earlier draft of this essay. I also benefited from comments delivered at the Yale conference by Robert Gordon and Reva Siegel and from comments and vigorous arguments following the subsequent presentation of the paper to a faculty colloquium at the University of California Law School (Boalt Hall). I am especially grateful to Jerome Culp, Sanford Kadish, Robert Post, and Leslie Green for their comments on that occasion. Finally, special thanks are due to Frederick Schauer for his copious suggestions; we turned out to be currently working on some very similar issues.

1. See Lief H. Carter, *Contemporary Constitutional Lawmaking: The Supreme Court and the Art of Politics* xiv (1985): "[W]e should evaluate the quality of a legal performance, using the same aesthetic guides we use to judge theatrical performances and other artistic acts."

2. An elegant demonstration of this separation can be found in Frederick Schauer, "Giving Reasons," 47 Stan. L. Rev. 633 (1995), which notes that courts are often most authoritative precisely when they give no reasons at all to justify their action. See, e.g., decisions, often important in social fact, to deny writs of certiorari or, at the trial court level, to sustain or deny an evidentiary objection. Even decisions accompanied by opinions, however, need not necessarily try to persuade, as opposed to announcing a rule to be followed by those who are presumed to be subject to judicial command. See Frederick Schauer, "Opinions as Rules," 62 U. Chi. L. Rev. 1455 (1995). I am reminded of Ring Lardner's immortal line " 'Shut up,' he explained."

3. See, most (in)famously, United States v. New York Times (The Pentagon Papers Case), 403 U.S. 713 (1971); Furman v. Georgia, 408 U.S. 238 (1972) (declaring unconstitutional existing death penalty systems in the United States).

4. See, e.g., Brandenberg v. Ohio, 395 U.S. 444 (1969).

5. After sending out a query on the Internet, I have learned, for example, that the Irish Supreme Court, when issuing a constitutional, but not a statutory, decision, speaks per curiam, with apparently no dissents allowed; the German Constitutional Court also speaks only as "the Court," although I gather that judges are allowed to dissent in their own name. In Greece, I am informed by George Katrougalos, "only the number of votes of the concurrences and dissenters are known, without the identity of either of them [being] revealed. For instance, we know that a decision has been taken with 7 votes against 2," but no one is identified. And, says Katrougalos, "all dissident opinions are incorporated in the corpus of the decision." Peter Hogg, in his book on constitutional law in Canada, notes that prior to 1966 the Judicial Committee of the Privy Council of the United Kingdom rendered "advice" to the monarch—which was, in fact, "binding judgment" "in the form of a single opinion. The theory was that advice to the Crown should not be divided." Thus "no dissenting opinion was ever filed, and there was no disclosure of a dissenting view in the single opinion filed." Peter Hogg, *Constitutional Law of Canada* 166 (2d ed. 1985).

6. This is also true of what might be termed standard-form legal scholarship, which adopts the perspective of the judge manqué and purports to offer a disinterested synthesis of existing legal doctrine (or, if one is an originalist, of what the framers happened to believe about some matter).

7. Minersville School District v. Gobitis, 310 U.S. 586, 596, quoted in Robert Ferguson, "The Judicial Opinion as a Literary Genre," 2 Yale J. L. & Hum. 201, 207 (1990).

8. This appears to be true, for example, of French judicial opinions. See Michael Wells, "French and American Judicial Opinions," 19 Yale J. Int'l L. 81 (1994). The confidence may reflect the Cartesian influence on French thought generally, in addition to the influence of the judicial role.

9. Id. at 206–7.

10. Richard Posner, "Judges' Writing Styles (and Do They Matter)," 62 U.Chi. L. Rev. 142 (1995). I am grateful to Judge Posner for sending me a draft of his article.

11. Id. n.48, citing Fishgold v. Sullivan Drydock & Repair Corp., 154 F.2d 785, 791 (2d Cir.), aff'd, 328 U.S. 275 (1946). One ought not interpret Hand as necessarily counseling such open confession of doubt. It was he, after all, who began his 1939 memorial to Benjamin Cardozo by noting that the judge "must pose as a kind of oracle, voicing the dictates of a vague divinity—a communion which reaches far beyond the memory of any now living, and has gathered up a prestige beyond that of any single man." And he argued that a judge "must preserve his authority by cloaking himself in the majesty of an overshadowing past." Learned Hand, "Mr. Justice Cardozo," in *The Spirit of Liberty* 129, 130 (Irving Dilliard, ed. 1952). I owe this quotation to Carl Landauer, "Scholar, Craftsman, and Priest: Learned Hand's Self-Imaging," 3 Yale J. of L. & Hum. 321, 241 (1991).

12. In a recent book, *Judicial Power and American Character* (1994), Robert Nagel refers to the "advocates' subjective sense that the preferred conclusion is inevitable, that it represents the one right answer," and that the contrary conclusion therefore represents a deficiency of either intellect or character (173 n.21).

13. Hans Linde, the distinguished former justice of the Oregon Supreme Court, in comments on an earlier draft of this chapter, noted an extremely interesting rhetorical feature of opinions involving criminal procedure. "Criminal law opinions routinely describe the crime, often quite horrible," even if the sole claim is an allegation that the police violated certain procedural rules—such as demonstrating probable cause to justify the issuance of a search warrant—that depend not at all on the facts of the crime. Linde suggests that this practice of beginning an opinion with the facts of the crime often reflects simple thoughtlessness. "But if a member of a collegial court begins an opinion with the issue presented by the motion to suppress evidence and never describes the crime (as I have done), another judge who wishes to reject the appeal is likely to object and describe the crime." I find Linde's comment fascinating; frankly, it never would have occurred to me, because I rarely read criminal procedure opinions. No doubt immersion in such opinions or in the opinions of other substantive fields—tax, torts, Texas administrative law, or whatever—would lead to other helpful insights about judicial rhetoric.

14. Philip Bobbitt, *Constitutional Fate* (1981), *Constitutional Interpretation* (1991).

15. Griswold v. Connecticut, 381 U.S. 479 (1965).

16. See, e.g., Walker v. City of Birmingham, 388 U.S. 307 (1967), which upheld the punishment of civil rights marchers for marching (on Easter Sunday) in defiance of a palpably unconstitutional injunction issued by a local Alabama judge prohibiting the march. Although the marchers would have been able to plead the unconstitutionality of a legislative statute prohibiting the march as a defense against prosecution for violating the statute, they were not allowed to plead the unconstitutionality of the judicial injunction as a defense for its violation. Thus judicial writings, even if substantively illegitimate as rhetorical performances, nonetheless can be the occasion for the imprisonment of those who refuse to respect them.

17. At least within the confines of the overall judicial role, for it is considered bad form to display openly one's talents as a legislative policymaker.

18. For counterthrusts, see e.g., opinions by Hugo Black or, more recently, Antonin Scalia. A fine source of angry accusations is surely former Justice Byron White. See, e.g., New York v. U.S., 112 S.Ct. 2408, 2444 (1992): "For me, the Court's civics lecture [based on the structural importance of federalism] has a decidedly hollow ring at a time when action, rather than rhetoric, is needed to solve a national problem [involving the disposal of low-level radioactive waste]."

19. Sanford Levinson, "On Positivism and Potted Plants: 'Inferior' Judges and the Task of Constitutional Interpretation," 25 Conn. L. Rev. 843, 850 (1993). Several of the points (and quotations) below are taken from this article.

20. "As applied in a hierarchical system of courts, the duty of a subordinate court to follow the laws as announced by superior courts is theoretically absolute." 1B James W. Moore et al., *Moore's Federal Practice* ¶ 0.401 (2d ed. 1993), quoted in Evan H. Caminker, "Precedent and Prediction: The Forward-

Looking Aspects of Inferior Court Decisionmaking," 73 Texas L. Rev. 1, 3 n.9. See also Caminker, "Why Must Inferior Courts Obey Supreme Court Precedents?" 46 Stan. L. Rev. 817 (1994). Not everyone agrees that inferior courts must obey Supreme Court precedents. See, e.g., Michael Stokes Paulsen, "Accusing Justice: Some Variations on the Themes of Robert M. Cover's *Justice Accused*," 7 J. L. & Rel. 33, 82–88 (1989).

21. Mary Ann Glendon, *A Nation Under Lawyers* 294 (1994).

22. See, e.g., Frank Michelman, "The Supreme Court, 1985 Term—Foreword: Traces of Self-Government," 100 Harv. L. Rev. 4 (1986).

23. Andrew Jackson, "Veto Message [of the Renewal of the Second Bank of the United States]" (July 4, 1832), reprinted in Paul Brest and Sanford Levinson, *Processes of Constitutional Decisionmaking* 50 (3d ed. 1992).

24. Hutto v. Davis, 454 U.S. 370 (1982).

25. Rummell v. Estelle, 445 U.S. 263 (1980).

26. *The Random House College Dictionary* at 1132 (rev. ed. 1988).

27. Hutto v. Davis, 354 U.S. at 375 (emphasis added).

28. I have treated this issue in Constitutional Faith, ch. 1 (1988).

29. Several of those who attended the presentation of an earlier version of this paper at Berkeley took issue with the starkness of this sentence. After all, isn't one of the attractions of precedent the principle of deciding like cases alike? Well, yes and no. See generally Frederick Schauer, *Playing by the Rules* ch. 6 ("The Force of Rules") (1991). Beyond strictly jurisprudential argument about the way we recognize cases A and B as being like or different, there is also the obvious practical fact, as noted later in the text, that the U.S. legal system has never adopted as a constitutive practice the following of precedent come what may, especially at the constitutional level. So the question becomes, When will we reject the importance of deciding like cases alike (assuming, that is, that we are confident in our ability to identify like cases) because the earlier case was decided wrongly or unjustly? I do not argue that this is an easy question, only that it is a legitimate question for some courts and apparently not for others—such as inferior courts. One can then turn to some version of rule utilitarianism to defend a restricted role for some courts, such as inferior courts, and not for others, such as those that we call supreme courts. But, once again, it is not self-evident why the best rule is that inferior courts never be free to assess the merits of existing doctrine.

30. Jeremy Bentham, "A Comment on the Commentaries," in *A Comment on the Commentaries and a Fragment on Government,* ed. J. Burns and H. L. A. Hart 196 (1977), quoted in Gerald J. Postema, "Some Roots of Our Notion of Precedent," in Laurence Goldstein, ed., *Precedent in Law* 14 (1987).

31. Hammond v. Bostic, 368 F.Supp. 732 (W.D.N.C. 1974) (McMillan, J.). See also the remarkable opinion by Judge Thomas Gee in Weber v. Kaiser Aluminum & Chem. Corp., 611 F.2d 133 (5th Cir. 1980); "Subordinate magistrates such as I must either obey the order of higher authority or yield up their posts to those who obey. I obey, since in my view the action required of me by the Court's mandate is only to follow a mistaken course and not an evil one."

32. Schauer, *Playing by the Rules.*

33. See Frederick Schauer, "Precedent," 39 Stan. L. Rev. 571, 600 (1987).

34. Planned Parenthood of Southeastern Pennsylvania v. Casey, 112 S.Ct. 2791 (1992). See, e.g., Frank Michelman, "The Supreme Court, 1985 Term—Foreword: Traces of Self-Government," 100 Harv. L. Rev. 4 (1986).

35. Richard Posner, *The Problems of Jurisprudence* 82 (1990).

36. New York Tribune, December 19, 1855, quoted in Carl Brent Swisher, V *History of the Supreme Court of the United States: The Taney Period, 1836–1864* 591 (1974).

37. Guido Calabresi, "What Clarence Thomas Knows," New York Times, July 28, 1991.

38. I ask myself as I write these lines, incidentally, if they manifest rhetorical excess or, what would be even worse, insult to a person I admire greatly, not least because of his willingness to engage in such candid, and correct, criticism of the current Court. I think not, although I would be interested in why someone

might dismiss my comments as mere bombast rather than an altogether-accurate, even if over-compressed, reflection of what is concealed in ordinary pious assurances to the Senate Judiciary Committee that inferior judges will of course enforce with no, or at least no disabling, compunctions the doctrines, however repugnant, articulated by the Supreme Court.

39. See, for a helpful recent discussion, Frederick Schauer, 24 Canadian J. Phil. 495, 506 (1994) (review of Roger Shiner, *Norm and Nature: The Movements of Legal Thought* [1992]).

40. *The Random House College Dictionary* at 91 (emphasis added).

41. See, e.g., Serrano v. Priest, 557 P.2d 929, 950-52 (1976), in which the California Supreme Court interpreted the California constitution's equal protection clause to invalidate the unequal financing of educational expenditures among school districts, although the Supreme Court had upheld such financing schemes against a federal equal protection challenge in San Antonio Independent School District v. Rodriguez, 411 U.S. 1 (1973). Similarly, the New York Court of Appeals construed the state constitution's due process clause to require "contact visits" with prison inmates even as it recognized that the Supreme Court would almost certainly not similarly construe the federal due process clause. Compare Cooper v. Morin, 399 N.E.2d 1188 (1979) with Bell v. Wolfish, 441 U.S. 520 (1978). I owe this point to Hans Linde.

42. Richard Neustadt, *Presidential Power: The Politics of Leadership from FDR to Carter* 9 (1980) (emphasis in original).

43. Id. at 10 (emphasis in original).

44. Id. at 9.

45. Responding to an earlier draft, Mark Tushnet took issue with this sentence, pointing out that it is extraordinarily unlikely that any president or judge "in fact" inflicts death upon hapless soldiers, civilians, or prisoners. In all cases, it is subordinates—ultimately extending to soldiers in the field or executioners who inject the solution into the arm of the prisoner tied to the gurney—who must be persuaded to obey the orders. To the extent that the orders are followed almost thoughtlessly, to view obedience as the outcome of a process of persuasion (other, perhaps, than persuasion that one's role includes fairly blind submission to the commands of one's superiors) is to miss something.

46. *Random House College Dictionary* at 1132 (emphasis added).

47. For the O'Connor-Souter-Kennedy opinion, see Planned Parenthood of Southeastern Pennsylvania v. Casey, 112 S.Ct. at 2808–16 (paean to precedent). For the critique, see especially id. at 2860–67 (dissenting opinion of Chief Justice Rehnquist).

48. "Augustus Noble Hand," in Charles E. Wyzanski, Jr., *Whereas—A Judge's Premises* 71 (1965).

49. Brown v. Board of Education, 347 U.S. 483 (1954).

50. See, however, Frederick Schauer, "Opinions as Rules," 62 U. Chi. L. Rev. 1455 (1995), for the valuable point that an opinion may be designed simply—and without much explanation—to set forth the rules that should ostensibly guide particular decisionmakers. He points out, for example, that one does not expect a statute to persuade. It is enough for many purposes if it sets forth with some clarity what is required of those legally obliged to obey it. The brunt of Schauer's extremely interesting article is to ask whether we should expect more of courts than of legislators in articulating legal rules.

51. Quoted in Joseph Goldstein, *The Intelligible Constitution* 58 (1992).

52. Richard Kluger, *Simple Justice* 697 (1975).

53. Id. at 698.

54. *Felix Frankfurter Reminisces* 344–46 (Harlan Phillips, ed., 1960).

55. See, e.g., the discussion of the travails that Justice Brennan underwent in writing the majority opinion in Patterson v. McLean Credit Union, 491 U.S. 164 (1986), in James F. Simon, *The Center Holds: The Power Struggle Inside the Rehnquist Court* 43–81 (1995). Significantly, these two chapters of Simon's book are entitled " 'Five Votes Can Do Anything' " and "Fine Phrases." The first title quotes a statement by Justice Brennan himself.

56. Walter Murphy, *Elements of Judicial Strategy* (1964).

57. See Joseph Goldstein, *The Intelligible Constitution* at 35, 40–41 (1992).

58. On the growing lack of use by judges of the writings of legal academics, see, e.g., Louis J. Sirico and Jeffrey B. Margulies, "The Citing of Law Reviews by the Supreme Court: An Empirical Study," 34 U.C.L.A. L. Rev. 131 (1986), cited in Pierre Schlag, "Normativity and the Politics of Form," 139 U. Pa. L. Rev. 801, 844 n.115 (1991). On the role of clerks, see Richard Posner, *Overcoming Law* 688–69 (1995). As Posner writes, with devastating effect, "With the vast majority of judicial opinions now being written by law clerks, almost all of whom are very recent law school graduates, increasingly the law professor's exegesis of the latest Supreme Court decision belongs to the same genre as his comments on his students' papers." Id. at 88.

59. I have previously acknowledged the importance of Michael McConnell's work in leading me to change my mind about the advisability—and constitutional legitimacy—of aiding parents who wish to send their children to parochial schools. See Sanford Levinson, "Some Reflections on Multiculturalism, 'Equal Concern and Respect,' and the Establishment Clause of the First Amendment," 27 U. Richmond L. Rev. 989, 999 n.18 (1993) (citing McConnell, "The Selective Funding Problem: Abortions and Religious Schools," 104 Harv. L. Rev. 989 (1991). I could also cite a plethora of articles by Frederick Schauer on the system by which we should protect freedom of speech. For one example, see Schauer, "Uncoupling Free Speech," 92 Col. L. Rev. 1321 (1992).

60. Youngstown Sheet & Tube Co. v. Sawyer, 343 U.S. 579, 592 (1952).

61. Id.

62. Antonin Scalia, "The Rule of Law as a Law of Rules," 56 U. Chi. L. Rev. 80 (1989). Sterile formalism is distinguished perhaps from an "unsterile" formalism resting on a self-conscious analysis of the costs and benefits of recourse to rules instead of standards. See especially Schauer, *Playing by the Rules.*

63. Probably the most famous example of self-reference in American judicial history is Felix Frankfurter's invocation of his own status (and anguish) as a "member of the most beleaguered minority in history" before going on to explain why he must, nonetheless, acquiesce, as a constitutional matter, in the power of West Virginia to compel, on pain of expulsion and criminal punishment of parents, flag salutes in the public schools. That opinion, too, was a lone dissent. See West Virginia Board of Education v. Barnette, 319 U.S. 624, 646 (1943). This suggests, among other things, that the decision to engage in self-reference always implies as well a decision of a judge in a multimember court to stand alone, with whatever institutional costs that carries.

64. James Boyd White, *Justice in Translation* (1990).

65. See Sanford Levinson, "Conversing About Justice," 100 Yale L. J. 1855 (1991).

66. West Virginia Board of Education v. Barnette, 319 U.S. 624, 646 (1943).

67. Dennis v. United States, 341 U.S. 404, 561 (1951).

68. Erving Goffmann, *Forms of Talk* 194–95 (1981).

PIERRE N. LEVAL, "JUDICIAL OPINIONS AS LITERATURE"

1. *Reynolds v. Sims,* 377 U.S. 533, 580 (1964) (Warren, C. J.).

2. *Jacobellis v. Ohio,* 378 U.S. 184, 197 (1964) (Stewart, J., concurring).

3. *Lynch v. Household Finance Corp.,* 405 U.S. 538, 552 (1972) (Stewart, J.).

4. *Lochner v. New York,* 198 U.S. 45, 75 (1905) (Holmes, J., dissenting).

5. For the history of the flag, see *Texas v. Johnson,* 491 U.S. 397, 421–30 (1989) (Rehnquist, J., dissenting); for the history of baseball, see *Flood v. Kuhn,* 407 U.S. 258, 261–64 (1972) (Blackmun, J.); for the rhapsody on wilderness, see *Sierra Club v. Morton,* 405 U.S. 727, 749–52 (1972) (Douglas, J., dissenting).

6. *Palsgraf v. Long Island R.R.,* 162 N.E. 99 (1928) (Cardozo, J.); *Miller S.S. Co. v. Overseas Tankship (U.K.) Ltd.,* The Wagon Mound No. 2, [1963] 1 Lloyd's Law List Rep. 402 (Sup.Ct.N.S.W.).

7. *Petition of Kinsman Transit Co.,* 338 F.2d 708, 725 (1964) (Friendly, J.).

My thanks to Jim Whitman for our many discussions, to Sanford Levinson for his comments on a previous draft, and to Stanley Fish, who originally spurred my interest in these matters.

1. The notable exception is the work of Stanley Fish, who came to the legal academy from the study of rhetoric and literary criticism. See, e.g., Stanley Fish, *Doing What Comes Naturally: Change, Rhetoric, and the Practice of Theory in Legal and Literary Studies* (Durham, N.C.: Duke University Press, 1989), pp. 471–502.

2. The art of rhetoric was developed in part in response to the legal demands of these societies. In ancient Greece, citizens were required to make speeches in the assembly and in the law courts; in ancient Rome, an advocate or patron would often speak on behalf of a client. See George A. Kennedy, *A New History of Classical Rhetoric* (Princeton, N.J.: Princeton University Press, 1994), p. 103. J. A. Crook puts the matter succinctly: "Ancient advocates employed and were masters of rhetoric: for some observers that is the most important and obvious fact about them. Rhetoric was then regarded as the theoretical foundation of forensic practice." J. A. Crook, *Legal Advocacy in the Roman World* (London: Duckworth Press, 1995), p. 3.

3. In saying this, one should understand that in ancient Greece there was no organized legal profession to speak of and hence no organized form of legal education. Citizens studied rhetoric in order better to defend their interests in the courts and in the assembly. In ancient Rome, one must distinguish between jurists who wrote about law and advocates who represented clients, usually in their capacity as patrons. Education in rhetoric (and hence legal advocacy) was thought of as part of general education but was nevertheless useful for the patron in his advocacy in courts of law as well as in political life.

Even after classical times, law's organic connections to the art of rhetoric continued in medieval schools that were the forerunners of the university. Indeed, as Richard Schoeck points out, it was not until the twelfth century that law ceased to be regarded as a subdivision of rhetoric and became a university subject in its own right. See Richard J. Schoeck, "Lawyers and Rhetoric in Sixteenth Century England," in James Murphy, ed., *Renaissance Eloquence: Studies in the Theory and Practice of Renaissance Rhetoric* (Berkeley: University of California Press, 1983), pp. 274–91. After the development of law schools, rhetoric continued to be an essential part of legal education both in England and on the Continent. During the development of the early common law in England, the classical tradition of rhetoric was enormously important and heavily influenced the education of lawyers. Id. at 275.

4. The other canons of rhetoric were arrangement (*dispositio, taxis*); style (*elocutio, lexis*); memorization (*memoria, mnēmē*); and delivery (*pronunciatio, hypokrisis*).

5. A position attributed to him by Cicero. See Cicero, *Topica*, II, 6–8, in *Cicero*, trans. H. M. Hubbell, Loeb Classical Library Edition, 28 vols. (Cambridge: Harvard University Press, 1976), 2:386–87 & note *b*.

6. Here we might compare the spatial metaphor of "topic" with the concept of a "horizon" as used in hermeneutic theory. Obviously, the nature and limits of one's horizon depend on the place where one stands.

7. Aristotle, *Rhetoric*, 1358a, 1396a–1397a.

8. Chaim Perelman and L. Olbrechts-Tyteca, *The New Rhetoric: A Treatise on Argumentation*, trans. John Wilkinson and Purcell Weaver (Notre Dame: University of Notre Dame Press, 1969); Theodor Viehweg, *Topics and Law: A Contribution to Basic Research in Law*, trans. W. Cole Durham (Frankfurt am Main: Peter Lang, 1993).

9. See especially Perelman, *New Rhetoric*, p. 190. Perelman and Olbrechts-Tyteca use the Latin equivalent for "topic," *locus* (also meaning "place").

10. Viehweg, *Topics and Law*, pp. 69–85. On the influence of Viehweg and the Mainz school, see Katharina Sobota, "System and Flexibility in Law," Argumentation 5:275–82 (1991); W. Cole Durham, Translator's Foreword to Viehweg, *Topics and Law*, pp. xix–xxii.

11. Durham, Translator's Foreword, pp. xix–xxv. As Durham points out, the early history of the common law was heavily influenced by the topical approach, particularly owing to the influence of Aristotle and the felt need to draw legal principles from ancient sources and legal rules. See Stephen Siegel, "The Aristotelian Basis of English Law," 56 N.Y.U. L. Rev. 18, 20–29 (1981). As a result, ancient sources became topoi for the discussion of legal problems. The educational system reinforced rhetoric's centrality. Law students studied ancient rhetorical texts and practiced their skills in moots and stylized disputations. See Schoeck, "Lawyers and Rhetoric in Sixteenth Century England," pp. 280–82.

12. As Viehweg notes, this conception of topics goes back at least as far as Aristotle. Viehweg, *Topics and Law*, p. 19.

13. The connection between law and problem solving is Viehweg's fundamental insight. See especially Viehweg, *Topics and Law*, p. 85.

14. I emphasize that these are not the only tasks of legal analysis, although they have been the primary focus of legal semiotics. In any case, the methods of legal semiotics can and have been extended to other areas, for example, statutory and constitutional interpretation—see, e.g., Philip Bobbitt, *Constitutional Interpretation* (Oxford: Basil Blackwell, 1991)—and factual characterization. On the latter, see, e.g., Mark Kelman, "Interpretive Construction in the Substantive Criminal Law," 33 Stan. L. Rev. 591 (1981); J. M. Balkin, "The Rhetoric of Responsibility," 76 Va. L. Rev. 197 (1990).

15. J. M. Balkin, "The Promise of Legal Semiotics," 69 Tex. L. Rev. 1831 (1991); Duncan Kennedy, "A Semiotics of Legal Argument," 42 Syracuse L. Rev. 75 (1991); Jeremy Paul, "The Politics of Legal Semiotics," 69 Tex. L. Rev. 1779 (1991); James Boyle, "The Anatomy of a Torts Class," 34 Am. U. L. Rev. 1003 (1985).

16. J. M. Balkin, "The Crystalline Structure of Legal Thought," 39 Rutgers L. Rev. 1 (1986), brings together these and many of the other standard arguments and provides examples drawn from judicial opinions and academic literature.

17. Vosburg v. Putney, 80 Wis. 523; 50 N.W. 403 (1891).

18. Balkin, "Crystalline Structure of Legal Thought," supra.

19. Karl N. Llewellyn, "Remarks on the Theory of Appellate Decision and the Rules or Canons About How Statutes Are to Be Construed," 3 Vand. L. Rev. 395 (1951).

20. For example, Philip Bobbitt's theory of constitutional argument lists six basic "modalities" into which, he claims, all constitutional arguments must fall. See Bobbitt, *Constitutional Interpretation*, supra. Bobbitt's modalities—history, text, structure, consequences, precedent, and national ethos—are topics for the analysis of constitutional law issues. Indeed, Bobbitt argues that one of the advantages of his classification system is that "if citizens and journalists (and politicians) know the basic modes, the fundamental ways of thinking about the Constitution as law, they can work through current problems on their own." Id. at 28. Going through the list of constitutional modalities, even mechanically, "ought to give one an idea of how to proceed to answer a constitutional question, rather than simply shrugging one's shoulders." Id. at 30. Bobbitt's rationales perfectly describe the point of a topical approach.

21. Karl N. Llewellyn, *The Common Law Tradition: Deciding Appeals* (Boston: Little, Brown, 1960), at pp. 77–91.

22. Finally, we should note that even the research tools of American lawyers have been structured in topical form. The West Publishing Company's digest and keynote system is self-consciously organized around topics, as are resources like American Law Reports and treatises like *Corpus juris secundum*. The gradual displacement of these tools by computer-assisted research, I predict, will be unlikely to change the common law's fondness for conceiving, categorizing, and imagining law in terms of topics. Rather, we are likely to see the topical sensibility arise in ever-new forms as new technology develops.

23. A familiar topic introduced by critical legal studies is the interrelation between public and private. Critical race theory and feminism have introduced such topics as unspoken norms of race and gender, analysis of law in terms of its reinforcement of caste, and the intersectionality of identity.

24. For a discussion, see Balkin, "Rhetoric of Responsibility," supra, at pp. 254–63.

25. A good example is Patricia J. Williams, *The Alchemy of Race and Rights: Diary of a Law Professor*

(Cambridge: Harvard University Press, 1991). Although Williams is perhaps best known for her emphasis on personal narrative, I have found her work invaluable for its detailed descriptions of the contrasting rhetorical frames that people use to describe and evaluate racially charged incidents.

REVA B. SIEGEL, "IN THE EYES OF THE LAW"

1. Sanford Levinson, "The Rhetoric of the Judicial Opinion," in this volume. The description of the judicial opinion provided in this and the following paragraph is drawn from Levinson's account.
2. For two quite different examples in recent legal theory, see Robert Gordon, "Critical Legal Histories," *Stanford Law Review* 36 (January 1984): 57–125; Angela Harris, "The Jurisprudence of Reconstruction," *California Law Review* 82 (July 1994): 741–85 (tracing influence of critical legal studies scholarship on new critical race theory movement).
3. John Hollander, "Legal Rhetoric," in this volume.
4. On the personhood of corporations, see *Santa Clara County v. Southern Pacific R.R.* 116 U.S. 394 (1886) (corporations are "persons" within the meaning of the due process clause of the Fourteenth Amendment); *Breslin v. Fries-Breslin Co.*, 58 A. 313, 316 (N.J. 1904) ("In the eye of the law corporations are entities separate and distinct from their constituent members and not bound by the individual acts of the latter. The law deals with the corporation as an artificial person."); and see generally Sanford A. Schane, "The Corporation Is a Person: The Language of a Legal Fiction," *Tulane Law Review* 61 (February 1987): 563–609. On the personhood of the unborn, see *Roe v. Wade*, 410 U.S. 113, 158 (1973).
5. Compare Reva Siegel, "Reasoning from the Body: A Historical Perspective on Abortion Regulation and Questions of Equal Protection," *Stanford Law Review* 44 (January 1992): 261–381.
6. James Kent, *Commentaries on American Law*, vol. II (New York: O. Halsted, 1827): 109 ("The legal effects of marriage, are generally deducible from the principle of the common law, by which the husband and wife are regarded as one person, and her legal existence and authority in a degree lost or suspended, during the continuance of the matrimonial union."). Compare *Wenman v. Ash*, 13 C.B. 837 (1853) ("In the eye of the law, no doubt, man and wife are for many purposes one: but that is a strong figurative expression, and cannot be so dealt with as that all the consequences must follow which would result from its being literally true."). See generally Norma Basch, *In the Eyes of the Law: Women, Marriage, and Property in Nineteenth-Century New York* (Ithaca, N.Y.: Cornell University, 1982): 42.
7. *England v. Dana Corp.*, 428 F.2d 385, 386 (17th Cir. 1970) ("[T]he unity concept of marriage has in large part given way to the partner concept whereby a married woman stands as an equal to her husband in the eyes of the law") (quoting *Troue v. Marker*, 252 N.E.2d 800, 804 [Ind. 1969]); *Karczewski v. Baltimore & Ohio R.R. Co.*, 274 F. Supp. 169, 174 (N.D. Ill. 1967) ("The removal of the disabilities of coverture put [the] wife on an equal footing in the eyes of the law."); cf. *Mengelkoch v. Industrial Welfare Commission*, 284 F. Supp. 950, 954 (C.D. Ca. 1968) ("Nearly all of woman's civil disabilities have been removed. In the nineteenth century she was viewed as physically, socially and economically inferior to man. The laws buttressed this view. In the eyes of the law today, she is man's equal and to be accorded the same rights and privileges as her male counterpart.").
8. *Black's Law Dictionary* defines a legal fiction as an "assumption of fact made by court as a basis for deciding a legal question. A situation contrived by the law to permit a court to dispose of a matter, though it need not be created improperly; e.g. fiction of lost grant as basis for title by adverse possession." *Black's Law Dictionary* (5th ed.) (St. Paul, Minn.: West Publishing Co., 1979): 804.
9. *Plessy v. Ferguson*, 163 U.S. 537 (1896).
10. Ibid., 559 (Harlan, J., dissenting) (emphasis added).
11. "Color blindness" is now a shorthand reference for opposition to affirmative action programs. See, e.g., Ana Puga, "Civil Rights Chief Cool to Policy Shift; Some White House Advisers Calling for 'Color Blindness,'" *Boston Globe*, March 7, 1995; Maria Goodavage, "Shot Fired on Affirmative Action," *USA Today*, June 1, 1995 ("[I]n an eight-page open letter to Californians, [Governor Pete] Wilson said

affirmative action 'pits group against group, race against race. Instead of moving us forward toward a color-blind society, it is holding us back.'").

12. *Adarand Constructors v. Pena,* 115 S.Ct. 2097, 2108 (1995) (applying strict scrutiny to federal affirmative action programs) ("'[t]he guarantee of equal protection cannot mean one thing when applied to one individual and something else when applied to a person of another color'") (quoting *Regents of Univ. of California v. Bakke,* 438 U.S. 265, 289–90 [1978] [opinion of Powell, J.]); see also *Adarand,* 115 S.Ct. at 2119 (Scalia, J., concurring) ("In the eyes of government, we are just one race here. It is American.").

In *Adarand,* the Court announced several "general propositions" concerning race-based state action. The first it called "skepticism": "'[A]ny official action that treats a person differently on account of his race or ethnic origin is inherently suspect.'" *Adarand,* 115 S.Ct. at 2110 (quoting *Fullilove v. Klutznick,* 448 U.S. 448, 523 [1980] [Stewart, J., dissenting]). The second it called "consistency": "'The standard of review under the Equal Protection Clause is not dependent on the race of those burdened or benefited by a particular classification.'" *Adarand,* 115 S.Ct. at 2110 (quoting *Richmond v. J.A. Croson Co.,* 488 U.S. 469, 494 [1989] [plurality opinion]). Applying these principles to the "minority preferences" in federal affirmative action programs, the Court declared its intention to scrutinize claims of race discrimination raised by white people as carefully as it has scrutinized claims of race discrimination raised by people of color. In other words, the Court construed the equal protection clause to protect privileges enjoyed by white people against remedial redistribution to minorities that have historically suffered discrimination at the hands of white people.

13. Personal Responsibility Act of 1995, 104th Cong., 1st sess., H.R. 4., Report #104-96. The Personal Responsibility Act and its various components are discussed in Ed Gillespie and Bob Schelhas, eds., *Contract with America: The Bold Plan by Rep. Newt Gingrich, Rep. Dick Armey and the House Republicans to Change the Nation* (New York: Random House, 1994): 66–69.

14. J. M. Balkin, "Some Realism About Pluralism: Legal Realist Approaches to the First Amendment," *Duke Law Journal* 1990 (June 1990): 375–430, 383 ("The radical ideas of the day often become the orthodoxy of tomorrow, and, in the process, take on a quite different political valence. I refer to this phenomenon as ideological drift.").

15. One need only consult Title I of the Personal Responsibility Act to appreciate the racialized referents of the welfare debate. The authors of *Contract with America* introduce the act as follows: "Today, one of every five white children and two of every three African-American children are born out of wedlock. The Personal Responsibility Act is designed to diminish the number of teenage pregnancies and illegitimate births. It prohibits AFDC payments and housing benefits to mothers under age eighteen who give birth to out-of-wedlock children. The state has the option of extending this prohibition to mothers ages eighteen, nineteen, and twenty." Gillespie and Schelhas, *Contract with America,* 70. The Personal Responsibility Act reflects years of race- (and gender-) infused opposition to welfare of the sort described by Jill Quadagno in her recent book, *The Color of Welfare: How Racism Undermined the War on Poverty* (New York: Oxford University Press, 1994): 117: "No program better exemplifies the racially divisive character of the American welfare state than Aid to Families with Dependent Children (AFDC). Conservatives attack AFDC for discouraging work and family formation and for rewarding laziness. Such comments are really subtly veiled messages about family structures and employment patterns among African Americans. However, often the attacks are neither veiled nor subtle."

16. Under current equal protection doctrine, governmental action that is explicitly race based is subject to strict scrutiny. So-called facially-neutral governmental action that has a disproportionate impact on minorities is only subject to heightened scrutiny if it can be shown that the challenged action is motivated by "discriminatory purpose." "Discriminatory purpose" is a restrictively defined term of art, akin to malice, which is very difficult to prove. See *Personnel Administrator of Mass. v. Feeney,* 442 U.S. 256, 279 (1979) ("Discriminatory purpose . . . implies more than intent as volition or intent as awareness of consequences. It implies that the decisionmaker . . . selected or reaffirmed a particular

course of action at least in part 'because of,' not merely 'in spite of,' its adverse effects."). In a recent voting rights decision, the Court bluntly observed that "[t]he distinction between being aware of racial considerations and being motivated by them may be difficult to prove." *Miller v. Johnson,* 115 S.Ct. 2475, 2488 (1995). Because it is so hard to prove discriminatory purpose under the equal protection clause, most institutions, practices, and values are constitutionally characterized as race-neutral. For example, in *Miller* the Court characterized the practice of drawing voting-district lines to reflect "compactness, contiguity, respect for political subdivisions or communities defined by actual shared interests" as an expression of "traditional race-neutral districting principles." Ibid.

    For a discussion of racially coded norms that might qualify as race-neutral under prevailing equal protection jurisprudence, see Kimberle Williams Crenshaw, "Race, Reform, and Retrenchment: Transformation and Legitimation in Antidiscrimination Law," *Harvard Law Review* 101 (May 1988): 1331–1478, 1387.

17. See Dorothy Roberts, review of Jill Quadagno, *The Color of Welfare: How Racism Undermined the War on Poverty,* and Linda Gordon, *Pitied but Not Entitled: Single Mothers and the History of Welfare,* in *Contemporary Sociology* 24 (January 1995): 1–4; Quadagno, *Color of Welfare,* v ("welfare reform is the policy issue that most readily translates into a racial code"). See also supra note 15.

18. See William Safire, "Wedge Issues: Each Party Has Topic with Which to Attack," *Fort Lauderdale Sun-Sentinel,* March 3, 1995 ("The key word is 'color-blind.' After three decades of penance for two centuries of discrimination, most whites [and many merit-conscious blacks] reject the compensatory reverse discrimination that has led to de facto quotas in hiring and favoritism in government contracts."). See also Robert Pear, "Report to Clinton Faults Programs to Aid Minorities," *New York Times,* May 31, 1995 ("A confidential report prepared for the President . . . analyzes the reasons for 'white male resentment' of [affirmative action]"; during a recent speech to the California Democratic Party, the President declared, " 'This is psychologically a difficult time for a lot of so-called angry white males,' who feel they have been treated unfairly.").

    Critical race scholars Cheryl Harris and Neil Gotanda have argued that the Supreme Court is now using concepts of color blindness to protect various forms of white privilege. See Cheryl I. Harris, "Whiteness as Property," *Harvard Law Review* 106 (June 1993): 1709–91; Neil Gotanda, "A Critique of 'Our Constitution Is Color-Blind,' " *Stanford Law Review* 44 (November 1991): 1–68.

19. Compare Rochelle Stanfield, "The Wedge Issue," *National Journal* 27 (April 1995): 790 (Clint Bolick, director of a conservative public interest law firm that opposes affirmative action, observes: "Those of us who are arguing for race neutrality have really claimed the mantle of the great civil rights advocates from Frederick Douglas to Martin Luther King Jr. and Hubert Humphrey."); Kevin Merida, "Rights Debate: Both Sides Uneasy," *Washington Post,* February 23, 1995 ("In his public comments, [Senator Robert] Dole has called for a 'colorblind society,' taking aim at programs that perpetuate quotas while simultaneously boasting of his civil rights record.").

    Thus, when the president recently attributed opposition to affirmative action to the resentment of "angry white males," see supra note 18, the editor of the *New Republic* publicly chastised him, complaining that "Mr. Clinton can only understand the opposition as a response of 'white males.' He doesn't seem to have noticed that there are other principles involved, like those of fairness and liberty." Andrew Sullivan, "Let Affirmative Action Die," *New York Times,* July 23, 1995. Apparently, Sullivan views the "response of 'white males' " as a principled basis for opposition to affirmative action, to be discussed alongside the "other principles involved."

20. *J.E.B. v. Alabama ex rel. T.B.,* 114 S.Ct. 1419 (1994); *Batson v. Kentucky,* 476 U.S. 79 (1986).

21. *J.E.B. v. Alabama ex rel. T.B.,* 114 S.Ct. 1419, 1432 (1994) (O'Connor, J.) (emphasis added).

CATHARINE A. MACKINNON, "LAW'S STORIES AS REALITY AND POLITICS"

1. See Elaine Scarry, "Speech Acts in Criminal Cases," in this volume, esp. p. 166.

2. David N. Rosen, "Rhetoric and Result in the Bobby Seale Trial," in this volume, p. 112.

3. Paul Gewirtz, "Victims and Voyeurs: Two Narrative Problems at the Criminal Trial," in this volume, p. 143.

4. Robert A. Ferguson, "Untold Stories in the Law," in this volume.

5. Alan M. Dershowitz, "Life Is Not a Dramatic Narrative," in this volume, p. 100.

6. Catharine A. MacKinnon, *Feminism Unmodified* 169 (1987). See generally Center for Women Policy Studies, *Violence Against Women as Bias-Motivated Hate Crime* (1991).

7. Each year, about four thousand American women are killed in battering contexts by husbands or partners who have abused them. E. Stark et al., *Wife Abuse in the Medical Setting:* In introduction for health personnel, National Clearinghouse on Domestic Violence, Monograph Series no. 7, USGPO, 1981. See also generally Senate Judiciary Committee, *Violence Against Women: A Week in the Life of America* (October 1992); Ann Jones, *Next Time, She'll Be Dead: Battering and How to Stop It* (1994).

8. Jean-François Lyotard, "The Differend, the Referent, and the Proper Name," 4 diacritics (Fall 1984).

9. Peter Brooks, "Storytelling Without Fear? Confession in Law and Literature," in this volume. Marion is the woman about whose entry into prostitution Rousseau fantasizes in his *Confessions,* the subject of Peter Brooks's essay, at 122 and following.

10. Martha Minow, "Stories in Law," in this volume, pp. 24–25.

11. Daniel A. Farber and Suzanna Sherry, "Legal Storytelling and Constitutional Law"; Martha Minow, "Stories in Law"; Harlon L. Dalton, "Storytelling on Its Own Terms," all in this volume.

12. Louis Michael Seidman, "Some Stories About Confessions and Confessions About Stories," in this volume.

13. Harlon L. Dalton, n.11 supra, p. 57.

14. See, e.g., Karin Obholzer, *Gespräche mit dem Wolfsmann* (1980).

15. See, e.g., Diana E. H. Russell, "The Incidence and Prevalence of Intrafamilial and Extrafamilial Sexual Abuse of Female Children," 7 Child Abuse and Neglect: The International Journal 2 (1983).

16. Janet Malcolm, "The Side-Bar Conference," in this volume.

17. Id. at 108 ("The juror, no less than the reader of a novel, needs to be protected from disbelief.").

18. Louis Michael Seidman, n.12 supra.

19. For studies that document this, see Catharine A. MacKinnon, "Prostitution and Civil Rights" 1 Michigan Journal of Gender & Law 27–28 (1993).

20. U.S. Merit Systems Protection Board, *Sexual Harassment in the Federal Workplace: Is It a Problem?* (1981).

21. Diana E. H. Russell, n.15 supra.

22. John Hollander, "Legal Rhetoric," in this volume, pp. 182–83.

23. Sanford Levinson, "The Rhetoric of the Judicial Opinion," in this volume, p. 194.

24. Collin v. Smith, 575 F. 2d 1187, 1210 (1976).

25. John Hollander, n.22 supra, p. 185.

Contributors

J. M. Balkin is Lafayette S. Foster Professor of Law at Yale Law School. He teaches and writes in the fields of constitutional law, jurisprudence, and torts.

Peter Brooks, Tripp Professor of Humanities and Chair of the Department of Comparative Literature at Yale University, is the author of *Reading for the Plot* and, most recently, *Psychoanalysis and Storytelling*.

Harlon L. Dalton is Professor of Law at Yale Law School and the author, most recently, of *Racial Healing*.

Alan M. Dershowitz is Felix Frankfurter Professor of Law at Harvard Law School and the best-selling author of *Chutzpah* and *Reversal of Fortune*. In his latest book, *Reasonable Doubts*, he examines the implications of the O. J. Simpson trial.

Daniel A. Farber, Henry J. Fletcher Professor of Law at the University of Minnesota, writes extensively about constitutional issues, edits the journal *Constitutional Commentary*, and is coauthor of the forthcoming book *On the Merits*.

Robert A. Ferguson is George Edward Woodberry Professor in the Department of English and the Law School at Columbia University. His books include *Law and Letters in American Culture* and *The American Enlightenment, 1750–1820*.

Paul Gewirtz is Potter Stewart Professor of Constitutional Law at Yale Law School. He is the author, most recently, of "On 'I Know It When I See It'" and "The Triumph and

Transformation of Antidiscrimination Law" and the editor of *The Case Law System in America.*

John Hollander is a poet and Sterling Professor of English at Yale University. His most recent books are *Selected Poetry, Tesserae,* and *The Gazer's Spirit.*

Anthony Kronman is Dean of Yale Law School and Edward J. Phelps Professor of Law. He has written widely in the fields of contracts, commercial law, jurisprudence, legal sociology, and professional ethics. His latest book is *The Lost Lawyer.*

Pierre N. Leval is a judge of the U.S. Court of Appeals for the Second Circuit. Previously, as a trial judge, he heard General William Westmoreland's libel suit against CBS, J. D. Salinger's suit to enjoin publication of a biography, and countless other cases.

Sanford Levinson is a professor at the University of Texas Law School and the author of *Constitutional Faith,* coeditor (with Steven Mailloux) of *Interpreting Law and Literature,* and editor of *Responding to Imperfection.*

Catharine A. MacKinnon is a lawyer, teacher, writer, activist, and expert on sex equality. She is Professor of Law at the University of Michigan.

Janet Malcolm is the author of *Diana and Nikon: Essays on the Aesthetic of Photography, Psychoanalysis: The Impossible Profession, In the Freud Archives, The Journalist and the Murderer, The Purloined Clinic,* and *The Silent Woman: Sylvia Plath and Ted Hughes.*

Martha Minow, Professor of Law at Harvard Law School, is the author of *Making All the Difference: Inclusion, Exclusion and American Law* and coeditor with Gary Bellow of *Law Stories* (forthcoming).

David Rosen practices law in New Haven, Connecticut, and is a lecturer at the Yale Child Study Center.

Elaine Scarry is Professor of English at Harvard University and was a Leff Fellow at Yale Law School in 1993. She has written *Body in Pain, Resisting Representation,* and a set of articles on war and the social contract.

Louis Michael Seidman is Professor of Law at Georgetown University Law Center. He is the author of *Constitutional Law* (with Geoffrey Stone, Cass Sunstein, and Mark Tushnet) and *Remnants of Belief* (with Mark Tushnet).

Suzanna Sherry is Earl R. Larson Professor of Civil Rights and Civil Liberties Law at the University of Minnesota. She is the author of many articles on constitutional law and coauthor of the forthcoming book *On the Merits.*

Reva B. Siegel is Professor of Law at Yale Law School. She teaches and writes in the fields of legal history, feminist and critical race theory, antidiscrimination law, constitutional law, and contracts.

Robert Weisberg is Professor of Law at Stanford Law School. He is the coauthor of the forthcoming book *Literary Criticisms of Law* (with Guyora Binder).

Index

Abolitionism, 80–81, 82
Abrams, Kathryn, 43
Adaptationism, 62
Adarand Constructors v. Pena (1995), 276*n12*
Adversarial system, 167, 170–71
Aeschylus, 3, 14, 259–60*n4*
Affirmative action, 229–30, 276*n12*,
    277*nn18–19*
Aid to Families with Dependent Children
    (AFDC), 276*n15*
Alaska, sentencing law, 169
Alexander, Larry, 50
Alfieri, Anthony, 72
Alibis, 162
American history, 80
American Revolution, 80, 91
American Revolution of 1800 (Sisson), 88
Anatomy Lesson (Rembrandt), 206
Anthropology, 76
Anti-Semitism, 242*n46*
Appellate courts, 18, 66, 68, 225
Arendt, Hannah, 26, 32–34, 35, 242*n41*
Aristotle, 17, 178–79, 181, 213–14
Arnold, Thurman, 202
Ashcraft v. Tennessee (1944), 116, 126–27

Attainder, bills of, 150
Austin, J. L., 123, 124, 130, 178, 191
Authority: of judges, 10, 12, 186, 196, 225,
    226; judicial opinions and, 10–11, 12, 20,
    21, 186, 187, 194, 195, 225–26; historical
    narrative and, 77–78; and persuasion, 186,
    195, 226

Bailey, Pearl, 185
Bakhtin, Mikhail, 131–32
Baldwin, James, 7
Balkin, J. M., 10, 20, 190, 230
Bankruptcy law, 66–67
Baron, Jane B., 43
Barthes, Roland, 19, 83
Batson v. Kentucky (1986), 230–31
Beard, Charles, 62
Benhabib, Seyla, 32
Benito Cereno (Melville), 97, 98
Bennett, W. Lance, 249*n1*
Bentham, Jeremy, 35–36, 192
Bhaba, Homi, 78–79
Billy Budd (Melville), 3
Black, Hugo L., 130, 196, 203
Black, Roy, 247*n11*

Blackburn v. Alabama (1960), 117, 128
Blackmun, Harry A., Jr., 128–29
Black Panther Party, 110–12
Blacks, 155, 156, 251n25
Black's Law Dictionary, 275n8
Black Thunder (Bontemps), 97
Bleak House (Dickens), 3
Board of Education of Kiryas Joel Village
    School District v. Louis Grumet (1994), 26,
    27–30, 31, 34
Bobbitt, Philip, 190–91, 196, 274n20
Bolling v. Sharpe (1954), 198
Bontemps, Arna, 97
Boorn, Jesse, 114–15
Boorn, Stephen, 114–15
Booth, Wayne C., 68
Booth v. Maryland (1987), 262–63n27, 263n29,
    266–67n10; prohibition of victim impact
    evidence, 139–42, 144–45, 147–48, 173;
    overruled in Payne, 140, 141, 261n15; vic-
    tim impact statement in, 140, 158–61, 264–
    65n45; state law in, 146
Borges, Jorge Luis, 132
Bostwick, Gary, 107–8
Boyle, Jamie, 216
Brennan, William J., Jr., 129–30, 144–45, 196,
    199
Brest, Paul, 146
Brewer v. Williams (1977), 125–26, 127–29,
    130, 258–59n24, 259n25
Brooks, Peter, 9, 20, 164, 166, 167, 168, 236
Brown, John, 79–82, 83
Brown v. Board of Education of Topeka, Kan-
    sas (1954), 50, 135–36, 184; Warren opin-
    ion in, 11, 197–99; and hate speech, 48
Buchanan, Patrick J., 254n8
Burger, Warren E., 125–26, 128
Burke, Kenneth, 178
Burns, George, 164

Calabresi, Guido, 194, 200, 237
California: sentencing law, 169; Supreme
    Court, 271n41
Camus, Albert, 132, 134
Canada, judicial opinions in, 236
Cannon, Walter B., 180–81
Capital cases, 119, 140, 262n24. See also Death
    penalty
Cardozo, Benjamin N., 207, 269n11

Cartesianism, 62
Catholic Church, 119, 121
Chekhov, Anton, 18, 99, 100, 104, 105, 256n22
Chicago Eight trial, 111
Children, 47–48; sexual abuse of, 237
Christian Burial Speech, 127, 128, 129, 132
Church-state separation, 28
Cicero, Marcus Tullius, 181, 214
Citizenship, 228, 229
Civil cases, 170
Civilization and Its Discontents (Freud), 89
Civil War, 80
Clark, Marcia, 104, 139
Cleaver, Eldridge, 253n45
Clinton, Bill, 277nn18–19
Coke, Sir Edward, 120, 191–92
Collin v. Smith (1976), 237
Colvin, Russell, 114–15
Commercial law, 62, 63
Common law, 219
Common Law Tradition (Llewellyn), 219
Compassion, individual and statistical, 166
Confession, 164, 167–70; voluntary and co-
    erced, 20, 115, 116, 120, 125–26, 130–31,
    173–74; Culombe v. Connecticut and, 115,
    117–18, 131; Escobedo v. Illinois and, 115,
    124–25; Massiah v. United States and, 115,
    128; Miranda v. Arizona ruling, 115–18,
    120–21, 125, 130, 131; police interroga-
    tions and, 116–18; Fifth Amendment and,
    117, 119, 120–21, 130, 257n13; Catholic
    Church and, 118–19, 121; medieval law
    and, 119–20; psychoanalytic model of, 121,
    124, 132–33, 258n18; Western literature
    and, 121, 129, 131–32; Rousseau on, 121–
    23, 125, 126, 132, 133; as speech act, 123,
    124, 133–34; false, 123–24; Talmudic law
    and, 124, 258n19; Brewer v. Williams and,
    125–26, 127–29; Ashcraft v. Tennessee
    and, 126–27; Camus on, 132, 134; and
    death penalty, 169
Confessions (Rousseau), 121–23, 125, 126, 132
Confessions of Nat Turner (Styron), 97
Conrad, Joseph, 17
Constitutional grammar, 190
Constitutional law, 21, 62, 274n20
Contract law, 267n6
Cooper v. Aaron (1958), 21
Cooper v. General Dynamics (1976), 185

Counternarratives, 86

Court TV, 84, 150

Cover, Robert M., 5, 167, 196, 266*n7*

Crime: public fear of, 135, 151, 157; language of law and, 226–27

Criminal Interrogation and Confessions (Inbau and Reid), 117

Criminal law, 62; John Brown trial and, 79; confessions in, 115, 124, 126; judicial opinions, 269*n13*

Criminal trials: narrative in, 2–3, 7, 64, 136–37, 249*n1;* public and, 135, 136, 149–57; crime victims and, 136, 137–38, 139; state versus defendant in, 166, 171; verdicts in, 166–67, 170

Critical legal studies (CLS), 13, 38, 39, 216

Critical legal theory, 242*n2*

Critical race theory, 42, 46, 50, 75–76, 223

Culombe v. Connecticut (1961), 115, 117–18, 131, 256*n3*

Cultural narratives, 75–76

Dahmer, Jeffrey, 147

Dalton, Clare, 41

Dalton, Harlon L., 5, 16, 208, 234, 235

Davis, David Brion, 80

Davis, Miles, 59

"Death of Ivan Ilych" (Tolstoy), 3

Death penalty: victim impact statements and, 139–40, 141, 144–45, 146, 148–49, 170, 173, 265*n51; Booth v. Maryland* and, 139–40, 141, 144–45, 263*n29; Payne v. Tennessee* and, 140, 158; defendants' mitigating evidence and, 142–43, 145, 262*n24;* confession and, 169

Defendants, 166–67; Fifth Amendment rights, 116, 130, 163, 265–66*n1;* confessions, 116, 130, 167–70; compulsion of evidence from, 129–30; victim impact evidence and, 141–43, 147, 170, 262–63*n27*, 263*n28*, 266–67*n10;* mitigating evidence, 142–43, 145, 262*n24*, 264*n44;* right to confront witnesses, 147

Defense lawyers, 69

De inventione (Cicero), 214

Delgado, Richard, 41, 43, 59

De Man, Paul, 123, 124

Democracy, 156–57

Dennis v. United States (1951), 204

Dershowitz, Alan M., 9, 18–19, 69–70, 233

Detective stories, 118

Dew, Thomas Roderick, 251–52*n26*

Dewey, John, 65

Dewey, Thomas E., 198

Diaspora, Jewish, 26–27, 32

Dickens, Charles, 3

DiGerlando, Benedict, 124–25

Discrimination law, 48

Dissenting opinions, 184, 188, 268*n5*

Donne, John, 182

Dostoevsky, Fyodor M., 129, 131–32

Douglas, Mary, 89, 91, 95

Douglas, William O., 130, 190, 202

Dred Scott v. Sandford (1857), 80

Due process of law, 74, 115

Dukakis, Michael S., 145

Dworkin, Andrea, 44, 255–56*n20*

Dworkin, Ronald, 15

Economics, 13

Eisenhower, Dwight D., 195

Ellison, Ralph, 7

Emerson, Ralph Waldo, 79, 82

Emotions, 55–56

English law, 119–20, 137

Enlightenment, 131, 234; and Jewish assimilation, 27, 29, 34; critical legal theory and, 38, 39, 50, 51–52; and slavery, 92

Equal protection law, 44, 48, 229, 230–31, 276*n12*, 276–77*n16*

Escobedo, Danny, 124–25

Escobedo v. Illinois (1964), 115, 124–25, 257*n6*

Essay Concerning the True Original, Extent, and End of Civil Government (Locke), 91

Establishment clause, 26, 28–29

Evidence, rules of, 9, 19–20, 119, 164; compelled evidence, 129–30

Fall, The (Camus), 132, 134

Farber, Daniel A., 5, 16, 54, 58, 59, 234

Fatal Vision (film), 106

Faulkner, William, 17

Federal Reporter, 191

Federal Supplement, 191

Feldman, Martha S., 249*n1*

Feminism, 42, 43, 50, 51, 223

Ferguson, Robert A., 8, 18, 233, 236; on trial of John Brown, 79, 81–82, 83; on judicial opinions, 189
Feynman, Richard, 255n12
Fish, Stanley, 15
Fiss, Owen, 15, 228
Formalism, 17
Fortas, Abe, 114, 121, 131
Frank, Jerome, 202
Frankfurter, Felix, 50, 272n63; Culombe v. Connecticut opinion, 115, 117–18, 131, 256n3; on judicial opinions, 188, 199, 200
Freud, Sigmund, 100, 118; on return of the repressed, 89, 97; on guilt and confession, 124, 133, 258–59n24; and child abuse, 235
Friendly, Henry J., 209–10, 257n7
Frye, Northrop, 67
Fugitive Slave Act (1793), 80, 81
Fundamentals of Criminal Investigation (O'Hara), 117

G., Mrs., 72–75
Gabriel's rebellion, 87–98, 110, 111, 252n28
Gant v. Aliquippa Borough (1985), 185
Garroway, David, 164
Garry, Charles, 111
Gates, Henry Louis, Jr., 50
Gee, Thomas, 270n31
Geertz, Clifford, 189, 250n9
German Constitutional Court, 268n5
Gewirtz, Paul, 9, 20, 164, 166, 267n12; on victim impact statements, 167, 170, 171, 173; on Brown v. Board of Education, 184; on storytelling, 233
Gide, André, 129
Gideon v. Wainwright (1963), 50, 246n60
Gilkerson, Christopher, 71–72
Gleick, James, 255n12
Glendon, Mary Ann, 191–92
Goffman, Erving, 178, 204–5
Goldberg v. Kelly (1970), 74
Goldstein, Joseph, 199
Gordon, Robert W., 41, 61
Gould, Stephen Jay, 101
Great Expectations (Dickens), 3
Greece, 268n5
Greeley, Horace, 194
Grenada Steel Indus. v. Alabama Oxygen Co. (1983), 185

Grisham, John, 2, 150
Griswold v. Connecticut (1965), 190

Hamlet (Shakespeare), 129
Hand, Augustus N., 196–97
Hand, Learned, 189, 207, 269n11
Harlan, John Marshall (the first), 228–30
Harlan, John Marshall (the second), 116, 120, 126, 134
Harvard University, 50
Hasidic school case. See Board of Education of Kiryas Joel Village School District v. Louis Grumet
Hate speech, 44, 46–47, 48, 51, 245n43
Hawthorne, Nathaniel, 80, 253n44
Hay, Douglas, 62
Hegel, Georg Wilhelm Friedrich, 77–78
Henry, Patrick, 90, 91
Heresy, 118–19
Historical narrative, 75, 76–78
Hoffman, Abbie, 111
Hogg, Peter, 268n5
Hollander, John, 10, 20, 226–27, 237
Holmes, Oliver Wendell, 105, 216; on "marketplace of ideas," 51; on public opinion, 158; and judicial opinions, 189, 198, 200, 207; on Fourteenth Amendment, 209
Holocaust, 27, 102
Horwitz, Morton, 63
Hot Shots! (film), 254–55n11
Huggins, Ericka, 111
Humanist view of law, 72

Illinois, sentencing law, 169
Immigration and Naturalization Service v. Chadha (1983), 50, 246n60
Inbau, Fred E., 117
Indeterminacy thesis, 38, 39–41, 42, 48–49, 52, 59
Indicia, 119
Inferior courts, 190, 191–92, 193, 225
Innocence, presumption of, 70
Inquisition, 119
Instrumental view of law, 72
Intelligible Constitution (Goldstein), 199
Irish Supreme Court, 268n5
Iser, Wolfgang, 117
Ito, Lance, 138, 155, 260n6

J.E.B. v. Alabama ex rel. T.B. (*1994*), 230–31
Jackson, Andrew, 192
Jackson, Robert H., 134, 196; on confessions, 116, 126–27; and *Brown v. Board of Education*, 198; *Youngstown Sheet and Tube* opinion, 202–3, 204
James, William, 68
Jefferson, Thomas: and slavery, 88, 90, 92, 250*n11*, 251*n20*, 251*n25;* on Washington, 94; Black Panthers and, 110
Johnson, Alex M., Jr., 242*n4*
Journalist and the Murderer (Malcolm), 106, 108
Judges: writing of opinions, 10, 11, 189, 196, 197, 199–200, 225, 226; authority of, 10, 12, 186, 196, 225, 226; and literature in law, 15, 206–7; and indeterminacy of legal reasoning, 41; and legal narrative, 66, 144; instructions to juries, 144; and victim impact evidence, 147; and losing party in cases, 197
Judicial opinions: coerciveness of, 5, 10; rhetoric of, 10, 11, 20–21, 176, 187, 190–92, 193, 199, 207–10; authority of, 10–11, 12, 20, 21, 186, 187, 194, 195, 225–26; and precedent, 10–11, 12, 185–86, 192–94, 225; self-certainty of, 11, 188–89; multiple, 11–12; authorship of, 12, 188; persuasiveness of, 20–21, 186, 187, 194, 195, 201–2, 207–8, 226; Supreme Court, 21, 188, 190–94, 197, 199, 210; audiences for, 21, 196–97, 199–201; obiter dicta, 184; dissents, 184, 188, 268*n5;* and rule of law, 188, 189, 226; of inferior courts, 190, 191–92; as literature, 206–7; description of crime in, 269*n13*
Juries: and stories, 8–9, 87, 104; side-bar conference and, 108; and victim impact evidence, 142, 144, 145, 146, 264*n44;* judges' instructions to, 144; sentencing decisions, 145; as representative of the public, 150, 152–54; nullification by, 153; rendering of verdicts, 178; selection of, 230–31
Jury consultants, 153

Kafka, Franz, 3, 14
Kamisar, Yale, 130, 259*n25*
Kansas-Nebraska Act (*1854*), 80
Katrougalos, George, 268*n5*

Kelman, Mark, 69
Kennedy, Anthony M., 28, 196
Kennedy, Duncan, 216, 218
King, Rodney, 153
Kiryas Joel case. See *Board of Education of Kiryas Joel Village School District v. Louis . Grumet*
Kornstein, Daniel, 107, 108
Kronman, Anthony, 5, 16
Kuhn, Thomas S., 65, 194–95

L.A. Law (television), 150
Language: in law and literature, 4; mindset theory and, 41; legal storytelling and, 42, 44, 49–50; in construction of oppression, 45; in rational argument, 51; of the law, 226–27, 228; nonpropositional, 243*n17*
Lardner, Ring, 268*n2*
Lateran Council (*1215*), 118–19
Law: as narrative, 2, 3, 63–65, 66, 67; public interest in, 2, 150; and literature, 3, 14, 65, 83, 182; in literature, 3, 14–15, 70; as literature, 3–4, 15; dissimilarities to literature, 5, 104, 105; narrative in, 15–17, 75–76, 136, 165; and reason, 50; historical criticism of, 61–62; humanist and instrumental views of, 72; in history, 77–78; metaphor and, 182; as trope, 183–84; precedent in, 186; rule of, 188, 189, 203, 204, 226; language of, 226–27, 228
Law clerks, 12, 200, 272*n58*
Law professors, 200, 272*n58*
Lawrence, Charles B., III, 47–48, 59
Law schools, 219–20
Lawyers: and clients' stories, 8, 71–72, 75, 239–40*n4*, 240*n5;* and trial narratives, 8, 86, 87, 112; indeterminacy thesis and, 40; and law as narrative, 63–64, 66; use of rhetoric, 64, 176; and victim impact evidence, 146, 147; and public opinion, 154; and coerced confession, 167; legal and topical reasoning, 215, 219
Learning (detective), 127, 128, 129, 130, 132
"Lecture, The" (Goffman), 205
Lectures on the Philosophy of History (Hegel), 77
Lee, Arthur, 90, 92
Legal counsel, right to, 128
Legal cultures, 222

Legal doctrines, 62, 219–20, 221
Legal fictions, 227–28, 237, 275n8
Legal narratives, 5, 61, 62, 66, 69, 71–72, 75,
    83
Legal reasoning, 220–21; indeterminacy thesis
    and, 39–40, 42, 49; hate speech and, 47;
    mindset theory and, 58; rhetoric and, 211–
    12, 214, 224; and problem solving, 215–16
Legal scholarship, 37, 43
Legal semiotics, 216, 218, 220
Legal storytelling movement, 5–6, 15–16, 37–
    38, 42–44, 47, 52, 142–43, 245n43
Leiris, Michel, 121
Lemon v. Kurtzman (1971), 28
Leontius, story of, 55–56
Leval, Pierre N., 10, 11, 20
Levinson, Sanford, 10, 20, 225–26, 237
Lévi-Strauss, Claude, 95, 232
Lincoln, Abraham, 82
Linde, Hans, 269n13
Literary theory, 13, 15, 17
Literature: law and, 3, 14, 65, 83, 182; law in,
    3, 14–15, 70; law as, 3–4, 15; dis-
    similarities to law, 5, 104, 105; confession
    in, 121, 129, 131–32
Llewellyn, Karl N., 6, 218, 219
Local Loan Co. v. Hunt (1934), 67
Locke, John, 91, 267n12
Lopez, Gerald P., 43
Lyotard, Jean-François, 233

MacDonald, Jeffrey R., 106–8
MacDonald v. McGinniss (1987), 106–8
McGinniss, Joe, 106–8
MacKinnon, Catharine A., 10, 20; on pornogra-
    phy, 44–46, 244n29, 245n34, 255–56n20
Madison, James, 190
Magna Carta, 119–20
Maimonides, 131, 258n19
Malcolm, Janet, 8, 18, 235–36
Mamet, David, 105
Marcus, Isabel, 67
Marital unity, doctrine of, 227, 275nn6–7
Marshall, Thurgood, 128–29
Marxism, 76
Maryland, victim evidence law, 146
Massiah v. United States (1964), 115, 128
Master narratives, 77
Matsuda, Mari J., 43

Medicine, 15
Melville, Herman, 3, 97, 98
Mendelssohn, Moses, 27
Menendez brothers, 151
Metaphor, 182, 237
Meyer, Carlin, 51, 247n64
Miller v. Fenton (1985), 131
Miller v. Johnson (1995), 276–77n16
Mindset theory, 41–42, 44, 47, 48
Minow, Martha L., 5, 16, 54, 57, 58, 234,
    262n25
Miranda v. Arizona (1966), 21, 115–16, 256n4;
    warnings required by, 115, 121, 130,
    258n22; Harlan-White dissents, 116, 120,
    125, 134; Warren opinion, 116–18, 120–21,
    130, 167; Brewer v. Williams and, 128,
    259n25; effects of, 131, 258n22
Missouri Compromise, 80
Monroe, James, 88, 96, 250n11
Moore, G. E., 254n8
Moral luck, 261–62n17
Morrison, Toni, 7
Moseley, Walter, 7
Movies, 2, 254–55n11
"Murders in the Rue Morgue" (Poe), 118
Murder trials, 138, 139, 142
Murphy, Walter, 199

Nagel, Robert, 269n12
Narrative: law as, 2, 3, 63–65, 66, 67; in law,
    15–17, 75–76, 136, 165; good and bad, 67;
    contest, 71; historical, 75, 76–78; theory of,
    144
Narratology, 17
Nationhood, 78–79
Nation-states, 77
Native Son (Wright), 138
Naturalistic fallacy, 101, 254n8
Natural law, 102, 190
Nazis, 27, 102, 237
Neuborne, Burt, 51
Neustadt, Richard, 195
New Rhetoric (Perelman), 214
New York (state): legislature, 28, 30; divorce
    law, 67; Court of Appeals, 271n41
Notes on the State of Virginia (Jefferson),
    90
Nozick, Robert, 41
Nussbaum, Martha, 33

Oath ex officio, 119
Obiter dicta, 184
O'Connor, Sandra Day, 196; on establishment clause, 28; on self-incrimination, 131, 259*n27;* on death sentencing, 144, 261–62*n17;* on peremptory strikes, 230–31
O'Hara, Charles E., 117
One Hundred and Twenty Days of Sodom (de Sade), 132
Oprah (television), 152
Ordeal, trial by, 119
Oresteia (Aeschylus), 3, 259–60*n4*
Original intent, 4
Origins of Totalitarianism (Arendt), 32

Papke, David Ray, 67
Parsons, Theophilus, Jr., 85–86, 249–50*n5*
Paul, Jeremy, 216
Payne v. Tennessee (1991): Booth overruled by, 140, 141, 261*n15;* and victim impact evidence, 141, 142, 143, 144, 158, 261*n15,* 262–63*n27*
Perelman, Chaim, 214
Perjury, 169
Perry Mason (television), 151
Personal Responsibility Act, 230, 276*n15*
Persuasion: rhetoric and, 14, 20–21, 177, 186, 196, 207–8; in judicial opinions, 20–21, 186, 187, 194, 195, 201–2, 207–8, 226; indeterminacy thesis and, 39, 40–42, 49; legal reasoning and, 39–40; storytelling and, 42, 49; authority and, 186, 195, 226
Philosophy, 34–35
Planned Parenthood v. Casey (1992), 11, 21–22, 193, 196
Plato, 54–56, 145, 212
Pleas, 169
Plessy v. Ferguson (1896), 228–29
Poe, Edgar Allan, 118
Poetry, 180, 183, 184
Police interrogations, 116–18
Politicians, 156, 157
Politics, paranoid style in, 80, 81
Pornography, 44–46, 47, 209, 245*n34,* 247*n64,* 255–56*n20*
Posner, Richard A., 15, 41; on judicial opinions, 189, 194, 195, 200, 272*n58*
Post, Robert C., 50, 51
Postmodernism, 77, 226

Postmodern jurisprudence, 216
Poverty law, 71, 75
Pragmatism, 68
Precedent, 270*n29;* judicial opinions and, 10–11, 12, 185–86, 192–94, 225; rhetoric and, 185–86, 193; Supreme Court and, 192, 193–94, 196, 225; topics and, 219. See also *Stare decisis*
Presidential power, 195–96, 203
Presidential Power (Neustadt), 195
Prettyman, Barrett, 198
Property rights, 209
Prosecutors, 137, 162
Proust, Marcel, 105
Psychoanalysis, 121, 132–33, 258*n18*
Psychology, cognitive, 47, 67
Public: interest in law, 2, 150; and criminal trials, 135, 136, 149–57; and victim impact evidence, 157–58
Punishments, cruel and unusual, 141
Puritans, 119–20

Quintilian, 181

Race relations: Simpson trial and, 155–56; *Brown v. Board of Education* and, 197; Harlan's *Plessy* dissent on, 228–30
Racial discrimination, 276*n12,* 277*n18*
Racism, 44, 251–52*n26;* hate speech regulations and, 46, 47–48, 246–47*n63*
Rackley, Alex, 110–11
Rae, William J., 107
Randolph, John, 252*n28*
Rape, and pornography, 245*n34,* 255–56*n20*
Rape laws, 68–69, 104, 227
Rawls, John, 35–36, 41
Reagan, Ronald, 6, 166
Reed, Stanley F., 198
Rehnquist, William H., 28–29
Reid, John E., 117
Reik, Theodor, 258*n18,* 258–59*n24*
Religion, 184
Rembrandt van Rijn, 206
Renaissance, 177, 182
Repressed, return of the, 89, 92, 97
Republic (Plato), 54–56
Rhetoric, 176–78; in judicial opinions, 10, 11, 20–21, 176, 187, 190–92, 193, 199, 207–10; and persuasion, 14, 20–21, 177, 186,

Rhetoric (*continued*)
  196, 207–8; and narrative, 64; lawyers' use
  of, 64, 176; classical art of, 177, 178–83,
  211, 212, 273*n3;* and precedent, 185–86,
  193; and legal reasoning, 211–12, 214, 224;
  topics in, 212–14, 222
Rhetorica ad herrenium, 181
Richards, I. A., 186
Roe v. Wade (1973), 227
Roman law, 119
Rorty, Richard, 65
Rosen, David N., 8, 18, 233
Ross, Thomas, 44
Roth, Philip, 121
Rousseau, Jean-Jacques, 114, 129, 131, 133,
  234; *Confessions,* 121–23, 125, 126, 132
Rubin, Edward L., 50
Rummell v. Estelle (1980), 192

Sade, Marquis de, 132
Saffle v. Parks (1990), 145, 263–64*n30*
Sartre, Jean-Paul, 18–19, 21, 101, 103
Scalia, Antonin, 28–29, 198
Scarry, Elaine, 9, 20, 232, 262*n21,* 265*n48*
Schauer, Frederick, 193, 268*n2,* 271*n50*
Scheppele, Kim, 68–69
Schlag, Pierre, 41
Schmerber v. California (1966), 129–30
Schoeck, Richard J., 273*n3*
School desegregation, 29, 135–36, 198
Schovkin, S. S., 100
Schulhofer, Stephen J., 258*n22*
Science, 76, 185, 194–95, 255*n16*
Seale, Bobby, 110–12
Searle, John, 178
Second Treatise of Government (Locke),
  267*n12*
Seidman, Louis Michael, 9, 20, 235, 236; on
  law of confessions, 131, 257*n13*
Self-incrimination, 125, 163; Fifth Amendment
  and, 117, 120–21, 162; *Miranda v. Arizona*
  and, 120–21, 130; *Schmerber v. California*
  and, 129–30
Sexism, 44, 46, 51, 68–69
Sexual harassment, 237
Shach, Rabbi Eliezer, 254*n8*
"Shape of the Sword" (Borges), 132
Shelley, Percy, 83
Sherry, Suzanna, 5, 16, 58, 59

Sherwin, Richard, 63
Side-bar conference, 106, 108–9
Siegel, Reva B., 10, 20
Simile, 182–83
Simon, David, 125, 131
Simon, William, 75
Simpson, Nicole Brown, 69, 103, 104, 138, 139
Simpson, O. J., trial of, 16, 168; spouse abuse
  issue, 69–70, 103, 260*n6;* dramatic narra-
  tives and, 103, 104; exclusion of evidence
  in, 138, 260*n6;* victims' stories in, 138–39;
  public audience for, 152, 154–55, 156; race
  relations and, 155–56
Singer, Joseph William, 41, 42
Sisson, Daniel, 88
Slave Power Conspiracy and the Paranoid Style
  (Davis), 80
Slavery, 80–81, 88, 89, 90–92
Sleeping Beauty (film), 104
Smith, Susan, 151
Smith, William Kennedy, 247*n11*
Social contract theory, 267*n12*
Social inequality, 45, 46, 233
Social reform, 37
Social sciences, 32–33, 34–35, 76–77
Social Statics (Spencer), 209
Sodomy laws, 226
Solum, Lawrence B., 40, 243*n8*
Souter, David H., 11, 21–22, 141, 196
South Carolina v. Gathers (1989), 173
Spargo, John, 256*n1*
Speech acts, performative, 63–64
Spencer, Herbert, 209
Spousal abuse, 103–4
Stare decisis, 16, 21–22, 176, 184, 186, 225.
  See also Precedent
State constitutions, 195
State v. Williams (1971), 70
Statutory interpretation, 218–19
Stein, Gertrude, 236
Stevens, John Paul, 28, 141–42, 158, 262*n24*
Stewart, Potter, 128, 209
Stone, Harlan Fiske, 198
Stone, Lawrence, 76–77
"Story and Transcription in the Trial of John
  Brown" (Ferguson), 79
Storytelling movement. *See* Legal storytelling
  movement
Strossen, Nadine, 246–47*n63*

Styron, William, 97
Sullivan, Andrew, 277*n19*
Sutcliff, Robert, 90
Sutherland, George, 67

Talmudic law, 124, 258*n19*
Technology, 156
Teleology, 100, 101
Television, 2, 151, 152
Tennessee Valley Authority v. Hill (*1978*), 50, 246*n60*
Theology, 183, 184
Thomas, Clarence, 28–29
Tison v. Arizona (*1987*), 261–62*n17*
Tolstoy, Leo, 3
Topics: in classical rhetoric, 212–14; legal reasoning and, 214–16, 220–24; and statutory interpretation, 218–19
Topics (Aristotle), 213–14
Topics (Cicero), 214
Tort law, 216–18
Torture, 119
Totalitarianism, 32, 33
Trent, Council of (*1551*), 121
Trial, The (Kafka), 3
Trials, 95; as narratives, 7–8, 9, 84–85, 87; side-bar conferences in, 106, 108–9; by ordeal, 119; murder, 138, 139, 142. *See also* Criminal trials
Trilling, Lionel, 239*n3*
Truman, Harry S., 195, 196, 202
Turner, Nat, 97
Turow, Scott, 2, 150
Tushnet, Mark V., 41, 59, 271*n45*

United Kingdom, Privy Council, 268*n5*
United States Congress, 203
United States Constitution, 100, 190; Supreme Court and, 21, 199; and religious schools, 29; and conduct of trials, 149, 150; and color blindness, 228–29, 230
—Amendments: First, 48, 51, 196, 209, 237; Fifth, 116, 117, 119, 120–21, 130, 162, 163, 257*n13*, 265–66*n1*; Sixth, 128, 147; Seventh, 254*n6*; Eighth, 141, 261–62*n17*; Fourteenth, 198, 209, 227
United States Court of Appeals, Fourth Circuit, 192
United States Justice Department, 137

United States Supreme Court, 16; judicial opinions of, 21, 136, 188, 190, 191, 197, 199; authority of, 21, 192; and constitutional adjudication, 21, 199; and religious schools, 26, 27, 28–29, 30; and school desegregation, 48, 197; and criminal confessions, 115–16, 118, 121, 125–31, 133–34; and compelled evidence, 129–30, 265–66*n1*; and victim impact evidence, 139–42, 144–45, 148, 158, 261*n16*; and death sentencing, 141, 142, 144–45, 261–62*n17*; and inferior courts, 191, 192, 193–94, 195, 225; and deference to precedent, 192, 193–94, 196, 225; conservative shift in membership, 196; politics and, 210; and racial discrimination, 228; and peremptory strikes, 230–31
United States v. Doe (*1984*), 257*n13*
United States v. Villasenor (*1990*), 185
Universities, 50

Verona, story of, 24–25, 57, 234
Victim impact evidence, 20, 136, 167, 260–61*n13*, 261*n16*; and death sentencing, 139–40, 141, 144–45, 146, 148–49, 170, 173, 265*n51*; *Booth v. Maryland* prohibition of, 139–42, 144–45, 147–48, 173; *Payne v. Tennessee* allowance of, 140, 141, 142, 143, 144, 158, 261*n15*, 262–63*n27*; victim impact statement in *Booth*, 140, 158–61, 264–65*n45*; three types of, 140–41, 173, 261*n15*; and defendants, 141–43, 147, 170, 262–63*n27*, 263*n28*, 266–67*n10*; juries and, 142, 144, 145, 146, 264*n44*; storytelling movement and, 142–43; as narrative, 143–44, 147–48; emotional responses to, 144–46, 147, 263*n29*; forms of presentation, 146–47; public opinion and, 157–58; arguments against allowing, 170–73, 262*n21*
Victimization, ethos of, 86–87
Victims' rights movement, 136, 139, 158
Victim stories, 31–32
Viehweg, Theodor, 214
Vinson, Frederick M., 202–3
Virginia, slavery in, 90, 91
Virginia Gazette, 90
Vosburg v. Putney (*1891*), 217

Walker v. City of Birmingham (*1967*), 269*n16*

Warren, Earl, 133, 196, 256*n3; Brown v. Board of Education* opinion, 11, 197–99; *Miranda v. Arizona* opinion, 116–18, 120–21, 130, 167

Washington, George, 88, 92–94, 252*n31*

Weisberg, Robert, 18, 131, 165, 257*n13*

Welfare reform, 230

West, Mae, 194

West, Robin, 43, 62

West Virginia State Board of Education v. Barnette (1943), 204

White, Byron R., 269*n18; Miranda* dissent, 116, 120, 122, 125–26, 127; *Booth* dissent, 148, 261–62*n17,* 262–63*n27*

White, Hayden, 77, 249*n3*

White, James Boyd, 33, 203

White, Lucie, 72–75

Wigmore, Dean, 126, 127

Williams, Patricia J., 243*n19,* 252*n36*

Williams, Robert, 127–28, 129, 130, 259*n25*

Winter, Steven L., 41, 43

Wisconsin, sentencing law, 169

Witnesses, 7; right to confront, 147

Wittgenstein, Ludwig, 41, 53

Women: and storytelling movement, 25–26, 67, 233–34; pornography and, 45; rape laws and, 68–69; child abuse and, 236; spouse abuse and, 255*n18*

Wonderful Life (Gould), 101

Wordsworth, William, 121

Wright, Richard, 7, 138

Yale Law Journal, 203

Yeats, William Butler, 177

Youngstown Sheet and Tube Company v. Sawyer (1952), 202–3, 204